THE
VISION OF
ISLAM

THE
VISION OF
ISLAM

by
Sachiko Murata
and
William C. Chittick

PARAGON HOUSE
St. Paul, Minnesota

VISIONS OF REALITY

A Series on Religions as Worldviews

Series Editor: Roger Corless, Duke University

Editorial Board: R. Ninian Smart, University of California,
Santa Barbara
Charles H. Long, University of California,
Santa Barbara

A common assumption behind many surveys of religions is that there is something called "religion" which is a uniquely classifiable phenomenon and which may be dealt with and written about according to recognized and agreed upon subdivisions. Systems identified as religions are then fitted into a prescribed format without considering whether the format is suited to the particular system under consideration.

This series is motivated by the awareness that, rather than there being something called "religion", there are many *religions*, and the more they are studied, the more each one manifests itself as equally profound, non-trivial, and adequate unto itself. Each volume will be an attempt to take each religion on its own terms. Comparison may be made with other religious traditions, but there will be no attempt to impose a single methodology in order to reduce the plurality of one basic scheme.

Published Volumes in the Visions of Reality Series:

THE VISION OF BUDDHISM   THE VISION OF ISLAM
Roger Corless   Sachiko Murata and William Chittick

Envisioned subsequent volumes on specific religions
or families of religions:

The Vision of China
The Vision of Christianity
The Visions of the Elders: An Anthology
The Vision of Hinduism
The Vision of Japan
The Vision of Judaism
The Vision of the West
and
Visions of Reality: Understanding Religions Understanding
Themselves (a methodological volume)

Published in the United States by
Paragon House
2700 University Avenue West
St. Paul, Minnesota 55114

Library of Congress Cataloging-in-Publication Data
Murata, Sachiko, 1943–
    Vision of Islam : reflecting on the Hadith of Gabriel / by Sachiko
Murata and William Chittick -- 1st ed.
        p.   cm. -- (Visions of reality. Understanding religions)
    Includes bibliographical references and index.
    ISBN 1-55778-516-3 (pbk.)
    1. Islam.   I. Chittick, William C.   II. Title.   III. Series.
BP161.2.M78 1994
297--dc20   94-16064
                                                                                  CIP

Manufactured in the United States of America
Typeset by AeroType, Inc.

The paper used in this publication meets the minimum requirements of
American National Standard for Information Sciences — Permanance of Paper
for Printed Library Materials, ANSIZ39.48-1984.

10   9   8   7   6   5   4   3

Table of
CONTENTS

So tell the tale—perhaps they will reflect.

Koran 7:176

Preface

This book grew out of an introductory course on Islam that one or the other of us has taught at least once a year since 1983 in the Program in Religious Studies at the State University of New York, Stony Brook. In teaching this course, we have dedicated our efforts to understanding the vision that animates the Islamic texts and to expressing it in the language of a Long Island classroom. From the beginning, we have been faced with the problem of presenting Islam to many kinds of students. Most of them come from Long Island or the New York City area, and they represent an extremely diverse cross section of Americans and other nationalities. Typically, about one-third are first or second generation immigrants from the Islamic world, ranging from China and Indonesia to Albania and Morocco.

The majority of non-Muslim students take a course on Islam because they need to fulfill a distribution requirement or because the hour was convenient. Muslim students attend for a variety of reasons. Some are quite distant from Islam but have developed enough disquiet about American society to have begun the search for their roots. Others have parents or grandparents who have insisted that they must learn something about their religion. Still others feel that, since they are Muslims, this course will provide them with an "easy A" (these students experience a rude awakening). Occasionally, an adherent of one of the political ideologies that are collectively referred to as "fundamentalism" attends the class in order to see for himself why non-Muslim scholars cannot be trusted in their evaluations of Islam.

This diverse audience has accentuated the problem of how to present Islam without distorting it. How is it possible to explain Islam both to Muslims, who—as a general rule—know nothing about their own religion but are defensive, and to Westerners, who also know nothing but are instinctively hostile? One way, which we always employ, is to have the students read various sympathetic accounts by contemporary scholars; fortunately the number of these is increasing.[1] Another way is to approach Islam not as an alien, third-world, outdated enterprise, but as one of the several, currently living world views that give meaning to the lives of billions of people. From the beginning, the basic goal of our lectures has been to provide Islamic self-understanding, and our lecture notes make up the substance of this book.

Many works on Islam acknowledge Islam's living relevance in the contemporary world, but few take notice of what the universe looks like through Muslim eyes. Or, if Muslim views are cited, they usually belong to those who have taken a political stance with full awareness of the importance of the modern media. Such people have replaced serious and leisurely discussion of the nature of things—the traditional approach in centers of learning in the Islamic world—with dramatic declarations and camera-wise media events.

The few studies of Islam that attempt to reveal the depth of Islamic thinking demand too much knowledge of the religion for beginning students and are usually couched in language that is primarily a derivative of the Western tradition. Even if an attempt is made to rely on Koranic terminology, seldom is much attention paid to the richness and diversity of Islam's own intellectual tradition.

Our approach in this book is focused on bringing out what Islam has thought of itself. By "Islam," we mean the great texts that have been universally acknowledged (until recent times) as the highpoints of the tradition. Like any great religion, Islam has its towering landmarks, and it is from these that we have sought to understand it. Such texts are rooted in the Koran. In a very deep sense, Islam is the Koran, and the Koran is Islam. The basic interpretation of the Koran is provided by Muhammad himself. Following in his wake, numerous great figures— sages, saints, philosophers, theologians, jurists—have elucidated and interpreted the nature of the original vision in keeping with the needs of their times.

In this book we try to pry open the door to the Islamic universe. We are not interested in evaluating Islam from within those dominant perspectives of modern scholarship that make various contemporary modes of self-understanding the basis for judging the subject. Instead, we want to portray Islam from the perspective of those great Muslims of the past who established the major modes of Koranic interpretation and Islamic understanding.

This is not to say that we will simply translate passages from the classical texts in the manner of an anthology. The classical texts ask too much from beginning readers. They were not written for people coming from another cultural milieu. Rather, they were written for people who thought more or less the same way the authors did and who shared the same world view. Moreover, as a general rule they were written for those with advanced intellectual training, a type of training that is seldom offered in our graduate schools, much less on the undergraduate level.

The classical texts did not play the same role as contemporary textbooks, which attempt to explain everything in a relatively elementary format. On the contrary, they were usually written to present a position in a broad intellectual context. Frequently the texts would present only the outline of the argument—the rest was supplied orally by the teacher. Students did not borrow these books from the library and return them the following week. They would often copy the text for themselves (by hand, of course), and spend several months or years studying it word by word with a master. We ourselves have attended sessions in which classical texts were being studied in the Islamic world, and we can attest to how easily a good teacher can choose a word or a sentence and draw out endless meaning from it.

Rather than present the texts themselves, we have tried to step backward from the texts and delve into the point of view that informs them. At the same time, we have attempted to avoid, as often as possible, the technical and abstract language that is typically used in many of the original texts and the erudite modern studies. We have also tried to keep in view the Koran's own mode of exposition and explain it by making use of quotations rather than summaries.

We are perfectly aware that many contemporary Muslims are tired of what they consider outdated material: they would like to discard their intellectual heritage and replace it with truly "scientific" endeavors, such as sociology. By claiming that the Islamic intellectual heritage is superfluous and that the Koran is sufficient, such people have surrendered to the spirit of the times. Those who ignore the interpretations of the past are forced to interpret their text in light of the prevailing world view of the present. This is a far different enterprise than that pursued by the great authorities, who interpreted their present in the light of a grand tradition and who never fell prey to the up-to-date—that most obsolescent of all abstractions.

The introductory texts on Islam that we have encountered devote a relatively small proportion of space to the Muslim understanding of reality. The reader is always told that the Koran is of primary importance and that Muslims have certain beliefs about God and the afterlife, but seldom do the authors of these works make more than a cursory

attempt to explain what this means in actuality. Usually the reader
encounters a short history of Islamic thought that makes Muslim intellectuals appear a bit foolish for apparently spending a great amount of
time discussing irrelevant issues. More sympathetic authors try to
explain that these issues were important in their historical context.
Rarely is it suggested that these issues are just as important for the
contemporary world as they were for the past, and that they are constantly being discussed today in our own culture, though with different
terminology.

We like to think that the Islamic tradition provides many examples of
great answers to great questions. The questions are those that all
human beings are forced to ask at one time or another, even if contemporary intellectual predispositions tend to dismiss them as irrelevant
or immature or unanswerable or self-deconstructing. We have in mind
the great whys and whats that five-year-olds have the good sense to
ask—though they soon learn to keep quiet in order to avoid the ridicule
of their elders. Why are we here? What is the meaning of life? Where
did we live before we were born? Where do we go after we die? Where
did the world come from? Where does God come from? What are
angels? Why is the world full of evil? What are devils? If God is good,
why did he create Satan? Why does God allow good people to suffer?
How can a merciful God predestine people to hell? Why do I have to go
through all this?

Texts on Islam often tell the reader, in extremely cursory fashion,
what Muslim thinkers have concluded about such issues; what they do
not address is the universe of discourse that informs Islamic thinking
and allows the conclusions to make sense. Studies usually highlight the
differences of opinion; what they do not clarify is that the logic of
either/or is not always at work. Perspectives differ in accordance with
differing interpretations of the sources, and the perspectives do not
necessarily exclude each other. We are told that people took sides, for
example, on free will and predestination. But any careful reading of a
variety of texts will show that the common intuition was that the true
situation is neither/nor, or both/and. The extreme positions were often
formulated as intellectual exercises to be struck down by the thinker
himself, if not by his followers.

In many ways this book responds to the texts that are normally
employed to introduce Islam to Western readers. Most of what we say
is designed to fill in the gaps in the works that are typically used on the
introductory level. The result is one-sided, but the other side can be
found by reading any of the readily available introductory textbooks,
or by taking an historical approach to Islam.

Readers need to be warned at the outset that this book is not designed
to provide the "historical facts." In the last section of the book, we will
say something about the Islamic view of history. That will help explain
why the concerns of the modern critical study of history are not our

concerns. To write history, after all, is to read meaning into the events of the past on the basis of contemporary views of reality. The events themselves cannot make sense until they are filtered through the human lens. If the Koran and the Islamic tradition are read in terms of contemporary scholarly opinions or ideologies, their significance for the Islamic tradition is necessarily lost to sight.

Naturally, we as authors have our own lenses. In fact, some people may criticize us for trying to find Islam's vision of itself within the Islamic intellectual tradition in general and the Sufi tradition in particular. But it is precisely these perspectives within Islam that provide the most self-conscious reflections on the nature of the tradition. If we did not take seriously the Muslim intellectuals' own understanding of their religion, we would have to replace it with the perspectives of modern Western intellectuals. Then we would be reading the tradition through critical methodologies that have developed within Western universities. But why should an alien perspective be preferable to an indigenous perspective that has survived the test of time? It does not make sense to us to employ a methodology that happens to be in vogue at the moment and to ignore the resources of an intellectual tradition that is still alive after a thousand-year history.

Finally, we take this opportunity to thank all the students we have had the pleasure of teaching at Stony Brook over the past ten years. Their constant interest and continual probing through intelligent (and sometimes not so intelligent) questions have forced us to keep rethinking our understanding of Islam's vision of itself and to reformulate it in terms that elicit responses of recognition.

Introduction

To talk about Islam we need to define some terms. *Islam* is an Arabic word that means "submission to God's will." More specifically, it designates the religion established by the Koran and the Prophet Muhammad. A *Muslim* is one who has submitted to God's will, or one who follows the religion of Islam. The Koran is a book that God revealed to Muhammad by means of the angel Gabriel. This is the basic story in its most simplified outline. Now we need to fill in some details.

The Koran

Islam today is the religion of about one billion people. It is far from correct to think that all Muslims are familiar with the story of how their religion became established. History as such has never held much interest for most Muslims. What is important about historical events is simply that God works through them. The significant events of the past are those that have a direct impact on people's present situation and their situation in the next world. From this point of view, the one event of overwhelming significance is God's revelation of the Koran. The actual historical and social circumstances in which it was revealed relate to an extremely specialized field of learning that few scholars ever bothered with. The fact that Western historians have devoted a great deal of attention to this issue says something about modern perceptions of what is real and important, but it tells us nothing about Muslim perceptions of the Koran's significance.

Most of this book will be dedicated to bringing out some of the more obvious implications of the Koran's teachings, including what the Koran has to say about itself. At this point, however, it may be useful to say something about the form of the Koran, since most of our readers have probably never seen the book itself, though some may have seen a translation.

Notice that we make a distinction between the Koran and a translation of the Koran. This is normal procedure in the Muslim view of things, in marked contrast with the Christian view, according to which the Bible is the Bible, no matter what language it may be written in. For Muslims, the divine Word assumed a specific, Arabic form, and that form is as essential as the meaning that the words convey. Hence only the Arabic Koran is the Koran, and translations are simply interpretations. Translations into the local languages of the Islamic world, particularly Persian, were made at a very early date. However, these were not independent books, but rather interlinear commentaries on the meaning of the text and aids to understanding.

The Arabic form of the Koran is in many ways more important than the text's meaning. After all, Muslims have disagreed over the exact interpretation of Koranic verses as much as followers of other religions have disagreed over their own scriptures. One of the sources of the richness of Islamic intellectual history is the variety of interpretations provided for the same verses. Muslim thinkers often quote the Prophet to the effect that every verse of the Koran has seven meanings, beginning with the literal sense, and as for the seventh and deepest meaning, God alone knows that. (The Prophet's point is obvious to anyone who has studied the text carefully.) The language of the Koran is synthetic and imagistic—each word has a richness having to do with the special genius of the Arabic language. People naturally understand different meanings from the same verses.

The richness of Koranic language and its receptivity toward different interpretations help explain how this single book could have given shape to one of the world's great civilizations. If everyone had understood exactly the same thing from the text, the religion would never have spread as widely as it has. The Book had to address both the simple and the sophisticated, the shepherd and the philosopher, the scientist and the artist.

The Koran says that God never sends a message except in the language of the people to whom it is addressed: Revelation conforms to the needs of its recipients. The Koran also tells us that Muhammad was sent to all the world's inhabitants. In order to present a message understandable to everyone in the world, the Koran had to speak a language that everyone could understand. And Islam did in fact spread very quickly to most of the civilizations of the world, from China and Southeast Asia to Africa and Europe. These people spoke a great diversity of languages — and we mean not only languages of the tongue, but also languages of the heart and mind. The Koran has been able to speak to all of them because of the peculiarities of its own mode of discourse.

Far from being a hindrance to the spread of Islam, as some have imagined, the Arabic language has been an aid. Although the form of the text was fixed, the meaning was left with fluidity and adaptability. People who did not know Arabic were forced to learn the Arabic text and then understand it in terms of their own cultural and linguistic heritage. But no one's interpretation could be final. The next generation could not depend exclusively upon the previous generation's translation and commentary any more than it could ignore the understanding of the text established by the tradition. Each Muslim needs to establish his or her own connection with the scripture. All serious Muslims were forced to enter into this Arabic universe of discourse — a universe, indeed, which they considered divine.

If, on the one hand, the Arabic Koran encouraged diversity of understanding, on the other, it encouraged unity of form. All Muslims recite the same scripture in the same language. They recite their daily required prayers more or less identically. Indeed, given the basic importance of God's revealed Word, recitation is the major way of participating in the Word. Understanding is secondary, because no one can fathom the meaning of God's Word completely. The most important task is to receive and preserve the divine Word. Its Arabic form is all-important. What one does with the form that one receives follows after receiving it.

A translation of the Koran is not the Koran, but an interpretation of its meaning. The Koran has been translated dozens of times into English. Each translation represents one person's understanding of the text, each is significantly different from the others, and none is the Koran itself. There is but one Word, but there are as many interpretations of that Word as there are readers.

This is not to say that Islam is a cacophony of divergent interpretations — far from it. By and large there is much less diversity of opinion on the fundamentals of faith and practice than, for example, in Christianity. Those who try their hand at interpretation have to undergo a great deal of training to enter into the Koran's world of discourse. Moreover, this training is accompanied by the embodiment of the Koran through recitation and ritual. The Koran possesses an obvious power to transform those who try to approach it on its own terms. This is precisely what Islam is all about — submission to the will of God as revealed in the Koran — but this is not simply a voluntary submission. The Koran establishes an existential submission in people so that they come to express its fundamental message through their mode of being, no matter how "original" their interpretations may be.

Of course, we are speaking of Koranic interpretation in the context of Islamic faith and practice. Many Westerners who have not been sympathetic toward Islam have offered their interpretations of the Koranic text. There is no reason to suppose that such interpretations will help non-Muslims understand the text that reveals itself to Muslims.

The Arabic book that goes by the name *Koran* is about as long as the New Testament. In most editions it is between 200 and 400 pages in length. In contrast to the Hebrew Bible and the New Testament, the Koran issued from the mouth of a single person, who recited what he heard from the angel Gabriel. Both the Jewish and the Christian scriptures are collections of many books that were written down by a large number of human beings, and opinions differ as to their status as revelation. Even if we say that the books of the Bible were all revealed, they were revealed to different people who did not live at the same time or in the same place.

The Koran is divided into chapters of unequal length, each of which is called a *sura*, a word that means literally "a fence, enclosure, or any part of a structure." The shortest of the suras has ten words, and the longest sura, which is placed second in the text, has 6,100 words. The first sura, the Fatihah ("The Opening"), is relatively short (twenty-five words). From the second sura onward, the suras gradually decrease in length, although this is not a hard and fast rule. The last sixty suras take up about as much space as the second.

The suras are divided into short passages, each of which is called an *aya*. Some of the longer *aya*s are much longer than the shortest suras. The word *aya* is often translated as "verse," but literally it means "sign." This is an extremely significant word, and we will discuss it in some detail.

The content of the Koran is reminiscent of parts of the Hebrew Bible and the New Testament. The Koran tells stories about many of the same persons and draws conclusions for its listeners' edification. The Koran calls the great human exemplars of the past *prophets* and mentions as the most important of these Adam, Abraham, Moses, and Jesus. Moses is mentioned by name more than any other person, followed by Pharaoh, his great enemy, who is the Koranic archetype of human evil.

The Koran elaborates on the ways in which the followers of the prophets, specifically the Jews and the Christians, have or have not lived up to the prophetic messages. It issues instructions on how to live a life pleasing to God. It tells people that they should pray, fast, and take care of the needy. It goes into great detail concerning human interrelationships—such as laws of inheritance and marriage—in a manner reminiscent of parts of the Hebrew Bible but foreign to the New Testament. It tells people that they should observe God's instructions purely for God's sake, not for any worldly aims. It warns those who deny God's messages that they will be thrown into the fire of hell, and it promises those who accept the messages that they will be given the bliss of paradise. Much more than the Judeo-Christian Bible, the Koran talks specifically about God. No matter what the topic may be, it finds occasion to refer the discussion back to God, if only by the device of attaching clauses mentioning God by one or more of his names, such as "And God is the Mighty, the Knowing."

For Westerners, the Koran is an extremely difficult text to appreciate, especially in translation. Even for those who have spent enough years studying the Arabic language to read the original, the Koran may appear as disorderly, inaccurate, and illogical. However, there is enough evidence provided by Islamic civilization itself, and by the great philosophers, theologians, and poets who have commented on the text, to be sure that the problem lies on the side of the reader, not the book. The text is undoubtedly one of the most extraordinary ever put down on paper. Precisely because it is extraordinary, it does not follow people's expectations as to what a book should be.

At the height of the imperialist era, when social Darwinism had convinced a large number of Westerners that they were situated at the peak of human perfection, many scholars looked upon Muslims with disdain for thinking that the Koran was worthy of respect. From that high point of human progress, the Koran appeared as a badly written mishmash of old sayings and superstitions.

Most Western scholarship of a more recent vintage has dropped the assumption of cultural superiority and looked at the Koran as a book that has its own unique genius. Positive evaluations are much easier to find than they were fifty years ago. Nevertheless, major barriers remain that prevent an appreciation of the Koran by non-Muslims or by those who do not have a thorough training in the Arabic language and the Islamic sciences. Even such training does not guarantee access to the book.

Many Muslims, especially those who are native Arabic speakers, feel a proprietary relationship to the Koran. However, it is not uncommon to meet people who know a great deal of the text by heart but have not the slightest understanding of the world view that permeates it. This does not necessarily hinder them from absorbing the Koran's transforming influence. But it does mean that they are unable to express the Koran's meaning in a way that harmonizes with their own tradition.

The nature of the Koranic world view presents a fundamental barrier to understanding the book. It is true that the Koran's view of things has a deep kinship with both the Jewish and the Christian world views, but most people in the modern world have little understanding of those world views either. Simply attending synagogue, church, or mosque does not mean that one sees things any differently from contemporary atheists. Our culture's dominant ways of thinking are taught to us not in our places of worship, but in our media and educational institutions. We may like to think that our education is scientific and unbiased, but this is a highly biased judgment, as many contemporary thinkers and social critics have told us.[1]

As a rule, it seems, when people with no grounding in the Islamic world view pick up a translation of the Koran, they have their prejudices confirmed, whatever these may be. No real entrance into the Koranic view of things is possible without some idea of the type of thinking that infuses the text. And that thinking is foreign to the way that we are taught to think in our own culture and in modern education in general.

We do not mean to suggest that people with a modern mindset—which includes practically all English-speaking or modern educated Muslims—will not be able to understand anything of the Koran, or that they should not bother reading the available translations. First of all, the very fact that the Koran has been translated means that the translator has accomplished the task of bringing it into the range of modern ways of thinking—and, of course, by that very fact may have severely distorted the meaning. In any case, everyone curious about Islam who cannot read Arabic should certainly read the book in translation. As a rule, it is much more useful to open it at random and read a few pages than to try to go through it systematically.

The Koranic world view is closely tied to the Arabic language, which, like Hebrew and Aramaic (the language spoken by Jesus), belongs to the Semitic family. The internal logic of Semitic languages is very different from that of Indo-European languages such as English, Latin, Sanskrit, and Persian. To begin with, each word derives from a root that is typically made up of three letters. From the three letter root, many hundreds of derived forms can be constructed, though usually only a few score of these are actually used. We will often discuss Arabic words in explaining the meaning of concepts. Without such discussion it would be impossible to suggest the richness of the associated meanings, the difficulty of translating words into English, and the interrelationships among Arabic words that are obvious in the original.

The Messenger of God

The story of Muhammad's life has often been told.[2] Few Muslims know all the details available to Western readers. For people who come from a Christian background, where the Gospel accounts of the life of Jesus play a major role in faith, it is well to keep in mind that Muhammad plays second fiddle to the Koran. He is enormously important for Islamic religiosity, but his importance stems from his relationship to the Koran. As F. E. Peters reminds us, repeating a point that has been made by many observers:

The Christian cannot but study the "Good News of Jesus Christ," since the sacred work of Jesus is revealed therein; the Muslim

*reads the "Life of the Prophet of God" simply as an act of piety: rev-
elation lies elsewhere.³*

Muhammad was born in about 570 C.E. into a respected family in the
city of Mecca in Arabia. The Meccans were connected to various Arab
tribes, some of whose members still lived as nomads. The city had a
certain importance as a trading center. More significantly, it marked
the location of the Kaaba, an ancient temple that, tradition said, had
been built by Adam and rebuilt by Abraham. In Muhammad's time, the
Kaaba was home for a large number of idols representing the gods of
the Arab tribes. Four months of the year were designated as sacred
months, when tribes were forbidden to war among themselves.

Ancient Arab warfare had no resemblance to modern warfare, although on occasion people were killed. Mainly, it was the means
whereby the culture stayed virile and periodically redistributed wealth.
It also encouraged attention to each tribe's distinctive characteristics
and heritage. The real heroes of battles were sometimes poets rather
than swordsmen. Tales exist of tribal warriors drawn up for battle who
turned away in despair after a great poet put them to shame.

Muhammad's father died before Muhammad was born, and his
mother died when he was six years old. He was raised by relatives. Like
many of the city people, he was placed for a time with a nomadic tribe
so that he could learn pure language and unspoiled habits. He grew into
a respected member of the community. He was known for his honesty,
integrity, and trustworthiness. He engaged in trading, and occasionally
accompanied caravans to Syria. When he was about twenty-five years
of age, his relatively wealthy employer, a widow of about forty years
old by the name of Khadijah, proposed marriage. He accepted, and
lived happily with her until her death twenty-five years later.

Muhammad was not content with the rituals of the local tribes and
preferred a monotheistic current of ancient Arabian religion, whose
scattered followers were known as *hanif*s. He used to go to a cave in the
mountains to be alone and meditate, and it was in this cave that an
event occurred that was to have enormous repercussions for world
history. He is said to have been forty years old, the age at which, in the
words of the Koran, "a man reaches full maturity" (46:15).⁴ While he was
meditating, an angel appeared to him, told him that God had chosen
him as his messenger, and revealed to him the first few words of the
Koran.

Muhammad underwent a period of self-doubt after this, especially
when the angel did not return. Khadijah, however, supported him,
being convinced that her husband was too stable to have lost his mental
balance. Some accounts report that in the absence of the angel, Muhammad reached the point of considering suicide. Finally, the angel returned and confirmed that he was God's messenger, and thereafter

came regularly. Reluctant at first, Muhammad submitted to God's will and began to proclaim his mission.

Little by little, people began to acknowledge the truth of Muhammad's message. What he told them was simple: God had chosen him to warn the people of the last judgment; people must accept God's sovereignty over them and mend their ways. This meant that they had to give God the worship that was his due and to adhere to certain ritual and moral instructions in both their individual and social lives.

Nowadays, many people find it difficult to imagine why such a message would be taken seriously. But Muhammad presented a supporting argument that many of his contemporaries found overwhelming: the language of the divine message; that is, the Koran itself, whose verses kept on arriving piecemeal until shortly before Muhammad's death.

In a society where poetry could be more powerful than swords, the awesome language of the Koran could be very convincing indeed. Not that the Koran was considered poetry, though many of its passages are highly poetical. But practically everyone who heard it had to acknowledge that its language was extraordinarily powerful. This was especially true of the verses that were revealed during the earlier period of the Prophet's career. The Koran was Muhammad's grand argument because it was, in effect, a living miracle.

Muhammad, after all, was a man whom everyone knew. He was recognized as a good man, but there was nothing very special about him. He was, if anything, rather ordinary, even if his honesty and reliability had earned him the title al-Amin, "the trustworthy." Like many of his fellow townspeople, he spoke the pure language of the tribes. But suddenly, this ordinary man began reciting a text of extraordinary power and beauty. Not only did the language surpass anything the Arabs knew—and remember, this is a society where language and power are intimately intertwined—but it confirmed something that they had heard before.

The Arab tribes considered themselves descendants of Ishmael, the son of Abraham. They counted Abraham as a prophet of old (though few people had clear ideas of what he had said). Moreover, there were Christians and Jews in the local environment. What Muhammad was saying was not unfamiliar to any of these three groups. The Koran often refers to the objections of the locals to the new message—they called it "fairy tales of the ancients," or "myths of those who came first." In other words, they reacted by saying that they had heard all this before, and it was nonsense:

The unbelievers say, "This is nothing but the fairy tales of the ancients." (6:25)

"We have been promised this, and our fathers before. This is nothing but the fairy tales of the ancients." (27:68)

What was convincing to the earliest Muslims was a combination of things: The sudden transformation of Muhammad, the incredible eloquence of his language, and the recognition that his message was something they had always known but somehow had stopped taking seriously. Or perhaps all of these remarks represent unwarranted psychologizing on the part of us moderns who have no way to appreciate what really happened in the minds of people living fourteen hundred years ago. After all, we hardly know what our next-door neighbors think. It may be that the best way to understand what happened is to cite, in good Muslim fashion, God's guidance and the resultant human faith. "Faith," as Muslim scholars have often said, "is a light that God casts into the heart of whomsoever He will." It is fundamentally inexplicable.

At first, the powers that be in Mecca simply thought that Muhammad had gone mad. But gradually, as their own friends and relatives started joining his small group, they took notice, and before too long they felt threatened. They did what they could to make life difficult for the converts, and Muhammad and his followers went through persecutions and trials.

The turning point came in the year 622 C.E. A delegation had come to Muhammad from the town of Yathrib, some two hundred miles to the north of Mecca. They were looking for a peacemaker to stop their internal quarrels, and they had heard good things about Muhammad's wisdom. They were willing to accept him as a prophet if he would come and rule their town. In the meantime, the Meccan oligarchy had decided that Muhammad had to be killed, because his teachings were becoming more and more of a threat to the status quo. A few hours before they put their plot into effect, Muhammad slipped out of the city with Abu Bakr, a close companion who was destined to take over Muhammad's political role after his death. After about ten days of following a circuitous route to avoid pursuers, the two of them reached Yathrib. Before long, it was called Madinat al-Nabi, "the city of the Prophet," or simply al-Madina (Medina), "the city."

The Prophet's move to Medina, called *al-hijra* (the emigration), was the grand turning point of his career. From then on, with some minor setbacks, the religion flourished. Islam was now established; a new civilization had been born. Hence the hijra is taken as the first year of the Islamic calendar. We will indicate dates both according to the hijra year (A.H., *anno hegirae*) and the Common Era (C.E.). Thus Muhammad died in the year 10/632, Constantinople (soon to be called Istanbul) fell to the Turks in 857/1453, and Napoleon invaded Egypt, marking the beginning of the colonial era in northern Africa, in 1213/1798.

The ten years in which the Prophet lived in Medina was a period of consolidation. By the time of his death, Mecca had surrendered to the Muslims without bloodshed—"poetry" had won another battle—and all of Arabia had embraced the new religion.

The consolidation of Islam that took place during the Medinan period meant that the focus of the Koranic verses that were being revealed shifted from threats of doom and promises of salvation to concrete instructions on how life should be lived in keeping with God's wisdom. Muhammad acted as prophet, king, judge, and spiritual counselor to the whole community. Hence he was the recipient of the divine message, he issued commands concerning political and social goals, he decided disputes and handed out punishment or pardon for transgressions of God's law, and he advised people in their personal attempts to gain nearness to God.

In short, the Muslims of Medina lived their lives in keeping with God's instructions as detailed by Muhammad. In later times, this period was looked back upon as Islam's golden age. God's messenger was present, and hence the truth was near at hand. There could be no differences of opinion, because Muhammad himself explained the Koran's meaning.

Just as people memorized and wrote down the text of the Koran, so did they memorize and record what Muhammad said and did. The records of his words and the reports about his activities (and the activities that he sanctioned) came to be called *hadiths*. We will refer to the whole body of this literature as the Hadith, and to each individual saying or report as a hadith. Both the sayings of Muhammad recorded in the Hadith and the verses of the Koran are words that issued originally from Muhammad's mouth. However, Muhammad himself always distinguished carefully between his words and God's words, and all Muslims have preserved this distinction, whose importance can hardly be overemphasized.

God's words are eternal and uncreated, while the words of his messenger are inspired by God, no doubt, but they must not be confused with God's own words. The Koran always takes pride of place. Muslims say and write, "God says," when referring to the Koran, but "the Prophet said," when referring to the Hadith. There is also a special category of Hadith in which Muhammad quotes the words of God. Then the formula reads, "Muhammad said that God says." These are often called *hadith qudsi* (holy sayings). They are totally distinct from the Koran, since they are Muhammad's sayings as contrasted with God's eternal Word. Often, however, they are given special respect—as indicated by the term "holy sayings"—because Muhammad possessed inspired knowledge about God's words.[5]

Medinan Islam was a way of life that did not exclude any human affair from God's domain. It may be that some affairs were considered indifferent, but this needed to be established by God and his prophet. Its indifference was itself a divine ruling. In later periods, the sense that everything had to be brought within the guidelines of the religion never left the Muslim consciousness. During most periods, governments pursued their own business with the usual worldly goals in view. Muslims accepted this as a fact of life, but they did not approve of it. In modern times, many political movements in Islamic countries have appealed to this time-honored sense that government should be run with God's guidance. Whether or not those in charge of the modern Islamic governments have really wanted to establish Islamic norms, and whether or not they have succeeded in doing so, are different issues altogether.

After the death of the Prophet, Islam underwent many growing pains and internal conflicts. The most significant of these was probably the split between the majority of Muslims and a minority over the issue of the Prophet's successor. The two groups came to be called the Sunnis and the Shi'ites.

When Muhammad died, a small group that centered around Ali and his wife, the Prophet's daughter Fatima, held that the Prophet had chosen Ali to lead the community after his death. But the majority took no notice, and the elders of the community met together and chose Abu Bakr as the Prophet's successor. His duty would be to rule over the community and act as its judge on the basis of God's law. The small circle around Ali at first refused to accept Abu Bakr as legitimate, but eventually Ali himself swore allegiance to him, and his partisans (*shi'a*, the source of the term Shi'ite) followed suit. Nevertheless, Ali did not give up his claim. In the Shi'ite view, the right order was only restored when the community selected Ali as the fourth successor of the Prophet in the year 35/656. But in 40/661 he was murdered by political opponents, and this marked the beginning of the period of the great hereditary caliphates, first the Umayyads and then the Abbasids.

Ali is recognized by Shi'ites as the first legitimate Imam (leader) of the community, while the Sunnis consider him the fourth of the four "rightly guided" caliphs (*khalifa*, "successor"). After him, political considerations took the dominant role in the dynasties that ruled the Islamic world. Islamic teachings had a say in determining a ruler's legitimacy, but government policy had no necessary connection with Islamic ideals.

Within one hundred years of the Prophet's death, Muslims had become a ruling elite throughout a good portion of the civilized world, from southern Spain to India. Political rule did not mean that all the subject peoples accepted Islam; far from it. The Koranic principle, "There is no compulsion in religion" (2:256), meant that no pressure was brought on local people to convert to the new religion. Outside the Arabian peninsula, most people were Christians, Jews, or Zoroastrians. Hence they were recognized as recipients of revealed books with the right to their own religious institutions. Moreover, the Muslim ruling elite did not encourage the subject peoples to convert, since it diluted their own privileges as Muslims.

Within three or four hundred years, Islam had become not only the dominant political power, but also the dominant popular religion in a region extending from Spain and North Africa into the Indian subcontinent. This, in any case, is another story, which should be sought in any of the many books that have been devoted to the history of Islam.

The Hadith of Gabriel

Any explanation of the beliefs, practices, and institutions that make Islam a major religion can benefit from a model that makes sense in terms of modern scholarship and has a basis in traditional Islamic learning. When we began teaching introductory courses on Islam several years ago, we chose as our model a famous and authentic hadith that Muslim thinkers have often employed for similar purposes in classical texts.[6] Typically, we ask our students to memorize the hadith, in the fashion of traditional Islamic learning. Even if they do not memorize it, by the end of the course they will find it hard to forget, since it contains in capsule form everything that they have learned in the semester. It also outlines everything that is written in this book. This is the text:

> *'Umar ibn al-Khattab said: One day when we were with God's messenger, a man with very white clothing and very black hair came up to us. No mark of travel was visible on him, and none of us recognized him. Sitting down before the Prophet, leaning his knees against his, and placing his hands on his thighs, he said, "Tell me, Muhammad, about submission."*
>
> *He replied, "Submission means that you should bear witness that there is no god but God and that Muhammad is God's messenger, that you should perform the ritual prayer, pay the alms tax, fast during Ramadan, and make the pilgrimage to the House if you are able to go there."*
>
> *The man said, "You have spoken the truth." We were surprised at his questioning him and then declaring that he had spoken the truth. He said, "Now tell me about faith."*
>
> *He replied, "Faith means that you have faith in God, His angels, His books, His messengers, and the Last Day, and that you have faith in the measuring out, both its good and its evil."*
>
> *Remarking that he had spoken the truth, he then said, "Now tell me about doing what is beautiful."*
>
> *He replied, "Doing what is beautiful means that you should worship God as if you see Him, for even if you do not see Him, He sees you."*
>
> *Then the man said, "Tell me about the Hour."*
>
> *The Prophet replied, "About that he who is questioned knows no more than the questioner."*
>
> *The man said, "Then tell me about its marks."*
>
> *He said, "The slave girl will give birth to her mistress, and you will see the barefoot, the naked, the destitute, and the shepherds vying with each other in building."*
>
> *Then the man went away. After I had waited for a long time, the Prophet said to me, "Do you know who the questioner was,*

'Umar?" I replied, "God and His messenger know best." He said, "He was Gabriel. He came to teach you your religion."[7]

To begin explaining the meaning of this hadith—a task that will occupy us until the end of this book—let us flesh it out by adding some background information that would be obvious to the original listeners but not to a reader situated many centuries and miles away.

Try to imagine the situation. The Messenger of God, at the time the greatest human being on the face of the earth (as far as his companions were concerned—and the historical record bears them out), is sitting at the edge of an oasis in Medina with a group of his companions, that is, people who have accepted that he is the mouthpiece of God. Suddenly a man appears whom no one recognizes.

Medina, at the time, is a tiny community in the midst of the desert (with a population of several hundred or perhaps a few thousand). Everyone knows everyone. If a traveler arrives, it is no small event, given the difficulty of travel and the small population. Everyone learns about new arrivals within hours. The system of personal relationships established by familial, tribal, and other bonds ensures that news is spread around much more efficiently than can ever be accomplished by today's six o'clock news. A man appears whom no one knows, but no one has arrived in town for several days, except the uncle of so and so, whom several of them have already seen.

Not only do the companions fail to recognize the man, but he also shows no signs of travel, which is very strange. If they do not know him, then he must be a newly arrived traveler. Someone would not be able to freshen up that quickly after several days of travel in the desert, even if he had traveled only by night on the back of a camel. (You think you feel bad after six hours in a car—think of six days in the hottest and dustiest environment you can imagine, with no air conditioned rest stops for coffee or soda.)

As soon as the man arrives, everyone is all ears. Who can this person be, and how did he get here without our knowing about it? Next strange fact: The man is obviously on familiar terms with the Prophet of God. He comes right up to him and kneels down in front of him, his knees against the Prophet's knees. Notice that the Prophet himself is kneeling, not in prayer as modern Westerners might kneel, but simply because kneeling is, for most Orientals, the simplest and at the same time the most respectful way to sit. Remember that, even in houses, chairs were unheard of. People sat on the ground, as they still do in much of the world—and this includes some of the richest and most sophisticated parts of the world, such as Japan. For most of the ancient world, chairs were the prerogative of kings.

You would not go right up to a person and kneel with your knees touching his unless he were, for example, your brother or a very close friend. The normal procedure, even if the person sitting there was just an ordinary person, would be to greet him from a respectful distance and keep the distance. But the stranger from the desert obviously knows Muhammad very well. He even places his hands upon Muhammad's thighs, which would be an unheard of piece of effrontery if the man were a stranger. Then the man addresses Muhammad by his name, whereas people always address him by his title, Messenger of God. The man begins talking without introduction as if he had been part of the conversation all along.

Once Muhammad answers the man's first question, the man says, "You have spoken the truth." 'Umar remarks, "We were surprised at his questioning him and then declaring that he had spoken the truth." This is an enormous understatement. More likely, the companions were flabbergasted. What kind of insolence is this? To come up to God's own messenger and begin to grill him, and then to pat him on the head as if he were a school boy! This is inconceivable. But then again, the companions took their clues from Muhammad. He was acting as if all this were perfectly normal and natural. What could they do but follow his example?

After the man leaves, Muhammad waits awhile, allowing his companions to think about this strange event. Finally, he tells them what had happened. They would not soon forget, and you can be sure that by that night, everyone in Medina had heard about Gabriel's appearance. No one was supposed to forget about this visit, for the Prophet had just presented them with their religion in a nutshell. If they ever wanted to know what was essential in Islam, all they had to do was remember the strange events of this day.

Religion

The hadith of Gabriel provides us with a picture of the *religion* of the followers of Muhammad. The first three questions and their answers suggest that in the Islamic view, religion comprises three main elements. We will be referring to these elements as dimensions. The fourth question raises another issue that also needs to be taken into account, and we will also deal with that. But let us first establish a picture of Islam as a three-dimensional reality. The issue raised by the fourth question can be set aside for the moment.

The first dimension of Islam is submission, and it comprises a series of activities, such as bearing witness, praying, and fasting. The word for submission is *islam*, the same word that is used to refer to the religion as a whole. We will see later that *islam* has other meanings as well. In this context, it refers to the activities that a Muslim must perform.

The second dimension is faith. The Prophet does not tell his listeners what faith itself is, no doubt because he assumes that they already know. Rather, he tells that what the objects of their faith should be.

What is it that they must have faith *in*? The answer is God, the angels, the scriptures, the messengers (i.e., the prophets), and so on.

The third dimension is doing what is beautiful. The Prophet does not look at the activity itself, but the motivation for the activity. An act cannot be beautiful if it is done without the awareness of God. God is the criterion for the beautiful, the good, and the right.

We will discuss the Prophet's answers in detail, and we will find out why it had to be Gabriel, among all the angels, who appeared. But first, we will look at a single word in this hadith, one that deserves special attention because it is employed to describe the whole. Muhammad, having just answered four questions, calls the four answers "your religion." The Arabic word he uses is *din*, and the translation as "religion" is more or less standard. However, it may not be the most appropriate translation in the context. The English word *religion* itself is notoriously vague, especially among people who make it their business to study religion. We cannot enter into the problems on the English side, but we can try to understand what, in this context, this word *din* would have meant to the Prophet and his listeners.

Our primary resource for understanding the Arabic language employed by Muhammad is the Koran and the various learned commentaries that have been written upon it. When Muhammad employed a word that is found in the Koran, he always had the Koranic meaning in mind. We will first look at dictionary definitions, then at the Koranic usage.

The root meaning of the word *din* is to obey, to be submissive, to serve. A closely related word, written the same way in Arabic script, is *dayn*, which means "debt." The connection between obedience and debt is not too hard to understand. If you lend someone some money and the person owes it to you, he is obliged to submit the money to you. We are dealing here with a society where personal relationships are everything. We are not talking about owing money to an impersonal entity like a bank. Rather, the person who lends the money is a fellow member of your community, and everyone knows that you are now indebted to him. Moreover, in this kind of community, a person's word is the person's honor, and to live without honor is to be less than human. Hence, when you owe someone something in the context of close personal relationships and the preservation of the honor, not only of the individual, but also of the family and the tribe, you are forced to be deferential toward that person. In effect, to be indebted to someone is, to some extent, to submit to that person's wishes. And, conversely, to submit to someone is to acknowledge that you owe something to that person.

The Arabic dictionaries provide us with a number of possible English synonyms for *din*, words that suggest the range of its meanings: obedience, abasement, submission; religion, that is, the means whereby one serves God; belief in the unity of God; the religion of Islam; a particular law, statute, or ordinance; a system of usages, rites, ceremonies, etc., inherited from the past; custom, habit; way, course, mode of activity; management of affairs. *Din* also has meanings that bring it close to the sense of *dayn*. Hence it can signify repayment, requital, recompense; retaliation; a reckoning; and the Day of Reckoning, the final judgment in the next world.

The word *din* has other meanings as well, but these few give us an idea of the problems that arise as soon as we translate *din* as religion. When Muhammad said, "He came to teach you your *din*," what exactly did he mean? The above definitions are helpful. He certainly meant "your religion" is "Islam," understood as the designation for the path set down by the Koran.

Muhammad also certainly had in the back of his mind—since it is demanded by the choice of this specific word—the connection with *dayn*. This connection suggests some of the moral weight that he wanted to give to what he was explaining to his companions. Muslims look at Islam as a debt that they owe to God. A debt is something that they are morally obliged to pay back. They are indebted to God first because he gave them existence and second because he offered them eternal happiness. There is a tremendous sense of "oughtness" carried in the word *din* when it is applied to Islam. It is the only moral thing to do, or rather, the only human and humane thing to do. Just as a person who borrows something and then runs out on the debt has no honor and is not even worthy of being called a human being, so also someone who shirks the religion is less than human and beneath contempt. If the hadith of Gabriel describes "your religion," so also it describes what you owe to God, and God is reality itself. We will see shortly that several of the other definitions that the dictionary offers for *din* easily fit into the category of what Muslims understand by the religion of Islam, but let us first try to gain a rough idea of what the Koran itself says about *din*, a word that it uses in ninety instances.

In the broadest sense, the Koran uses the term for a set of rules and regulations, or a collection of norms for correct activity. In this broad sense, we do not know if the religion in question is right or wrong, true or false, until we look at the context. For example, Joseph employs a ruse to keep his brother Benjamin with him in Egypt, because "he could not have taken his brother according to the king's religion" (12:76). Translators usually render the term *din* in this verse as "law," thereby suggesting the modern distinction between sacred and profane. But given what we know about ancient world views in general and the Egyptian world view in particular, there is no reason to suggest that the king's law was outside his religion, or that his religion was any different from his law.

In another example of the general use of the term, the Koran employs it to refer to the ways followed by the people of Pharaoh, and Pharaoh is the Koran's most important human villain. Pharaoh says to his council:

> *Let me slay Moses, and let him call to his Lord. I fear that he may*
> *change your religion, or that he may cause corruption to appear in*
> *the land. (40:26)*

In other words, if you listen to what Moses says, you will leave the
religion that we all follow, and thereby our social fabric—the rules
and regulations that we follow in order to maintain harmony and
stability—will be ruined.

In a slightly more specific sense, the word *din* refers to the message
brought by all the prophets, including Muhammad. Thus the Koran
addresses Muhammad and his adherents with the words that appear
below. Notice the distinction between "you" (plural) and "thou" (singular) in the verse. Throughout this book, we will usually preserve the
Koranic distinction between second person singular and plural, because it often adds an important nuance to the verse, as in the following. Notice also the switch between first and third person references to
God, a peculiarity of the Koranic style:[8]

> *God has laid down for you as religion that with which He charged*
> *Noah, and what We have revealed to thee, and that with which We*
> *charged Abraham, Moses, and Jesus: "Perform the religion, and*
> *scatter not regarding it." (42:13)*

What is this religion that God has set down as a duty for Noah,
Abraham, Moses, Jesus, and Muhammad? In the Islamic view, these
prophets share the declaration, "There is no god but God," along with
the worship of the one God who is designated by this declaration. This
declaration and worship are called *tawhid*, which means literally "the
assertion of God's unity." *Tawhid* is a major topic of this book. The
Koran says specifically that all God's messengers were charged with
tawhid:

> *And We never sent a messenger before thee save that We revealed*
> *to him, saying, "There is no god but I, so worship Me." (21:25)*

In the Koranic account of the prophet Joseph's imprisonment, Joseph
gives the following advice to his fellow prisoners. In effect, he defines
right religion as *tawhid*:

> *Judgment belongs only to God. He has commanded that you wor-*
> *ship none but Him. That is the right religion, but most people do*
> *not know. (12:40)*

The word *islam*, like *din*, has a wide range of meanings, as we will see
later. In a broad sense, it designates the submission of every prophet to

God. Abraham in particular is looked upon as having been perfect in his submission:

> *When [Abraham's] Lord said to him, "Submit," he said, "I have submitted myself to the Lord of the worlds." And Abraham charged his sons with this, as did Jacob: "My sons, God has chosen the religion for you, so do not die unless you have submitted." (2:132)*

In this and other passages of the Koran, "the religion" refers to *tawhid* and submission to God in the most general sense. It includes both Islam and pre-Islamic religions. What is especially important in such verses is that this religion has been established by God and that it functions for God's purposes. This suggests the sense of several Koranic verses that insist that religion must belong to God. In other words, any religion—such as that of the Koranic Pharaoh—that was not established by God is not a true religion. Likewise, any religion that people do not live up to in God's terms (not their own terms) cannot function as a true religion:

> *What, do they desire another religion than God's, while to Him has submitted [islam] whoso is in the heavens and the earth, willingly or unwillingly? (3:83)*

> *God says: "Take not two gods. He is only one God. So fear Me!" To Him belongs all that is in the heavens and the earth. His is the religion forever. (16:51-52)*

> *Worship God, making thy religion pure for Him. Does not pure religion belong to God? (39:2-3)*

Still more specifically, "religion" refers to that form of religion that God revealed through Muhammad:

> *Today I have perfected your religion for you, and I have completed My blessings upon you, and I have approved for you Islam as a religion. (5:3)*

It is in this sense that the word is employed in the hadith of Gabriel. "Religion," or more properly, "the religion" (*al-din*), is a set of teachings, including *tawhid* and submission to God, that God perfected for Muhammad and his followers. In other words, their religion has been given a seal of completion and approval by God himself.

The Koran also uses the word *din* to refer to specific prescriptions or regulations of Islam. Thus, for example, verse 24:2 refers to the punishment specified for those who engage in fornication as "God's religion."

In conclusion, we can suggest that when the Prophet said to his companions, "Gabriel . . . came to teach you your religion," he was defining, first of all, the Islamic idea of Islam itself. By implication, however, he was also telling us how Islam understands religion in general. Certainly, any authentic religion will have to have the three dimensions that the Prophet mentioned. Hence, while we will be discussing Islam's vision of itself, we will also be discussing—sometimes explicitly but more often only implicitly—Islam's vision of a more universal reality, called "religion," of which Islam is but a single instance.

Three Dimensions of Islam

We said that religion in the Islamic view has three dimensions. These are *islam* (submission), *iman* (faith), and *ihsan* (doing what is beautiful). The translations of the three terms are problematic, and we will need to discuss these terms in more detail. For the moment, however, we want to look at the metaphor that is implicit in the use of the word *dimension*.

When we say that Islam has three dimensions, we are implying that it is helpful to think of Islam in geometric imagery. The spatial reality with which we have contact has three dimensions (leaving aside the fourth dimension for the moment). It is possible to study physical reality in one-, or two-, or three-dimensional terms, and it is possible to study the first dimension independent of the second, or the first and the second independent of the third. In other words, we can study reality purely in terms of lines, or we can study it in terms of surfaces and area, or we can study it taking depth into account as well.

Each of Islam's three dimensions can be studied independently. For the purposes of our research, we might ignore the fact that a given dimension does not offer a complete view of reality. The "mathematical operations" are simplest this way, so it is the route that most people are tempted to follow. If we pay attention to too many things at once, it becomes impossible to draw a picture that makes any sense.

We will deal with Islam's three dimensions separately, but we will suggest all along that this is simply a heuristic device. The point is that Islam's self-understanding is complex, and that in order to gain the whole picture, we need to develop it a little at a time. We separate out the dimensions only to suggest that they fit together as a whole. In the same way, we talk about height, breadth, and depth only to suggest that space needs to be considered in terms of all three before we can have a proper picture.

We have arranged the three dimensions in the order in which they are found in the specific text of the hadith of Gabriel that we have cited, though other arrangements would also have been possible.[9] We think that this arrangement is particularly appropriate, because it begins with what is most obvious and easy of access. Here, however, the spatial metaphor becomes less and less helpful, and one could more profitably think in terms of dimensions of human existence.

We can think of human beings in terms of three basic dimensions or domains or levels of selfhood. The most external dimension is connected to what appears. People do things, and these actions can be analyzed and discussed without reference to the people themselves. We may look simply at the activity: Someone hits a home run that decides the World Series; someone wins the lottery; someone collects his pay check. What is important in the first place is the act or event — we can study personalities and motivations later, if we care to at all.

We may also wish to take into account the inner dimensions of a person. There are basically two questions that we can ask, one having to do more with knowledge, and the other having to do with intention and will. When we look at an activity, we might be interested in what sort of understanding lies behind the activity. How many times have we heard it said — parents in particular are fond of this line — "How could you have been so stupid?" Someone does something, and it is clear that only ignorance of the actual situation could have led to the act. However, a major problem arises as soon as we ask, "How does one gain knowledge of the actual situation?" How can the "actual situation" be defined? Should we define it in terms of the person and the act, the social or cultural context, the biological determinants, the historical moment? What about the structure of the cosmos, the structure of the human psyche? What about God, angels, devils? Knowledge of which of these, if any, will provide us with an understanding of the actual situation? This then is a dimension of human experience having to do with knowledge, understanding, and world view. Islam approaches these issues from the vantage point of faith, for reasons that will become clear.

We can also ask a very different set of questions about the inner dimension of human beings and their activity: What was the motivation? What choices were involved? What was the intention behind the act? People may well have all the requisite knowledge, but then do things that others consider unacceptable. Moreover, they may perform these acts precisely because they know that they are unacceptable. The question of motivation frequently arises in courts of law. If someone meant to do what was done, it is a crime. However, if the person did not intend to commit a crime, then the whole issue has to be examined more carefully.

Religion is a right or correct way. The hadith of Gabriel suggests that in the Islamic understanding, religion embraces right ways of doing things, right ways of thinking and understanding, and right ways of forming the intentions that lie behind the activity. In this hadith, the Prophet gives each of the three right ways a name. Thus one could say that "submission" is religion as it pertains to acts, "faith" is religion as it pertains to thoughts, and "doing the beautiful" is religion as it pertains to intentions. These three dimensions of religion coalesce into a single reality known as Islam.

In the living actuality of a person, we differentiate acts, understanding, and intentions only for our own purposes. We are dealing with a single human personality for which this differentiation does not necessarily have any meaning. People simply live out their lives. Then we, as external observers, may divide what we observe or fail to observe into different categories.

In the same way, Muslims or followers of other religions live out their religions. Theologians, philosophers, historians, psychologists, and other scholars may categorize. In doing so, they distort the whole. Nevertheless, by dividing things up, they may give us what we need in order to put things back together again and come to a fuller understanding.

Islamic Learning

In discussing how religion is defined in the Islamic context, we left out institutions, such as a priesthood or a church. Nowadays, many people identify religion with everything that the church does, or with everything that keeps priests busy. Islam has neither churches nor priests.

In place of churches, Islam has mosques. These are locally established places of worship without any central authorities that might allow us to talk about "the Mosque" as people talk about "the Church."

In place of priests, Islam has *ulama*. Priests, in a religion like Christianity, perform a function that ordinary people cannot perform. In the case of Islam, there are no religious functions that cannot be performed by every adult member of the community. At the same time, certain Muslims have a specifically religious vocation. Everyone has heard of *ayatollahs* and *mullahs*. Without trying to sort out the different names that are used, let us just say that the generic term for individuals who play a special religious role is *ulama* (Arabic *'ulama'*, plural of *'alim*). The word simply means "the learned." Those who devote their lives to Islamic learning come to play a special role because they preserve and maintain the knowledge that the tradition needs in order to survive. Fundamentally, their function is to be—as contemporary jargon has it—"resource people." They have gained specialized knowledge about Islam and are willing to employ it for the good of the community. They are much more like rabbis than priests or ministers.

No ordination is involved in becoming one of the ulama. Anyone who studies may become learned, and, to the extent that people make their knowledge available to others, they will become known as learned people, that is, ulama. Women rarely become ulama, but there are enough examples of famous women ulama to show that there have been no theoretical barriers to their gaining the requisite knowledge. There have always been certain social barriers, but those were not necessarily supported by the basic religious teachings.

To be a person of learning is a relative affair. As the Koran puts it, "Above everyone who is learned [or, has knowledge] is someone who knows [more]" (12:76). In a small village, someone may have gone off to the big city for a year or two and come back with a smattering of Koran and Hadith. That would make him a learned person in the eyes of the villagers, and they would be happy to have him lead their prayers and provide them with instructions on how to do things in keeping with God's commandments as provided by the Koran.

In Islamic cities that were great centers of learning, such as Cairo, Damascus, Baghdad, Istanbul, Najaf, and Delhi, there were many classes of ulama, and each class was ranked in degrees. Not that there was necessarily anything formal about this ranking, but it was not difficult to find out who was a good scholar and who was not.

The great centers of learning were supported by pious donations. In many of them, anyone could become a student, and anyone could teach. It would be impossible in the Islamic context to discourage learning, given that the Prophet said, "The search for knowledge is incumbent upon every Muslim." A student was typically called "a searcher (for knowledge)." To become a student, you found out when and where a class was being taught and you went. Often classes were held at a certain pillar in a large mosque. Once you started attending, no one would pay any attention to you unless you showed yourself. You were free to join the discussion, but if you did not know what you were talking about, you would be laughed out of court, or simply told by the other students to shut up. There were no degrees offered. However, if you spent a few months or years with a given teacher and mastered the book he was teaching, he would write out a certificate giving you formal permission to teach it. One of the questions that is asked about ulama when people want to find out how much they know is what certificates of permission they have, and from whom. The source of the permission was extremely important, since some scholars handed out certificates easily, while others were much stricter.

Many students were sent to a large *madrasah* (Arabic *madrasa*, "place of study") in the city by their teachers in the towns or villages, and they were not sent if they did not have the qualifications. Simply to have an introduction from known teachers was often enough to secure room and board—there was no tuition. But someone who came in off the street could also receive financial help. Teachers were always happy to have a talented student and, once he showed himself to be capable, would arrange support for him.

Not only could anyone be a student, but also anyone could teach. This does not mean that everyone would have a stipend from the madrasah. It simply means that you could go into a mosque and sit down by a pillar with a book, and tell anyone who would listen that you were there to teach. A good teacher could quickly gain a gathering and before too long—politics permitting, of course—be given a stipend. But to be a good teacher, you had to be learned, and this was a place where learning was put to the test. A person who was simply making claims to learning would quickly be found out, and then he would have no students.

Although what we have said might suggest that Islamic learning was localized in madrasahs and mosques, in fact it was an informal affair that could be carried on anyplace. No degrees were offered, so the motivation was the learning itself (contrast this with the situation in the modern university—if no degrees were offered, most students would quickly disappear). Learning was looked upon as a religious activity, and all people in society were expected to participate to the extent of their abilities. Since there were no formal institutions, the opportunity to study the religion was available in one form or another to everyone. Jonathan Berkey has described how this worked in his fascinating study of the transmission of knowledge in medieval Cairo. As he writes in his conclusion:

> *Education in the medieval period was never framed in any system of institutional degrees. Despite the proliferation of schools devoted to the religious sciences, instruction was never limited to particular institutions: it could go on wherever a scholar sat down, and could be shared by all those to whom he chose to speak. It was its personal and oral character that, in some form, made education accessible to all.*[10]

Islamic learning can be divided into three major categories, represented by Islam's three dimensions, and into numerous subcategories, especially in the case of the second dimension. The majority of the ulama hardly get past right activity (the first dimension), which itself is an enormously complex and detailed field of learning. If you feel like dedicating your life to it, you can easily do so. Moreover, the ulama who specialize in the first dimension are those who usually become most closely involved with the affairs of this world, because they tell people about right and wrong activity. In a traditional Islamic society, they are the legal experts and the judges. They are typically referred to as jurists (*fuqaha*). Just as lawyers have a great deal of power and influence in Western society, so also did the jurists in Islamic society, often functioning as advisors to kings on legal matters. In fact, the jurists played such an important role in Islamic society that, in the minds of most Muslims, to say "ulama" is to say "jurists," even though the term *ulama* has a much broader meaning.

The foundation of all Islamic learning is the Koran. The word *tafsir*, meaning Koran commentary or exegesis, is itself a specialized field of learning. Typically, a Koran commentary provides a verse by verse explanation of the whole book, but often scholars wrote commentaries on single suras or on selected portions of the Koran. Scholars wrote all sorts of commentaries, depending upon their own interests. Some commentaries simply explained the literal meaning of the text by expanding upon it in detail either in Arabic, or in one of the other Islamic languages such as Persian or Turkish. There were commentaries that focused on grammar, historical background, juridical implications, theological teachings, moral edification, allegorical meanings, and so on. Any scholar could write a Koran commentary from the perspective of his own specialty and explain his own understanding of the text. But everyone recognized that the meanings of the Koran were inexhaustible.[11]

If, from one point of view, investigation of the meaning of the Muslim scripture is called *tafsir*, from another point of view, all Islamic learning represents Koran commentary. However, jurisprudence, for example, focuses on the systematic elaboration of Koranic teachings on activity. Hence the Koran becomes the primary source or "root" (*asl*) of jurisprudence. Building on the Koranic teachings and adding to them the Hadith and certain other sources, the jurists established a major branch of Islamic learning. A similar thing was done in other fields, such as theology and ethics. Some fields of learning, such as philosophy, have a less obvious relationship to the Koran, but even there, one can make a case for saying that the Koran is the primary inspiration.

In the modern West, most people think of scripture as something one reads for edification, for learning about God and right living. In the Islamic context, the Koran was much more than that. Learning the Koran was the primary goal of traditional education, and it normally began early in life. No one thought it important for children to understand the meaning of the Koran—after all, even adults, even great theologians, understand only snippets of its total significance. What was important in education was memorization of the Word of God. The actual, spoken words should be learned by rote such that their recitation becomes second nature.

Note that we say "recitation." The text was recited, not simply read out loud. The Koran should always be pronounced carefully, according to the rules of beautiful enunciation and expression. Many children can be found in the Islamic world who can recite—sing, it might seem to us—dozens of chapters of the Koran if not the whole book, without understanding a single word. No one thinks this strange or unfortunate. Education begins by setting up a foundation upon which a structure can be erected. The foundation has to be built slowly but firmly. Children have their whole lives ahead of them to understand the book. And if they had ten lifetimes ahead of them, that still would not be enough, because this is the infinite and eternal Word of God.

In the modern West, most people seem to think that children should be allowed to learn at their own pace and their own level. The material that they are taught is—in one word—infantile. In traditional Islamic education, it was recognized that the enormous capacity of children for rote learning is a divine gift that should not be wasted through teaching them trivia. In any case, life is full of trivia, and children will absorb enough of that on their own. The relatively small amount of time that they can devote to formal education should be expended on what is most important and most essential in life, the divine guidance that makes ultimate happiness possible.

Rote learning was not such a difficult activity, because a good teacher made it fun. Children learned to recite the Koran beautifully, often in unison. In other words, as far as they were concerned, they were learning some nice songs or chants, and frequently they had a good time singing them together. Children do the same thing everywhere. But in this case, the children were taught to have special respect for these chants. For theological reasons, these were not thought of as songs but rather as recitations, and they were never accompanied by instruments of any sort, not even clapping. But such recitations are music nonetheless, and there is no instrument that plays more beautifully than the human voice.

The Koran provides a firm basis for subsequent learning. The traditional curriculum gradually added other elements, based on the Koranic text. In order to understand the meaning of the text, children had to know the stories of the prophets, for example. Elaborate versions of the Koranic narratives, with a great deal of material interpolated from all sorts of other sources, are very much part of popular culture. All Muslims have heard stories about Abraham, Joseph, Moses, Solomon, David, Jesus, Muhammad, and other prophets.

On a more formal level of education, one important prerequisite for understanding the Koran was Arabic grammar. Once students had memorized part or all of the text, they had examples of every grammatical rule in their heads. Then it was relatively easy to learn the intricacies of this complex topic. Other subjects were gradually added in keeping with the student's aptitude. But it was always recognized that the most essential formal learning was memorization of the divine Word, whether or not its meaning was understood. And the most essential parts of the divine Word were those parts that have to be known in order to perform the basic rituals. The stress was always on bodily activity, the body being the indispensable support for everything human, not least the mind and heart.

A Fourth Dimension

We left out the last section of the hadith of Gabriel. There, as we saw, the Prophet provides a rather cryptic description of the signs that will occur at the end of time, such as the slave girl giving birth to her mistress. The tone is typical for many hadiths and a few Koranic verses.

The implication is that religion includes knowledge of the way in which time will unfold and come to an end. Hence there is an allusion to an Islamic view of history. Given the geometrical metaphor of dimensions, where time is a fourth dimension, it is appropriate to think of the Islamic conception of time and history as a dimension of the religion. And time also has something to do with the dimensionality of human beings, since everyone has a beginning and an end.

If the main body of this book explains Islam in terms of *islam* (submission), *iman* (faith), and *ihsan* (doing what is beautiful), the final section looks at some of the implications of the Islamic view of history. However, this will not be the history one reads about in modern history books, where the underlying world views are of rationalistic types that have only recently come into existence. Rather, we will be dealing with a view that sees history full of divine meaning and that makes definite statements about beginnings and, especially, ends.

Part I:

ISLAM

The Word *Islam*

The Arabic word *islam* means "to turn oneself over to, to resign oneself, to submit." In religious terminology, it means submission or surrender to God, or to God's will. The Koran uses the term and its derivatives in about seventy verses. In only a few of these verses can we claim that the word refers exclusively to "Islam," meaning thereby the religion established by the Koran and the Prophet Muhammad.

We have already seen that the Koran and the Hadith use the word *din* ("religion") in a range of meanings. This is typical for many important terms employed in the Koran and the Islamic tradition. Incomprehension often occurs because people think they are talking about the same thing, whereas in fact they are merely using the same words. For example, when non-Muslims speak about Islam, they usually have in view the specific religion established by Muhammad. Muslims mean that religion too, but they frequently have one or more of the other meanings of the term in mind as well, and this tends to make mutual understanding difficult.

In the broadest sense, *islam* means "submission to God" as an undeniable fact of existence. If God is understood as the only reality truly worthy of the name—or Reality with an uppercase R—then nothing else is truly real. In other words, everything else is dependent upon God for its reality. Or, to use less philosophical and more theological language, all things in the universe, and the universe itself, are creations of God. Since God made them the way they are, they depend totally upon God. Hence they are "submitted" to God.

In the first verse quoted below, a verse that we have already cited, this broadest sense of the term *islam* is used to prove that true religion is established by God alone. The other verses illustrate the Koranic view that everything in the natural world praises and glorifies God. Simply by existing, all creatures demonstrate their Creator's glory and perform acts that acknowledge God's mastery over them:

What, do they desire another religion than God's, while to Him has submitted whoso is in the heavens and the earth, willingly or unwillingly? (3:83)

Have you not seen how whatsoever is in the heavens and the earth glorifies God, and the birds spreading their wings? (24:41)

Have you not seen how to God bow all who are in the heavens and all who are in the earth, the sun and the moon, the stars and the mountains, the trees and the beasts, and many of mankind? (22:18)

Notice that "many of mankind" bow to God. This means, conversely, that many do not. Although from one point of view human beings are included in "the heavens" and "the earth" and hence are creatures of God and submitted to him, from another point of view they are free not to submit to him. This is the great mystery. It is here that human problems begin. People are not like mountains and trees, which simply submit to God's will and give no thought to it. People are always faced with the fact of their freedom, the fact that they can choose to obey or disobey when someone tells them to do something, whether that someone be God, their parents, the government, or whoever. If there were no choices to be made, everything would be fine, because no one would be able to conceive of any other situation.

The Koran says in the verse just cited that "many of mankind" bow to God. It frequently refers to these many as *muslims*, that is, "those who have submitted to God." Although "Muslim" normally means a follower of the religion established by the Koran, in the Koranic context it frequently means those who follow any of God's prophets. In translating the word in this sense we will employ the term *muslim*, rather than Muslim.

When [Abraham's] Lord said to him, "Submit," he said, "I have submitted to the Lord of the worlds." (2:131)

Jacob said to his sons, "What will you worship after me?" They said, "We will worship your God and the God of your fathers, Abraham, Ishmael, and Isaac, one God, and we will be muslims toward Him." (2:133)

And when I revealed to the Apostles [of Jesus], "Have faith in Me and in My messenger," they said, "We have faith, and we bear witness that we are muslims." (5:111)

All prophets submitted themselves to God's will and hence were *muslims*. In the same way, all those who follow the religions brought by the prophets are *muslims*. But clearly this does not mean that they follow the religion established by the Koran, which appeared in Arabia in the seventh century. Hence, in a still more specific sense, the word *islam* refers to the historical phenomenon that is the subject of this book, the religion that goes by the name "Islam." Surprisingly, none of the eight Koranic verses that mention the word *islam* itself refers exclusively to this religion, since the wider Koranic context of the term is always in the background. It is probably true that most Muslims read these verses as referring to Islam rather than *islam* in a wider sense, but as soon as one understands the broad Koranic context, one can easily see that the verses have more than one meaning.

> *Religion in God's view is the* submission. *(3:19)*

> *If someone desires other than the* submission *as a religion, it will not be accepted of him. (3:85)*

In these two verses, both the word religion and *al-islam* ("the submission") can be understood in broader or narrower senses. Most Muslims read them to mean that the right way of doing things is that set down by the Koran and the Hadith. Others understand the verses to mean that every revealed religion is one of the forms of *islam*, just as the message of all the prophets is *tawhid*. If someone rejects God's religion — that is, "the submission" revealed to all the prophets — and follows instead a human concoction, God will not accept that from him. Having one's religion rejected by God is the same as being sent to hell.

Some of the verses that speak of *islam* might well be read as referring exclusively to the religion brought by Muhammad, because he is mentioned in the context:

> *They count it as a favor to you that they have submitted. Say: "Do not count your* islam *as a favor to me. No, rather God confers a favor upon you, in that He has guided you to faith." (49:17)*

> *Today I have perfected your religion for you, and I have completed My blessing upon you, and I have approved* islam *for your religion. (5:3)*

Several other Koranic verses that refer to *islam* or *muslim*s can be read as referring to the historical religion of Islam. But at least one verse refers to *islam* in a still narrower sense. Apparently a group of bedouins — that is, tribespeople who lived a nomadic existence in the desert — had seen that the new religion was the rising power in their region and that they could gain advantages by joining up with it. Hence they came before the Prophet and swore allegiance to him, in the time-honored manner of the Arabs. But of course, Islam came with a set of conditions that were completely unfamiliar to the bedouins; that is, the five practices of the religion that are mentioned in the hadith of Gabriel. Part of swearing allegiance to the Prophet was agreeing to observe these practices. At some point, after having sworn allegiance, the bedouins told the Prophet that they had faith in Islam. Now God enters the discussion by revealing the following verses to Muhammad:

> *The bedouins say, "We have faith." Say: "You do not have faith, rather say, 'We have submitted,' for faith has not yet entered your hearts. If you obey God and His messenger, He will not diminish you anything of your works." (49:14)*

In this verse, it is clear that submission is not the same as faith (*iman*), since submission means obeying God and the Prophet, whereas faith is something deeper, having to do—as we will see later—with knowledge and commitment. Obeying God and the Prophet pertains to the domain of activity, to the realm of commands and prohibitions. The Prophet has come with specific instructions from God for the people. If they obey the Prophet, they obey God's instructions. "Whosoever obeys the Messenger, thereby obeys God" (4:80). God, in turn, will pay them their wages.

It is this fourth meaning of the word that is the topic of the present chapter and is made most explicit in the hadith literature. Thus the hadith of Gabriel, in defining submission, simply lists a set of activities that must be performed in order for people to obey God:

> *Submission is that you witness that there is no god but God and Muhammad is His messenger, that you perform the prayers, you pay the alms tax, you fast during Ramadan, and you make the pilgrimage to the House if you are able to go there.*

In short, we have four basic meanings for the word *islam*, moving from the broadest to the narrowest: (1) the submission of the whole of creation to its Creator; (2) the submission of human beings to the guidance of God as revealed through the prophets; (3) the submission of human beings to the guidance of God as revealed through the prophet Muhammad; and (4) the submission of the followers of Muhammad to God's practical instructions. Only the third of these can properly be translated as *Islam* with an uppercase I. The other three will be referred to as "submission" or *islam*.

It should not be imagined that these four meanings are clearly distinct in the minds of Muslims, especially those who live in the ambiance of their religion. It is common for Muslims to think of Islam as their own practices, and to think of their practices as the same as the practices of all religions (since all religions are *islam*). If other practices are different, it must be because they have become corrupted. In the same way, it is common for traditional Muslims to think that their own religious activities are the most normal and natural activities in the universe, since they are simply doing what everything in creation does constantly, given that "to Him has submitted whoso is in the heavens and the earth." In other words, the various meanings of the term become conflated, and it is not always easy to separate them.[1]

Chapter 1.

THE FIVE PILLARS

A pillar is a support, something that holds up a structure. The structure is the religion of Islam, with its three dimensions. If the five fundamental practices of Islam are called "pillars," the implication is that everything else depends upon them.

Practice: Embodied Submission

Practices pertain to the domain of the body. Our bodies determine our configuration within reality, so much so that there have always been people who claim that bodies make up the whole of existence, or at least everything significant. The Koran sometimes cites the criticisms that such people make of those who follow the prophets:

> If you obey a mortal like yourselves, then you will be losers. What, does he promise you that when you are dead, and become dust and bones, you shall be brought forth? Away, away with what you

are promised! There is nothing but our life in this world. We die,
and we live, and we will not be raised up. (23:34–37)

If bodies were not of such profound importance for human existence, people would not think in such terms. But bodies play a determining role in all the individual characteristics that give us our identity. Our meeting with our surroundings always begins on the bodily level, through the intermediary of the senses. If philosophers and theologians can speak of nonbodily realities, their words may have no meaning for children or unreflective people.

From the beginning, Islam set out to build a society. What Islam has always understood is that people are united by common practices at least as much as by common ideals. Islam has functioned socially by harmonizing people's activities.

The body is a lived reality for everyone, but nonbodily realities do not make much sense to many people. "Show me," they say. And the Koran simply replies that salvation will be achieved by those who "have faith in the unseen." At this first level, people are not asked to understand the unseen, simply to accept that it is there and to act accordingly, by performing the Five Pillars and the other activities set down in the revealed guidance.

For the most part, people are born into the religion they profess. Islam recognizes that correct practice makes people Muslims and that, for most people, correct belief follows upon correct practice. Muslim children are rarely taught a catechism. Rather, they are taught to pray and to perform other rituals. They grow up performing basic purification rites, because these determine the nature of toilet training. And like children everywhere, they enjoy doing what grown-ups do, so they frequently follow along in the movements of the ritual prayer when their parents or other family members perform it. No one cares if they lose interest in the middle and go off to play. The point is for the practices gradually to become a natural and organic part of the human configuration.

Behind all the stress on practice is the recognition that the Koran must become flesh and blood. It is not enough for people to read the Koran or learn what it says. They have to embody the Book. It must become the determining reality of what they do (*islam*), what they think (*iman*), and what they intend (*ihsan*).

The First Pillar: The Shahadah

The pillars are practices, which is to say that they are described and defined in terms of activity. What do you do to be a Muslim? This question does not pertain to the level of faith, understanding, or intention. Questions on that level belong to Islam's second or third dimensions, not the first.

The first pillar is the fundamental act upon which all Islamic activity depends. It is to acknowledge verbally that one accepts the reality of God and the prophecy of Muhammad (and hence the truth of the Koran, the message with which Muhammad was sent). It is known as the Shahadah (Arabic *shahada*, which means "to testify" or "to bear witness").

The Koranic usage of the term *shahada* throws interesting light on its significance. One of God's Koranic names is "Knower of the *ghayb* and the *shahada*." *Ghayb* means "the absent, the unseen, the invisible, the hidden." *Shahada* in this context means "that which is visible or witnessed." By employing this divine name and in other ways as well, the Koran divides reality into two realms, that which is absent from our senses, and that which our senses are able to witness. We know only the witnessed realm, while God knows both the witnessed and the invisible realms. Included in the unseen realm are God and spiritual beings. Included in the witnessed domain are all bodily things. Another of God's names is *al-shahid*, the Witness, for God is witness to everything that happens, because, as the Koran puts it:

> He is with you wherever you are. (57:4)

> God is Witness of what they do. (10:46)

> Suffices it not as to thy Lord, that He is Witness over everything?
> (41:53)

The Koran also frequently uses the term *shahada* in the sense of giving witness. For example, it tells people that when someone borrows money, two witnesses should be present and the whole transaction should be recorded. "That is more equitable in God's sight, and more reliable as *shahada*" (2:282).

The act of bearing witness to God's unity is the most basic act of Muslims. By performing it, they imitate God and the angels, who also perform it, and they enter into the ranks of those who have been given knowledge:

> God bears witness *that there is no god but He—and the angels,*
> *and the possessors of knowledge—upholding justice; there is no*
> *god but He, the Inaccessible, the Wise. (3:18)*

In its briefest form, Islam's first-pillar is simply to say the two sentences, "There is no god but God" (*la ilaha illa'llah*) and "Muhammad is God's messenger" (*Muhammadun rasul Allah*). Normally, the words "I bear witness that" (*ashhadu an*) are added before each sentence.

Theoretically, it is only necessary for a Muslim to utter the Shahadah once in his or her lifetime, but in practice, Muslims recite it frequently,

initiation

especially because it is incorporated into the daily required prayers. Traditionally, a child's father whispers the Shahadah into its ear at birth. Thus the child is exposed to the first pillar at the very beginning of life. The formula is recited by Muslims on all sorts of occasions, and a child is taught to say it as early as possible. No one supposes that the child understands the Shahadah. It is the act itself that is important.

The Shahadah's primary importance comes out clearly in the fact that reciting the Shahadah is the ritual whereby one submits oneself to God, that is, becomes a Muslim. In this ritual, the formula must be recited in Arabic, with the intention of submitting oneself to God, in the presence of two Muslim witnesses.

Most Muslims agree that pronouncing the Shahadah is all that is absolutely necessary for one's Islam to be accepted by God. However, they add that Islam is not genuine and sincere if it remains simply verbal. By reciting the Shahadah, one makes the remaining four pillars incumbent upon oneself, and if one does not observe them, one's Islam is lacking, if not unacceptable.

The Second Pillar: *Salat*

Although uttering the Shahadah is the fundamental act of Muslims, performing the *salat* (ritual prayer) is, in a certain sense, even more basic. The Prophet called *salat* the "centerpole" of the religion, suggesting the image of a tent with a single pole holding it up in the middle and with other poles as secondary supports. The Koran commands performance of the *salat* more than it commands any other activity, and prophetic sayings suggest that God loves the *salat* more than every other human act. It is not accidental that performing the ritual prayer in communion has come to symbolize Islam on television. For TV producers, the reason is simply that the *salat* makes good footage. But for Muslims, this act embodies what it means to be a Muslim more than any other, and Muslims have always recognized that this is the case.

Like many other Koranic terms, the word *salat* has several meanings. The basic sense of the word in Arabic is to pray or bless. Just as God and the angels utter the Shahadah, so also they perform the *salat*. And just as people bear witness to God's oneness in imitation of God, so also they perform the prayer in imitation of God.

In Koranic usage, there are at least four forms of *salat*. First, God and the angels perform a *salat* whereby they bless God's servants:

> *It is He who performs the* salat *over you, and His angels, that He may bring you forth from the darknesses into the light. (33:43).*

Second, all creatures in the heavens and the earth perform *salat* as the expression of universal *islam*:

*Have you not seen that everyone in the heavens and the earth glo-
rifies God, and the birds spreading their wings? Each one knows
its* salat *and its glorification. (24:41).*

Third, every voluntary *muslim* performs the *salat*, which is to say that
the term is applied to one of the specific forms of worship revealed to all
the prophets:

*And We delivered [Abraham], and Lot. . . . And We gave him Isaac
and Jacob as well, and every one We made wholesome. . . . And We
revealed to them the doing of good deeds and the performance of
the* salat. *(21:71-73)*

Finally, in the most common usage of the term, *salat* refers to the
specific form of ritual that is the second pillar of Islam.

Although the Koran repeatedly commands Muslims to perform the
salat, it says little about what the *salat* actually involves. How to perform the *salat* was taught by the Prophet, and thus Muslims today,
wherever they live, pray in essentially the same way that Muhammad
prayed and taught them to pray. In the following, we provide a general
description of the *salat*, without noting various minor differences that
exist among the schools of Islamic law.

Salat is divided into two basic kinds—required and recommended. The
required *salat* is the second pillar, while other *salat*s are recommended
on all sorts of occasions. The primary required *salat* is performed five
times a day, while there are other occasional forms, such as the congregational prayer on Fridays. After sunset (the beginning of the day in
Islamic—as in Jewish—time reckoning) and before the disappearance of
the last light from the horizon, the first of the five daily prayers, the
evening *salat*, is said. The next prayer is the night *salat*, whose period
extends from the end of the time of the evening prayer to the beginning of
the time of the morning prayer. The morning *salat* can be said any time
between the first appearance of the dawn and sunrise.[2] The fourth *salat* is
said between noon and midafternoon. Noon is the time when the sun
reaches the meridian—not clock noon, which seldom coincides exactly
with solar noon. Midafternoon is usually defined as the time when something's shadow is slightly longer than the thing itself. The period for
saying the fifth *salat* extends from midafternoon until sunset.

Each prayer consists of a certain number of cycles (*rak'a*). The evening *salat* has three cycles, the night four, the morning two, the noon
four, and the afternoon four. Each cycle involves a number of specific
movements and the recitation of a certain amount of Koranic text and
various traditional formulas, all in Arabic.

If we were to observe a group of people performing the *salat* together,
we would see the following (perhaps with slight differences from place
to place): First, those performing the *salat* stand up straight. After a

minute or two, they bow at the waist with backs straight. After a few seconds, they stand up straight again, then almost immediately they place their knees, hands, and foreheads on the ground. They remain in this position of prostration for a few seconds, then come up for a second or two to a sitting position, then prostrate themselves for a second time. This is the end of the first cycle.

From the position of prostration, they go back to a standing position and begin a second cycle, exactly like the first. After the second cycle, instead of standing again, they come up to a seated position and recite formulae of blessing and peace directed to the Prophet and the faithful. Here they also recite the Shahadah in an elongated form.

If this prayer that we have just observed is the morning *salat*, it now comes to an end with greetings of peace to the right and the left. If it is any of the other prayers, it goes into a third cycle. The evening prayer ends after the third cycle, with the seated Shahadah, blessings, and greetings. The other three *salats* have four cycles, so they correspond to the morning prayer performed twice.

During the two, three, or four standing parts of the prayer, Muslims recite the Fatihah, which is the first chapter of the Koran, consisting of seven short verses. In the first two cycles, they also recite another chapter or some verses from the Koran.

In order to perform the *salat*, people must be in a state of ritual purity (*tahara*). For practicing Muslims, maintaining ritual purity is a daily concern, since it involves preserving the body and clothing from con- tamination by excretions and blood. Muslim toilet training is deter- mined by the rules of ritual purity. Although children are not expected to perform the prayers until puberty, even infants are taught to clean themselves in a way that keeps them ritually pure. What this cleaning involves is basically careful elimination of all traces of bodily wastes, preferably with water.

There are two main categories of impurity, and two basic kinds of ablution to remove impurity. The major ablution (*ghusl*) is required after sexual intercourse or emission of semen, menstruation, child- birth, and touching a human corpse. A person in need of a major ablution cannot perform the ritual prayer and should not enter a mosque or touch the Koran. In order to perform the *salat*, one has to be free from minor impurity as well. This kind of impurity occurs if one sleeps, goes to the toilet, breaks wind, and in certain other ways as well. It is removed by a minor ablution (*wudu*).

The major ablution involves washing the whole body from head to toe, making sure that every part of it gets wet. The minor ablution involves rinsing or wiping the following with water, in this order: the hands, the mouth, the nose, the right and left forearms, the face, the head, the ears, and the right and left feet.

If there is no access to water, or if a person should not touch water because of illness or some other reason, and if the time for prayer arrives, a simpler form of ablution is made with clean sand or a stone. Called a *tayammum*, it can replace both major and minor ablutions.

The five daily prayers are incumbent on all Muslims who have reached puberty. However, women who are impure because they are menstruating or have just given birth should not perform the *salat*. People who are too ill to pray are excused; if they are well enough to recite the prayers seated or lying down, they should do that.

Just as people must have been purified through the ablutions before they can perform the *salat*, so also their clothing and the place where they perform the *salat* must be pure. Clothing is pure as long as it has not been tainted by human or animal excrement, urine, semen, or blood. Following the Sunna of the Prophet, Muslim men traditionally squat when they urinate, in order to avoid splashing their clothing with urine. If clothing becomes impure, it must be rinsed before it can be worn while one performs the *salat*.

In the same way, the place of prayer must be kept pure. Practicing Muslims normally keep their homes pure, which explains why they (like Far Easterners) remove their shoes before entering the house. They will commonly pray in their homes wherever purity is preserved. In places inside or outside the house that are impure or of questionable purity, people put down a piece of cloth or a prayer carpet, which they then fold up and put away when they finish. This cloth or carpet is called a *sajjada*, a "place of much prostration."

Nature is by definition pure, and it is common in Muslim countries to see people praying in the fields by the side of the road. The main way to purify clothing or carpeting that has become impure is to wash it, but if the impure substance itself has been removed, placing the article in the sun for two or three days will also purify it.

Saying prayers in congregation is highly recommended. According to the Prophet, a *salat* said in congregation is rewarded with seventy times the reward of a *salat* said alone. A congregation is defined as two or more people praying together. Hence a husband and wife or a mother and her child are a congregation when they pray together. But in general, it is felt that the larger the congregation, the better, and this fits in nicely with the social dimension of much of Islamic practice.

The places in a community where congregational prayers are held are called "mosques." This English word is derived from the Arabic *masjid*, which means "place of prostration." The social house of worship is called a *masjid* because prostration is understood as the *salat*'s highpoint, as it were. It symbolizes the utter submission and surrender (*islam*) of the human being to God.

Men must attend the mosque once a week for the Friday congregational prayer, which is held in place of the noon prayer. Women are not required to go. Shi'ite Muslims maintain that the Friday prayer, although recommended, is not incumbent.

The rhythm of life in a traditional Islamic society is largely determined by the five daily prayers. Even today, one is made aware of this rhythm in any Muslim city by the call to prayer—the *adhan*—that is made at every mosque to summon the faithful to *salat*. Except for the first sentence, which is recited four times, and the last, which is recited once, each sentence is recited twice.

> *God is greater.*
> *I bear witness that there is no god but God.*
> *I bear witness that Muhammad is the messenger of God.*
> *Hurry to the* salat.
> *Hurry to salvation.*
> *God is greater.*
> *There is no god but God.*

In the morning *adhan*, the sentence "The *salat* is better than sleep" is usually added after "Hurry to salvation."

The person who recites the *adhan*, the muezzin, is typically selected for his strong and beautiful voice. In a traditional city, where there are many mosques located not far from each other, one hears a symphony of beautiful voices, each reciting the *adhan* in a slightly different rhythm and tune. This is particularly striking and moving at the time of the morning *adhan*, when the city is otherwise silent.

Nowadays, most people in charge of mosques have lost their sense of beauty and harmony. Instead of hearing a variety of beautiful voices issuing from the minarets, people hear the sound of loudspeakers. Often every mosque broadcasts the recorded voice of the same muezzin. Although the voice may be beautiful, loudspeakers make even the most beautiful recording ugly. The *adhan* becomes an electronic imposition that can be quite disturbing, not only to travelers, but also to the locals who have preserved their taste.

A great deal can be said about the significance of the *salat* for Muslim life. Here we will only remark that observing it has a deep effect on both the individual and collective psyches. The whole color of a society in which most people perform five daily prayers is profoundly different from one in which there is no time for God, or in which religion is a private affair, or reserved only for one day a week. The following hadith puts the prayer's effect into a nutshell:

> *God's messenger said, "Tell me, if one of you had a river at his door in which he washed five times a day, would any of his filthiness remain?"*
> *The people replied, "Nothing of his filthiness would remain."*
> *He said, "That is a likeness for the five* salats. *God obliterates sins with them."*

The Third Pillar: *Zakat*

Zakat is commonly translated as "alms tax." It is defined as a certain percentage of one's acquired property or profit for the year that is paid to the needy. In keeping with the Koran (9:60), there are eight categories of people to whom *zakat* should be given: the needy, the poor, those who collect the *zakat*, those whose hearts are to be reconciled to Islam, captives, those in debt, those who are fighting in God's path, and travelers. The rules and regulations for calculating *zakat* are quite complex. Depending on the nature of the property and the conditions under which it was acquired, it can range from 2.5 percent to 10 percent of one's profit.

The root meaning of the word *zakat* is "purity." The basic idea behind *zakat* is that people purify their wealth by giving a share of it to God. Just as ablutions purify the body and *salat* purifies the soul, so *zakat* purifies possessions and makes them pleasing to God.

Zakat has an obvious social relevance. Purification of an individual's possessions takes place through helping others. In order to pay it, one has to concern oneself with the situation of one's neighbors and discover who the needy are. *Salat*, like *zakat*, has a social significance, but what is required is that the *salat* be recited, not that it be recited with others. In contrast, *zakat* depends totally upon social interaction. One cannot pay *zakat* to oneself.

Paying *zakat* depends not only on the circumstances of those who receive, but also on the circumstances of those who pay. In other words, people pay *zakat* only if they fulfill the required conditions. They must have had an income over the year and made a profit. Those who do not fulfill these conditions cannot pay *zakat*. If they give charity in spite of their own need, this is praiseworthy, but it is not the required *zakat* because it does not fulfill the conditions.

This way of looking at *zakat* is a typical example of how Islam sets up priorities. Certain things are absolutely obligatory, like the Shahadah and the ritual prayer. Others depend upon circumstances, like the *zakat*. Notice that what is absolutely essential pertains to the individual, because there is always a person who stands before God. What is secondary pertains to society, because one is not necessarily a part of any given social conditions. This means, in brief, that Islam asks Muslims to put their own houses in order first. Only then are they expected to look at other people's houses, according to the instructions given by God.

In short, the primary task is to set up a right relationship with God, and this begins with the individual. A healthy society can only exist when its members are healthy. The individuals who make up the society are the primary focus of attention. But their religious well-being demands that they accept some measure of social responsibility. If, as the Prophet said, "A person who marries achieves one-half of his religion," this is because the family is the fundamental building block of society. If the family can be kept healthy—and this depends on the spiritual health of its members—then society can be kept healthy.

The Fourth Pillar: Fasting

The fourth pillar is "to fast during the month of Ramadan." Ramadan is the ninth month of the Islamic calendar. Since this is a lunar calendar of 355 days, each month lasts twenty-nine or thirty days. For a month to be considered as having twenty-nine and not thirty days, the new crescent moon must have been *sighted*. This helps explains why day begins at sundown: the new moon is seen at sunset on the western horizon, and then it sets. If it is cloudy and people have to depend upon calculation to decide if the new month has begun or not, the month is counted as lasting thirty days.

The month of Ramadan begins when the new crescent moon is sighted, or when the previous month reaches thirty days. Fasting begins at dawn the next morning. Dawn is defined as the time when the earliest light shows on the eastern horizon, or the time when one can see the difference between a black and a white piece of string by natural light. This is the time of the morning *adhan*, about an hour and a half before sunrise. The fast comes to an end when the sun sets; that is, when the evening *adhan* is sounded.

Fasting consists of refraining from eating, drinking, smoking, and sexual activity. All Muslims who have reached the age of puberty are required to fast, although there are several valid excuses for not fasting, such as illness and travel, and, while pregnant or menstruating, women are forbidden from fasting. Missed fasting needs to be made up for at another time, at the discretion of the person.

Ramadan is a time of heightened attention to the rules of right conduct. For example, the Prophet said, "Five things break the fast of the faster—lying, backbiting, slander, ungodly oaths, and looking with passion." In other words, at a time when certain normally permitted acts are forbidden, acts that are always forbidden ruin a person's fast.

The fact that Ramadan is a lunar month has interesting consequences. Except for the spring and autumn equinoxes, every daytime period of the year is of a different length in different locations on the face of the earth. The daylight hours in June are long in the northern hemisphere and short in the southern hemisphere. A solar month when every Muslim in the world would fast the same amount of time cannot be found—especially when one remembers that the pre-Islamic Arab solar calendar was observed by adding an extra month every three years to the lunar calendar, similar to what is done with the Jewish calendar. But the use of the lunar calendar demands that all Muslims who fast for a period of thirty-three years will have fasted for the same amount of time, no matter where they live.

Because of the lunar calendar, Ramadan moves forward in the solar calendar about eleven days every year. Thus in the year 1998 c.e., the first day of Ramadan corresponds to December 20 (give or take a day); in 1999, to December 9; in 2000, to November 28; and so on. People living in northern latitudes who will be fasting for only eight or nine hours a day during December will be fasting for seventeen or eighteen hours a day after seventeen years when Ramadan comes in June. Thus most people's lives follow a cycle regulated by Ramadan, where fasting becomes easier and then more difficult.

Like the other pillars, fasting has a strong social component. When the pattern of individual life changes, the effects are multiplied in society. In a traditional Islamic community, all places of eating are closed during the daylight hours of Ramadan. People usually have a good-sized meal just before the beginning of the fast in the early morning. Depending on the time of the year and their own habits, they may then stay awake or go back to sleep after saying their morning *salat*. For the rest of the day, they go about their activities more or less as usual.

Those who have not experienced the fast of Ramadan may think it is easy to skip breakfast and lunch, but what about that morning cup of coffee? Even a sip of water makes a difference after a heavy sleep, since it helps turn the metabolism around. In winter it is not difficult to go eight hours without food or drink, but what about June or July? One day may be easy, but what about one week, two weeks . . . ? Unless people are firm in their faith, they are not likely to make it through the whole month, summer or winter.

But to suggest that fasting during Ramadan is difficult does not mean that Muslims find it to be a hardship. By and large Ramadan tends to be the happiest time of the year, although this does not become obvious until the night. During the daytime, people are too subdued to show their happiness. Traditional Islamic cities are sights to behold during the month of fasting. Daylight hours and nighttime exhibit a total contrast. During the day there is relatively little activity, many shops are closed, and people tend to be quiet, if not morose. But as soon as the cannon sounds or the *adhan* is proclaimed, the whole atmosphere changes. Everyone has been anxiously waiting for the day's fast to end. If they follow the example of the Prophet, they immediately eat a date or two or have a drink of water, then say their evening *salat*. In public areas, right before sundown, the tea houses and restaurants are full of people sitting patiently, food and drink before them.

In many parts of the Islamic world it has become the custom to have a feast as soon as the fasting ends. In any case, the nights of Ramadan are festive occasions. The city streets come alive with the activity that is reserved for daylight hours at other times of the year.

According to Islamic law, not observing the fast is a serious sin. In order to make up for a single day missed intentionally, a person must fast for two months. However, as is often the case, there is no way to enforce this rule. People have only themselves and God to answer to. In traditional Islamic society, everyone carefully observed the fast in public. In private, they could do whatever they wanted, and no one but God was the wiser.

Today, in some of the larger cities in the Islamic world, one may have the impression that few people fast. Restaurants are busy and life seems to be going on as usual. But even in the West, many Muslims who do not observe the pillars of Islam fast for at least a day or two. (In a similar way, residual Christians are likely to go to church once a year at Easter). Part of the reason for token shows of fasting is that the fast is the one ritual that is strictly between the individual and God. Though it has social dimensions, God alone sees whether or not a person observes it. Hence, Ramadan is usually considered to be the most personal and spiritual of the pillars. It is a test of people's sincerity in their religion. The *salat* can be seen by other people, and in a tight-knit society, everyone knows how well others observe it. But no one can check on your every movement during the day to see whether or not you have taken a sip of water or nibbled a snack. Many otherwise lapsed Muslims sense this, and so they fast for a day or two just to let themselves and God know that they have not left the fold.

The Fifth Pillar: Hajj

The fifth pillar is to "make the pilgrimage to the House of God if you are able." The hajj is a set of rituals that take place in and around Mecca every year, beginning on the eighth and ending on the thirteenth day of the last lunar month, Dhu'l-Hijja (The Month of the Hajj). Mecca was a sacred center long before Islam, and according to Muslim belief, Adam himself built a sanctuary at Mecca. Eventually it was rebuilt by Abraham, and by the time of the appearance of Islam, the Kaaba (cube) had long been a place of pilgrimage for the Arab tribes. The Koran and the Prophet modified and resanctified the rituals performed at the Kaaba, making them a pillar of the religion.

Muslims are required to make the hajj once in their lifetimes, but only if they have the means to do so. To understand some of the significance of the hajj, one needs to remember that steamships, airplanes, and buses are products of the past one hundred years. For thirteen hundred years, the vast majority of Muslims made the journey to Mecca on foot, or perhaps mounted on a horse or a camel. It was not a matter of taking a two-week vacation, and then back to the office on Monday morning. Rather, for most Muslims the hajj was a difficult journey of several months if not a year or two. And once the trip was made, who wanted to hurry? People stayed in Mecca or Medina for a few months to recuperate and to prepare for their return, to meet other Muslims from all over the Islamic world, and to study. Often they stayed on for years, and often they simply came there to die, however long that might take.

Today, one can go to Mecca in a few hours from anyplace in the world. Some people decide to do the hajj this year because they did Bermuda last year. In the past, most Muslims had to fulfill strict conditions in order to make the journey. In effect, they had to be prepared for death. They had to assume that they would never return, and make all the necessary preparations for that eventuality. One of the conditions for making the hajj is that people have to pay off all their debts. If a man wanted to make the hajj, but his wife did not want to accompany him, he had to make sure that she was provided for in the way in which she was accustomed. He had to see to the provision of his children as well, and anyone else for whom he was responsible.

Traditionally, the hajj was looked upon as a grand rite of passage, a move from involvement with this world to occupation with God. In order to make the hajj, people had to finish with everything that kept them occupied on a day-to-day basis. They had to answer God's call to come and visit him. The hajj was always looked upon as a kind of death, because the Koran repeatedly describes death as the meeting with God, and the Kaaba is the house of God. The hajj, in short, was a death and a meeting with God, and the return from the hajj was a rebirth. This helps explain why the title "hajji" ("one who has made the hajj") has always been highly respected throughout the Islamic world. Hajjis were looked upon as people who were no longer involved with the pettiness of everyday life. They were treated as models of piety and sanctity, and no doubt most of them assumed the responsibilities toward society that the title implies, even if some took advantage of the respect that was accorded to them.

A Sixth Pillar? Jihad and *Mujahada*

Some authorities have held that there is a sixth pillar of Islam: jihad. This word has become well-known in English because of the contemporary political situation and the focus of the media on violence. Hence, a bit more attention has to be paid to it than would be warranted if we were simply looking at the role that jihad plays in Islam.

The first thing one needs to understand about the term *jihad* is that "holy war" is a highly misleading and usually inaccurate translation. In Islamic history, the label has been applied to any war by "our side." Until very recently in the West, the situation was similar; every war was considered holy, because God was on our side. By employing the term, Muslims condemned the other side as anti-God. In short, the word has played the role of patriotic slogans everywhere. To undertake a jihad is, in contemporary terms, "to fight for the preservation of democracy and freedom." It is to do what the good people do.

The Koranic usage of the term *jihad* is far broader than the political use of the term might imply. The basic meaning of the term is "struggle." Most commonly, the Koran uses the verb along with the expression "in the path of God." The "path of God" is of course the path for right conduct that God has set down in the Koran and the example of the Prophet.

From one point of view, jihad is simply the complement to *islam*. The word *islam*, after all, means "submission" or "surrender." Westerners tend to think of this as a kind of passivity. But surrender takes place to God's will, and it is God's will that people struggle in His path. Hence submission demands struggle. Receptivity toward God's command requires people to be active toward all the negative tendencies in society and themselves that pull them away from God. In this perspective, submission to God and struggle in his path go together harmoniously, and neither is complete without the other.

Within the Islamic context, the fact that submission to God demands struggle in his path is self-evident. *Salat, zakat*, fasting, and hajj are all struggle. If you think they are easy, try performing the *salat* according to the rules for a few days. In fact, the biggest obstacles people face in submitting themselves to God are their own laziness and lack of imagination. People let the currents of contemporary opinion and events carry them along without resisting. It takes an enormous struggle to submit to an authority that breaks not only with one's own likes and dislikes, but also with the pressure of society to conform to the crowd.

The place of jihad in the divine plan is typically illustrated by citing words that the Prophet uttered on one occasion when he had returned to Medina from a battle with the enemies of the new religion. He said, "We have returned from the lesser jihad to the greater jihad." The people said, "O Messenger of God, what jihad could be greater than struggling against the unbelievers with the sword?" He replied, "Struggling against the enemy in your own breast."

In later texts, this inward struggle is most often called *mujahada* rather than jihad. Grammatically, the word *mujahada*—which is derived from the same root as jihad—means exactly the same thing. But the word *jihad* came to be employed to refer to outward wars as well as the inward struggle against one's own negative tendencies, while the word *mujahada* is used almost exclusively for the greater, inward jihad.

Those Muslim scholars who have said that jihad is a sixth pillar of Islam have usually had in mind the fact that struggle in the path of God is a necessity for all Muslims. At the same time, they recognize that this struggle will sometimes take the outward form of war against the enemies of Islam.

But it needs to be stressed that in the common language of Islamic countries, the word *jihad* is used for any war. In a similar way, most Americans have considered any war engaged in by the United States as a just war. But from the point of view of the strict application of Islamic teachings, most so-called jihads have not deserved the name. Any king (or dictator, as we have witnessed more recently) can declare a jihad.

There were always a few of the religious authorities who would lend support to the king—such as the scholar whom the king had appointed to be chief preacher at the royal mosque. But there have usually been a good body of the ulama who have not supported wars simply because kings declared them. Rather, they would only support those that followed the strict application of Islamic teachings. By these standards, it is probably safe to say that there have been few if any valid jihads in the past century, and perhaps not for the past several hundred years.

The Shariah

The Five Pillars are the basic practices of Islam. They are relevant to every Muslim, though it may happen that many people never have to pay *zakat* or do not make the hajj because their personal circumstances make it impossible for them to do so. But all Muslims have uttered the Shahadah, because that is what makes them Muslims. The *salat* is incumbent upon all adults every day, although women are excused during certain times of the month. Fasting during Ramadan is also an annual practice for everyone, though there are several valid reasons for not observing it.

There are many other Koranic and prophetic injunctions that Muslims have to observe. Many of these pertain to moral prescriptions and have a universal applicability. Among forbidden activities are lying, stealing, murder, adultery, and fornication. Other injunctions relate to domains that in modern Western usage are usually considered to lie outside the pale of religion, such as inheritance, marriage, business transactions, and foods that may or may not be eaten.

The whole body of rules and regulations set down by the Koran and the Prophet gradually came to be codified as the Shariah, or "the broad path leading to water," the road of right activity that all Muslims have to follow. The water here is the heavenly water that purifies and saves, a water that is alluded to in many Koranic verses:

> *He sends down on you water from heaven, to purify you thereby,*
> *and to put away from you the defilement of Satan. (8:11)*

The term *Shariah* is often translated as "Islamic law" or "revealed law." The study of this domain of Islamic learning is called *fiqh* ("jurisprudence"). The specialists in this kind of learning are the *fuqaha'* ("jurists") to whom we have already referred. Practically all ulama—all Muslims learned in Islam—have a wide knowledge of jurisprudence, but some of them have specialized in other areas, such as theology, philosophy, or Sufism. As already indicated, the vast majority of those who are recognized as ulama in Islamic countries—the mullahs as they are called in many places—are in fact jurists, since they have little or no learning in other domains. This is to say that knowledge of Islam's first

dimension is required of all Muslims, but knowledge of the second and
third dimensions, though in many ways as important, is much less
widely disseminated.

The primary importance of activity in the Islamic view of things
appears completely natural to Muslims. After all, everyone must be
involved with activity because of the human body, and hence everyone
has need of guidelines for doing things. Of course it is also true that
everyone has a mind and a heart, but it is in the nature of things—at
least in the historical eras of which we have knowledge—that most
people do not get involved with too much thinking, nor do many people
devote themselves to purifying their hearts and their intentions in
order to prepare themselves for the vision of God. These endeavors
have always been the domain of a minority, and Islam is no exception.

One of the reasons that the word *law* is not quite appropriate to refer
to everything dealt with in the Shariah is the connotations of the
English word. To begin with, we think of law as commands and prohibitions. For example, the law tells you that you have to pay taxes and that
you are not allowed to commit murder. At the same time, there is a third
category of human activities, the category of things that are not regulated by law.

Islamic jurisprudence deals with these same three categories, but it
adds two more domains that it considers important. Not only does the
Shariah tell people what they must do and what they must not do, it also
tells them what they should do and what they should not do, and it tells
them explicitly that many things are indifferent. Hence we are faced
with five categories of actions: the required, the recommended, the
indifferent, the reprehensible, and the forbidden.

As a result of this way of looking at things, the Shariah covers a great
deal of ground that in modern terms seems to belong outside a legal
system. As an example, let us take a look at the category of "recommended." As we have seen, the Five Pillars are all required. But in
addition to the five required *salat*s, there are a large number of recommended *salat*s. For example, it is recommended that, before saying the
two cycles of the morning prayer, people should perform two other
cycles. Each of the daily prayers has a certain number of recommended
cycles that accompany it.

In the case of fasting, people are required to fast only during Ramadan.
But it is recommended that they fast during certain other days of the
year, certain days of each month, and even certain days of each week.
Likewise, those who pay the *zakat* are not required to give more than a
certain amount of their profit, but it is recommended that they give
away much more. It is also recommended to make loans—without
interest, since interest (according to most opinions) is forbidden. Some
authorities maintain that lending money is more meritorious than
giving it away, because the person who borrows the money has a moral
obligation to pay it back, and thus he or she is encouraged to find steady

employment. And when the money is paid back, it can be loaned to someone else, thus doing more good work.

The fifth pillar also has a recommended form, which is a pilgrimage to the House of God outside the season of the hajj, a ritual called the 'umra. People should make the 'umra if they have the opportunity. And since it is a recommended act, it needs to be described in all its details in the textbooks on the Shariah.

Many things are considered reprehensible, such as divorce, using more water than is necessary while making an ablution, scratching oneself while making the salat, and eating until one is satiated.

The attention that the Shariah pays to food often appears strange to Christians (in contrast to Jews). Muslims are forbidden to consume intoxicating beverages and narcotics. They are also forbidden to eat pig, dog, domestic donkey, and carrion, which is defined as the meat of any animal that has not been ritually slaughtered. Animals are slaughtered ritually by cutting their throats while mentioning the name of God. This ritually slaughtered meat is then called halal (permitted). Many jurists maintain that meat prepared by Jews or Christians is halal for Muslims, while others disagree. On this point the Koran gives a general ruling: "The food of the People of the Book [those who have been given scriptures, such as Jews and Christians] is permitted to you" (5:5), although it is understood that this food, if meat, must be slaughtered in the name of God. Kosher meats in particular seem to fit this category. In general, the Shariah declares that it is forbidden to eat any wild animal that has claws, nails, or tusks with which it overcomes its prey or its enemies, such as lion, tiger, wolf, bear, elephant, monkey, and cat. However, one school of law maintains that it is reprehensible to eat these animals, not forbidden. Minor differences of opinion among the jurists are quite common. Thus, most of them maintain that all animals that live in the sea are permitted, whereas one school makes an exception for sea animals that do not take the form of fish—such as shellfish, crabs, alligators, or walruses.

Because of the existence of five categories instead of three, Islamic law goes into all sorts of details about everyday life that would not otherwise be discussed. It has many branches and subfields, expertise in which can require years of study. Many Muslims accord so much importance to the Shariah that it seems to become for them the whole of their religion, at least in practice. Nevertheless, many of the greatest Muslim authorities have warned against spending too much time studying the Shariah, since this can blind people to the other dimensions of the religion, which are also essential to Islam.

Al-Ghazali (d. 505/1111), one of the most famous of the great authorities, held that each Muslim must have enough knowledge of the Shariah to put it into practice in his or her own life. But if Muslims do not need a given injunction in their circumstances, they have no need to know about it. There will be, in any case, people who devote their lives to the study of the Shariah, and they can be consulted when the need arises. This explains the basic function of the jurists in society: to explain the details of the Shariah to those who need to observe it in any given circumstances.

To take a simple example, when a youngster wants to learn how to say the *salat*, the normal route is to ask a family member how to do it. There is no need to consult books, since most people are familiar with the basic rules, but it may happen that one person says you hold your hands this way, and another says you hold your hands that way. What do you do? Of course you ask someone else. Soon, by asking, you will reach the imam (prayer leader) of the local mosque, who is normally the most knowledgeable person about these things. But the imam may not be an expert in jurisprudence, and if the question is good enough, he may send you to a jurist, who will then explain the details. Not that this is necessarily the last word. There are other jurists, and jurists, like scholars everywhere, have differences of opinion. Basically, it is your duty to keep on asking until you are satisfied with the answer.

Sin

The Shariah sets down rules for right activity. These are God's rules as specified in the Koran and explained by the Prophet. The Koran and the Hadith are the two basic sources of the Shariah. If the ulama consult these sources and a question still remains, they can consult the opinions of the great Muslims, the recognized authorities in the Shariah. Hence consensus *(ijma)* is recognized as a third source of Shariite rulings; Sunnis consider reasoning by analogy *(qiyas)* a fourth source, while Shi'ites put reason *('aql)* in its place.

If people accept the instructions of God as set down in the Shariah and put them into practice, this is called "obedience" *(ta'a)*. A correct act is an obedient act. God or his Prophet say, "Do this" or "Don't do that," and a good Muslim obeys these instructions. The Koran frequently employs the word *obey* to refer to right activity:

> *Obey God and the Messenger; perhaps you will be shown mercy.*
> *(3:132)*

> *Obey God and obey the Messenger, and beware. But if you turn your backs, then know it is only for Our Messenger to deliver the clear message. (5:92)*

> *Whoso obeys God and His Messenger, He will admit him to gardens through which rivers flow, therein dwelling forever. (48:17)*

> *Whosoever obeys God and the Messenger—they are with those whom God has blessed. (4:69)*

It is not for any man or woman of faith, when God and His Messenger have decreed something, to have a choice in the matter. Whosoever disobeys God and His Messenger has been misguided with a clear misguidance. (33:36)

If obedience is right activity, then disobedience (*ma'siya*) is wrong activity. Human disobedience began with Adam, who ate the forbidden fruit. "Adam disobeyed his Lord and went astray" (20:121). Disobedience is the attribute of anyone who fails to obey God and his messengers. The Shariah codifies the instructions of God and the Prophet, so disobedience to the Shariah is considered disobedience to God. This is one of the meanings understood from the following verse, where "the possessors of the command" can be interpreted to mean those who have the requisite learning to explain the Shariah to Muslims:

O you who have faith! Obey God, and obey the Messenger and the possessors of the command among you. If you should quarrel on anything, refer it to God and the Messenger. (4:59)

The Koran uses the verb *to disobey* in several verses, almost always in discussion of the reaction of the wrongdoers to past prophets. But the underlying message for Muslims is clear:

These are God's bounds. Whoso obeys God and His Messenger, him He will admit to gardens through which rivers flow, therein dwelling forever; that is the mighty triumph. But whoso disobeys God and His Messenger, him He will admit to a Fire, therein dwelling forever, and for him awaits a humbling chastisement. (4:13-14)

Scholars writing on Islam frequently translate *ma'siya* as "sin," and of course this word does mean sin in a general sort of way. But disobedience is a special kind of sin, one that is defined in terms of God's commands and prohibitions; and it always calls to mind its opposite, which is obedience. The Koran uses several other words that are commonly translated as sin, including, among others, *dhanb*, *ithm*, and *khati'a*. Each of these terms has nuances that differentiate it from the others. All this is to say that the English word *sin* is, from the Islamic point of view, extremely vague, since it encompasses several types of activity.

What all these terms have in common is that talk of sin involves judgments about activity, and this is the domain of the Shariah. The Shariah cannot ignore the issue of intentions, but it deals with them almost exclusively in relation to acts. Those of the ulama who look at intentions from the perspective of Islam's third dimension have a far broader view of the deep moral and spiritual issues that are involved in sin.

It would be appropriate to round out this discussion of disobedience and sin with a discussion of the general Koranic view on the good works that people perform in order to be obedient. However, we will leave this discussion for Part III of the book. At that point, we will have enough background to relate good works to all three dimensions of Islam. For the time being, we will simply say that the most common term that the Koran employs for good works is *salihat*, which can be translated as "wholesome deeds." Those who perform these deeds are often called *al-salihun* (the wholesome).

When the Koran and the Islamic tradition mention wholesome deeds, what is meant is activity that represents obedience to God's command. The primary wholesome deeds are the Five Pillars, but every sort of good deed is included in the category, that is, all those deeds that the Shariah recognizes as good. In addition, the authorities of the second and third dimensions of Islam often broaden the term to include a wider definition of good.

Chapter 2.

THE HISTORICAL EMBODIMENT OF *ISLAM*

ع

The ulama are those who have knowledge of the religion. By this definition, the most knowledgeable person is God Himself, and indeed, one of His names is *al-'alim*, the Knowing. Among human beings, the Prophet Muhammad is considered to have had more knowledge than anyone else, and he himself said, "I came to know everything in the heavens and the earth." Naturally, the primary teachers of the Shariah are God and the Prophet – as represented by the Koran and the Hadith.

The Koran and the Sunna

The role of the Prophet in codifying Muslim learning should not be underestimated. In principle, everything is in the Koran. But actually, an enormous number of details concerning Islamic practice can be found only in the Hadith. For example, the Koran repeatedly commands people to perform the *salat*, and one can probably understand from various verses that this performance involves standing, bowing, prostrating oneself, and sitting. Likewise, the Koran makes it clear that people need to be pure before they perform the *salat*. But nowhere does the Koran provide precise instructions on how to perform the prayers or make the ablutions. Here the Sunna — the exemplary practice — of the Prophet becomes absolutely essential for the religion. The Sunna in turn is recorded in the Hadith. It is the Prophet who told people that they should stand, bow, and prostrate themselves in such and such a manner and while reciting such and such Koranic verses or words of praise and thanksgiving.

Many of those who were especially close to the Prophet played an extremely important role in the transmission and dissemination of Islamic learning. They heard what the Prophet said on various occasions, or they saw what he did, and later they reported his words or described his actions to others. Among the most important of these companions were his wife, A'isha, and his cousin and son-in-law, Ali. The reports of hundreds of the Prophet's companions are recorded in the books on Hadith.

Islam is fundamentally a practice, a way of life, a pattern for establishing harmony with God and his creation. Just as *islam* signifies, in its most universal meaning, the submission of all things to the divine wisdom and command, so also in its more specific, human senses, it signifies the proper functioning of the human being and human society through submission to the divine pattern. This pattern for right life is manifested first and foremost in doing. It is true that doing depends upon knowing and willing, on choices differentiated and courses of activity consciously followed, but that is another issue — which will be discussed in its own place. For now we want to stress the fact that the criterion for being a Muslim is fundamentally the outward activity that people perform.

Hence, to be a good Muslim means following the Sunna of the Prophet — doing things in the way that Muhammad did them. The most important thing that Muhammad did was to receive the Koran from God, thereby establishing the religion of Islam. His followers cannot receive the Koran directly from God, but they can receive it indirectly from him through the Prophet's intermediary. They receive it by learning it, memorizing it, and reciting it.

Memorization of the Koran is considered one of the most beneficial religious acts, and, as we have seen, it provides the basis for traditional Islamic education. All Muslims memorize at least some of the Koran, because without knowing the Fatihah and certain other verses, they cannot recite the *salat*. The *salat* itself is the daily renewal of the Koran in the Muslim. It is the first and primary embodiment of the Koranic revelation in human existence.

Given the foundational nature of activity for human existence, it is not surprising that Muslims look first to activity in judging the extent to which Islam is observed. Historically, what is certain is that the fundamental activities go back to the prophetic period, and that Muslims have always been extremely attentive to what exactly should be done in every circumstance. They observed the Prophet carefully, and they listened to him attentively, and they put what they had learned into practice in their own lives. The Shariah was later elaborated and codified on the basis of what pious and sincere Muslims were doing. And these people traced the pattern for their own activities back to the Prophet's Sunna.

We will not go into the historical details of how exactly Islamic practice was passed down among the early generations of Muslims. These things are not known for certain, and modern historians have expended a good deal of effort in trying to map this out, without too much success. But we can summarize the net result of the transmission of the Sunna—the birth of several recognized ways of observing the Shariah.

The *Madhhabs*

As the years and centuries passed, the living memory of Muhammad and his Sunna gradually weakened, and it became more and more necessary to record the details of his life and practice so that they would not be lost. At the same time, the areas within which Islam became established continued to go through the vicissitudes that mark human existence—the differences of opinion, the struggles for power, the loves and hates, the natural and man-made catastrophes. In other words, history went along as usual, but now the Koran and the Sunna of the Prophet became added factors in human relationships.

The picture of those times was the picture of all times. Ali summed up the reports of all the historians to come when he said, "Time is two days: A day for you, and a day against you." But he did not leave it at that. Following the example of the Koran, which deals with historical events only insofar as they teach something about the human relationship with God, he reminded people of two of the primary virtues that need to be cultivated: "When time is for you, give thanks to God, and when it is against you, have patience."

At the beginning of Islam, observing the Sunna of the Prophet was part and parcel of being a Muslim, and one learned it by following the example of those who were Muslims before. This explains the sense of such prophetic sayings as the following: "My companions are like stars. Whichever you follow, you will be guided." After the companions came the "followers," those who had met the companions. As long as Islam was a relatively small community in which faith and practice remained intense, it was perfectly feasible for people to be good Muslims by following the example of their companions and teachers. But gradually the community—as religious community, rooted in Islam's three dimensions—became dissipated, especially when the early conquests brought enormous wealth. Many Muslims lost sight of the original goals of the religion and became caught up with other activities. At this point religious learning became more and more the domain of a limited number of people, and they found it feasible to pass on their learning only to a relatively small number of students and perhaps to write a book or two to preserve some of the essentials of knowledge.

Knowledge of the Sunna, in short, gradually became a specialized field of learning. Moreover, as the community expanded, the vicissitudes of life and fortune meant that Muslims came face to face with all sorts of human experience that had to be sorted out. The idea that *islam* is the attribute of right activity and embraces the whole of creation meant that nothing could be ignored by those who were trying to put the Sunna into practice.

But what did people do when they met a situation that had never arisen during the Prophet's lifetime? Or, from another direction altogether, what did they do when they met two or more contradictory reports about the Prophet's activity? How did they decide which report is correct? Issues such as these gradually led to the formation of a number of different "trodden paths," each representing a slightly different understanding of what exactly the Sunna of the Prophet was and how it could be applied to human life. We say "slightly different" from a modern perspective. Within the context of the times, the differences often appeared major, and on occasion conflicting views could lead to pitched battles (although this is true only if various social and political factors were mixed into the brew). At first there were scores of these paths, each focused on the teachings of someone thoroughly knowledgeable in the Sunna. Gradually some of the ways disappeared or became consolidated with others. Eventually four paths became recognized among Sunnis as equally valid. Muslims could follow any path they chose, and it has not been uncommon for them to combine the paths, following one on one issue and another on some other issue.

The word that came to be employed for the different versions of the Prophet's Sunna was *madhhab*, which derives from a root meaning "to go." A *madhhab* is a way of going, a route, a road that is walked, a trodden path. It is sometimes translated as "school of law" or "school of jurisprudence." Each correct way of practicing Islam is a way of walking in the Sunna. Each represents one way of interpreting and applying the Shariah.

The four *madhhab*s of Sunni Islam are named after those who are looked back upon as their founders, the ones who took the most important steps in codifying the rules and regulations of the *madhhab* and differentiating it from other ways of interpreting the Sunna. The four founders are Abu Hanifa (d. 150/767), Malik ibn Anas (d. 179/795), al-Shafi'i (d. 204/820), and Ibn Hanbal (d. 241/855). Most Shi'ites follow a fifth *madhhab* named after the sixth Imam, Ja'far al-Sadiq (d. 148/765), who was, incidentally, one of the teachers of Abu Hanifa.

There are no major differences separating the *madhhab*s, at least not from the external perspective that we naturally have to take. A non-Muslim unfamiliar with the Shariah would find it extremely difficult to see any difference, for example, between the way two Muslims who follow two different *madhhab*s perform the *salat*. But specialists in jurisprudence can point out tiny differences in practically every stage of the ritual. The different schools very often agree on certain points, while differing on others. Ja'fari or Shi'ite law is no different here, and it tends to be especially close to the Hanafi position. However, there are two specific instances where Ja'fari law establishes minor practices that set it apart from the four Sunni schools. The first is the permissibility of a form of temporary marriage (*mut'a*), and the second is in the establishment of a specific form of alms-tax (the *khums*), which is the share of the Imam.

Although there were many *madhhab*s in early times, eventually all Sunni Muslims came to observe one of the four just mentioned. Once these became established as the right ways, no major changes in the Shariah took place. So much is this true that it has often been said that the "gate of effort" in determining the rulings of the Shariah was closed. Many of the great ulama, however, took no notice of this opinion and continued to exert effort as they saw fit. As for the Shi'ites, they reject this opinion absolutely, saying that the "gate of effort" is always open and that it is forbidden to follow the juridical rulings of someone who is dead.

Early Western scholarship on Islam tended to make a big point of this closing of the gate of effort, often with the intention of criticizing Islam for an alleged stultification of legal thinking. Scholars often like to suggest that modern people like themselves are very smart and dynamic, while people in olden times were rather dull and unimaginative. More recent scholarship has become aware of the self-congratulation implicit in many earlier judgments of non-Western cultures and has begun to reevaluate the sources. As a result, it has been shown that in the case of Islamic juridical thinking, a great deal has been going on in many areas, especially when it has been a question of new situations—situations that naturally occur because of historical change. Where the judgment about closure is more or less valid, however, is in the area of the Five Pillars, the fundamental acts established by the Sunna.

Jurisprudence and Politics

The jurists are those ulama who specialize in the Shariah. Each jurist is typically a specialist in one *madhhab*, although some may be familiar with other *madhab*s as well. In a certain Christian and post-Christian way of looking at things, jurisprudence appears to have no relevance to what today is often called "spirituality." There is a certain truth in this judgment, and many Muslim authorities over the centuries have made the same point. After all, the jurists are very careful about looking at all the details of activity, and typically they drone on and on in the manner of lawyers. Jurisprudence is a science that revels in nit-picking. Although it is a necessary science in Islam, if too much stress is placed upon it, it can discourage the attention that should be paid to Islam's second and third dimensions.

Like modern lawyers, many of Islam's legal authorities were intensely interested in and involved with political affairs. The Shariah, after all, sets down many rules and regulations that have a general social relevance, especially the teachings on transactions and contracts. In addition, the Koran says a great deal about the importance of justice and honesty in human relationships. It establishes concrete rules for redistribution of wealth through *zakat* and encourages other forms of charity.

There is no doubt that the Koran and the Prophet provided guidelines for society and that these have been put into effect with some success throughout Islamic history. But neither the Koran nor the Hadith is explicit on methods of government. Some of the early Muslim philosophers proposed political theories, but these were never influential in practice. What occurred in Islamic history is that the institutions of the time, which were basically monarchical, continued to function as before. The Umayyad and Abbasid caliphates ruled ostensibly as Islamic governments, but they were hereditary monarchies nonetheless. Since the caliphs appealed to Islam for their legitimacy, they were forced to acknowledge the Shariah as the law of the community. Some of them also observed the Shariah carefully in their own lives, and, by most accounts, many of them did not. For the majority of Muslims, however, kings and caliphs retained their legitimacy so long as they did not reject the Shariah in public.

It is commonly said that Islam does not exclude government from the realm of the sacred. This is true. Islam does not exclude anything under the sun from the realm of the sacred, but this does not mean that every government in Islamic history has been a government run by sincere Muslims intent upon observing the Shariah. Kings tend to be worldly people, as do those who become involved with government in general. Muslims have always recognized that government *should* put the Shariah into practice and be run by good Muslims, but they have also recognized that this has been the exception rather than the rule. Some Muslims would claim that the last example of a good Muslim ruling the community is provided by the fourth caliph, Ali, and from the time of the Umayyads to the present, the extent to which government has heeded Islamic teachings has steadily decreased. Today's Islamic republics are no exception to this general rule. By and large, religion has simply become the latest tool of those who crave power.

Many Islamic authorities have criticized the jurists for their tendency to congregate in centers of power. The jurists always have something to say about government policies. In many cases, they are simply doing their duty, which is to try to provide guidance as to how the Shariah can be properly observed, but like lawyers everywhere, the jurists know how to manipulate the law for their own ends, and there have always been jurists who would sell their skills to the powers that be. Every king has had an official mullah or two who was willing to issue whatever "Islamic" edicts were necessary for the government to function in the way that the king desired.

In the modern world, Muslim scholars have devoted an extraordinary amount of attention to theories of government and political science, often in the attempt to make Islam fit the mold of "democracy" dictated by Western models (and remember that Marxism has always presented itself as the best form of democracy). There is no lack of books on politics in the Islamic context, and readers who are interested can consult any decent library.

In our view of things, politics was never a very important issue for the vast majority of Muslims throughout history. Many Muslim thinkers were intensely interested in establishing social harmony and equilibrium on the basis of the Shariah, but they did not see this as something that should be or could be instituted from above. People had to conform themselves to the Shariah and the other dimensions of the religion. If they did so, society would function harmoniously.

The Koran repeatedly commands "bidding to honor and forbidding dishonor," and this has always been taken as a command to take a certain responsibility for one's social surroundings. But this is one of many commands, and other commands take precedence. It is difficult to read this as meaning that God has now empowered a few politicians to take control and put into effect policies that "society needs."

The ideal of Islamic life has always been organic rather than mechanical. The best way to gain a feeling for this is simply to look at the physical structure of traditional Islamic cities, which are reminiscent of luxuriant jungle growth. The modern ideal is rather the grid, a "rational" order imposed from outside. In many parts of the Islamic world, the secularizing governments have imposed the grid on the old city. One of the aims has been, of course, to destroy the traditional social structure so that it can be remade in the image of the industrialized West. So also, modern Muslim political thinkers have been attempting to rationalize the traditional teachings on government and society with specific social goals in view. We will suggest, when we discuss the last part of the hadith of Gabriel, why this excessive stress upon a specific kind of modern rationality is simply aiding in the dissolution of Islamic values and the Islamic world view.

PART II:

IMAN

Islam and *Iman*

In the hadith of Gabriel, the Prophet said that faith was "that you have faith in God, His angels, His books, His prophets, and the Last Day, and that you have faith in the measuring out, both its good and its evil."

At first sight, this looks like a definition of faith. But notice that the Prophet repeats the word *faith*. A proper definition cannot repeat the word being defined in the definition. Hence, the Prophet is assuming that his listeners already know what faith is and that they need to be told what they should have faith *in*. It is not enough to have faith and leave it at that, nor is it enough to "have faith in God." Faith must also have other objects, and unless one has faith in all the mentioned objects, one's faith will not be counted as Islamic faith, but rather as some other kind of faith.

Before we turn to the objects of Islamic faith, we need a definition of the word *faith* itself, or rather of the Arabic term *iman*, because some common ideas about *faith*, as the term is employed in English, do not apply to *iman*.

In English, we usually make no distinction between faith and belief. However, Wilfred Cantwell Smith has pointed out that the word *faith*— even without considering the Arabic context—needs to be differentiated from the word *belief*.[1] When we say that people believe in something, we mean that they have confidence that something is true, but frequently we are implying that they are mistaken and are flying in the face of all the evidence. In Islamic languages, the word *iman* has no such negative connotation. *Iman* involves confidence in a truth that is really true, not a supposed truth. There is no suggestion that people have faith in a falsehood. The object of their faith expresses the objective reality of things. Moreover, faith means that when people have this confidence, they commit themselves to acting on the basis of the truth that they know.

The Prophet defined the word *iman* by saying, "Faith is a knowledge in the heart, a voicing with the tongue, and an activity with the limbs." Thus faith involves knowing, speaking, and doing.

Someone who has *iman* first knows or recognizes in the heart that something is true. The *heart*—a term which is often used in such contexts in the Koran—is not primarily the place of emotions. Rather, it is the specific faculty or spiritual organ that separates human beings from nonhuman beings. Usually we refer to it by words such as *intelligence*. In philosophical language, it can be associated with what the word *rational* refers to when the human being is defined as a rational animal.

In the Koranic view of things, a rational animal is an animal with a heart. A human being without a functioning heart is an animal, or worse. It is in reference to such people that the Koran says, "They are but as the cattle, or rather, they are further astray from the truth" (25:44). A healthy heart is able to understand the nature of things, but many hearts are, in Koranic terms, "sick" or "rusted" or "locked." Only a healthy heart has faith and is able to see things the way they are:

> *They have hearts, but do not understand with them. (7:179)*

> *It is not the eyes that are blind, but blind are the hearts within the breasts. (22:46)*

> *What, do they not ponder the Koran? Or is it that there are locks on their hearts? (47:24)*

> *They would trick God and the faithful, and only themselves they deceive, but they are not aware. In their hearts is a sickness. (2:10)*

> *No indeed; but what they were earning has rusted upon their hearts. (83:14)*

> *Those—He has written faith upon their hearts. (58:22)*

> *It is He who sent down tranquillity into the hearts of the faithful, so that they might add faith to their faith. (48:4)*

Faith is also a "voicing with the tongue." The human quality of intelligence becomes manifest in rational speech, a faculty possessed only by human beings, at least in our world. The heart's recognition of the truth must be expressed, and its first expression must be in the most human of ways—through speech.

It is difficult to overestimate the importance of speech in the Islamic perspective. God himself creates the universe through speaking. "Our only word to a thing, when We desire it, is to say to it 'Be!' and it is" (16:40). God provides guidance by speaking through the prophets. Hence, all the scriptures are the speech of God. The Koran is God's speech to Muslims and the foundation of everything Islamic. Moreover, human beings return to God by speaking to Him; that is, through prayer. As we saw earlier, the Shahadah, the first pillar of Islam and the fundamental act of Muslims, is a speech act. It is not sufficient simply to think that there is no god but God and Muhammad is His messenger. One must also say so. The ultimate importance of this speech act is indicated by the fact that it alone suffices for a person to be a Muslim. The centerpole of Islam, the *salat*, is a series of bodily actions accompanied by speech, and if, for some reason, a person cannot perform the bodily movements, it is sufficient to recite the words (mentally if necessary). In sum, "voicing with the tongue" is the most important act a person performs: It marks the person's humanity and makes possible the establishment of a relationship with God.

But speaking, of course, is not the only requirement for faith. We all know people who say one thing and do something else, and we do not usually have much respect for them. The Koran makes it clear that God Himself dislikes this quality in people: "Very hateful is it to God that you say what you do not do" (61:3). Hence we come to the third element in the Prophet's definition of faith, "activity with the limbs." Having recognized that something is true and acknowledged its truth verbally, people must commit themselves to this truth and show their commitment in their activities. They must live in conformity with the truth that they know. The necessity of "activity with the limbs" for complete faith explains why most Muslim theologians include *islam* as part of *iman*. *Islam* is precisely activity with the limbs—not just any activity, but activity as commanded by God, or in conformity with the truth of the Koran.

The fact that *iman* demands *islam* is important. Faith includes submission to God's instructions, but submission to God's instructions does not necessarily include faith. A person can act outwardly as a Muslim without having the faith that the Prophet describes in the hadith of Gabriel. This does not necessarily nullify the activity, but it does call its value into question.

A simple example can help clarify the relationship between *iman* and *islam*. Today in America there are several million Muslims. Most of them are immigrants or the children of immigrants. American Muslims go to the same schools as other Americans, and it frequently happens that a Muslim will fall in love with a non-Muslim and want to get married. If the family observes the Shariah, then the marriage has to take place according to Islamic law. If a Muslim man wants to marry a Christian or Jewish woman, the general opinion of the jurists is that the marriage can take place without any difficulty, so long as the children are raised as Muslims. But if a Muslim woman wants to marry a non-Muslim man, the Shariah says that this is not permissible. What to do? The most common solution to this problem is formal conversion to Islam. The man simply recites the Shahadah before two Muslim witnesses. Then the marriage can go ahead with no objections. Normally, no one asks if the man has faith in what he says, because the Shariah is concerned with activity, not with faith. As the Prophet said in a famous hadith, criticizing a companion for judging that someone's profession of faith was false, "Did you open the heart and look?" Faith is a matter between God and human beings. It is not for people to judge. Only activity can be judged by others, not the contents of the heart.

The distinction between *islam* and *iman* is mentioned in a passage from the Koran that we have already quoted:

> *The bedouins say, "We have faith." Say, "You do not have faith. Rather say, 'We have submitted,' for faith has not yet entered your hearts. If you obey God and His messenger, He will not diminish you anything of your works." (49:14)*

There are a number of points that need to be noticed in this Koranic passage: First, *iman* and *islam* are two different things. The fact that people have submitted to the commands of God does not mean that they have faith in God. They may have submitted out of fear, or to make friends and allies, or to marry a girl.

Second, faith is located in the heart. In another verse the Koran says, "They will give you satisfaction with their mouths, but refuse in their hearts" (9:8). Muhammad is told to inform the bedouins that they have no faith, because it is not found in their hearts, which is to say that they do not have the required recognition of the truth and commitment to it. Moreover, notice that Muhammad tells them this not on the basis of his own judgment, but on the basis of God's instruction. God alone can look into people's hearts and judge their intentions and thoughts. "God knows what is in your hearts" (33:51), but we do not know what is in other people's hearts.

Third, submission is the domain of obedience and works (*a'mal*). People obey God by doing what He asks them to do. If the works follow God's command, they will be rewarded, even if these works are not accompanied by recognition of the truth and genuine commitment to it. This is not to say that anything people do, if it happens to coincide with God's command, will be rewarded. The works in view here are the basic acts of obedience set down by the Koran; that is, the pillars of Islam. The bedouins have come and submitted—they have become Muslims. Hence, their intention is to follow the religion and obey the Prophet, and they will be rewarded in keeping with their intention.

Some of the significance of *iman* can be understood by considering its opposite, *kufr*, a word that is usually translated as "infidelity" or "unbelief." It is true that in ordinary language a *kafir*—a person who has the quality of *kufr*—is someone who does not accept Islam. Hence, if the Muslims are believers, the *kafirs* must be unbelievers or infidels. But we have already suggested that "belief" is not the best translation for *iman*, and so also "unbelief" is only a rough try at *kufr*. When we study the use of the word *kufr* and its derivatives in the Koran, we see that it has certain nuances that are difficult to catch in English.

To begin with, the Koran employs *kufr* not only as the opposite of *iman*, but also as the opposite of *shukr*, which means "gratitude." In the Islamic view of things, the fact that human beings are God's creatures and have received their existence and everything that they possess from his creative activity means that they should be grateful to him. Without God's generous giving, they would not exist. Gratitude is the first character trait that people owe to God.

After the formula of consecration, the first words of the Koran are "Praise belongs to God" (*al-hamdu lillah*), and this Arabic expression of gratitude is as commonplace in Islamic languages (not only in Arabic) as "thank you" is in English. It is, so to speak, common courtesy to acknowledge one's debt to God. This sentence sets the tone for the whole Koran and provides its message in a nutshell.

Notice that this phrase, "Praise belongs to God," is not an exclamation, although people may employ it as such. It is not equivalent to the English sentence "Praise be to God!" which would be uttered on some special occasion. Rather, it is a simple statement of fact. No one else deserves praise, because no one else is the source of good and benefit. Everything positive and praiseworthy comes from God, even if talent or the weather or luck seem to be the immediate causes. The Prophet expressed the view that everything good comes from God in his short prayer of praise, "The good, all of it, is in Thy hands, and evil does not go back to Thee."

Given this sort of world view, ingratitude appears as the ugliest of human failings. It is to shut one's eyes to the obvious. God is the source of all good, so people must thank him for it. When someone is ungrateful to God, he appears in Muslim eyes like a person who is invited to a grand feast through no merit of his own and who then sits down at the table, eats his fill, burps, and walks out, with no thought of thanking his host.

In the Koranic view of things, as in the Muslim understanding in general, the two meanings of *kufr*—as the opposite of both faith and gratitude—are practically inseparable. Faith is nothing but a form of gratitude, and gratitude is a form of faith. *Iman* is the natural and normal reaction of human beings to the marvelous fact of their own unwarranted existence. When they see that there is a reality above and beyond them that has made them what they are, they should acknowledge that reality. They should thank their host for inviting them to lunch. They should realize that if they walk out without expressing thanks, their good fortune will come to an end. Considering that this is the only free lunch in town—or rather, the only lunch there is—they had better express their gratitude and make themselves available in case their benefactor wants them to run some errands.

Remember that faith begins with recognition of the truth in the heart. Hence *kufr* begins with denial of the truth in the heart. Just as *iman*, for Muslims, is the acceptance of self-evident truths and commitment to them, *kufr* is the rejection of the same truths and refusal to abide by them. Wilfred Cantwell Smith summed up the Muslim view of faith nicely with his words, "The object of faith being thought of as pellucid and incontrovertible, the issue is, what does one do about what one knows?"[2] Since *kufr* represents a rejection of objects that are "pellucid and incontrovertible," that are completely self-evident and utterly undeniable, it is looked upon with contempt.

The original sense of the term *kufr* is to conceal something. People who are ungrateful conceal the good that has been done to them by not mentioning it. A person who has no faith conceals the self-evident truths of existence. *Kufr*, in short, is understood as a covering over and a concealing of the truths that one knows. Hence we will not employ such words as *unbelief* or *infidelity* in translating it, but rather the term *(ungrateful) truth-concealing*.

People may object that "unbelief" is a better translation because it is not so judgmental. Moreover, some will say, the issue has to do with what Muslims believe, not with objective truths. But if Muslims accept that the issue is simply a matter of belief, the ball will be back in the non-Muslims' court, because they will have thereby agreed that the discussion has to do with beliefs that may or may not be true. But once again, this falsifies the meaning of the word *iman*, which has nothing to do with belief in that sense.

Someone might object to the use of the word *truth-concealing* by saying, "I don't know these 'truths,' nor do I accept that they are truths, so how can I be called a 'truth-concealer?'" Traditional Muslims would typically reply that such people have simply not understood what the Koran is saying. If they would pay more attention to the message, they would realize that they know perfectly well that "There is no god but God," since it is human nature to know this. People who claim not to know it are denying their humanity.

Although this answer may appear unsatisfactory from the viewpoint of non-Muslims, an attempt should be made to understand the logic behind it. Once one gains a basic grasp of the implications of the Islamic understanding of God and human beings, one will see that the answer makes sense. By the end of Part II, we hope that readers will at least be able to see that this perspective is rooted in a coherent world view.

To summarize this discussion of the word *iman*, we can say that faith is a state of mind and heart that has to do with recognition of truth, commitment to the truth one recognizes, and activity on the basis of one's commitment.

Discussion of faith necessarily brings forth the discussion of truth. What is it and how do we recognize it? This is one of the most difficult of all questions to answer, and we cannot enter into the details of the Islamic answer here. Our goal is simply to suggest how Muslims have understood the truth that they recognize through faith, the truth that the Prophet summarized in the hadith of Gabriel.

The Three Principles

The truth that Muslims recognize and to which they commit themselves is expressed through the objects of faith mentioned in the hadith of Gabriel: God, the angels, the scriptures, the prophets, the Last Day, and the measuring out. When theologians and philosophers undertook the classification and organization of religious knowledge, these six objects were divided up and placed in three broad categories known as *tawhid*, prophecy (*nubuwwa*), and eschatology or the Return (*ma'ad*). These came to be known as the three principles or roots (*asl*) of the religion.

Shi'ite theologians typically added two more principles — justice (*'adl*) and imamate (*imama*). We will discuss the three principles that are common to all Muslims and leave the two specifically Shi'ite principles for another occasion. It is sufficient to know that these two pertain to Shi'ite understandings of the implications of *tawhid* and prophecy. In other words, justice is looked upon as specifying the nature of *tawhid*, while imamate explains how certain dimensions of prophecy are extended through the Imams.

We have defined *tawhid* as accepting that there is no god but God and worshiping him. As a principle of faith, *tawhid* explains the nature of God and how the various creatures, including angels, are connected to God. Prophecy explains who the prophets are and the function of their scriptures. The Return explains the Last Day, or what happens after death. Hence the term is often translated as "eschatology"; that is, knowledge of the last things.

The word *tawhid* is derived from the same root as the word *wahid*, which means "one." God is one, and *tawhid* means "to recognize and acknowledge that God is one." Sometimes the term is translated as "unity" or "divine unity." More correctly, it can be rendered as "the assertion of divine unity," or "the declaration of God's oneness." But *tawhid* implies far more than the simple fact that God is one, and no single English expression could possibly render the full range of its nuances.

Tawhid is concerned primarily with three of the six objects of faith: God, the angels, and the measuring out, although this does not begin to exhaust what it entails.

God is the foundation and beginning of everything Islamic. The angels are the creatures nearest to God in the cosmic hierarchy, and they play a central role in God's interrelationship with human beings. The "measuring out, both its good and its evil" refers to how God interacts with creation. To each thing, God measures out a certain limited amount of good and, as the negative consequence of exactly the same act, a certain amount of evil. Unlimited good belongs to God alone, and limited good is inseparable from a touch of evil.

When we ask how God determines who gets what and whether or not his creatures have anything to do with this determination, we enter into the thorny domain of free will and predestination. Moreover, any mention of good and evil brings up the question of how a good creator can create a universe that seems to have too much evil. These are issues that people have stumbled over for centuries, and we will not be able to resolve them here, but it will be useful to have some idea of how Muslims approach them.

Prophecy is concerned with the prophets and the books. Why did God send prophets? What is their function in human society? More specifically, what roles do Muhammad and the Koran play?

The Return looks at human destiny in terms of *tawhid*. Since people come from the One, they also go back to the One. And this going back has everything to do with the human response to prophecy. Once people know about God through the prophetic messages, how do they react? What fruits does human activity yield in the worlds after death? What happens when blindness disappears at death and people come face to face with the reality of God?

The second and third principles are implied in the first principle. *Tawhid* is an all-embracing concept, in keeping with the all-embracing nature of the divine reality which it expresses. It is impossible to discuss prophecy and the Return without referring back to *tawhid*. In the Koran and the Hadith, of course, no attempt is made to set up these three principles, and this should be enough to alert us to the fact that discussion of the three principles is simply a way of conceptualizing the objects of faith. There is nothing final about this approach but, like the idea of Islam's three dimensions discussed in the Introduction, it provides us with a way of seeing how things fit together.

Islam's three principles make up the primary subject matter of a vast number of books and an enormous amount of learning. We will suggest in Chapter 6 how three major schools of thought developed in response to the various ways of understanding the objects of faith. For the time being, we will try to provide a basic understanding of the three principles so that readers can become familiar with Islamic ways of looking at reality.

Chapter 3.

TAWHID

ع

W e have already discussed the primary importance of the Shahadah for Islamic practice: Without it, a person is not a Muslim. In
the same way, the Shahadah has a fundamental importance for Islamic
faith, since it expresses the first and second principles of faith in a
nutshell.

The First Shahadah

The Shahadah consists of two statements, which we can call the first
and the second Shahadahs. Through the first Shahadah, one bears
witness that "There is no god but God," and through the second, one
testifies that "Muhammad is the Messenger of God." The first Shahadah
expresses *tawhid*, while the second speaks of prophecy. Hence we will
discuss the second Shahadah when we reach the second principle of
faith.

For Muslims, the first Shahadah has no special connection with the
religion brought by Muhammad. Rather, it expresses *islam* in the
widest sense — it explains why everything in the heavens and the earth

is submitted to God. It also expresses *islam* in the narrower sense of the religion of all the prophets. The most explicit Koranic verse here is, "And We never sent a messenger before thee save that We revealed to him, saying, 'There is no god but I, so worship Me' " (21:25). All prophets have come with the message of *tawhid*.

The universality of the first Shahadah is at first difficult for non-Muslims to understand. One problem lies in the concepts of god and God. What do people understand when they hear the words, "There is no god but God"? Nowadays especially, when institutionalized religion has relatively little effect upon the way people think, everyone has his or her own idea about what the word *god* means. What is certain is that ordinary understandings of the word do not help much in grasping its meaning in the Islamic context.

When someone says, "I don't believe in God," Muslims familiar with their own religion's teachings find it easy to reply, "I don't believe in the God you don't believe in either." People are usually quite right not to believe in the god that they have come to understand, since that god is far from the reality to which the first Shahadah refers. That is why it is necessary for us to spend quite a bit of space explaining the Islamic concept of God.

A second problem that makes it difficult for non-Muslims to understand the first Shahadah's universality is the common use of the word *Allah*. When people hear this word, they naturally think that it means that Muslims believe in a god, Allah, just as the ancient Greeks believed in Zeus, many Hindus believe in Vishnu, and every tribe has its own god. To think of Allah in these terms is to imply that the Jews and/or Christians believe in the real God, but Muslims have their own local god, or a false idea about God.

In Arabic, *Allah* simply means "God." The Koran, the Hadith, and the whole Islamic tradition maintain that the God of the Jews, the Christians, and the Muslims is a single God. Arabic-speaking Muslims cannot imagine using a different word than Allah when referring to the God worshiped by Christians and Jews. Arabic-speaking Christians and Jews themselves worship God using the word *Allah*.

Use of *Allah* in English is especially misleading in discussions of the first Shahadah. If it is translated as "There is no god but Allah," this has very different connotations from the sentence "There is no god but God." For example, it does not sound totally unreasonable to claim that Moses and Jesus taught that "There is no god but God," but it sounds ridiculous to say that they were preaching that "There is no god but Allah." English speakers unacquainted with Islam naturally tend to understand Allah to be some false, alien god of the same sort that pagans and other nonbelievers worship (whoever they might be).

Some Muslims insist on using the word Allah when they speak English for several reasons. First, it is the primary name of God in the Koran, so the word itself is considered to have a special blessing.

Second, most Muslims who speak English are not native speakers of the language, and at the same time it is perfectly obvious to them that Islam is a true religion. Hence they cannot imagine the misunderstandings that arise in the minds of non-Muslim, native speakers of English simply by the mention of the word Allah. Third, many Muslims have little grasp of the theology of their own religion. Hence they think that Allah is the true God, and the word *God* as used in English refers to a false god worshiped by Jews and Christians. Such Muslims represent the mirror image of those English speakers who think that God is the true God and Allah is a false god worshiped by pagans.

GOD

The first article of Islamic faith is God. But who or what is God? Practically all Muslim authorities maintain that a true understanding of the word *god* is impossible without divine revelation. In other words, God himself must tell people who he is. After all, it is difficult enough to understand other *people*, and almost impossible to do so unless they express themselves through speaking. People we can see and touch, but God lies beyond the range of our vision. If we are to understand who God is, he himself must tell us. God tells people who he is by speaking through the prophets. His words are recorded in the books of the prophets, that is, the scriptures. What distinguishes Muslims from followers of other religions is that they accept Muhammad as God's messenger and the Koran as God's message; in contrast, people who follow other religions have other prophets (or so the traditional Islamic view maintains).

The fundamental message of all the prophets is the same—"There is no god but God." In brief, Muslims understand this word *God* to refer to the reality that reveals itself through the Koran, and they understand *god* to refer to anything that is falsely described by any of the qualities that the Koran ascribes to God.

Clearly, the first step in understanding God is to understand the Koran. But the Koran is not an easy book to understand. One can say without exaggeration that Muslims have been explaining the Koran for the past fourteen hundred years and that they have not begun to exhaust its meaning. In other words, no matter how much you say about God, there is still more that can be said.

Before suggesting some of the things that the Koran says about God, we can usefully look at the Arabic words *ilah* (god) and *Allah* (God). A god, the Arabic dictionaries tell us, is anything that is taken as an object of worship, adoration, or service. The Koran uses the word in both positive and negative senses, which is to say that it may denote the true god or a false god. The Koran frequently uses the term in a positive sense, as in the verses "No god is there but one god" (5:73), "God is but one god" (4:171), and "Your god is one god, so submit to Him" (22:34).

The Koran also uses the word *ilah* in a negative sense, meaning a false god or an idol. For example, in the Koranic account of the Children of Israel and the Golden Calf, the people say to Moses, "O Moses, make for us a god, as they have gods" (7:138). In his reply Moses says, "What, shall I seek a god for you other than God?" (7:140). With this sense of the term *god* in mind, it is easy to understand that "There is no god but God" means that all gods that people worship other than God are false.

The Koran uses the term *ilah* in other negative senses as well. After all, a god is anything that you worship or serve, whatever that thing might be. This does not imply that this god is the only thing that you serve, since people can have many gods—and the Koran frequently criticizes them for doing so. The god you worship does not have to be an external god. We tend to think of a god as something "out there," something up in heaven, some being of a higher order than ourselves. But the Arabic word *ilah* does not demand that. You can perfectly well worship a god that is within yourself or less than yourself.

The Koran vehemently stigmatizes those who worship their own inclinations and moods as gods. The word it employs is *hawa*, which we will translate as "caprice." It is almost identical in meaning and derivation with the word *hawa'*, which means "wind." Caprice is an internal wind that blows this way and that, a whim of the moment. One day you want one thing, the next day you want something else. For the Koran, caprice is the worst of gods. When you worship it, you never know what is up and what is down. Practically every day your ideas, feelings, and emotions change. The wind keeps on blowing and, the Koran assures us, if you let it take you along with it, it will take you to destruction. A few Koranic verses can help offer a picture of the wind of caprice:

> As for him who feared the station of his Lord and forbade the soul its caprice, surely paradise shall be the refuge. (79:40-41)

> Have you seen him who has taken his own caprice to be his god? (25:43)

> Who is more misguided than he who follows his own caprice without guidance from God? (28:50)

> Have you seen him who has taken his caprice to be his god, and God has misguided him in spite of [his] knowledge? (45:23)

The Koran employs the plural of *hawa* (caprices) in the same sense. In sixteen of the seventeen instances in which the plural is used, it is paired with the verb *to follow*. Those who are ignorant follow their own caprices—the little gods inside themselves—and as a result they end up in hell. The message is clear. People must avoid false gods by following guidance from God, which comes in the form of prophecy.

This same word *caprices* came to be used in later times to mean "heresies" or "sects." People who are members of sects follow the winds of their own desires and pay no attention to the message of the prophets. Or they follow their own whims—or the whims of their leader—in deciding how to understand the scriptures. The use of the word *caprices* to mean sects parallels the use of the word *heresy* itself, which derives from a Greek root meaning "to choose." A heresy is a way that you choose for yourself, without guidance from God.

If a god can be a false god or a true god, God is by definition a true God. If a god is anything that can be worshiped, God is that which should be worshiped. To say that "There is no god but God" means that no service or worship should be rendered to anything other than God, since everything other than God can only be a false god.

Shirk

The first principle of faith is *tawhid*, the assertion that God is one. The meaning of *tawhid* is expressed most concisely in the first Shahadah, which is called "The sentence of *tawhid*" (*kalimat al-tawhid*). "There is no god but God" means that there is only a single true and worthy object of worship, God. All other objects of worship and service are false. To serve anything else is to fall into error and misguidance. It is to be guilty of the sin of *shirk*.

Shirk means "to share, to be a partner, to make someone share in, to give someone a partner, to associate someone with someone else." In the theological context, *shirk* means to give God partners and, by implication, to worship them along with God or exclusive of God. The Koran employs the word in seventy-five verses. We will be translating it as "associating others (with God)."

> *Worship God, and do not associate any others with Him. (4:36)*

> *Do not associate others with God; to associate others is a mighty wrong. (31:13)*

> *Say [O Muhammad!]: Surely God is one god. Surely I am free of the others you associate. (6:19)*

> *Say: I have only been commanded to worship God, and not to associate anything with Him. (13:36)*

The avoidance of associating others with God is thus a central part of the Koranic message, because it is nothing but the reverse side of *tawhid*. Given the fact that the sentence of *tawhid* is the first pillar of Islam and *tawhid* itself is the first principle of Islam, one begins to understand why *shirk* is so strongly criticized and why, according to the Koran, it is the only unforgivable sin:

> *God forgives not that any others should be associated with Him,*
> *but less than that, He forgives to whomsoever He will. (4:48, 4:116)*

> *If someone associates any others with God, God will prohibit para-*
> *dise to him. (5:72)*

Since understanding *tawhid* is so basic to Islam, a little more reflection on the nature of *shirk* will be useful. As the Arabic proverb puts it, "Things become known through their opposites." We understand day through night, and night through day. So also, we can understand *tawhid* if we can understand what *shirk* is all about.

The literal sense of the term *shirk* may suggest that one has to be conscious of associating others with God in order to be guilty of it. How can I give a partner to someone if I do not know the someone? Then, one might reason, if we do not know about God and we worship something else, we are not guilty of *shirk*. This is a complex issue, and various approaches can be taken to it. We will attempt a very basic reply, without entering into the theological fine points.

Most Muslim thinkers hold that knowledge of *tawhid* pertains to what it means to be human. It lies in the original human nature (*fitra*), since human beings were created knowing that "There is no god but God." The prophets were sent to remind them of what they already know. Hence, to associate others with God is to go against the most fundamental instincts of the human species. It is, so to speak, to betray human nature and even to leave the domain of human existence. This explains why it is such a grave sin: It is the overturning of what makes us human. In this view of things, claiming ignorance of *tawhid* is tantamount to claiming not to be human. In the next world, paradise is the human realm, while hell is the realm of those creatures who began as human beings but did not live up to their humanity.

In discussing *shirk*, one needs to keep in mind the nature of the things that can be associated with God. It is not only a question of worshiping a being or beings other than God, or serving idols in the crude and literal sense of the term. Remember that caprice is a god and that those who follow caprice are *mushriks* (associators of others with God). To follow one's own opinions and feelings, then, is a form of *shirk*. According to many authorities, it is a worse form of *shirk* than idol-worship, because idol-worship is clear and plain and therefore relatively easy to deal with and to cure. But the worship of caprice is hidden and often found in people who appear outwardly to be very pious.

The way to cure obvious *shirk* is to observe the Shariah. In other words, when people follow the first dimension of Islam, they obey the instructions of God. Hence their activities are put in right order. However, hidden *shirk* does not pertain to the domain of *islam*, but rather to *iman* and *ihsan*, the second and third dimensions. It is much more difficult to recognize and to remedy than obvious *shirk*. No longer must one simply perform certain activities to establish the outward form of *tawhid*; now it is a question of bringing one's thoughts, understanding, attitudes, and moral qualities into conformity with *tawhid*.

The Prophet said that he was commanded to war against people until they say the Shahadah. Then, with this verbal acknowledgment of Islam, they became members of the community. The good standing of their membership was confirmed when they observed the rest of the Five Pillars. As the Prophet said (and here again we see the primary importance of the ritual prayer), "Abandoning the *salat* throws a man into *shirk* and truth-concealing." But observing the *salat* is outward and external, and it does not necessarily tell us anything about what is going on inside. People may observe the Shariah, but that does not mean that faith has entered their hearts. A number of hadiths express the Prophet's worry about people's attitudes and thoughts. One of his companions reported as follows:

> *The Prophet came out to us from his house while we were discussing the Antichrist. He said, "Shall I tell you about something that is more frightening to me than the Antichrist?"*
>
> *The people replied that he should.*
>
> *He said, "Hidden* shirk. *In other words, that a man should perform the* salat *and do it beautifully for the sake of someone who is watching."*

Another hadith makes it completely obvious that idolatry or paganism in the ordinary senses of these terms does not begin to exhaust what is at issue in discussions of *shirk*:

> *The most frightening thing that I fear for my Community is associating others with God. I do not mean to say that they will worship the sun, or the moon, or idols. I mean that they will perform works for other than God with a hidden desire.*

To summarize, Muslims understand God as the only object truly worthy of worship and service. To serve anything other than God is to betray the fundamental impulse of the original human nature. *Shirk*, or associating others with God, implies not only worshiping more than one god, but also following one's own desires or anything less than the guidance of God.

In this first view of things, *tawhid* has an eminently practical application, because it refers to the everyday course of life. It explains what sort of motives should govern activity, and hence it is intimately related to *ihsan*, Islam's third dimension. *Shirk* is the underlying cause of all wrong motives. It is to see two or more when there is only one. It results in every sort of misguidance, error, and loss.

If *tawhid* means to worship only God, while *shirk* is to worship other gods, we can rightly ask how we should go about worshiping God and avoiding worship of others. The first answer, of course, is *islam* in the narrowest sense — the Shariah. But the Shariah applies only to activity. What about motives, understandings, attitudes? How can they be altered and brought into harmony with *tawhid*? To answer questions of this sort, we must have a clearer understanding of what we are talking about when we use the word *God*. This is the task for the rest of this section.

The Signs of God

The Koran is God's speech, directed at human beings. Whatever God says in the Koran is an expression of himself. In the same way, when we speak, we express ourselves. We may be playing a role, but we ourselves have chosen the role, and no one else would play it the same way. Even the roles we play express something of ourselves.

When Muslim scholars study the Koran, they look at every chapter, every verse, every word, and every letter as God's self-expression. There is nothing in the Koran that is not full of significance, because God has spoken with full awareness of what he is saying. In the case of human beings, we may not be aware of what we are expressing through our words, but God is not negligent and forgetful like us. Hence, he knows exactly what he is saying, and people can come to understand his speech to the extent of their capacity. Ultimately, the whole religious enterprise in Islam involves understanding the Koran and embodying its message through everyday life.

The Koran gives people news of God, since it is God's purposeful and intentional speech, directed at them. Everything in the Koran is an indication or an intimation of God's self. This helps explain why the Koran refers to its own words and sentences as *signs* (*ayat*):

> We have sent down upon thee signs, clear indications, and none denies their truth save the transgressors. (2:99)

> These are the signs of the Wise Book. (10:1)

> These are the signs of the Manifest Book. We have sent it down as an Arabic Koran. (12:1–2).

If the Koran expresses God, however, it is not the only thing that expresses him. Other scriptures also express him, and so do his creatures. The Koran employs the word *aya* (sign) in almost four hundred instances, in the most general sense to anything that gives news of something else. In a slightly more specific sense, the word is used to refer to everything in the heavens and the earth, inasmuch as it gives news of God. All things are signs of God for the same reason that they are *muslim*—because they submit to God's creative power. Everything that happens tells us something about God's activity within creation. Signs are found not only in the natural world and historical events, but also inside ourselves:

> *We have appointed the night and the day as two signs. (17:12)*

> *And a sign for them is the dead earth, which We brought to life and from which We brought forth grain that they eat. (36:33)*

> *And of His signs is the creation of the heavens and earth, and the variety of your tongues and colors. (30:22)*

> *And of His signs are the ships that run on the sea like landmarks. (42:32)*

> *In the earth are signs for those having certainty, and in your selves. (51:20-21)*

The Koran uses the term *sign* in a still narrower sense, to refer to the miracles and scriptures that are given to the prophets as proof that they have come with messages from God. Through signs, God's messengers show people the significance of history. Just as all prophets and all followers of the prophets are *muslim*s, so also all the prophetic activities give signs of God's wisdom and power:

> *They said [to the prophet Salih], "You are merely one of those who are bewitched. You are merely a mortal, like us. Then produce a sign, if you are one of the truthful." (26:153-154)*

> *And We sent Moses with Our signs, and a manifest authority, to Pharaoh and his council. (11:96-97)*

> *So when Moses came to them with Our signs, clear indications, they said, "This is nothing but a forged sorcery." (28:36)*

> *In Joseph and his brethren are signs for those who ask questions. (12:7)*

Finally, in the specific sense that we have already encountered, the Koran refers to its own words as signs, and the term came to be applied technically to each of the subunits of the suras.

In short, the word *sign* can be applied to anything at all, since all things are God's creatures. Everything in the universe is an ayatollah (a sign of God), though this particular expression—which has become well known because of modern political events—has recently come to be applied to some of the ulama. Even Satan is an ayatollah, a sign of God. His activity, as we will see later, also manifests God's wisdom in creation.

Before leaving the term *sign*, it is important to state explicitly something that is implicit in the word: A sign is put there for people to read. People do not set up signs or give indications unless they want to convey a message. The Koranic use of this term in at least three main senses alerts us to a fundamental insight of Islam, a point that Muslims find so self-evident they are often nonplused when non-Muslims do not grasp it immediately: All of nature and scripture speaks to us directly, with a specific message, and God expects us to read the message and to react appropriately. When the Koran mentions God's signs, it typically concludes with something like "Perhaps you will take heed," or "Will you not understand?" or "Do you not see?" The worst thing that human beings can do is to ignore the message that is before their eyes wherever they look—the message of *tawhid*:

> How many a sign there is in the heavens and in the earth that they pass by, turning away from it! Most of them have no faith in God, and they associate others with Him. (12:105-106)

> Who does greater evil than he who is reminded of the signs of his Lord, then turns away from them? (32:22).

Interpreting the Signs

The signs of God give news of God within the matrix of history. There are two basic kinds of signs: prophetic and natural. Prophetic signs can be divided into oral or written (scripture) and physical (miracles). The natural kind can be divided into external (pertaining to the world around us, whether nature or society) and internal (pertaining to our own selves). We will return to some of the prophetic signs when we discuss prophecy, and we will look more closely at external and internal signs when we discuss the cosmos and its relationship with the human being. At this point we want to ask how the signs can help us understand the meaning of the word *God*.

By definition, signs are signs of God. If we understand the signs, we are understanding something about God. One way to grasp the message of the signs would be to look at the natural world and try to understand its language. In a certain sense, this is what modern science does; it is trying to understand the message of nature and the cosmos. However, science has certain presuppositions about the nature of reality, and hence it leaves aside the question of God, considering it irrelevant to the scientific enterprise.

The fundamental difference between the traditional Islamic approach to the natural world and that of modern science is that Muslims begin with the faith that "There is no god but God." In other words, Muslims already know that the signs are signs of God, but they are trying to understand what God is saying. The scientists feel that understanding natural phenomena has nothing to do with whether or not there is a god. The result is two radically different points of view that cannot easily be brought together.

Without pursuing this issue further, let us suggest an analogy for the difference between the Islamic and the scientific approach to things. Most people look at a painting—let us say a Michaelangelo—and try to understand what the painter is saying. Opinions differ as to the exact message, but everyone agrees that what is important about the painting is what the painter is trying to get across. However, we could also study the painting from the point of view of any of a dozen different sciences. We could analyze the canvas, the paint, the colors, the geometrical relationships among the objects, and so on. In these tasks we would have to make use of physics, chemistry, biology, geometry, and other sciences, and we could also make use of various other approaches that assume the validity of modern scientific knowledge, such as sociology, history, and psychology. This is all well and good, and there is no contradiction between looking at things in these ways and looking at them from within the Islamic perspective. But suppose that a group of the scientists began claiming that the painting had come to exist spontaneously. There was no painter, and if there was, he had no message to express, he was just throwing around tints haphazardly. And even if he had a message, we would have no way of understanding it.

For Muslims, the proof of *tawhid* is the way things are, just as for most people, the proof of the artist and his message is the existence of his painting. It is just as self-evident to traditional Muslims that God created the universe as it is self-evident to any sane person that someone painted the pictures hanging in a museum. This most basic insight of Muslims is sometimes referred to as "the religion of old women," not to disparage it, but to suggest that there is no one so unintelligent as to miss the point. The expression derives from a story that is told about the Prophet.

One day, Muhammad was walking through town with some companions, when he met an old and decrepit woman from one of the tribes who was making wool into thread with a spinning wheel. He greeted her and began speaking to her. He asked her if she had faith in God. She replied that she did. The Prophet asked her why. She replied that a spinning wheel does not turn unless there is a hand to turn it, and the heavens cannot turn unless someone is turning them. The Prophet looked at his companions and said, "You should have the religion of old women."

But how much can people understand about God from the signs in the universe? This has been a perennial issue in philosophy and theology for a number of religions, and it is intimately tied to the question of whether or not human beings need revelation from God. The general Muslim view is that divine help is necessary to understand the signs. Trying to read the signs without prophetic guidance is like trying to understand speech without knowing the language, or without recognizing that it is speech.

The basic position of Muslims concerning knowledge of God, the world, and themselves is that people are ignorant. There are uncounted mysteries that can never be solved by human reason. However, that does not mean that people should give up trying to understand. Ignorance is curable, to some degree. The way to reach the remedy is to listen to the words of the prophets. More specifically, it is to accept that the Koran is the speech of God, full of the signs of God. To understand what the Koran says about God is to understand what God is telling human beings about himself. This position directly follows the acceptance of Muhammad as the messenger of God. In other words, God has a message, known as the Koran; Muhammad has brought it, and in order to understand what it has to say, we have to read it and study it. The theme of this message, as we saw above, is *tawhid*.

To the extent that generalizations are meaningful, we can say that Western scholars who have studied the Koran have searched for its significance in its historical context, the Judeo-Christian background, social relationships, economic considerations, and linguistic factors. They have felt that the discovery of the historical and social circumstances surrounding the Prophet and the early community is of fundamental importance. Verses that refer to historical events need to be understood in terms of those events.

Certain elements of this modern Western approach to interpretation have been known to Muslims from earliest times, and often Western scholars are simply following in the footsteps of their Muslim predecessors. The great difference between this approach and the traditional Islamic approach is that Muslims never imagined that the meaning of a verse could be exhausted by its historical significance. If one wants to argue that the Koran has to be understood in terms of historical circumstances, the Muslim commentators can reply that the historical circumstance themselves are signs of God, and hence they have a significance that transcends the mundane: How can you understand the historical circumstances if you do not understand what these circumstances tell us about *tawhid*? The difference between signs found in scripture and signs found in nature is that the scriptural signs tell us explicitly and in so many words that this is a message of God. But human beings cannot grasp the divine message in historical signs without understanding the scriptural signs.

Both the modern and the traditional Islamic approaches to the interpretation of scriptural and historical signs agree that history has a meaning and that it can be understood if we grasp the causes of what occurred. In the modern Western approach, causality moves "from down to up"; that is, the meaning of concepts such as God, religion, community, human being, and history has to be sought in the constitutive elements that brought these concepts into existence. These elements can be natural, environmental, social, psychological, economic, and so on. In contrast, the Islamic approach works "from up to down." It begins with *tawhid*, and then, on the basis of *tawhid*, attempts to situate everything else in relation to God. The *meaning* of a thing is found in its *sign*-ificance. The thing is a sign, and the sign speaks of God.

Muslims do not deny that the historical elements are important; the Koran itself makes their importance clear. When the Koran says that God sent every messenger speaking "the tongue of his people" (14:4), this is a specific reference to the idea that divine messages are adapted to the cultural, historical, and linguistic circumstances of the people to whom they are revealed. But to say this is also to affirm that they are divine messages. It is God who is speaking—Arabic or Hebrew or Sanskrit or Chinese as the case may be—and it is human beings who are listening. It is a far cry from this position to the position that humans made up the language and God along with it.

At the risk of oversimplifying, one can summarize the difference between the traditional Islamic perspective on interpreting signs and the various modern approaches to historical understanding by reference to the Biblical saying, which the Prophet repeated, "God created human beings in his own image." Muslim scholars have taken this to mean that everything in the universe with which human beings have contact has to be understood in terms of the divine reality that determines human nature. Modern scholarship, however, takes a different view of the matter by reversing the saying. God is no longer taken as an active participant, but rather as a human construction. Hence, modern scholarship maintains that "Human beings created God in their own image." For modern scholarship, the human origin of religion then explains the tremendous diversity of religious belief and practice found throughout history.

If we moderns are to grasp the logic of the Islamic vision of things, we need to keep in mind that, for Muslims, things begin with God and come down. For us (by and large), things begin with us and go up (or, what is more likely, in every which way). From the modern perspective, even speaking of up and down becomes problematic, since we have to choose a standard by which to judge directions, and people do not easily agree on such things.

Divine Names

It should be clear that the workaday concept of God cannot do justice to a religion that uses its own idea of God as the absolute center from which everything else is judged. To begin to understand what Muslims mean by God, we need to turn to the Koran.

Since the Koran itself is God's speech, everything within it expresses God, just as everything you say—even if you are quoting someone else—expresses who you are. But in order to understand God's self-expression, we need a vantage point from which to begin our survey. The obvious vantage point to take is the first pillar of the religion, the Shahadah, the fact that "There is no god but God."

What sort of being is designated by this word *God*? The typically Islamic way of answering this question is to refer, in the first place, to what the Koran says *explicitly* about God (since everything it says refers *implicitly* to God). Here we find that the Koran has a great deal to say.

One way to find out what the Koran says about God is simply to read the book; but we have already suggested that a number of barriers stand in the way of making this an easy approach for modern people. This task can be made easier by classifying, with the help of some standard categories found in Islamic theology, the types of things that are said about God.

It needs to be kept in mind that the Koran is an infinitely rich book that has inspired countless philosophers, theologians, jurists, poets, and artists over the centuries, not to speak of its effect on people from every other walk of life. In other words, we cannot begin to do justice to the Koran; what we have to say on any topic is always preliminary and schematic. In the actual text, and in the way development takes place over history, things are enormously more complex. With this caveat in mind, we can say that the Koran summarizes its teachings about God in what it calls the "most beautiful names" (*al-asma' al-husna*). The word *al-husna* is the superlative adjective from *hasan*, which means "beautiful" and "good." By calling God's names "the most beautiful," the Koran is implying that, just as God himself is good and beautiful, so also the names he gives to himself in the Koran are good and beautiful, because they express his beauty. And, just as God's beauty and goodness infinitely surpass those of his creation, so also the beauty of his names is far greater than the beauty of the names of other things.

In a famous hadith, the Prophet said that God has ninety-nine names. Books about the ninety-nine names of God have played an important role in Islamic theology. As many authors of these books point out, the number should not be taken too literally, since there is no completely dependable list of the names, and it is easy to find more than ninety-nine names of God in the Koran (although determining which Koranic expression is to be considered a most beautiful name of God is a task with important theological implications). In any case, there is no disagreement on the fact that the Koran often ascribes names to God. Among commonly employed Koranic names are Merciful, Compassionate, Knowing, Desiring, Alive, Powerful, Creator, Forgiver, and Loving. Notice that these are not personal names, in contrast, for example, to Jupiter or Shiva. God has no personal names, with the possible exception of Allah. We say "possible," because the issue is not addressed in quite the same way in Islamic theology.

Many Muslim theologians think that Allah is a proper name (*ism 'alam*) that God has given to himself, but there is no word that corresponds exactly to the English *personal*. As a proper name, *Allah* has no specific meaning, any more than *London* has a specific meaning that would demand that every town called London has certain qualities. Other theologians prefer to derive the name Allah from one of several roots, making it a name with a meaning. Then it would be similar to names like Knowing, Willing, and Compassionate. For example, some theologians derive the word *Allah* from *ilah* and hold that it means simply "the God," although there are several other suggestions as well. Modern philologists typically consider this particular opinion to be correct. But this is not simply a question of philology, because it also has theological implications, and this helps explain why many Muslim authors ignore what modern scholars consider obvious.

In polytheistic religions, each god typically presents a personal face that embodies one or more qualities. Thus, for example, Hindu mythology presents us with many accounts of the acts and exploits of gods such as Brahma, Vishnu, and Shiva, and these accounts are presented as if the gods were persons. At the same time, Hindus often say that Brahma is the Creator, Vishnu the Preserver, and Shiva the Destroyer. But each of these gods has many other qualities as well, and the qualities often overlap with those of other gods.

The Koranic names of God play a role in the Islamic world view that is in certain ways analogous to the role of the multiple divinities in some forms of polytheism, with the important and fundamental difference that the names are never personified or looked upon as separate beings. Each name represents an attribute or a quality, not a concrete thing. For example, God is never referred to as "father" or "heaven," much less as "sun" or "moon."

The divine name with perhaps the most concrete sound is King. But this name, like other divine names, does not imply that God is pictured in concrete terms. Rather, the name means that God is a reality that possesses the attributes of kingship to such a degree that nothing else really deserves the name. If God is King, this means that all power and ruling authority belong to him, while earthly kings, presidents, and dictators represent at best pale reflections of God's kingly power.

Tawhid means that the qualities denoted by God's names belong truly to God and only secondarily or metaphorically to the creatures. Any divine name can be placed in the sentence of *tawhid*, "There is no god but God." Thus the first Shahadah can be utilized as a quick formula for stating the various implications of *tawhid*.

If God is the Merciful, then there is no god but the Merciful. A god, we said, is "anything that is taken as an object of worship, adoration, or service." The Merciful is the source of mercy, which is goodness, kindness, and love directed toward others. The Merciful is the object of worship and service because everyone needs mercy to survive. Without mercy, we would have no goodness, kindness, and love. Or rather, we would not even be here, since our existence itself is a gift, for which gratitude is due. Hence the Shahadah tells us that all mercy is the gift of the Merciful. "There is no god but the Merciful" means that "There is no mercy but God's mercy," or "There is none merciful but the Merciful." God's mercy overshadows all the mercy in the universe. His mercy is true mercy, and other mercy is not worthy of the name. The Prophet expressed this idea in the following hadith:

> God created a hundred mercies on the day He created the heavens and the earth, each mercy of which would fill what is between the heaven and the earth. Of these He placed one mercy in the earth. Through it the mother inclines toward her child, and the birds and animals incline toward each other. When the day of resurrection comes, He will complete those mercies with this mercy.

God is the Praiseworthy. In other words, as the first sentence of the Koran says, "Praise belongs to God." What is praiseworthy in this world is what is good, true, and appropriate. It is, in short, anything real; that is, anything that corresponds with the underlying nature of reality, which is God himself, who is goodness, beauty, and praiseworthiness. To say "Praise belongs to God" is to say that God alone deserves the name "praiseworthy."

God is the Knowing. There is no god but the Knowing. All knowledge derives from the Knowing. No one has any knowledge but the Knowing. There is none that knows but God. All human knowledge is simply one degree or another of ignorance.

God is the Strong. There is none strong but the Strong. All strength belongs to God. All physical, worldly, political, and cosmic strength is nothing before the infinite strength of God. "The strength, all of it, belongs to God" (2:165). "There is no strength but in God" (18:39). As the Prophet put it, in a formula that Muslims frequently repeat, "There is no power and no strength but in God, the High, the Tremendous."

God is the Creator. None creates but God. As the Koran expresses it, turning the Shahadah into a rhetorical question, "Is there any creator apart from God?" (35:3)

God is the Permanent. There is nothing permanent but God. "Everything is perishing except His face" (28:88). "Everyone in the earth disappears, but there remains the face of your Lord, the Possessor of Majesty and Generous Giving" (55:26-27).

God is the Independent. None is independent but God. Everything in the heavens and earth depends utterly upon God for its existence and subsistence. "O people, you are the dependent upon God, and God—He is the Independent, the Praiseworthy" (35:15).

God is the "Owner of the kingdom" (3:26). God alone is owner of things, and nothing owns anything for itself. "To God belongs the kingdom of the heavens and the earth" (3:189, 5:17, etc.). "God has no associate in the kingdom" (17:111). "Blessed is He in whose hand is the kingdom, and He is powerful over everything" (67:1).

We will not go through all the ninety-nine names of God, but let us look at one more name which, in a sense, brings home the meaning of *tawhid* more clearly than any other. That is *al-haqq* (the Real). God is the Real; there is nothing real but the Real; everything other than God is unreal, ephemeral, transitory, illusory, vanishing, nothing. In short, every quality and characteristic of things that has a positive side to it derives from a divine quality and owes its existence to God. Everything good, praiseworthy, permanent, and real belongs to God. Therefore "Praise belongs to God," and to no one else.

The cosmos or universe is commonly defined as "everything other than God." The first Shahadah means that the cosmos is unreal. In the last analysis, it is nothing compared to the Real, but this perspective does not lead to nihilism. Nihilism demands that the nothingness and illusory nature of our existence yield a sense of meaninglessness and despair, but *tawhid* leads to confidence, faith, and joy.

If the world and ourselves are unreal, how do we explain the fact that we are here, aware of our own unreality? How can we say we are unreal when *we* are saying it? Our selves, our speech, and our understanding must have some sort of reality, or else the self could never understand and never say that it is unreal. Hence, in the midst of the unreality of the world, there is some sort of reality. If there were no reality whatsoever, why would God bother talking to us? However, this reality that is found in the world does not belong to ourselves or to the world. The reality belongs to God—"Praise belongs to God." We are—as "we"—unreal, but inasmuch as God shows mercy and generosity to us, we are real as a result of mercy and generosity.

One way to sort out this confusing situation is to say that God's reality is absolute, but our reality is relative. God's reality is permanent and unchanging; it is the standard by which all things are judged. All other realities exist as a function of God's reality. Hence other things can only be understood in relation to God—their reality is relative. "There is no god but God" means that everything other than God has to be understood in relation to God.

If we do not take God—the absolute point of reference—into account when trying to understand something, we can only understand that thing in relation to other unreal things. Our knowledge will remain unreal, uncertain, changing, and undependable. We will be thrown into doubt and perplexity. People can have sure knowledge only if they have perceived the absolute point of reference, and this depends upon *tawhid*. *Tawhid*, in turn, brings about a commitment known as faith. Once again, we are brought back to the coincidence of knowledge and faith.

It is no accident that Sura 2 of the Koran begins with the words, "This is the book in which there is no doubt." In the Islamic view, doubt can only be removed through *tawhid*, which allows people to recognize that every positive quality is rooted in the Absolute Reality.

Speech

God manifests his signs through speaking. As already mentioned, Muslims view the Koran and other scriptures as God's speech. The words and sentences of God's speech are known as signs. But just as God reveals the signs of scripture through speaking, he also reveals the cosmic and natural signs through speaking. In the Hebrew Bible, God begins creation by *saying*, "Let there be light." In the view of many Muslim theologians, all creativity is a function of God's speech.

Many Koranic verses mention God's word or words. Take, for example, the following verse:

> *Though all the trees in the earth were pens, and the sea and seven seas after it supplied it with ink, yet the words of God would not be spent. God is Mighty, Wise. (31:27)*

At first sight, this verse seems to be talking about scripture. But many commentators understand it as a reference to God's creative power. Every creature comes into existence when God says to it "Be!" so each creature is a word of God. God's creative power is infinite, so his creatures never cease coming into existence.

Because of the Koranic theme of creation through speaking, many Muslim thinkers employ the imagery of speech as a means to suggest the relationship between God and the world. Human speech is taken as a sign of divine speech. How do we create words? God creates creatures in a similar way.

When we speak, we begin with the intention of saying something, even if the intention is not clear to us. Speech does not appear unintentionally—even sudden expressions are a communication of an inner feeling or idea, such as surprise or pain. We want to express an idea, so we speak. Of course, we are just human beings, with all sorts of imperfections, so our words often come out muddled, and we find that we are not able to say what we want to say. The situation is different with God, since he is free of our limitations. His words come out just as he wants them. But that does not mean that we necessarily understand them. The Koran repeatedly instructs people to ponder the signs of God in order to find out what God is saying. God is speaking clearly, but his listeners are not so bright.

If we continue using human speech as an analogy, we find many interesting parallels between it and God's speech. For example, what is the relationship between a spoken word and its speaker? The word is certainly not the same as the speaker, since the word is there for an instant and then disappears. But the word is not completely different from the speaker either, because there could be no word without the speaker. The words are utterly dependent upon the speaker for their existence. In the same way, each of God's creatures exists only for an instant (from the point of view of eternity), and each of them is utterly dependent upon God for its existence. He speaks a word, and it may seem to us to last for ages, but in God's view of things, "Everything is perishing but His face" (28:88).

Some theologians have compared the universe to a book that is being written out by God. Each thing in the universe is a letter. The letters join to become words. Birds, flowers, stones, and trees are all words composed of letters. The letters may be the same in each case, but they are put together in different combinations, thus giving us different words. We could call heads, tails, arms, legs, hearts, and livers "letters." Most animals have these letters, but they are put together somewhat differently in each case. Plants and minerals are spelled with altogether different letters.

Letters have no meaning on their own. When you put them together, they are words, which have meanings. However, words really have no meaning except in the context of a sentence. Without a context, we can never be completely sure what a word means. And if we want a sentence—that is, an expression that makes sense—we cannot string words together haphazardly. In the same way, God's cosmic words, such as elephant, garlic, and cockroach, have meaning only in the context of the natural world in which they are found.

Continuing with the image of a universe as a book, we can say that each sentence needs to be placed within a chapter, or a *sura*, which, as we saw earlier, means literally an enclosure. The suras of the universal book are like the worlds of our universe. But each world is related to other worlds in some way. In terms of modern astronomy, each star and galaxy interrelates with all the others, though we may not be quite sure how the relationships work. In Islamic terms, any world only makes sense in relation to the worlds that surround it, whether spatially or temporally. As we will see later, Islamic cosmology looks at our own experienced world as one of several worlds that exist simultaneously, and it also looks upon it as one in a series of worlds that come one after another. The whole significance of our world can only be grasped if we see how it fits into those other worlds, just as the whole significance of a chapter depends upon the book of which it is a part.

In short, by comparing the universe to a book of God, Muslim thinkers are saying that the universe is a collection of signs that has a message. But we have to be able to see the signs in the context of the whole in order to understand the message. The theme of God's book is of course *tawhid*, the declaration that God is the unique reality underlying all appearances.

Essence and Attributes

The Koranic names of God have provided Muslims with an endless source for meditation on the nature of reality. Discussion of the names of God does not entail some abstract and irrelevant endeavor having nothing to do with the real world. Quite the contrary, the signs of the divine names are present in everything we do and everything we are. If the universe and our own existence are nothing but a panorama of divine signs, these signs are telling us who God is, or what his names are.

God's names are also referred to as attributes, since they designate qualities and characteristics. God has the attributes of generosity and justice, so two of his names are the Generous and the Just. We might also say that Elizabeth is generous and just. The difference is that in the case of God, these attributes are absolute, while in the case of Elizabeth, they are relative. To say that God is generous means that "There is none generous but God," and nothing else truly deserves to be called generous. But to say that Elizabeth is generous simply means, "relative to most people." We are saying, for example, that she is free with her time and enjoys helping people, whereas most people are not willing to devote that much of their attention to others.

Muslim thinkers have frequently classified the names of God into different categories in order to illustrate what we can know about God. For example, the names can be divided up into three groups. The first group of names tells us what God is not; the second tells us what he is; and the third tells us how he interrelates with the universe. These can be called the "names of God's essence," the "names of his attributes," and the "names of his acts."

The essence (*dhat*) of something is its reality, its innermost core that defines it and makes it what it is. For example, we can ask what the essence of a cow is, and if we study the matter we may come up with a statement that defines what is absolutely essential to a cow in order for it to be a cow rather than a horse or a donkey.

In the case of God, the question is, What is God's very self? What is the fundamental reality of God that makes him God and nothing else, or that differentiates God from everything in the cosmos? A typical answer is that God is not like anything else, while everything in the universe is like something or other. What distinguishes God from the things is precisely that he is utterly distinct from them in every way. But human beings, for example, are like cows and donkeys and other animals; they are also like minerals in certain respects. Everything in the universe has some sort of similarity with human beings. More precisely, everything is similar to everything else in some way or another. God alone is distinct from all things. Hence we can say that his essential characteristic is that he is not similar to anything else. In brief, "Nothing is like Him" (42:11).

God's essence is what he is and what everything else is not. But what exactly is that? He is not any exact thing, or else he would be similar to other exact things through this exactness. But nothing is like God.

This type of discussion always sounds a bit puzzling, since it is a complicated way to say that we are unable to grasp what God is. But admitting that we do not know what God is means that we know that we do not know. How do we know? Because the Koran says, "Nothing is like Him." We know things by knowing what they are like. If we know that they are like nothing at all, then we know that we do not know them. But this ignorance is itself wisdom, because it allows us to understand a fundamental sense of *tawhid*. "There is no god but God" means that "There is no knowledge but God's knowledge," and "None truly has knowledge but God." As Muslim theologians have expressed the idea, "None knows God but God."

When people know that they do not know, this is called, in Islamic texts, *simple ignorance*. In contrast, when they do not know that they do not know, this is called *compound ignorance*. Muslims see simple ignorance in the face of God as wisdom. In contrast, they consider compound ignorance the worst of fates. One who is compoundly ignorant about God thinks that he knows what God is. Anyone who thinks this has missed the point of the first Shahadah, and therefore stands outside the pale of humanity. This is why we said earlier that many Muslims find it easy to agree with those who say, "I do not believe in God," because, simply by asking those people what they mean, they find out that such people have a very definite idea of *what* God is, and this idea is always unacceptable.

We began by saying that there are names that are used to designate God's essence. These are names that tell us what God is not. Since God's essence cannot be explained to human beings in positive terms, negative names help people understand their own limitations. An example of a negative name is *quddus*, which is usually translated as "Holy." The Arabic term means that God is beyond every imperfection and stain that is imaginable for created things. Another negative name is *subbuh*, (Glorified). In other words, God's glory, greatness, and transcendence is such that he is beyond all creaturely understanding. Another is *salam* (Peace). This name means that God is free of every sort of disharmony and disequilibrium, every strife and war. Still another negative name is *ghani* (Independent). God does not depend upon anything in the universe and is free of all the dependencies that define the natures and limitations of creatures.

If names of the essence tell us what God is not, names of the attributes tell us what God is. Although God in his very self cannot be fathomed, we can know what sort of qualities he chooses to reveal to us through his signs. There is no contradiction between God's unknowability and knowability. After all, the same thing can be said about any human being. We can say that Bob is alive, knowing, desiring, powerful, seeing, and hearing. Fine, but how much does that tell us about Bob's uniqueness, or about Bob as he really is in himself? Would Bob be satisfied that we have mentioned everything important about him by listing those attributes?

Again, what exactly defines the human species, of which Bob is one example? At one time, anthropologists might have told us that a human being is a tool-making animal, but that is simply a rough description. None of us would be ready to say, "All right, I am a tool-making animal, and that's that. The rest of me you can have. From now on, I will make tools. My family is irrelevant, my pains and complexes are irrelevant, my loves and hates are irrelevant. Take it all!" Of course, we could not give away the rest even if we wanted to. And we still do not know what we are. Everyday, if you pay close attention, you will find new facets to your own existence.

In short, we can say about a person that he is this or that, but whatever we say, we cannot exhaust the reality of that person. In the same way, to say that God is this or that does not exhaust God's reality—far from it. God is the infinitely and absolutely Real, about which the relatively real can know but little. We can understand reality to the extent that we are real. And that raises the question of how real we are. That is what *tawhid* is all about.

The limitations of human knowledge are obvious in the scientific sphere. Despite all the discoveries that are constantly being made, few people really imagine that the universe is near to being understood. The human race has still not fathomed an infinite number of phenomena on the face of the earth and in its depths. How can we really fathom our own star, for example, or our galaxy, or the trillions of galaxies in the universe? Compared to what is potentially knowable in scientific terms, present human knowledge might as well be called pure ignorance. As for God, "Nothing is like Him." Knowledge of the whole universe would not necessarily help us understand God.

In short, names of attributes are names that designate what God is, at least for practical purposes of human understanding. The attributes we just gave to Bob are also names of God's attributes: Alive, Knowing, Desiring, Powerful, Hearing, Seeing. Again, the difference between God and Bob is that God's attributes are real, while Bob's are a pale reflection of reality. Human life is not really life, since it disappears very quickly, but God's life is eternal. Thus, "Nothing is like Him" applies also to the names of God's attributes. Having said that God is Alive, we also have to remember that his life is not like our life or any other kind of life we might understand.

A third category of names can be called names of acts. The acts are God's creatures, or the results of his activity. Names of acts are distinguished by the fact that they make sense only in terms of creatures and that they have opposites that are also God's names. Examples are Life-giver and Slayer, Exalter and Abaser, Forgiver and Avenger.

In the case of names of attributes, it is not necessary to suppose that there be a creation. God is Alive, but this does not demand that anything else be alive. God is Knowing, but this does not mean that there has to be a universe that he knows. Perhaps he knows only himself. Moreover, the opposites of the names of attributes cannot be applied to God. God is not dead, nor is he ignorant.

In contrast, the names of acts demand creatures. God cannot give life to himself, since he is already alive. Nor can he slay himself, since his life is eternal by definition. Hence the name Life-giver only makes sense in terms of God's acts. And so also, if he can perform one act, he can perform its opposite. If he can give life, he can also take it away. He exalts some creatures, but he abases others. He forgives some people for their sins, but he exacts vengeance from others for their disobedience.

Finally, to prevent any possible misunderstanding, let us repeat that this classification is one of many possible ways of meditating upon God's names. There is nothing final about it, and we present it simply as an example of the type of thinking that goes on when Muslim theologians consider the fact that God ascribes many names to himself in the Koran.

Mercy and Wrath

The names of acts are names whose opposites are also applied to God. Many people, on hearing that God is called by opposite names, ask an obvious question: How can a single God have qualities that are contradictory? How can God be both merciful and wrathful? The simplest answer is that, as we have just explained, God is one, but he is dealing with many creatures. As the governing and controlling Lord of all creation, he interrelates with each creature in different ways. Moreover, with any given creature, the ways in which he interrelates change over time.

God is Life-giver and Slayer, but he does not give life to a single creature and take it away at one and the same time under the same relationship. In other words, he gives someone life, sustains that life for a period of time, and then takes it away. He may be giving life to some people and taking it away from others at one and the same time.

Relationships become much more subtle as soon as we ponder the situation. Every birth—every giving of life—is also a death, a slaying. A child is born into the world, but dies from the womb. A person dies from this world, but is born into the next world. Life-giving and slaying are not so different after all. All the opposite qualities have subtle relationships that allow us to show that their opposition is not absolute. Rather, their opposition might better be called complementarity. As soon as we understand that the two opposite names are in fact two sides of the same coin, we come closer to *tawhid*, or to showing that unity underlies multiplicity.

Because many of the divine names can be paired as opposites, they are often divided into two groups. The first group designates attractive and gentle attributes that instill a sense that it would be nice to be close to someone who possessed them. One might call these qualities motherly, since they are warm and embracing. They include such divine names as Merciful, Compassionate, Loving, Kind, Forgiving, and Beautiful. The second group of names is not so appealing, because they instill in those who think about them a sense of awe and fear. They include names such as Wrathful, Vengeful, Severe, Majestic, Just, Harmer, and Slayer.

It is difficult to overestimate the importance of these two categories of names for Muslim thinking about *tawhid*. Because of the two different perspectives these names allow, Muslim discussion of God's relationship to the world and its inhabitants frequently waffles between two standpoints. One standpoint considers God as distant and severe, the other as near and kind. A person's first reaction may be, "Why don't you make up your mind?"

The more you think about it, the more it should become clear that most important questions cannot be answered "yes" or "no." And in this case, we are dealing with the most important of all questions, that of the nature of reality itself. If we can usually say yes or no about everyday affairs, that does not mean that we can always make categorical statements about the Real. Indeed, it would be nice if everything were simple and straightforward, with no complications. But life and existence are not simple and straightforward. People who think that they are, frequently do so by blocking out much of the world around them. Many forms of fundamentalism head in this direction, but this is an approach quite alien to the Islamic intellectual tradition, which allows for subtleties and shifts of perspective.

Nearness and Distance

Tawhid can be looked at from two basic points of view. From the first point of view, *tawhid* means that everything real and good belongs to God. "There is nothing real but the Real." "Praise belongs to God." Everything other than God, by the fact of being *other*, is unreal, and hence it has nothing intrinsically good about it. From the second point of view, *tawhid* means that every trace of good and reality that can be found in ourselves and the world derives from God, the only true reality. From the first standpoint, God is real and the world is unreal. From the second standpoint, the world partakes of God's reality to some degree.

These two standpoints or perspectives can be correlated with the divine names. If we think about the names of majesty, we can see that they affirm God's reality and the world's unreality. God is Majestic, Great, and Magnificent, while the world is small, paltry, and insignificant. Why? Because God is real and permanent, but compared to his reality, the world is like a vanishing shadow.

God is the King who has power over all things. He is the absolute Ruler. He is Independent of the worlds, since he has no need of anything in the cosmos. But the cosmos has every need for God, because he is the source of its existence.

The name King does not make the point as strongly as it would have in premodern times, when there were still kings. A constitutional monarch is not a king, nor is a president or a dictator. A king in the ancient perspective—which is present in Islam and certainly implicit in the fact that God is called King—was this world's absolute authority. His word was a final command. Frequently, an executioner stood next to him with an ax, and it was enough for him to point his finger for one of his subjects to lose his head (literally). Sometimes, the king was veiled from his subjects, since no one was worthy of seeing his face save his intimates. To see his face without permission or by accident could be a death sentence.

Kings, in short, were powerful symbols for God's sovereignty over the whole of existence. And it was characteristic of kings to be distant from ordinary people, to be awe-inspiring and frightening. From one point of view, God is considered a powerful king worthy of such names as High, Mighty, Transcendent, Exalted, Holy, and Distant. In keeping with his distance and aloofness from creatures, the king often shows his wrath through terrible manifestations of power. He sends out his armies against all those who dare to lift their heads in protest against his commands, and his retribution is truly terrible. When people look at God in terms of these attributes of majesty and wrath, their natural reaction is to cringe and tremble. If this were all the Koran had to say about God, Islam would be a terrifying religion, but God also has names of beauty and mercy. God is concerned for each and every one of his creatures. He is like a mother with many children who wants each one to have the best.

One day, the Prophet was traveling with some companions and they stopped at an encampment of bedouins. He asked who these people were, and he was told that they were Muslims. As they rested in the camp, a woman was baking bread in an oven carved in the ground. She carried an infant on her hip. Suddenly, as she was fanning the oven's fire, its flames leapt up, and she jumped back quickly to protect her child.

A few minutes later, the woman came to the Prophet and asked, "Are you God's Messenger?" He replied that he was. She said, "Is it not true that God is the most merciful of the merciful?" He replied that it was true. She said, "A mother would not throw her child into the fire."

The Prophet looked at the ground and wept. After a few moments, he looked at her and said, "God will only chastise the one who is defiant and rebellious, the one who rebels against God and refuses to say, 'There is no god but God.'"

In other words, the Prophet is saying that God will only chastise those who deny *tawhid* and insist on remaining distant from God's mercy.

The Koran says, "Do not despair of God's mercy. Verily God forgives all sins" (39:53). This is the other side of the Koranic message. If God is a stern king, he is also a caring nurse. All the merciful and gentle names point to the reality of God's concern: Loving, Compassionate, Forgiving, Pardoner, Overlooker, Life-giver. These are qualities that illustrate God's nearness to his creatures, the fact that he never leaves them on their own. "We are nearer [to the human being] than his jugular vein" (50:16). "He is with you wherever you are" (57:4). "Wherever you turn, there is the face of God" (2:115). The natural human response to a God who is conceived in these terms is to feel close to him and to love him.

One could say that God has two faces—a merciful face and a wrathful face, or a gentle face and a severe face, or a near face and a far face. People must fear the wrathful face and love the merciful face. But how should they express these feelings? Normally, if people fear something, they run away from it. But one can hardly hide from God when his face is found wherever you turn. Hence, the Koran commands people, "Flee to God" (51:50). The Prophet used to pray, "I seek refuge in Thy good-pleasure from Thy anger, I seek refuge in Thy pardon from Thy punishment, I seek refuge in Thee from Thee." When you fear God, you do not run away from him, you run toward him. And when you love God, you also run toward him. This is precisely the implication of *tawhid*. However you approach things, you are led back to God.

It may be helpful to think of the viewpoints of nearness and distance in terms of the relationship between unity and multiplicity, or oneness and manyness. *Tawhid* affirms that God is one. Since God is infinitely beyond the universe, the universe can have no share in his oneness. Hence, the universe is divisible into an infinite number of parts. God is unity, while the world is multiplicity. From the second point of view, God's unity is reflected within the universe. This means that the universe is a single whole, and that all its parts share in harmony, balance, and equilibrium.

Tanzih and Tashbih

In the technical language of theology, especially as it developed after the seventh/thirteenth century, two terms are commonly employed to express the contrast between the perception of God's nearness and mercy and that of his distance and wrath. These terms are *tanzih* (declaring incomparability) and *tashbih* (affirming similarity).

Tanzih means literally "to declare something pure and free of some-thing else." It is to assert that God is pure and free of all the defects and imperfections of the creatures. In the perspective of *tanzih*, God is so holy and pure that he cannot be compared to any created thing, includ-ing concepts, since all our ideas are created. The Koranic verse that expresses *tanzih* most clearly is "Nothing is like Him" (42:11).

Divine names that are taken as expressing *tanzih* are the names of God's essence already mentioned, such as Holy, Glorified, Independent, and Transcendent. But all the majestic and wrathful names can also be called names of *tanzih*, because they stress God's difference from cre-ation, the fact that he is infinitely beyond the petty affairs of the creatures.

Tashbih means "to declare something similar to something else." It is to assert that God must have some sort of similarity with his creatures. If he did not, how could they have anything to do with him? God's signs within the cosmos and scripture designate his attributes, such as life, know-ledge, desire, power, mercy, generosity, and provision. These attributes belong to God, but they are also found in created things. All divine names suggest some sort of *tashbih*, because they allow us to think that God is such and such. Although we know that "Nothing is like Him," as soon as we name God we create a concept in our minds of what he is like. For example, as soon as we read in the Koran that God is Compassionate, we think of God in terms of our own understanding of compassion. Even when we name God by a name of the essence, such as Independent, we understand that name in terms of our own ideas of independence.

Every divine name suggests a certain *tashbih*, but the beautiful and merciful names of God stress *tashbih* much more than they stress *tanzih*. Hence names that tell us about God's nearness to creation and concern for his creatures can be classified as names of *tashbih*. To say that God is merciful and loving is to stress that he is not distant and aloof; instead, he is close to and concerned with people's everyday affairs. Names of gentle-ness and mercy describe a God whom people can understand and love. These names suggest that, like a caring mother, God stays close to his creatures and watches out for their every need. When someone is gentle, good, and loving, the normal human response is to reciprocate.

The perspective of *tanzih* affirms God's oneness by declaring that God is one and God alone is Real. Hence everything other than God is unreal and not worthy of consideration. God's single reality excludes all unreality. In contrast, the perspective of *tashbih* declares that God's oneness is such that his one reality embraces all creatures. The world, which appears as unre-ality and illusion, is in fact nothing but the One Real showing his signs. Rather than excluding all things, God's unity includes them.

Often *tanzih* and *tashbih* are associated with the two divine names *ba-tin* (Inward or Nonmanifest) and *zahir* (Outward or Manifest). Inas-much as the Real is Inward, all outwardness is unreal, and oneness is found only in the Real himself. But inasmuch as God is Outward, all outwardness is the Real. Hence the universe itself is real through God's realness and one through God's oneness.

Both God's incomparability and his similarity need to be kept in view. If God is far, he is also near. Although he is beautiful and stirs up love in the heart because of his beauty, his beauty is not like the beauty of any created thing. "Nothing is like Him." In the midst of his nearness he is far, and in the midst of his similarity he is incomparable.

One way to understand the idea of incomparability is to conceive of an infinitely vast circle (Figure 1). God is at the center; he is the dimensionless central point that serves as the origin of the circle. The world that we experience is at the periphery, infinitely distant from the center. There are many worlds, and these can be pictured as a series of concentric circles, some closer to God and some farther away. All worlds have the same center, and all are cut off from the center because of God's incomparability. Only the central point has no dimensions, and "Nothing is like Him." At the same time every concentric circle is similar to every other circle. Created things share the same qualities, but God shares none of their qualities.

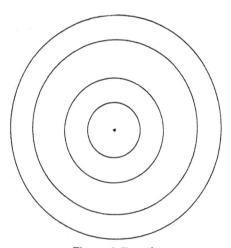

Figure 1: Tanzih

In order to picture *tashbih*, we can use the same dimensionless point, but now we need to imagine that the point has an infinite number of radii extending outward (Figure 2). Each creature in the universe is situated on a radius and is connected directly to the center, gaining its reality from the central point. The radii suggest God's concern for creation through love, mercy, compassion, and kindness.

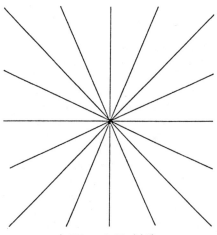

Figure 2: Tashbih

However, neither *tanzih* nor *tashbih* provides a complete picture of reality. The universe needs to be understood in terms of both perspectives simultaneously (Figure 3). Then we see that each thing is at once near to God and far from him, at once similar to God and incomparable with him. Each thing is confronted simultaneously with mercy and wrath, gentleness and severity, life-giving and slaying, bestowal and withholding, reality and unreality. This is *tawhid*.

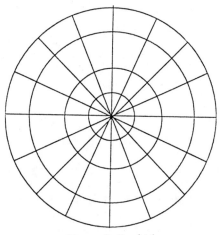

Figure 3: Tawhid

The two perspectives of *tanzih* and *tashbih*, or God's distance and nearness, are met constantly in Islamic texts and in the everyday life of

Muslims. Let us cite one simple example. We have already referred to the Koranic formula "Praise belongs to God," which is recited by Muslims on all sorts of occasions and in all sorts of contexts, since it expresses gratitude to God. People recite it when anything good happens, when they eat or drink something, when they see something that pleases them. If they are a bit more careful in observing the Prophet's Sunna than most, they will thank God for everything, for the bad as well as the good, for suffering as well as joy. They will recognize that everything that comes from God should be acknowledged with gratitude. The Prophet said, "Praise belongs to God in every situation."

The formula of praise ties blessings back to God. It takes the signs in the cosmos and in the soul and ascribes them to their divine origin. Hence it affirms the perspective of *tashbih*, the nearness of God and his activity in all situations, his care and concern for human beings.

Another commonly recited Koranic formula is "Glory be to God" (*subhanallah*). In contrast to "Praise belongs to God," this formula stresses *tanzih*. It is uttered when any thought of ill occurs toward God or his activity, or when any suggestion is made that God might have motivations like human beings. The Koran often employs the phrase with this meaning, as when it rejects various opinions of pre-Islamic peoples. For example, "They have set up a kinship between Him and the jinn. . . . Glory be to God above what they describe!" (37:173).

These two formulas, which Muslims recite habitually and often without thinking about their meaning, express *tanzih* and *tashbih* in everyday life. What is significant is that both formulas are needed, since the human situation demands that God be perceived as both absent and present.

In short, *tanzih* and *tashbih* represent the two poles of *tawhid*. As we shall see, these two complementary perspectives need to be taken into account whenever we discuss such basic issues as the role of human beings in the cosmos, the nature of prophecy, and the return to God.

Mercy's Precedence

The perspective of *tawhid* asserts the oneness of God, who is the only true reality. It recognizes that God is related to all things in the universe: without some contact with reality, the things could not exist. It asserts that God is infinitely beyond all things (*tanzih*), but it also declares that he is present within all things (*tashbih*).

We suggested that the names of majesty and wrath are more closely connected to *tanzih* than to *tashbih*, because the majestic names assert the utter otherness of God, his grand power and magnificent tremendousness. Names like All-Compeller, Intensely Severe, All-Subjugating, and Terrible in Punishment give news of a distant king who runs his kingdom the way he likes, without a thought for your feelings or mine.

In the same way, the names of beauty and mercy are more closely connected to *tashbih* than to *tanzih*, since they give news of someone who is intensely concerned for even the smallest details of everyday life. If God were not "closer than the jugular vein," why does he say "Call upon Me, and I will answer you" (40:60)?

If we understand God to be both near and distant, both caring and unconcerned, both gentle and severe, we may soon find ourselves bewildered about God. Should we fear his wrath or hope for his mercy? As indicated above, the traditional answer has always been that people should have both fear and hope. Without fear, people become bold and do whatever they want, not worrying about the consequences. Without hope, they shrivel and die.

Is either hope or fear to be preferred above the other, or should people have them in equal measure? If God's majestic and beautiful attributes stood in exact balance, then it would have to be said that people need fear and hope in equal measure. But in fact, the tradition says that majesty and beauty do not stand on the same level.

We showed earlier that the fear of God does not produce the same reaction as fear of a creature. In this world, when you fear something, you run away from it, but if you hope to receive some benefit from it, you go toward it. However, the only logical way to act when you fear God is to go toward him, since there is nowhere to run. Likewise, hope and love for God encourage people to go toward him. Every relationship with God encourages seeking out nearness with him. The human reaction to God's distance should be to seek nearness to him, and the human reaction to his nearness should be to seek greater nearness. Nearness is an attribute of *tashbih*, not *tanzih*.

The message of God's incomparability is that people should strive to achieve similarity. And the message of similarity is that they should strive to achieve greater similarity. Similarity, not incomparability, is the desired goal.

Of course, God is distant from human beings. And once again, this is the God of *tawhid*, not the God of contemporary popular culture. This is the God who is the source of life, knowledge, desire, power, speech, mercy, good, and everything real. To say that God is distant is to affirm that people dwell far from reality, because their life, knowledge, desire, power, and other positive qualities are exceedingly faint and fleeting.

But God is also near, because nothing can escape reality. To speak of human beings is to speak of life, knowledge, desire, and so on, no matter how faint these attributes may be. There can be no escape into an absolute nothingness, because these qualities do not belong to people in the first place. How can you throw away what you do not possess? These are God's qualities, and they stay with us as he decides. As we will see when we discuss the Return, Islam insists that death is merely transferal from one abode to another. Circumstances change, but not the basic attributes of existence.

All this is to say that God is real, whereas created things are unreal. Any reality that creatures may possess has been given to them by God and remains in his power and control. They have no way to escape their God-given reality. Reality is everything, while unreality is nothing. Reality pertains to God. The more real a thing is, the closer it is to God. The less real it is, the farther it is from God. But even in distance, things are near to God, since to be real is to be a sign of God, a ray of his light.

The Koran and the Hadith normally discuss nearness and distance in terms of their human consequences. To be distant from God is to be controlled by the attributes of majesty and wrath, and this can be a painful situation. To be near is to be controlled by the attributes of beauty and mercy, and this is a pleasant place to be. We will see how the Koran associates hell with distance and paradise with nearness. Here our point is that beauty and mercy are more real than majesty and wrath, because beauty and mercy represent closeness to God. That which is close to God is more like him than that which is distant, and thus more real. Hence the attributes of *tashbih* are a better representation of the Real than the attributes of *tanzih*.

One of the ways in which the Koran refers to the fact that the names of beauty and mercy represent God's true nature more accurately than the names of majesty and wrath is in the statement that God's mercy embraces all things. "I strike with My chastisement whom I will, but My mercy embraces all things" (7:156). The Koran never suggests that God is wrathful toward all things. He is wrathful only toward those creatures who refuse to accept his nearness to them, who fly in the face of reality through their thoughts and actions.

The Prophet reported that God has written upon his Throne, "My mercy takes precedence over My wrath." This precedence is not temporal, it is ontological. In other words, mercy is more fundamental to reality than wrath. Mercy pertains to the very nature of the Real, whereas wrath is a secondary attribute that rises up because of the specific situations of certain creatures.

The idea that God's mercy takes precedence over his wrath is one of the most important principles of Islamic thought. It has innumerable repercussions both in theory and in practice. We will often come back to it, but for the time being, it is important to see this principle as establishing a relationship between *tanzih* and *tashbih*. God's incomparability is a fact of existence, but his similarity is a more fundamental fact. *Tawhid* tells us that God is different from us, but it also tells us that God is not different in every respect, and this second statement has the final say. Mercy takes precedence, and mercy establishes nearness to the Real.

Islam begins with the perception of difference. We are different from God and far from him. God is utterly other, and created things are totally helpless because of their lack of any positive qualities. But the purpose of Islamic teachings is not to leave people in wrath (distance), but rather to take them to mercy (nearness). People are supposed to do something about their distance from God, and if they do, they will move toward nearness. Nearness is desirable, because it is nearness to everything that is real, good, beneficial, and enjoyable.

As a divine attribute established in relation to the creatures, mercy is everything that God does to allow people to benefit from the good and the real. Mercy represents God's fundamental motive, since mercy is God himself. Wrath is an accidental affair that will eventually disappear, since wrath pertains to things that are isolated from God, and nothing can be isolated from God in a real sense. As soon as nearness is achieved, wrath is effaced.

With these remarks on the fundamental role that mercy plays in Islamic thought, we end our discussion of God's names and attributes. In no way are we implying that this discussion could ever be completed, since exploring the names and attributes is merely a way of explaining *tawhid*. And *tawhid* is the explication of how God is connected to his creatures, who are the infinite signs. For every sign of God, there is a lesson to be learned about God, something to be understood about his nature. But the signs have no end, because the universe, which is everything other than God, has no end.

Acts

The attributes of God can be discussed endlessly, but they are normally summarized in ninety-nine names. In the same way, the attributes of the universe can be discussed endlessly—as modern science illustrates—but the Koran and the Hadith provide clear organizing concepts that have allowed Muslim scholars to picture the cosmos as a grand, coherent panorama of the signs of God, or a vast collection of verses announcing a single message.

In the language of Islamic theology, the use of the term *acts of God* to refer to created things indicates that all things are creations of God and signs of his attributes. As we saw earlier, the term *acts* is employed in the context of the terms *essence* and *attributes*. The essence of God is God's very self, his reality as he alone knows it. The attributes of God are those qualities of God's self—his names—that he reveals to his creatures through the signs, whether scriptural or natural. The acts are the things and events of the universe that appear through God's activity.

The relationships among these three terms can be understood if we apply them to ourselves. The essence of a person is the person, without regard to qualities such as male or female, old or young, pleasant or unpleasant, intelligent or stupid, strong or weak. The attributes are the qualities possessed by the person, such as maleness, youth, pleasantness, and intelligence. The acts are everything the person does or makes manifest that leads us to the conclusion that he is young, pleasant, and intelligent.

Notice that the acts depend on the attributes, and the attributes depend on the essence, whether we are talking about God, or people, or anything else. A student attends class, which is an act, on the basis of a large number of attributes, such as life, knowledge, desire, power, and speech. All these attributes depend on someone being there—the essence. If no one is there, we cannot discuss attributes.

Take another example: You are a carpenter who builds a house. The essence is you. The attributes include knowledge of carpentry, the desire to build the house, and the power to lift hammers and saws. The acts are all the things you do to build the house. The final act, which is analogous to the whole universe, is the house.

In short, when we discuss God and *tawhid*, the discussion takes place on three different levels. First, we recognize that a single reality is there (the essence), hidden behind the diversity of appearances. Second, we describe the ways in which that thing appears to us, and our descriptions are called attributes. Third, we describe the things that are apparent before our eyes as acts and we recognize that these acts depend upon those attributes.

God's acts are all the things that he creates in the universe throughout time and space. The universe, or cosmos—in all its temporal and spatial extension—is a single infinite act that externalizes everything that God knows about it in his infinite knowledge.

From one point of view, we can say that only two things exist: God, and his act. Normally, this perspective is expressed by saying that we have God and everything other than God. "Everything other than God" is thus a synonym for the cosmos, or for the sum total of all God's acts. The attributes, or names, then describe the perceived relationship between God and the cosmos. The attributes do not exist as entities; rather, they are understood by the mind as designating how the acts are related to the essence.

Take yourself as an example. In all of existence there is you and other than you. Your attributes do not exist as a third set of things, different from yourself and others. Examples of your attributes are small and large, mother and daughter, intelligent and stupid, strong and weak, forgiving and vengeful, and so on. You are small compared to mountains, planets, and stars, and large compared to insects, microbes, and atoms. You are mother in comparison to your children, and daughter in relation to your mother. You are intelligent compared to some of your friends, your dog, and bugs. You are stupid compared to some of your acquaintances and people like Aristotle and Einstein. You are forgiving when a puppy nips you, but vengeful when a mosquito drinks your blood.

All our attributes depend upon our relationships to other things. In the same way, God's attributes can only be conceived of in terms of his relationship to other things, and those things are everything other than himself, his acts.

The Unseen and the Visible

Everything the Koran says about the world can be considered a description of God's acts. But some statements are more general and some more specific. Some verses refer to many of the acts or all the acts, while others refer only to one or a few. Meditating upon the Koranic accounts and taking help from the Hadith and the prevailing world view of their time, Muslim thinkers deduced that the acts can be divided into two basic categories.

The Koran tells us in several verses that God is "Knower of the unseen and the visible." Clearly, everything that exists is either seen by us or not seen by us. Our knowledge extends as far as we can see, grasp, encompass, investigate, and analyze—and this leaves practically the whole universe unknown to us, since we have no way to see it and grasp it. In contrast to us, God knows everything, whether we see it or not.

But when the Koran speaks about the "unseen," it does not seem to mean that which our eyes do not reach in practice, but rather that which our eyes do not reach in principle. Our eyes can only see material things. However, not only is the universe infinitely vast on the level of these material things, it is also infinitely vast on the immaterial level.

At the beginning of Sura 2, the Koran speaks about itself as guidance for those who are careful in their dealings with God and "who have faith in the unseen." Thus, if we need to express the objects of faith in one word, we can say the "unseen." Of course the scriptures are visible to us in their written form, but the meaning of the scriptures is unseen to us, which explains why people of all religions have spent an enormous amount of time and energy investigating the meaning of their scriptures, and why they continue to do so.

In short, Muslims have discerned two basic kinds of reality, the unseen and the visible, or the absent (*ghayb*) and the witnessed (*shahada*). The unseen can be divided into two basic categories: God and the angels. God is not seen by anyone except himself, whereas the angels are seen by other angels, by God and by certain exceptional human beings, like prophets. Hence, angels are unseen in relation to most human beings, but visible in relation to themselves and God.

The visible is the sensory world, which includes everything we see in fact or can see in principle. The visible can also be divided into two kinds: those things that all of us can see, like the external world, and those things that all of us do not share in seeing, like dreams and hallucinations. Dreams are visible to the dreamer, but not to anyone else in our world. Of course, God sees our dreams, and so also do those angels whose business it is to see them (given that angels are divided into many kinds in keeping with their functions). There are also other kinds of beings that belong to the semivisible world, beings that for the most part cannot be seen, but on occasion show themselves. The jinn fit into this category (we will have more to say about them as we go along).

Heaven and Earth

Another pair of Koranic terms that is frequently employed in discussions of the universe is *heaven* (or heavens) and *earth*. In discussing heaven, it is important not to confuse it with paradise. In Islam, paradise is always juxtaposed with hell, while heaven is always contrasted with earth. Paradise and hell pertain to the Return to God. They cannot be experienced in their fullness until after the Last Day. But heaven and earth refer to the situation of the cosmos from the time of this world's creation until the Last Day. At the Last Day, heaven and earth will be transformed: "Upon the day the earth shall be changed to other than the earth, and the heavens, and [people] shall go forth unto God, the One, the Intensely Severe" (14:48).

The Koran refers to seven heavens, and these are marked by the seven planets (a term which, in Greek and Arabic, means "wandering celestial body"). It is important not to think of these planets in terms of modern astronomy. Although the Muslims developed scientific astronomy to a high degree, the Koranic astronomy is an astronomy of signs. What we see with our naked eyes is used as a means to teach us about the unseen—God, the angels, and the Last Day. Hence, Koranic discussion of the heavens remains at the level of what people can observe by going out in their backyards on a dark night.

It is useful to keep in mind that the heavens were always full of meaning for people who lived with nature and that they could be seen clearly, given the lack of atmospheric pollution or interference from man-made light sources. In the modern world, scientific knowledge has removed us from the direct experience of nature. We can no longer see things as they present themselves to us. On the contrary, we see things as we were taught to see them in grammar school. Not only that, for the most part we have no interest in seeing things, because we think that the scientists—the specialists—know it all, and we cannot discover anything of significance ourselves. If we need to know something, we can look it up in a book. In any case, the fluttering electronic light of our television sets is much more dynamic and fascinating than the stars, which hardly move. (What did people do at night before television anyway?)

In ascending order, the seven planets are the moon, Mercury, Venus, the sun, Mars, Jupiter, and Saturn. Each planet swims in its own heaven. The tradition usually adds two more heavens to this list—the Footstool and the Throne. Sometimes these two are said to be identical with the sphere of the fixed stars and the starless sphere. The Koran mentions the Footstool only once, in one of its most famous verses, which is often found inscribed in mosques or monuments:

God—there is no god but He, the Living, the Self-subsistent. Slumber seizes Him not, neither sleep. To Him belongs all that is in the heavens and the earth. Who is there to intercede with Him save by His leave? He knows what is before them and what is behind them, but they encompass nothing of His knowledge save such as He wills. His Footstool embraces the heavens and the earth, and preserving them does not burden Him. He is the High, the Tremendous. (2:254)

Notice that the Koran is not talking about the cosmos but about God's attributes. God knows all things, but people know only as much as God lets them know. Their knowledge, in other words, is measured out, while his knowledge is beyond measure. Then the verse mentions the universe in passing—the heavens and the earth. And it says that God's Footstool encompasses them. The Footstool is obviously the place where God puts his "feet." If God's feet are resting beyond the universe, where could his "head" be? Not that God has head or feet, or at least in the sense that we have them, but the imagery is suggestive of relationships. What is lowest in God stands beyond what is highest in the universe. God has to stoop way down in order to interact with us, and we have to stretch high up in order to find God.

The Footstool is located below the Throne of God, where God the King sat down after he created the heavens and the earth. The Koran refers to the Throne in twenty-one verses, all of which suggest God's kingship and power. However, perhaps to offset the majestic and severe connotations of kingship, the Koran associates only one divine name directly with the Throne, and that is Merciful.

God is not similar to other kings, whose primary attribute is majesty and severity. On the contrary, God is a king whose gentleness predominates over his severity. Remember that the inscription on the Throne reads, "My mercy takes precedence over My wrath." God's rule brings nothing but good to his creatures. Hence the Koranic idea of the divine Throne combines attributes of majesty and beauty. This is highly appropriate for something that encompasses the whole universe, for the universe is ruled by both kinds of attributes.

It should not be imagined that the Koran is talking about the solar system when it mentions the heavens. Although the heavens are marked by the planets, which are visible, the heavens themselves are unseen. A set of hadiths that bring this out clearly recount Muhammad's journey to God, which is referred to in the Koran (17:1, 53:1-21, 81:19-25). This journey is known as the *mi'raj*, which means literally "ladder." The image here is not unconnected to the ladder that Jacob saw extending to heaven, with angels ascending and descending (Genesis 28:12). Muhammad was taken up the ladder to God, and then he came back down on the ladder to his people, to continue his mission to them.

Briefly, the accounts of the *mi'raj* tell us that Muhammad was woken one night by Gabriel, who told him to come along. Gabriel mounted him on Buraq, a winged horse whose every stride was equal to its glance. In a few quick steps they reached the Temple at Jerusalem, where all the prophets from Adam down to Jesus were assembled. At the Temple, which the Koran calls the Further Mosque, Muhammad performed a *salat*, and all the prophets prayed behind him, with him as their imam.

Then Gabriel took Muhammad by the hand and they went up to the heaven of the moon. Gabriel knocked on the door, and a voice asked who was there. Having assured the voice that the two of them had been sent for, Gabriel was let in, Muhammad following. Waiting for them was Adam, and Gabriel performed the introductions. Adam said, "Welcome to a good son and a good prophet." Then Gabriel and Muhammad continued the journey. In each of the remaining six heavens they met one or more of the prophets. After traveling through the heavens, they visited hell and then paradise. Some modern scholars have suggested that the accounts of the Prophet's *mi'raj* provided the inspiration for Dante's depiction of hell and paradise in the Divine Comedy.

Having reached the outermost edge of paradise, located perhaps just below the Throne itself, Gabriel said that from this point on, Muhammad would have to go on alone to meet God, because, if Gabriel were to fly any farther, his wings would burn. Muhammad went to meet the ineffable light, and here the report turns silent. On the way back down, Muhammad rejoined Gabriel and then stopped in every heaven to say farewell to the prophets who reside there.

This account should make clear that discussion of the heavens does not necessarily have much to do with the planets with which we are familiar. As some Muslim authorities have pointed out, this is a symbolic narrative that refers to various levels of existence and the fact that each level manifests different divine attributes. Each of the prophets that Muhammad meets represents part of the overall divine message, or a segment of the totality of the signs that God reveals in the scripture and in the cosmos. No Muslim has ever imagined that Adam, Moses, Abraham, and other prophets are living on the planets, or at least not on the planets as we conceive of them in modern astronomy. Rather, the planets that wander through the sky are signs of God that fill existence with the light of his messages. They are signs that point to higher realms of existence that can be visited by those who go to meet God. As we will see later, all the faithful are taken up through these same heavens immediately after death, before settling down in the grave to wait for the day of resurrection.[3]

When heaven and earth are discussed, the basic issue is the nature of the relationships that are established among things of the created universe, or the hierarchy that is set up in the cosmos as a result of its subordination to God. We learn about God's relationship to the cosmos both by contrasting his qualities with its qualities (*tanzih*) and by showing that the qualities of the two sides are in certain respects similar (*tashbih*). In the same way, we learn about the relationships among God's creatures by drawing consequences from the fact that heaven and earth reproduce in miniature the relationship between God and the cosmos.

When Muslim thinkers look at heaven and earth in terms of the attributes of incomparability, they describe the two in opposite terms: high and low, bright and dark, strong and weak, active and passive, giving and receiving. When they stress the attributes of similarity, they illustrate that the qualities of heaven are also found in the earth, but in a diminished sense.

God is Creator. "Is there any creator apart from God?" (35:3). The question is rhetorical, and no one doubts that the answer is "No." The verse is meant to stress God's incomparability. But another Koranic verse says, "God is the best of creators" (23:14). Hence we learn that other things share in the attribute of creativity. Within the cosmos, heaven is the primary place where the attributes of creativity appear. In contrast, the earth's qualities depend upon receptivity toward heaven. Moreover, heaven also depends upon earth, because without earth, heaven has no place to display its art.

Heaven represents a concentrated, undifferentiated, and immaterial power, while earth represents a dispersed, differentiated, and material collection of signs, manifesting the invisible power of heaven. The basic Koranic symbol for the qualities of heaven is water, which is pure and undifferentiated. When heavenly water falls down, it yields a tremendous diversity of living things. As the Koran puts it, "Of water We fashioned every living thing" (21:30). Many Muslim thinkers maintain that this verse refers not only to animals and plants, but also to all created things, for everything in the heavens and the earth sings the praise of God, as the Koran says repeatedly. How can something sing without being alive?

It is He who sent down out of heaven water, and thereby We have brought forth the shoot of every plant. (6:99)

You see the earth blackened. Then, when We send down water upon it, it quivers, and swells, and puts forth herbs of every joyous kind. (22:5)

We sent down from heaven pure water, so that We might give life to a dead land. (25:48)

If heavenly water is pure, it is also "one," because of its undifferentiated nature. Only after being drunk by the earth can it give rise to diversity: "And in the earth are . . . gardens of vines, and fields sown, and palms in pairs, and palms single, watered with one water" (13:4).

Earth, then, represents the place where heaven displays its properties, just as heaven and earth together (the cosmos) display the signs of God. Heaven is near to God, and earth is far away. Hence heaven alerts us to attributes of *tashbih*, while earth is dominated by attributes of *tanzih*. Nevertheless, earth also, inasmuch as it displays fruitfulness and bounty, is displaying God's gentle and merciful qualities, so earth also has to be thought of in terms of *tashbih*. And heaven is not exempt from *tanzih*, because "Everything is perishing except the face of God" (28:88), and that includes heaven.

Koranic teachings on how heaven and earth display God's signs could be discussed endlessly, and all of it would be an expression of *tawhid*, but we will focus on a specific concept that is mentioned in the hadith of Gabriel—the angels. We said that the angels pertain more to *tawhid* than to prophecy or eschatology, though they have important roles to play in those domains as well. We now turn to explaining how the Koranic idea of angels helps shape the Islamic vision of God, the cosmos, and human beings.

ANGELS

In the hadith of Gabriel, the Prophet said that people should have faith in God's angels. Just as faith in God is meaningless without a concept of God, so also faith in angels has no sense unless we know what angels are. Ideas about angels current in our society, like common ideas of God, will not help us much in understanding the Islamic concept. Better to discard from the outset all those winged little boys shooting arrows or Grecian maidens playing harps.

The Arabic word for angel, *malak*—like its Hebrew cousin *mal'ak*—means the same as the Greek *angelos*; that is, "messenger." The Koran employs the term, usually in the plural, about ninety times. In addition, the Koran mentions several angels by name—including Gabriel, Michael, Harut, and Marut—and refers to quite a variety of angels by words that seem to designate their functions. Thus we have reciters, glorifiers, scarers, dividers, casters, pluckers, severers, ascenders, writers, watchers, envoys, outstrippers, and so on. The Koran usually mentions these angels only in passing. For explanation, one has to refer to the Koran commentaries. In any case, it is important to know at the outset that the Koran has a great deal to say about angels.

Nowadays in our own culture, few people take angels very seriously, even if popular books on the subject are increasingly common. Many Christian theologians think that angels are a remnant of a superstitious age or, at best, some sort of symbol no longer needed. But angels are an ever-present reality in the traditional Islamic mind, and the more that Muslims learn about their religion through faith and practice, the more seriously they take them. One cannot even perform the *salat* without acknowledging the existence of angels. After finishing the ritual prayer, the person turns to the right and says, "Peace be upon you," even if he or she is praying alone. The reason is that it is necessary to greet the angels who, according to the Prophet, pray along with everyone who performs the prayer.

Angels are found everywhere. There are angels with God who carry his Throne and others who circle around it praising and glorifying him. Angels witnessed the creation of the human being, and an angel entrusts the human soul to the embryo in the womb. The first thing people see when they die is angels, chief among them Azrael, the angel of death.

God's Unseen Messengers

What do angels do? Basically, they bring messages. More broadly, they carry out God's commands. It is important that we give the word *message* implicit in the name *malak* a wide meaning, just as we have to give *islam* and other important terms wide meanings. There are many different kinds of messages, some of which we would not normally think of as messages. For example, few messages brought by the angels involve the actual handing over of an oral or written text. Only prophets receive scriptures and tablets.

The scriptures that are given to prophets are brought by one specific angel to whom God has entrusted prophecy: Gabriel. Again, we should not take ourselves too literally when we say that it is Gabriel's function to deliver scriptures. We need to understand scripture in a broad sense. Scripture is the speech or word of God revealed to human beings with the goal of guiding them to happiness. Hence, a scripture does not have to be a book in the usual meaning of the term; the words of God, whatever form they take, can be called scripture.

Since God's message does not necessarily take the form of a book, it may take the form of a human being. This is one way we can understand the Koranic verses that describe Gabriel's relationship with Jesus. The Koran refers to Jesus, alone among all the prophets and messengers, as God's "word," so he is comparable to a scripture. And one of the terms that the Koran employs to refer to certain angels is *casters*, because they "cast" or toss God's messages to human beings. Hence it seems natural that Gabriel, the angel who brought the Koran to Muhammad, should be the angel who acted as the intermediary for God's casting his word into Mary. It was he who announced to Mary that she would give birth to the Messiah.

> *We sent to her Our spirit [Gabriel], and he appeared to her in the image of a mortal without fault. (19:17)*

> *The Messiah, Jesus son of Mary, was only the messenger of God, and His word that He cast to Mary, and a spirit from Him. (4:171)*

Most messages brought by the angels take the form of a concrete occurrence or event, not a scripture. We learned earlier that all creatures can be considered words of God. In that case, all creatures are messages sent by God. In other words, everything is a sign of God, which is to say that each thing teaches us about God. This teaching about God is not haphazard. The teacher is God himself, who creates the signs in order to reveal himself. Hence the term *sign*, which refers to natural phenomena, scriptures, and miracles, is nearly synonymous with *message*.

If the angels deliver God's messages, then the angels must have something to do with God's signs. Behind every sign—every created thing—stands an angel. Some texts report that everything has an angel and that an angel descends with every drop of rain. How could it be otherwise, if the angels deliver God's messages, and if all things are his messages?

In short, by pondering the signs in the light of *tawhid*, we come to the conclusion that angels play the important role of acting as intermediaries between the visible universe and God himself, the creator of that universe. But since the angels themselves are invisible, they pertain to the domain of the unseen. Hence they are heavenly creatures, suspended halfway between God and earth.

Looking back on the Koran and the Hadith, Muslim authors have come up with various classifications of the kinds of angels that fill the cosmos. One account gives us fourteen major categories, with no attempt to make connections (we could, for example, consider numbers 2 through 7 as archangels):

1. *Those who carry the Throne of God (40:7).*

2. *The Spirit, who is said to be the greatest of the angels.*

3. *Seraphiel, who will blow the Trumpet twice at the end of time. At the first blow, everyone in heaven and earth will faint away, and at the second blow, all will be brought forth to meet their Lord.*

4. *Gabriel, the angel of revelation.*

5. *Michael (2:98), who provides nourishments for bodies and souls.*

6. *Azrael, the angel of death.*

7. *The cherubim, who have no knowledge of created things and spend all their time contemplating God.*

8. *The angels of the seven heavens.*

9. *The guardian angels (82:11), two of whom are charged with each human being; one writes down good deeds, and the other writes down evil deeds.*

10. *The attendant angels (13:11), who bring down blessings and go back to God with news of the creatures.*

11. *Nakir and Munkar, who question the dead in their graves.*

12. *The journeyers, who travel in the earth searching out assemblies where people remember God's name.*

13. *Harut and Marut, two angels who came down to Babylon and taught its inhabitants sorcery (2:102).*

14. *The angels charged with each existent thing, maintaining order and warding off corruption. Their number is known only to God.*[4]

Light

The Prophet tells us that God created angels out of light. Light is a name of God, and the Koran tells us that "God is the light of the heavens and the earth" (24:35). In order to understand what angels are, we have to understand what light is. It will not help us much to think about light in physical terms. Rather, we have to grasp the signs that are revealed to us when we observe light.

Normally, we think of light as visible, but in fact, it is invisible. We can only see light when it is mixed with darkness. If there were only light and no darkness, we would be blinded by its intensity. Look at what happens when you gaze at the sun, which is 93 million miles away and is viewed through the earth's atmosphere. If we moved outside the atmosphere, just a few miles closer to the sun, we could not possibly look at it for a moment without losing our eyesight. What we call visible light is pretty pale stuff. It can hardly compare with unfiltered sunlight, much less with the divine light, which illuminates the whole cosmos. Hence, it is said in Islam that God's light is so bright that people have all been blinded by it.

God is unseen, angels are unseen, and light is unseen. Thus it should not be surprising that God and angels are light. You might object and say that we see light shining everywhere, but we don't see angels or God. Don't we? *Tawhid* is telling us that the signs are nothing but God's radiance, and the creatures are nothing but the outward marks of God's creative power. "God is the light of the heavens and the earth" (24:35), and the heavens and the earth are the radiance or the reflection of that light.

Light is invisible, but without light we see nothing. Hence, light can be defined as an invisible something that makes other things visible. So also, God and the angels are invisible, but without them there would be no universe. Hence, God and the angels can be described as invisible somethings that make the universe visible.

The opposite of light is darkness, and darkness is simply the absence of light. In other words, light is something, but darkness is nothing. We see things because a nothing has mixed with a something. We would not be able to see if there were only light, or if there were only darkness. Light and darkness must come together for vision to occur.

God is Light. The opposite of light is darkness, which is nothing. In other words, God has no real, existing opposite, since nothing is not really something. If nothing is there, how can we talk about opposites? Of course, we say that nothing is the opposite of something, but this nothing does not exist except as a figure of speech or as an object of supposition for the purpose of discussion and explication.

Are creatures light or darkness? The answer, of course, is that they are neither, or that they are both. If they were light and nothing but light, they would be God, and if they were darkness and nothing but darkness, they would not exist. Hence they live in a never-never land that is neither light nor darkness.

In respect of *tashbih*, the creatures are light, but in respect of *tanzih* they are darkness. In other words, to the extent that things are similar to God, they are luminous, but to the extent that they are incomparable with God, they are dark. They must have some luminosity, or else they could not exist.

To dwell in darkness (relative darkness, that is, since absolute darkness does not exist) is to dwell in distance from God; it is to be dominated by the divine qualities of majesty and wrath, which keep things far from God. To dwell in light is to live in nearness to God; it is to be dominated by the qualities of beauty and mercy, which bring things close to God.

There is one light, and that light is God. There are many darknesses, since each creature represents darkness in relation to God. The deeper the darkness, the greater the distance from God. Absolute darkness does not exist, because it would be cut off from God in every respect. How can anything exist if it has no relationship whatsoever to the Real, which is the source of every quality?

Created things dwell in distance from God, in difference, in otherness. This is to say that they dwell in relative darkness. Relative darkness has many modes and forms, since there are an infinite number of ways in which things can be different from God. "Nothing is like Him," but each thing is unlike him in its own unique way.

Dwelling in difference means perceiving God from the perspective of *tanzih* and hence to be dominated by the attributes of severity, majesty, and wrath. The goal of religion is to bring about a movement from *tanzih* to *tashbih*, from distance to nearness, from difference to sameness, from manyness to oneness, from wrath to mercy, from darkness to light.

The Koran frequently explains that God's goal in creation is to bring about unity, and often it employs the terms light and darkness to make this point. The broad significance of such verses becomes clear as soon as one grasps the meaning of *tawhid*. Notice that in the following verses light is one, since light is an attribute of God, but the darknesses are many, since darkness is an attribute that assumes many forms in keeping with the diversity of creation:

> Are the blind and the seeing man equal, or are the darknesses and the light equal? (13:16, 35:20)

> It is He who sends down upon His servant signs, clear explications, that He may bring you forth from the darknesses into the light. (57:9)

> Why, is he who was dead, and We gave him life, and appointed for him a light to walk by among the people, as one who is in the darknesses, and comes not forth from them? (6:122)

> It is He who performs the salat over you, and His angels, that He may bring you forth from the darknesses into the light. (33:43)

This last verse brings us back to the angels, who are created from light and are therefore able to assist God in giving light to the creatures who dwell in the visible world.

Angelic Luminosity

God is light. The opposite of God's absolute light is absolute darkness, which cannot exist, since there is no reality outside of God to support its existence.

The angels are *created* of light. Hence they differ from God, who is uncreated light. Angelic light can have an opposite, a created darkness. This darkness is not absolute darkness, because then it would not exist and hence would not be a created thing. The opposite of created, angelic light is a created, nonangelic darkness; that is, something dark in relation to the light of the angels.

The Koran refers both to created light and to created darkness in the verse, "Praise belongs to God, who created the heavens and the earth and who made the darknesses and the light" (6:1). Notice that the verse speaks of created light in the singular. This alludes to the fact that, in the last analysis, "There is no light but God." All light is merely the radiance of God's light, so all light is ultimately one. In contrast, dark-nesses are many, because they represent the infinite ways in which things can be distant and different from God.

Invisible, uncreated light (God) has no opposite. Created light is also invisible, but it has an opposite, which is anything visible—everything that can be seen with the eyes. You might say, sunlight can be seen with the eyes. Is that darkness? The answer is "Yes and no." Yes in relation to angelic light, but no in relation to material things. Remember that talk of absolutes refers to God, who is absolute light. When we are discuss-ing creation, everything is relative. Angels are luminous in relation to other creatures, but dark in relation to God. The moon is bright in relation to a star, but dark in relation to the sun.

Angelic light is not the same as physical light, but it shares many of its characteristics. Light is that which removes darkness, dispels shadows and obscurities, illuminates, irradiates, unveils, and reveals. Both angelic and physical light do all that. However, there are also important differences, relatively speaking. Physical light is lifeless, while angelic light is alive. Physical light illuminates, but angelic light also enlightens. To turn on a lamp is one thing, to be given knowledge through an angelic apparition—as the Prophet was given the Koran by Gabriel—is something else. For knowledge is light, and the Koran is "a clear light" (4:174). This is not knowledge as information, but knowl-edge as awareness. When the Buddha awoke to reality and reached enlightenment, he saw light, but it was not the lifeless and lusterless light of lamps, nor even of stars and suns. Reading the account in Islamic terms, one can say that the Buddha saw Light itself, which is the source of all life, awareness, knowledge, and joy.

We said that the opposite of created light is created darkness. If light and dark are relative terms, every created thing can be darkness or light, depending on the point of view. An angel is darkness in relation to God, while a stone is luminous in relation to nothingness. Everything in the universe is both light and darkness, and this follows directly from *tanzih* and *tashbih*: If we consider God, who is light, as infinitely distant and incomparable, then all things are darkness, but if we consider God as similar and near, then all things are light.

There are many traditional expressions of this ambiguous status of everything in the universe. For example, the Prophet said, "This world is accursed—accursed is everything within it, save the remembrance of God." Briefly, "remembrance" (*dhikr*) is everything that reminds people of God and every effort that they exert in order to bring God to mind.

This hadith tells us that everything other than God, everything that people experience in life, has, in itself, no positive value, because it is darkness. To the extent that things are darkness, people should pay no attention to them. However, all things are also light, that is, they are luminous inasmuch as people recognize them as signs of God and make use of their *significance* to establish *tawhid*. This hadith explains the personal, existential significance of such Koranic verses as:

> *He clarifies His signs for the people so that perhaps they may remember. (2:221)*

> *This is the path of your Lord, straight—We have differentiated the signs for a people who remember. (6:126)*

If people do not recognize the signs as the radiance of God's light, they have lost contact with reality. For them this world is a dark and accursed place, because it gives no news of God, which is to say that it has been cut off from the Real. If the world does not help people establish *tawhid*, it can only keep them in *shirk*.

Let us go back to the angels. The Koran makes many statements about them that provide hints as to their nature, but people have to meditate on the Koranic signs before the meaning of these hints starts to become apparent. Take this verse as an example:

> *Praise belongs to God, Originator of the heavens and the earth, who appointed the angels to be messengers, having wings two, three, and four. God increases creation as He wills. (35:1)*

Angels, we learn, have wings. In Islamic art, as in Christian art, they are typically depicted as having two wings. It would not be too difficult to paint them with four wings, since we have the example of butterflies and other insects. But how would you paint an angel with three wings? Already we learn that angels are not quite like the winged creatures that we know from everyday life.

Why do angels need wings in the first place? Obviously, to fly. If they act as messengers, and if God is depicted as dwelling some great distance away so that he has to send messages, they need wings to come and go. The fact that they have wings tells us that they move much faster than we do, because we only have feet.

This verse has other meanings as well. A bird or an insect needs wings to fly up, because it has weight. Without wings it would not be able to leave the ground. If it wants to come down, it stops beating its wings and glides back to earth. But angels are luminous and dwell in heaven or God's proximity. By nature they are close to God. They need wings not to fly up, like birds, but to fly down. Then, having delivered their messages, they glide back up to their natural home.

We can make the same point in the language of Islamic philosophy by saying that the "wings" refer to the faculties or powers of the angels, the means whereby they perform their appointed functions. There are many kinds of angels—some who perform simple functions, and others who perform more complex functions. They need at least two wings, corresponding to their knowledge and their activity. But their activity may be subdivided into many different types. Notice that the just-quoted verse says, "God increases creation as He wills." Some commentators say that this means God adds wings to his angels in keeping with their functions. They cite as evidence a hadith in which the Prophet said that he saw Gabriel with seven hundred wings. That sounds like a reasonable number of functions for one of God's most important angels.

Clay

The Koran employs the word *clay* in ways that suggest that it, like darkness, can be considered the opposite of light. Clay is water mixed with earth. The angels were created from light, but the human body was created from clay. If we thought that the Koran provided scientific information in the modern sense, we might understand it to mean that the body is made out of food, and food is basically water and earth that reaches us through the intermediary of plants and animals. Hence, the body is clay. No doubt this is one of the meanings of the teaching, but much more is at issue here. We have to ask what the Koran and the Islamic world view in general have understood by water, earth, and the clay that represents their combination.[5]

We understand the essences of things by looking at their attributes. The attributes of clay are those of earth and water, plus an added something that results from the combination. Earth is heavy, dark, dry, and infinitely divisible. Water is also heavy, but it allows light to penetrate it, so it is not as dark as earth. Water is also infinitely divisible, but it holds together naturally as a single body. If you put water and earth together, you have a substance which is heavy and dark, but which has the potential to receive light, because of the water within it, and which also holds together rather well, especially if you bake it. In one verse the Koran says, "God created the human being from dry clay, like pottery" (55:14).

Earth and water have various qualities that are reflected in things made out of clay. For example, bodily things come in a variety of colors, and human beings are no exception. This has something to do with water and clay. Take the following Koranic verse:

> *Have you not seen how God sends water down out of heaven, and therewith We bring forth fruits of diverse hues? And in the mountains are streaks white and red, of diverse hues, and pitch black; people too, and beasts, and cattle—diverse are their hues. (35:28)*

Some of the Prophet's companions connected this diversity of the color of the earth and people in a suggestive way. They reported that when God wanted to create Adam, he sent the angel Seraphiel down to earth to collect some soil. The earth, however, protested. It did not want to give up anything of itself (earthly creatures, especially humans, tend to be like that; they are very concerned about themselves and their integrity). The earth begged and pleaded with Seraphiel, who finally felt sorry for it and went back to God, asking what to do. God said it was not important. He would send another angel. So he sent Michael. But the same thing happened, and Michael came back empty-handed. Then God sent Gabriel, but it was the same story. Finally God sent Azrael, giving him special instructions. Azrael went down and explained to the earth that he was merely going to borrow some earth for a short period of time, and that he would take personal responsibility for returning it. Having received this guarantee, the earth agreed, and Azrael took handfuls of soil from the earth's four corners, some of it red, some white, some black, and some yellow. God then took the earth and mixed it together with water and molded the clay of Adam. This explains the diversity of human colors, and it also explains why Azrael is the angel of death. It is his responsibility to return the earth to its proper place. Hence, he has to take away the human spirit and give the earth back to its rightful owner.[6]

Spirits and Bodies

Angels are made of light, bodies of clay. This means that angels are luminous, invisible beings who share in the qualities of divine light, such as life, knowledge, and power. In contrast, bodies are dark, visible things, which—relative to angels—have none of the characteristics of divine luminosity. They are dead, ignorant, and weak.

If bodies are dead, why do we see so many of them walking around? In the case of human beings, the Koran tells us that God gave life to Adam's clay by blowing something of his own spirit into it: "He originated the creation of the human being out of clay, . . . then He proportioned him and blew into him of His spirit" (32:7-9). Human bodies are alive because the divine spirit animates them. Without the spirit, they would be water and earth. When Azrael takes away the spirit, the body shows its true nature, since it returns to dust. Muslim thinkers agree that in nonhuman animals and plants also, qualities such as life and desire pertain to spirit and not to the bodies themselves.

What then is spirit? We are given some hint by the Arabic word itself, *ruh*, which derives from the same root as *rih*, which means "wind." A wind is something whose presence is made visible only through its effects. It makes a tree's branches move, or picks up dust, or presses against the face. We know that it is there, but we cannot see it; we only see or feel its effects. So also a spirit (from Latin *spiritus*, also meaning wind) cannot be seen, but it makes its presence felt by its effects. A body, which is water and earth, shows all the signs of life. A sleeping and a dead body may appear the same, but there is an enormous difference between the two. The difference lies in that invisible something that is called a "spirit."

Spirits are akin to angels. The Koran makes this clear by sometimes referring to Gabriel as the "Holy Spirit." It also refers to "the Spirit," which the commentators say is the greatest of the angels. Most authorities maintain that angels are a kind of spirit, but that the word spirit is broader in meaning, because not all spirits are angels. One way to explain the difference between spirits and angels is to say that all spirits are connected to bodies, but not all bodies are made of the same substance. If the spirit is connected to a body made of light, then the configuration of the two is called an angel, but if the spirit's body is made of clay, then it is the spirit of an animal or a human. Some authorities maintain that plants and inanimate objects also have spirits, while others say special angels are given charge of them. In either case, the basic point is that physical things cannot exist without some spiritual reality acting as an intermediary between them and God.

The basic function of a spirit is to govern and control a body. No bodily thing can hold together without a spirit or an angel to give it wholeness and coherence. After all, bodily things are made of clay, which breaks down easily and has no inherent unity. Baked clay may appear solid, but it can be smashed. In contrast, spirits are made of light, which is a single reality—the radiance of God. The light is one, as the Koran frequently reminds us, but the darknesses are many. The many cannot hold together since they do not consist of a unified reality.

The Koran makes allusions to the idea that each level of structure in the universe is governed by specific spirits. For example, it is clear that the human spirit results from God's blowing his own breath into the human body. The human spirit gives wholeness and integrity to a collection of cells, organs, and bodily parts. But each of these parts has a certain independence, which is maintained by the spirits of the individual organs.

The Koran refers to this independence in several verses in which it is discussing the day of resurrection, when people are questioned about their activities in this world. Since this is a judgment, comparable to a court of law, witnesses are called. Among those witnesses are angels. But the bodily organs and limbs will also witness against their owners, thus showing that each has an autonomy that is difficult to explain in Islamic terms unless each organ has its own governing spirit:

There awaits for them a mighty chastisement on the day when their tongues, their hands, and their feet shall witness against them concerning what they were doing. (24:23-24)

Today We set a seal on their mouths, and their hands speak to Us, and their feet bear witness as to what they have been earning. (36:65)

It might be asked how all spirits can be differentiated and at the same time be held together by greater spirits. One way to answer this question is to study the signs in the human self. "In the earth are signs for those having certainty, and in your own selves. What, do you not see?" (51:20-21). Just as we can compare the whole universe to a book, so also we can compare the human being to a book made up of letters, words, sentences, and so on.

Each cell of the body can be compared to a letter. A letter takes a specific shape so that it can express a meaning; it is not a haphazard line. The spirit of that letter gives it its shape. On the next level, letters join together to form words, which themselves have an integrity and wholeness, given to them by their governing spirits. These words can be compared to the various subunits that make up the bodily organs.

Then each organ of the body performs a specific function; each is a sentence within the human body, while the body itself is a paragraph. But the paragraph expresses meaning only within the context of a chapter, which we can take as a family. Then the chapter has a role to play within the context of a book, which is the human race. Letters, words, sentences, paragraphs, chapters, and books can be studied on their own level, but the meaning of each level only becomes clear when it is situated in a broader context. By themselves, letters are simply alphabet soup. Only when words are formed do they make any sense. But words do not really have meaning outside the context of sentences, and sentences are incomplete unless situated within still larger units, such as paragraphs and chapters.

From the Islamic perspective, it is ridiculous not to recognize the wholes that hold together the parts. If we stop at any level, we miss the greater meaning. Ultimately, even to understand the full significance of a single letter, we have to be able to read the whole book. And the author of the book is God, which is to say that *tawhid* provides the book's final meaning. We can understand the letters, words, and sentences outside the context of the book's author, but we will be missing the message if we do so. We will be like our imaginary chemists who say that the meaning of the Mona Lisa lies in the composition of the paint.

Each level of coherence and meaning (such as letters, words, and sentences) is built into the structure of existence. Each can be grasped by human intelligence, which itself partakes of the nature of the greatest of all spirits, the spirit of God blown into Adam. It is significant that one of the several words often employed synonymously in Islamic texts for spirit is *meaning* (*ma'na*). The spirit is that which gives meaning, coherence, unity, and comprehensibility to a thing. But there are many levels of spirits, distinguished by the extent to which they comprehend and embrace lower realities. The spirit of a cell is one thing, of an organ something else, and the spirit of the human being as such—the rational or divine spirit—is the supreme organizing principle that holds all the lesser spirits together.

Spirits do not make sense outside the context of bodies. In traditional Islamic texts, to say "body" is to imply "spirit," and vice versa. Just as we can only speak of darkness in relation to light, and just as light can never be seen unless darkness is present, so also body and spirit are inseparable. Even a dead body or an inanimate thing is governed by a spirit, and the soul that departs from the body at death does so in a subtle bodily form.

The primary attribute of spirit is usually said to be life. If, on the one hand, mention of spirit calls to mind body, on the other hand it calls to mind life. In the Persian language, for example, jan means both "spirit" and "life." The reason is clear. Without the spirit, the body is dead. Or rather, it is simply clay.

Clay cannot have life until God kneads it, shapes it, and blows his spirit into it. God, of course, does not have to knead it directly. He uses intermediaries to do his work. In the case of an animal, he normally kneads the clay in the womb of its mother. According to a hadith, the human infant is not sufficiently shaped to support a spirit until the fourth month of pregnancy. Only after four months does God blow his spirit into the embryo.[7]

The spirit belongs to God, just as light and life belong to God. There is no life but God's life, and no light but God's light. So also, all the characteristics of the spirit are divine characteristics. Otherwise, God would not have referred to the human spirit as "My spirit." Nevertheless, most theologians maintain that the spirit is a created reality. Although it belongs to God, it is not identical with God. In the same way, angelic light is the radiance of God, not God himself.

It is important to grasp the characteristics of the spirit. Without knowing what the spirit is, we cannot know what the body is, since body and spirit are defined in terms of each other. We already said that the spirit is luminous and alive, and of course, invisible, like light and angels. Notice that Light, as a name of God, is usually said to be a name of God's essence, of his very self. What is God? Light. Once, when the Prophet was asked if he had seen God, he replied, "He is a Light. How could I see Him?"

If the spirit is light, that means, in respect of tashbih, that it possesses all the attributes of God's essence, all the characteristics denoted by his names. Hence, in itself, the spirit is alive, knowing, desiring, powerful, speaking, generous, just, compassionate, loving, and so on. If you object that most people, though they have spirits, do not display such qualities as generosity and justice, the answer is simply that people are not only spirits, they are also bodies. God breathed his own spirit into the clay, and the result was human beings. Are people spirits? Yes and no. Are they light? Yes and no. Are they clay? Yes and no. Do they have knowledge? Yes and no. Are they generous and just? Yes and no.

In short, when we speak about the meeting of light and clay in human beings and other creatures, we are simply explaining in different language the two principles of tanzih and tashbih. In respect of their spirits, people are similar to God, but in respect of their bodies, they are incomparable with God. Of course, in another respect, the spirit is also incomparable and the body is also similar. But here we are simply discussing the dominant characteristics of the two sides.

The spirit is dominated by the characteristics related to *tashbih*. Hence, it is closely connected with nearness, mercy, gentleness, beauty, and bounty. In contrast, the body is dominated by the attributes of *tanzih*. Hence, it is connected with distance, wrath, severity, majesty, and justice.

The fact that the body functions more as a sign of the attributes of wrath than the attributes of mercy does not amount to a denigration of the body. All these attributes associated with the body, after all, are divine attributes. It is true that mercy takes precedence over wrath, and this explains why the spirit is, in a sense, superior to the body. But spirits must have bodies in order to display the attributes of mercy and beauty. If human bodies were made of light instead of clay—that is, if the bodies themselves were of a spiritual nature—people would be angels, not human beings. If they were angels, they could not achieve the greatness for which they were created. (We will come back to God's goal in creating human beings shortly.)

Fire

Created light is the opposite of created darkness, which is to say that the attributes of spirit are the opposites of the attributes of clay. The attributes of spirit are the divine attributes. The primary attributes of God, when envisaged in relation to creation, are often said to be life, knowledge, desire, power, and speech. These qualities are inherent to the spirit, but they are not found to any appreciable degree in the body.

Spiritual things such as angels are alive, knowing, desiring, powerful, and speaking by their very nature. Again, these qualities are not absolute, since spirits are dead and ignorant compared to God. When we discuss spirits, we have in mind their contrast with bodies. The words *spirit* and *body*, as said above, form a conceptual pair, so you cannot discuss one without at least implicit reference to the other.

In contrast to spirits, bodies—such as stones or corpses—are dead, ignorant, desireless, weak, and mute. As for living bodies, they are not simply bodies, since the presence of life proves that a spirit is present within the body. However, the life and knowledge of living bodies are pale compared to the pure life and knowledge of spirits. The combination of spirit and body in effect produces a third thing that is neither spirit nor body, but something in between. In order to understand the nature of that third thing, it will be useful to go back to the contrast between angelic light and bodily clay.

Angels are created of light, while bodies are created of clay. The Koran also speaks of certain kinds of beings who are made neither of light nor of clay, but of fire. Notice that fire is luminous and dark at the same time. Fire ascends toward heaven, yet it is earthly. Fire can never be separated from clay, since it needs a fuel to burn. Fire rises up, as if striving for the freedom of light, but it never escapes its clay. If we change the composition of the clay—the material fuel—we can modify the nature of the fire. Green wood burns differently from dry wood or gasoline. If we mix in various salts and other substances derived from earth, we can easily change the color of the fire.

Most often the Koran refers to the creatures made from fire as *"jinn,"* a term that means literally "hidden, concealed." It says a good deal about these jinn, and one could write a book simply investigating these Koranic statements. Here we will simply say that the jinn are ambiguous creatures, somewhat like human beings, and somewhat like angels.

The most famous member of the jinn race is Iblis, also known as Satan. His career epitomizes the ambiguity of the jinn. Most accounts say that he was the first of the jinn to be created, and hence he plays a role for the jinn like that of Adam for human beings. For thousands of years before the creation of Adam, Iblis was extremely pious and spent all his time in acts of devotion.

The angels, the Koran tells us, dedicate their lives to serving God and to praising and glorifying him. They never forget God, so they are always striving to show their gratitude to him by mentioning his greatness, grandeur, and kindness. When Iblis was created, his luminous nature drew him toward the angels, and he joined in their activities. Gradually, his tremendous devotion brought him into a select group of servants. Although he was created of fire, God allowed him to mix freely with the creatures created of light. Everything went well until God created Adam. Iblis watched the whole process, observing how Adam's clay was collected and how God kneaded it for forty days. But he seems to have missed the crucial event, when God blew of his own spirit into Adam. After all, the spirit is invisible, and God is even more invisible, so even careful observers might miss some of the subtleties.

Having created Adam, God said to all the angels—and of course Iblis by this time was standing in their ranks—"Prostrate yourselves before Adam" (2:34, 7:11, and elsewhere). They all did so immediately, since the angels "do as they are commanded" (16:50). But Iblis was not an angel, so he could disobey if he wanted. And on this occasion, for the first time in his life, he decided to do just that.

God said to Iblis, "What prevented you from prostrating yourself to him whom I created with My own two hands?" Iblis replied, "I am better than he. You created me of fire, but You created him of clay" (7:12, 38:76). (The great Persian poet and sage Rumi [d. 673/1274] suggests that Iblis had only one eye, and with that eye he saw Adam's clay, but he was lacking a second, different kind of eye, to see Adam's divine spirit.)

From here on, the story is well known. God sent Iblis down out of heaven in disgrace, and Iblis busied himself with trying to deceive the children of Adam. We will return to these events later, since they provide important keys for understanding Islamic anthropology. For now, it is sufficient to note that Iblis has both the luminous nature of angels, and a dark, deceptive, and devious nature that can only come from a lack of light. This dark nature shares darkness with clay, but it possesses something that clay does not have.

Clay, after all, is neutral. There is nothing evil about clay. It is a good substance for making pots (if you are a potter) or bodily things in general (if you are a god). Clay has its drawbacks. It is dark and dense, so when you pour liquid light into the pot, the light is hidden, and some people might imagine that the pot is empty. But without pots, you would have no containers for light. Clay is not devious and deceptive, it is simply dull.

When spiritual luminosity mixes with the impermeability of clay, one result may be a perverted, deceiving game of light and shadow, a game that can lead ever further into the world of darkness. Iblis represents this possibility. Nevertheless, fire does not have to go bad. The Koran makes clear that there are jinn who have faith in the prophets and, in general, the tradition differentiates between the faithful jinn and the truth-concealing jinn. The latter are called satans, while their chief is Iblis, called in Arabic *the* Satan (*al-shaytan*).

Fire is ambiguous. If light dominates in its nature, then it is similar to the angels and participates in God's mercy and gentleness. If darkness dominates, then it is distant like bodies and falls under the sway of the names of wrath and severity.

Fire in any case tends more toward wrath than toward gentleness. It rises up and asserts its own power and wants to wipe out everything in its path. Translated into a human (or satanic) attribute, fire becomes self-assertive arrogance. Iblis says, "I am better than he." Satan's game is "Me, me, me." Do your own thing—follow caprice and ignore your God-given intelligence.

Fire's negative nature is nicely summed up in the Koranic word *istikbar*, which means "to seek greatness, magnificence, or eminence." From the same root we have the word *akbar* meaning "greater." "God is greater" is one of the most common formulas heard on Muslim lips, and it marks every movement of the *salat*. It means simply "There is no greatness but God's greatness." Everything that appears great in your eyes is small compared to God.

From the same root we also have the divine name *al-mutakabbir*, "he who is great in himself," or "the magnificent." As a human quality, the word means "arrogant," since no one deserves magnificence but God.

Iblis and those human beings who have the qualities of fire seek greatness and magnificence for themselves. Like fire, they assert their own reality and try to destroy that of others. The Koran ascribes this quality of claiming greatness to Iblis, to Pharaoh and his council, and to truth-concealers in general. All of them will be thrown into hell, which is precisely a fire that corresponds to their own nature. The fact that Pharaoh was drowned in the sea is certainly an appropriate worldly end for fiery claims.

> *Then the angels prostrated themselves [before Adam] all together, except Iblis. He claimed greatness and was one of the truth-concealers. (38:73-74)*

> *And [Pharaoh] claimed greatness in the land, he and his hosts, wrongfully. . . . Therefore We seized him and his hosts, and cast them into the sea. . . . And We appointed them leaders, calling to the Fire. (28:39-41)*

> *Those who cry lies to Our signs, and claim greatness against them—those shall be the inhabitants of the Fire. (7:36)*

Just as the Koran attributes the act of claiming greatness to Iblis and his followers, so also in several verses it negates it from the angels.

> *Those who are with thy Lord do not claim to be too great to worship Him. (7:206)*

> *The angels—they do not claim greatness. They fear their Lord above them, and they do as they are commanded. (16:49-50)*

Soul

Spirit has the qualities of light, and body has the qualities of clay. Neither spirit nor body is fire, since fire combines the qualities of light and clay. Hence, in order to complete our picture of the human being, who came into existence when spirit was blown into clay, we need something fiery, something that is neither spirit nor clay, but something that is produced when spirit and clay are brought together. That something is typically called *nafs*, which can be translated as "soul" or "self." Before spirit meets body, there is no human self, no human soul. Only after the two conjoin does a person come to exist, a person who perceives himself neither as spirit nor as body, but simply as self.

In Arabic, the word *nafs* is written the same as the word *nafas*, which means "breath" (compare the Hebrew *nephesh*, a sister word). Just as a spirit is a wind that animates a body, so also a soul or self is an invisible power that allows a thing to have the breath of life. When this side of the meaning of the term is considered, soul is often used as a synonym of spirit. For, in relation to the body, the soul has all the primary qualities of the spirit, such as life, knowledge, desire, and power.

The soul is frequently viewed in respect of its difference from the spirit, its immersion in the body, and its ignorance of the fact that its reality does not reside in the body but in the spirit and in God. In this sense of the term, the word *nafs* is used with a negative connotation. It refers to all the darkness within people that keeps them wandering in ignorance and distance from God.

In short, the term *nafs* in Islamic texts is full of ambiguity, in keeping with its kinship with fire and the jinn. But if we want to have an overall picture of what the human soul represents, we need to keep both sides of the *nafs* in view. If the soul is contrasted with the luminous spirit, it is seen to be dark, dead, ignorant, and weak. Like the spirit, the soul has desires, but these are perverted and distorted desires. The angel can think of nothing but God and it desires nothing but God, so its desire is good. But the soul in this negative sense of the term is forgetful of God and desires anything but God. This perspective, which makes the soul something negative, correlates with *tanzih*. In other words, the soul is looked upon as incomparable with the divine Reality.

However, if the soul is contrasted with the body, then the soul is seen to be luminous, intelligent, desiring, powerful, and so on. The divine attributes are present within it, but absent from the body. This perspective correlates with *tashbih*.

If we take any given human individual, the picture looks something like this: Except for minor differences, the body made of clay is similar to other human bodies. The spirit made of light is, in the last analysis, identical in some mysterious way with all human spirits, since human spirits are the divine spirit blown into the bodies, and there is only one divine spirit. But the soul of each individual is both similar to and different from that of other individuals. What makes up each human personality is a unique combination of divine signs. Some people have little of the divine attribute of knowledge (intelligence and awareness), while others have more. No two people are the same. So also is the situation with every divine attribute.

Take, for example, the attribute of speech. The most perfect speech is God's speech, which we perceive as his signs; that is, the universe and the scriptures. But among human beings, people actualize the attribute of speech in different degrees and modes. Moreover, any given individual possesses this divine attribute in differing degrees in various stages of his or her life. A newborn infant knows nothing of human speech, but gradually learns. One never knows for sure what sort of development will take place. We may have here a poet, a novelist, the next Shakespeare, a boor. Who knows?

Naturally, speech is intimately connected with knowledge. In fact, all the divine attributes are intimately connected with each other. The more you investigate, the more you find that some attributes depend upon other attributes, and eventually they all depend upon the essence of God. This is *tawhid*, the assertion that all reality is rooted in a single being, who is the Real. Since Reality is one, the attributes of Reality are also one in a certain respect.

Imagination

Many Muslim thinkers employ the Arabic words for "imagination" (*khayal* or *mithal*) to refer to the intermediate domain of fire or soul. The Koran and Hadith provide ample support for employing these words. For example, when the Koran describes Gabriel's appearance to Mary at the annunciation, it says, "He appeared to her in the image of" — or, more literally, "he *imaginalized* himself to her as" — "a mortal without fault" (19:17). The Prophet used this term *imaginalize* in a number of interesting hadiths. In the most famous of these, he said, "Satan cannot imaginalize himself in my form." Most people understand this to mean that when someone sees the Prophet's image in a dream, it is truly his image and not a satanic deception. In another hadith he said, "The Garden and the Fire were imaginalized for me in this wall"

When something is imaginalized, it appears to someone as an image. This apparition is considered to be "imaginal," not "imaginary," which is to say that it has a certain reality that needs to be considered. We cannot simply say, "You are imagining things," and dismiss the images from further consideration.

Imaginal things share the attributes of two sides, just as the soul shares the attributes of spirit and body. The most common example of a concrete, imaginal thing is the image in a mirror. Your mirror image is both yourself and not yourself at the same time. In certain respects, and for certain purposes — for example, as a guide when you are combing your hair — you can treat the image as yourself. Nevertheless, the image is not you, since it is simply light rays reflected from a piece of glass.

If we look inside ourselves, the best place to find imaginal things is in our dreams. Here we have a tremendous diversity of objects and people that are both themselves and not themselves, or both ourselves and not ourselves. The tree you see in a dream is a tree — it is not a frog or a baseball. Yet, it is not a tree, if we mean by tree something that grows in the ground in the physical world. Or again, the tree that you see in a dream is both you and not you. It is not you because it is a tree. And it is you because it is simply the picture of a tree as imagined by you.

Notice that the domain of dreaming is the soul. Hence, the soul is often called the "microcosmic world of imagination," while the world where jinn and satans live is called the "macrocosmic world of imagination." The microcosm is the human individual, while the macrocosm is the whole cosmos.

One of the important characteristics of imaginal existence is constant change. Imagination does not stay the same for two successive moments. Nothing in the world of intermediacy is fixed. Every dream image is constantly in the process of being transformed into other images.

Lack of fixity is important to keep in view when we discuss the soul. People tend to think of the soul as something solid and defined, on the analogy of the body, with which it is usually paired. Even the body, of course, is not fixed, but it is relatively solid and constant, especially when compared to a dream image.

The soul is born from the meeting between a relatively fixed body and the divine breath, which is pure, unchanging luminosity. Hence, the two sides of the soul are relatively constant. But the soul itself is a flux, a continual flow of impressions, a running stream of consciousness and awareness. Muslim cosmologists often say the soul is "an ocean without shore." The soul is like the ocean because the ocean has hidden depths and moves constantly, as the waves on its surface make clear. However, unlike the ocean, the soul has no boundaries, no fixed limits. When we discuss the Return, we will see that the nonfixity of the soul has important consequences for human becoming. It means that because human beings are not this or that, they can be anything, and what they become in this world determines the form they take in the next world.

Summary

We have come a long way from the premise "angels are messengers of God," but we have not wandered far from the various ideas and concepts that Muslims consider when they want to have more than just a superficial faith in angels. And we have hardly begun exploring these ideas. Some of them will come up again in what follows, and naturally so, because *tawhid* demands the interrelationship of all things. Before moving on, let us summarize what we have learned about angels.

Angels play the role of intermediaries between the physical world and God. Because they are made of light, they represent the closest things to God, who is Light. The attributes of angelic light are the same as the attributes of God's light, except that the angels' light is created and contingent, while God's light is uncreated and eternal. The attributes of light can best be understood by contrast with the attributes of darkness, which is the absence of light. The opposite of created light is created darkness. One kind of created darkness is clay, which is the substance from which all material things, such as stones, plants, and the bodies of animals, are made.

Angels are one kind of spirit, and spirit is ultimately the breath of God. Just as we understand light in terms of darkness, so also we understand spirit in terms of body. The two represent opposite poles on the spectrum of existent things—those which are near to God and those which are distant from God. Though bodies are distant, they are good, since they are creatures of God and manifest his attributes, even if the attributes of severity and wrath are more clearly displayed within them than the attributes of gentleness and mercy. The qualities of spirits are strongly, but not exclusively, associated with *tashbih*, while the qualities of body are strongly, but not exclusively, associated with *tanzih*.

If we investigate the contrasting qualities of light and clay, we find that fire embodies both sets of qualities. In the world outside us, there exist creatures who are neither spirits nor bodies, called jinn. In our own inner worlds, there is a dimension of us that is neither spirit nor body, called self, or soul, or imagination. Our souls are ambiguous and ever-changing, like fire or dream images. The attributes of our souls are neither those of our bodies nor those of our spirits; alternatively, they are a combination of the attributes of the two sides. Whenever imagination is discussed, the stress of the discussion is on the ambiguity of the situation, the fact that light and darkness are mixed, that *tashbih* and *tanzih* are intertwined.

THE MEASURING OUT

The Prophet said that faith includes faith in "the measuring out, the good of it and the evil of it." The term *measuring out* (*qadar*) is frequently translated as "predestination," and in some contexts, this is a good translation, but this will not help us much to understand the broad significance of the word in the Koran and the Hadith. In this section we will emphasize the wide meaning of the term by following up its implications into domains that are rarely discussed in treatments of the Muslim idea of predestination. To be fair to the concept, one needs to understand how its logic fits into *tawhid*.

Creative Power

The word *qadar* comes from the same root as *qadir*, which is a divine name that we have been translating as "Powerful." The noun *qudra*, which designates the divine attribute of power, is close to *qadar* both in derivation and in meaning. To have power is to have the ability or capacity to do or make something, to perform an act, to achieve a goal. God, the Koran tells us repeatedly, "is powerful over all things," so his power—in contrast to ours—is unlimited.

Qadar is sometimes used synonymously with *qudra*, so it also means "power" and "ability." But the word *qadar* puts stress on the basic meaning of the root, which is to measure or determine the size or quantity of something. This may be done physically, with a scale or a tape measure, or it may be done mentally, through computation and reckoning. The term may mean not only "to take something's measure," but also "to determine its measure." To measure something, in this sense, is to control it and govern it, to have power over it. Hence we come back to power.

God is powerful over all things, while human beings have a certain limited power inasmuch as they reflect God's power. Obviously they have no power over God, any more than a ray of light has power over the sun. Nor are they able to understand God in a true sense without God's guidance, for understanding something gives us a certain power over it:

> *They comprehend nothing of His knowledge, save such as He wills. (2:256)*

> *They measured not God with His true measure. (6:91, 22:74, 39:67)*

The Koran uses the term *qadar* in ten verses, and these provide part of the basis for the later formulation of a doctrine that can fairly be called that of predestination. But the theological understanding of *qadar* has had much less importance in determining the way Muslims in general have understood *qadar* than the Koranic verses. We will look at a few of these verses, since they provide a convenient introduction to basic Islamic ideas about the relationship between God and the cosmos and God and human beings:

> *Surely We have created everything with a measuring out. (54:49)*

> *There is nothing whose treasuries are not with Us, and We send it down only with a known measuring out. (15:21)*

These two verses illustrate the basic Koranic themes that God is Knowing, Powerful, and Creator. He is the source of all things, so all things are found with him. Whether they are with him in the Unseen or with us in the Visible, he knows them:

> *With Him are the keys to the Unseen; none knows them but He.*
> *He knows what is in land and sea; not a leaf falls, but He knows it.*
> *Not a grain in the earth's shadows, not a thing, fresh or withered,*
> *but it is in an explicit Book. (6:59)*

When God creates something, he brings it into existence. At the same time, he keeps with himself the treasuries from which he provides for the thing's existence. These treasuries represent the good and the real, which belong only to God. "There is nothing real but the Real." In more detail, the treasuries represent the divine attributes, which are the sources for all good and real qualities in the world. Hence, a thing's life is supplied from God's treasury of life, a thing's power from his treasury of power, a thing's compassion from his treasury of compassion.

Who decides what it is that things receive from the treasuries? The owner of the treasuries. What is his decision called? Measuring out. He measures out knowledge, power, mercy, good, and so on. No created

thing is able to control its share of these qualities. Everything participates in the real qualities of existence only to the extent that Reality
allows it to participate; God is on the giving end, and created things are
on the receiving end. *Tanzih* demands that God alone have reality, but
tashbih demands that he give of his reality to creation—in the manner
that he chooses. The measuring out is his, not ours.

> *Had God expanded His provision to His servants, they would have
> been insolent in the earth. But He sends down whatsoever He will
> with a measuring out. Surely He is aware of and sees His servants.
> (42:27)*

Like many important Koranic terms, *servant* has several levels of meaning. In the broadest sense, its meaning is equivalent to "creature."
Anything at all is a servant of God, since God created it to do his work,
and it does his work, whether it knows it or not, and whether it wants to
or not. Just as everything in the heavens and the earth is a *muslim*
because it is submitted to God, so also everything is his servant. "None
is there in the heavens and earth but he comes to the Merciful as a
servant" (19:93). In a narrower sense, a servant is someone who consciously serves God by following a prophet. In a still narrower sense, a
servant is a human being who serves God perfectly and with full
awareness and total freedom of choice. It is in this last sense that
servant is considered the most exalted title of the prophet Muhammad.

The just-cited verse (42:27) is saying that God measures out carefully
what he gives to his creatures. Otherwise, they would overstep their
bounds and work corruption in the created order. In a wide sense, the
verse means that the limitations imposed upon creatures by their
created attributes give them their identity. "He gave everything its
creation" (20:50). If the moon had too much light, nighttime would be a
rare thing. If cats had too much strength, we could not domesticate
them and there would be no one to take care of the mice. God's wisdom
is always in the background, determining what is good for all creatures. As the Persian proverb puts it, "God knew the donkey when he did
not give it horns."

In the human context, this Koranic verse means that poverty, need,
and suffering are necessary for the maintenance of social order. If
everyone were rich, who would bake the bread? For that matter, who
would plant the crops? Differentiation among people is utterly necessary for the welfare of society. Moreover, if God had made everyone
rich and independent, this would have turned them away from the most
basic of human tasks, which is to establish *tawhid*. If God were to give
people everything their lower natures wanted, why would they turn to
God for their needs? They would consider this world a paradise and
forget about *tawhid*. They would rise up in revolt against God, since
they would follow other gods, mainly their own caprice.

In short, one of the implications of the verses on measuring out is that God has his own purposes for giving people what he gives them. There is wisdom and mercy behind his activities, even if we fail to see the wisdom and even if we suffer because we feel that our share has been stinted:

> *It may happen that you will hate a thing which is good for you,*
> *and it may happen that you will love a thing which is evil for you.*
> *God knows, and you know not. (2:216)*

All good reaches the creatures through God's measuring out. The Koran often makes this point by referring to the "water" that God sends down out of heaven. In reading such verses, we need to remember that heaven is the dwelling place of angels and spirits. It is the created source of light, purity, nourishment, and everything that grows up in the earth. Without water, there is no life. Without heaven, the earth is dead. And without earth, heaven has no place to display its bounties. The verses are saying that within this created realm, every blessing and bounty that reaches us in the earth has been measured out by God:

> *And We sent down out of heaven water with a measuring out and*
> *lodged it in the earth; and We are able to take it away. Then with it*
> *We produced for you gardens. . . . (23:18-19)*

> *[God is He] who sent down out of heaven water with a measuring*
> *out, and We gave life thereby to a land that was dead. (43:11)*

> *He sends down out of heaven water, and each dry streambed flows*
> *with its own measure. (13:17)*

The dry streambeds are the creatures of the earth, which have no life, knowledge, desire, power, compassion, or any other positive quality without the water of heaven, which must flow down on them. Then each streambed flows in its own measure. Here the emphasis is placed not on God's measuring out, though the same word is used, but on the fact that once God has measured out identity to a thing, it can hold only so much water. "God gave everything its creation" (20:50). "There is no changing the creation of God" (30:30). Elephants do not become bees. However, human beings are more complicated creatures. Although all this talk of measuring out seems to make it clear that human beings have nothing of their own, the situation is not so straightforward. For one thing, God also measures out freedom, and he gives by far the largest portion of it to human beings.

Good and Evil

Faith in measuring out allows no exceptions. The hadith of Gabriel says, "measuring out, the good of it and the evil of it." That which is measured out, whether good or evil, is measured out by God. Modern sensibilities often find this point particularly offensive. How can a supposedly good God parcel out evil? This reaction is understandable, but a bit premature. Before such a judgment is made, one has to attempt to see this teaching in its Koranic context, and this means that we must grasp the nature of the good and the evil that are at issue here.

The Arabic word for good is *khayr*, while the word for evil is *sharr*. *Good* and *evil* in English are exceedingly broad terms, but typically they involve a moral judgment. In contrast, the Koranic context of *khayr* and *sharr* does not usually imply a statement about right and wrong, but rather about the benefit or loss that something brings.

The human being never wearies of praying for good, but when evil touches him, he is desperate and loses hope. (41:49)

If God should hasten unto people evil as they would hasten good, their term would already be decided for them. (10:11)

The good and evil that are measured out have to do with the things that people wish to have or to avoid. The issue here is not a moral good and evil, but rather a good and evil relative to the view of the person who is receiving it. Thus, in the hadith of Gabriel, when the Prophet referred to both the good and the evil of the measuring out, he had in view human judgment about the situation. We suffer a loss, so that is evil for us. We receive a benefit, so that is good.

Typically, your loss is someone else's gain. What is evil for you is good for someone else, and vice versa. In the same way, what appears as evil today may turn out to have been good in the long run. All of us experience situations that are difficult and trying at the time, but when we look back, we realize that they were good for us. Even death, which appears evil for the individual—though it is not difficult to see that it is necessary for the good of the world as a whole—may in fact be good for people.

The Koran often points out that people may be mistaken in their judgments about good and evil. You might think it is good for you to win the lottery, when in fact it may be evil. When people judge good and evil by their own standards, they are frequently mistaken: "As for those who are stingy with the bounty God has given them, let them not suppose it is good for them; no, it is evil for them" (3:180).

People think that what they desire is good and what they dislike is evil. For most people, this means that the benefits of this world are good. But the Koran insists that these things are not necessarily good for people, especially if such things cause them to forget their human responsibilities: "Made attractive to people is the love of the things they crave—women, children, heaped-up heaps of gold and silver, horses of mark, cattle, and tillage" (3:14).

The list has not changed much since the time of the Prophet. To update it, we could make the first item nonsexist by saying "lovers" and replace the last three with "cars, electronic gadgets, and property." These are all good in people's eyes, and if God did not have the attributes of a wise parent, he would give the foolish children of this world what they want. That at least seems to be what the Koran means in the following passage, which is discussing God's mercy, a term that in many ways is synonymous with good; thus, to divide up mercy among people is to measure out good:

> *What, is it they who divide up the mercy of your Lord? We have divided among them their livelihood in the life of this world, and raised some of them above others in rank, so some take others in forced labor. But the mercy of your Lord is better than what they collect.*
>
> *Were it not that people would be a single community [through ingratitude and truth-concealing], We would have appointed for those who have* kufr *toward the Merciful roofs of silver to their houses, and stairs whereon to mount, and doors to their houses, and couches whereon to recline, and ornaments. Surely all this is but the enjoyment of the life of this world. And surely the next world with your Lord belongs to the god-wary. (43:32-35)*

It is important to keep in mind that the Koran employs several different terms that are frequently translated as "good" and "evil," in particular the pair *husn* and *su'*, which have a strong moral connotation. Partly to differentiate these two terms from *khayr* and *sharr*, we will translate them as "beautiful" and "ugly." Koranic usage of "beautiful" and "ugly" reflects a judgment on the rightness and wrongness of human activity, rather than a consideration of the benefit and loss that a person may perceive. The meanings of the terms *good* and *evil* sometimes overlap with *beautiful* and *ugly*, since in the long run, benefit and loss depend upon right and wrong activity.

One way to understand the nature of the good and evil that is measured out is to place the discussion back into the context of the Shahadah. We suggested earlier that the Real coincides with everything that is good, and we had in mind the Arabic term *khayr*. This means that the unreal corresponds with *sharr*, evil. We could also say that good is light, and evil is darkness. Just as darkness is nothing but the absence of light, so also evil is nothing but the absence of good. "There is no god but God" means that "There is no good but God." We cannot place the word *evil* in the Shahadah, however, because evil is nothing.

The Prophet expressed the relationship of good and evil to God with his short prayer of praise, "The good, all of it, is in Thy hands, but evil does not go back to Thee." To what then does evil go back? To the lack of good, the lack of light, the lack of reality, the lack of the divine qualities. In other words, evil pertains to everything other than God, while good pertains to God alone. "There is no good but God." Jesus says the same thing in the Gospel: "Why do you call me good? No one is good but God alone" (Mark 10:18).

Evil is inherent to the universe in respect of *tanzih*, but good is inherent to the universe in respect of *tashbih*. Inasmuch as God is totally other than the cosmos, the cosmos has nothing of good, because God alone is good. But inasmuch as God displays his signs and activity in the cosmos, the cosmos is good through God's good.

Notice that on this level of discussion, good and evil have nothing to do with moral considerations, and this, as remarked above, is also true of the basic sense of the terms *khayr* and *sharr*. To say that something is good is to say that it shares in the divine attributes to some degree. To say that something is evil is to say that it lacks the divine attributes to some degree. All things are both good and evil in this sense. God alone is good, so everything other than God is evil. But things are not absolutely other than God, as *tashbih* teaches us. Hence, to the extent that they are not other, they are good. All things are mixtures of good and evil, light and darkness, high and low, knowledge and ignorance, power and weakness.

When some Muslim thinkers say that the whole universe is imagination, they have in mind the ambiguity of things caused by the fact that the Real is neither fully absent from creation nor fully present within it. Each thing in the universe, ourselves included, is like an image in a mirror. The object that throws the image is the divine Reality, the source of every positive quality, the one who displays the signs. The mirror is nonexistence, which simply is not there, except as a concept that helps us to think. The mirror image is identical to the Real inasmuch as it reflects the Real's attributes, but it is other than the Real inasmuch as it is supported by nonexistence.

The situation of the Real and its image is caught nicely by our own experience of looking at ourselves in the mirror. How real is your image? Do you care if the mirror breaks and the image disappears? Do you feel sorry for the image? This is the perspective of *tanzih*, illustrating how utterly real God is, and how utterly unreal we are. But this is not the whole story, because there is a major difference that is brought out in the perspective of *tashbih*. God cares about his images and will not allow the mirror to break. He is after all, as the Koran reports, "The Most Merciful of all those who have mercy."

It is worth stressing here the close connection between the Koranic concepts of good and mercy (*rahma*). The word *khayr*, like the word *good* in English, functions both as a noun and an adjective. But it also has a comparative sense. When the Koran says, "The mercy of your Lord is better (*khayr*) than what they collect" (43:32), it is affirming the identity of God's mercy with good. But it is also reminding us that there is no good but God's good. The things that people gather during their lives in the attempt to achieve happiness—things like friends and possessions—can be no more than transitory and illusory goods. Notice the following verse, which paraphrases a verse we have already cited about good: "If We let the human being taste mercy from Us, and then We take it away from him, he is desperate, ungrateful" (11:9). People are allowed to "taste" mercy, not to have it and keep it. In other words, mercy is parceled out to them. It does not belong to them, it belongs to God, and God gives of his mercy to whomsoever he desires.

Trial

The Koran often says that God measures out good and mercy to test people's faith and to allow people to prove their own nature—not to God, of course, because he already knows their nature. They are demonstrating their nature to themselves, so that they will have no objections when they reach their destination in the next world.

People who have faith in the measuring out—both the good of it and the evil of it—will recognize that God knows what he is doing, even if their personal desires are constantly thwarted. They will show their gratitude to God when he gives and they will have patience when he withholds. Such reactions will prove their faith. But they will not have demonstrated faith if they act in the way that the Koran repeatedly stigmatizes (employing words such as *good* and *evil*, *mercy* and *wrath*): "When We bless the human being, he turns away and keeps aloof, but when evil touches him, he is in despair" (17:83). The proper response to good, mercy, and blessing is gratitude, while the proper response to evil, wrath, and harm is patience and hope.

When the Koran takes the benefits of both good and evil into account, it sometimes employs the words *trial* (*bala*) and *testing* (*fitna*): "We try you with evil and good as a testing, and then unto Us you shall be returned" (21:35).

The Koran says that human beings have been placed in the earth to prove themselves, to show their stuff. Once they have undergone the test, their final resting place will be known to everyone:

> We split them up in the earth into nations, some of them wholesome, and some of them otherwise; and We tried them with the beautiful things and the ugly, that perhaps they should return [to tawhid]. (7:168)

*Surely We will try you with something of fear and hunger, and
diminution of goods and lives and fruits. Yet, give good news to
the patient who, when visited by an affliction, say, "Surely we belong to God, and to Him we return." (2:155-56)*

Trial does not involve only evil, pain, and suffering. Benefits and pleasure are also trials. If people forget God, whether in suffering or joy,
they have failed the test. And even remembering God must take the
right form. Simply recognizing God's gifts is not sufficient. Gratitude
(*shukr*), after all, is inseparable from faith (*iman*), and faith demands
submission to the Shariah. In the following, the Koran criticizes people
for failing both the test of blessing and the test of affliction. Notice how
the passage immediately turns to a criticism of those who fail the test
by alluding to various wholesome deeds that they need to perform in
order to demonstrate their faith:

*As for the human being, when his Lord tries him, and honors
him, and blesses him, he says "My Lord has honored me." But
when He tries him and stints his provision, he says, "My Lord has
despised me." No indeed, but you honor not the orphan, and you
urge not the feeding of the needy, and you devour the inheritance
greedily, and you love wealth with an ardent love. (89:15-20)*

God tests human beings to find out which of them have faith and do
wholesome deeds and which of them conceal the truth and work
corruption:

*We have appointed all that is on the earth as an adornment for it,
and that We may try them, which of them is most beautiful in
works. (18:7)*

*Blessed is He . . . who created death and life, that He may try you,
which of you is most beautiful in works. (67:1-2)*

One of the recurring themes of the Koran, alluded to in the above
verses, is that people fail to acknowledge their own proper places. If
they experience good, they think they deserve it, but if they experience
evil—that is, lack of good—they think they are being mistreated. This is
kufr (truth-concealing and ingratitude), since it contradicts the necessi-
ties of both faith and gratitude:

*When harm touches the human being, he calls upon Us. Then,
when we confer on him a blessing, he says, "I was given it only because of a knowledge." No, it is a trial, but most of them know not.
(39:49)*

Tawhid means that people have nothing positive that is strictly their own; on the contrary, all good is in God's hands. If people experience good, they experience it on God's initiative through no merit of their own. If they do not experience good, that is simply what they deserve, since—apart from God's blessing and mercy—they are literally nothing. Hence, the Koran pictures human pretensions to good as distortions of the way things are.

No one is hurt, however, by human pretensions, except those who make the pretensions. Justice (*'adl*) is a divine attribute, defined as putting a thing in its proper place. The usual opposite of *'adl* is *zulm*, which in the Koranic context we translate as "wrongdoing." Wrongdoing is a human attribute, usually defined as putting a thing in the wrong place. The Koran repeatedly stigmatizes human wrongdoing. Interestingly, when it mentions those who are harmed by the wrongdoing, it almost always employs the word *self* (*nafs*). People cannot wrong God. A mosquito cannot sting the sun. But people can and do wrong themselves every time they put something in the wrong place. They distort their own natures, and they lead themselves astray.

The following is a typical verse in which wrongdoing is mentioned. It occurs in a story of the destruction of earlier peoples who denied their prophets. Remember that a god is anything that is served or worshiped other than God. The ultimate wrongdoing is *shirk*, to serve things that are not worthy of service, to put false divinities in place of God.

> *And We wronged them not, but they wronged themselves. The gods that they called upon apart from God were of no use to them when the command of your Lord came. The gods increased them only in destruction. (11:101)*

In sum, when the Prophet said "the measuring out, the good of it and the evil of it," he had in view people's perception that some things that reach them are good and some things that happen to them are evil. Human beings should have faith that whatever reaches them comes from God. Whether they perceive it as a benefit or a loss, they should accept it with gratitude, always remembering that God's mercy predominates over his wrath. Everything that occurs tests their faith: "Do the people reckon that they will be left to say, 'We have faith,' and will not be tried?" (29:2).

Freedom

Faith in the measuring out means to understand that all good belongs to God. Everything other than God is lacking in good in some or many respects. People who have such faith will be grateful for the good they have, and they will trust God in respect of the good that they lack. They will be confident that the Real, who is the Merciful, measures things out with wisdom while keeping the ultimate good of all things in view:

> *When evil touches him, he is in despair. (17:83)*

> *Those who have* kufr *toward God's signs and the encounter with Him—they have lost hope in My mercy, and there awaits for them a painful chastisement. (29:23)*

> *Do they not know that God outspreads His provision to whomsoever He will, and straitens it? Surely in that are signs for a people who have faith. Say: O My servants who have been immoderate against yourselves, do not despair of God's mercy! Surely God forgives all sins. Surely He is the Forgiving, the Compassionate. (39:52-53)*

Brief statements of the measuring out always suggest a logical contradiction: If all things, whether good and evil, are measured out, then is it not true that our business is over and done with? After all, the Prophet said that a person's ultimate abode—paradise or hell—is already written for him in his mother's womb. Therefore, what use is religion, since everything is already decided?

This is the issue of free will and predestination, a problem that has vexed theologians of various religious persuasions for centuries. We will not present the Muslim theological solutions to this problem, though many have been proposed. Instead, we will simply stick to the Koranic level of things and suggest that, as in the case of all important problems, there is no clear and simple answer. Just as often as the Koran affirms that God has measured things out and that he knows all things even before they occur, it also affirms that human effort is meaningful:

> *Whoso desires the next world and strives after it as he should while having faith—those, their striving shall be thanked. (17:19)*

> *The human being will have only what he has strived for, and his striving will be seen. (53:39-40)*

The Koran is nothing if not a book of exhortations directed at people to get them striving on the path to God. Just as it demands a voluntary *islam* over and above universal and compulsory *islam*, so also it demands jihad and *mujahada*—struggle in the path of God. If human beings were mere puppets, with no self-control whatsoever, the Koran would be a silly book, since it would be telling stones to fly.

Free will and predestination need to be understood as complementary expressions of the human situation. Neither explains the situation fully. One useful way to understand how the two ideas are related is to think again in terms of *tanzih* and *tashbih*.

In respect of *tanzih*, human reality is sheer unreality, since God is the only reality there is. Human beings have no knowledge, power, desire, or freedom, since these are divine attributes and belong exclusively to God. But in respect of *tashbih*, human beings reflect these divine attributes. The attributes belong to God, but they are put into effect through human beings. If God can "do whatever He desires," so also, in respect of *tashbih*, human beings can do whatever they desire.

In any case, human freedom has enormous limitations, as everyone recognizes. People cannot choose their place of birth, their parents, their race, their culture, their mother language, their fundamental physical characteristics, and so on. All these are givens. But within the context of these givens, choices remain. To the extent that these choices are real, people are free.

Notice that predestination pertains to the side of *tanzih* and the attributes of wrath. One of the most important theological terms employed to refer to predestination is *jabr* (compulsion), and one of God's Koranic names is *al-jabbar* (All-Compeller). This name fits into the category of majestic and severe names. But we know that God's mercy takes precedence over his wrath. The names of beauty and gentleness will overcome the names of majesty and severity. Love and mercy will conquer compulsion. The beautiful names bring about nearness to God, and the closer people are to God, the more they share in his freedom.

In modern society we think highly of freedom and consider it a worthy goal in life. Of course there are two basic modes of freedom, "freedom from" and "freedom for." We want freedom from oppression, and we want freedom for speech and for the things that we enjoy. In human affairs, these two kinds of freedom often conflict. When we gain freedom to enjoy a wealth of consumer goods, for example, we may bring about terrible oppression for peoples in other parts of the globe who have to suffer the consequences of exploitation and ecological devastation. The flip side of freedom's coin may well be slavery. What is good for you may be evil for someone else. Your freedom can be another's slavery, or it even can be your own slavery. Look at all the people who, in their desire to be free to have a good time, enslave themselves to demeaning jobs.

Muslim thinkers also take into account both freedom from and freedom for. Their concept of freedom is distinguished from the modern concept because it is rooted in the Shahadah. "There is none free but God." God is free of any sort of outside constraint, "a sovereign doer of what He desires" (11:107, 85:16), but no creature can have this attribute. Compared to God, all creatures dwell in utter slavery. In order for human beings to be free, they must partake of God's freedom.

God is free of everything other than himself. He is "independent of all the worlds" (3:97). Human beings can never be free of God. "O people,

you are dependent upon God, and God is Independent, Praiseworthy"
(35:15). All power, reality, and praise belong to God alone.

Since human beings can never be free of God—they are *muslim*s and
*'abd*s by nature—they need to recognize this and submit to him voluntarily. Then they will not be flying in the face of reality. Submitting
themselves to God, they free themselves from everything other than
God. Freeing themselves up *for* God, they become free *from* everything
else. To be free from everything other than God is to be free from all
unreality and to be free for Reality. It is to reject every form of *shirk* and
establish *tawhid*.

Hence, in the Islamic view, "freedom from" is to be free from the
constraints placed on us by created things and to serve God. "Freedom
for" is to choose the Real over the unreal in every case. To be free for the
unreal is meaningless, because the unreal does not exist. People should
desire to be free for knowledge, desire, power, good, and everything
positive and real. Nothing is real but the Real. Hence freedom from the
unreal comes down to the same as freedom for the Real. There can be no
contradiction. Both are *tawhid*.

Are we free? The answer is, "Yes and no." We are free to the extent
that we are similar to God, but our similarity is always tempered by
incomparability. *Tawhid* demands both *tanzih* and *tashbih*. Freedom is
a reality, and it is a reality that has degrees. The closer people move to
God, the freer they become. The purpose of Islam is to show the way to
tawhid, where *tanzih* and *tashbih* dwell in proper balance. To be human
is to be relatively free. But to be as free as it is humanly possible to be
free can only come about when full submission and surrender to Reality is achieved.

One final point needs to be made on the issue of free will and
predestination: When people criticize the contradictions involved in
attributing absolute power to God, it is important to keep in mind
their intentions; in other words, we have to ask why people object.
Often the intention is simply to convince others that they are stupid
and naive to think that the idea of God or prophetic guidance has any
meaning.

To use some modern jargon, when people protest against the idea of
predestination, they are often motivated by a hermeneutics of suspi-
cion. The protesters assume the worst. In their view, the real issue is
power. They think that what has really happened is that certain people
have manipulated religious teachings in order to preserve their own
power and keep others subjugated.

Without denying that there may be such manipulative people, we still
have to recognize that there are other ways of reading the situation, and
that the Islamic way has always been rooted in a hermeneutics of trust.
This trust is not directed at human beings, however, but at God. The
Koran speaks of trust (*tawakkul*) in forty verses, and in every case the
object is God.

God is their Friend, so in God let the faithful put their trust. (3:122)

Truly, I have put my trust in God, my Lord and your Lord. There is no creature that crawls, but He takes it by the forelock. Surely my Lord is on a straight path. (11:56)

Judgment belongs to none but God. In Him I have put my trust, and in Him let all who put their trust put their trust. (12:67)

And whosoever puts his trust in God, He shall suffice him. (65:3)

Satan has no authority over those who have faith and put their trust in their Lord. (16:99)

A famous *hadith qudsi* suggests that trust in God means that people should always have a good opinion of him. They should never be suspicious of God's motives: "I am with My servant's opinion of Me." They should have a good opinion of him so that they will meet him inasmuch as he is Merciful, Loving, and Gentle.

Muslims have a good opinion of God because they recognize that he is the Real, and that reality itself demands that mercy must predominate over wrath. They have always held that God's good intentions in revealing the Koran are clear. He wants to guide people to ultimate happiness, or to the fulfillment of human destiny. By asserting that all things are measured out, the Koran is simply stating that God is in charge — or that Reality is what it is — and nothing can be done to change it.

Among the things that God measures out are freedom and guidance. Hence, human beings are free to accept or reject the offered guidance. They carry a burden of responsibility: they will be called to answer for how they employed the freedom that they were given and how they reacted to the guidance that they were offered. This is also the limit of their responsibility. To the extent that they were not free and guidance was not offered to them, they will not be held responsible.[8]

Creaturely Diversity

God measures out all things. "There is nothing whose treasuries are not with Us, and We send it down only with a known measuring out" (15:21). Measuring out pertains not simply to the issue of whether or not people have the ability to make free choices. It has far wider implications, since it is the principle of creation itself. No matter what there might be in existence, God has measured it out and determined its nature. "He gave everything its creation" (20:50).

The net result of all this measuring out is that God produces an inconceivably enormous cosmos with an infinite diversity of created things. If we investigate the creatures one by one, the task can never be completed. But if we speak in general terms, it is possible to classify created things into categories. Such classifications are not meant to be exhaustive, simply to indicate in general terms what people observe or may observe if they have the necessary insight.

We have already mentioned that the cosmos can be divided into two basic worlds, the unseen and the visible, sometimes referred to as "the heavens and the earth," or "the spiritual world and the bodily world." We also said that there is a third world that is both similar to and different from these two basic worlds, called the "world of imagination." And we pointed out that, if these three worlds represent the general structure of the total macrocosm, the human being can be called a microcosm, since three parallel domains are found within each individual: spirit, soul, and body.

At this point, we want to look at other bodily creatures; that is, those physical things that fill the visible universe. Muslim authorities follow the standard Greek classification by dividing the visible things into three broad categories: inanimate objects, plants, and animals. What is interesting for our purposes is how these three kinds of creature manifest the signs of God.

We suggested earlier that one way to read the signs is to meditate upon the divine attributes that become visible through them. Which attributes become visible in inanimate objects? Perhaps the best way to answer this question is to say that more than anything else, inanimate objects conceal God's attributes instead of revealing them. They tell us what God is not rather than what he is. Of course, everything in the universe, by being something, is other than God, and hence we learn from each thing that God is not like that. This is the perspective of *tanzih*.

All things also say something in terms of *tashbih*, and *tashbih* is weakest in inanimate things. It is extremely difficult to see divine attributes in a stone, although stones do suggest something of the divine permanence and eternity. But for the most part, stones tell us that God is infinitely distant and different from themselves. However, stones—especially big stones, like planets—teach us that God is the Powerful, the Majestic, and the Magnificent King, who throws around big stones, not to speak of suns and galaxies, as if they were sand.

In contrast to inanimate things, plants display several obvious divine attributes. It is easy to see that plants are alive, and life is the first of the Seven Leaders, the seven divine attributes that predominate in creation. Plants have a certain knowledge. They know where to hunt for nutrients and where to find the sun. They certainly have desire: they want water, sunlight, fertilizer, trace elements. If you treat them well and give them what they really desire—like nice, rich manure—they even show their gratitude by producing enormous crops; they are not ungrateful truth-concealers. Plants have power and can destroy stones and concrete, but they need time. But all these divine attributes are found rather feebly within plants, so *tanzih* outweighs *tashbih*.

In contrast, the divine attributes found in animals are much more intense. Moreover, animals add other attributes that are difficult to find in plants. The knowledge possessed by animals can be extraordinary, though it is always rather specialized. Bees can tell their hive-mates exactly where to find the best honey, but they don't know much about vinegar. Monarch butterflies know the precise location of their valley in Mexico, but they cannot be trusted to take you to New York City. The animal kingdom represents an incredible diversity of knowledge and skills, divided among a vast number of specialized organisms. Desire is also clearly present in animals, but each species desires different things, and thus a great natural harmony is created where, as Rumi puts it, "Everything is both eater and eaten."

Both plants and animals represent a tremendous variety of specific signs. Each plant or animal species is a special configuration of divine attributes that is not reproduced in any other species. Hence, oak trees produce acorns, and we are never surprised that we don't get apples. If we did get apples from an oak tree, we would know that something extraordinary had occurred.

Each animal species is defined by the specific knowledge, desire, power, and other divine attributes that differentiate it from every other animal species. Because the attributes are specific, we always know what to expect from peacocks and elephants and cats. There may be a certain element of surprise involved, but we know that this is traceable to our ignorance of the species or of certain external factors, such as a disease, that complicate the picture.

Human beings are a species of animal, and they share many characteristics with them. But there is one remarkable characteristic that differentiates them from all other animals: Each animal is what it is, with little or no confusion. We never mistake a dragonfly for an eagle, or even a cat for a dog. But human beings are unknown factors. We never know what a human being is, because a human being can be practically anything.

A dog is a dog, but a human being may be a dog or a pig. We use such terms as insults, but they contain a profound wisdom that every culture has recognized. Each species of animal is dominated by one or a few characteristics. For the animal, all these characteristics are good, since they define its very nature. But if the same characteristics dominate over human beings, they may be good or bad.

A dog has a number of characteristics. It is faithful, and this is a good quality when found in people. But dogs also have a strong streak of rapacity and viciousness, and this is usually what people have in mind when they call someone a dog.

The human being is infinitely malleable. We never know what we have when faced with a roomful of people. We could have saints and serial killers, and never be able to tell the difference. When we are faced with a dog or a lion or a slug, we know what to expect and how to act. But with people we never know.

The Human Being

What then is a human being? What brings about this fundamental difference between human beings and other animals? Muslims answer these questions in many ways. The easiest approach within our current discussion is to investigate the nature of the relationship between human beings and the divine attributes. Every creature other than a human being is a sign of God in which a specific, limited, and defined configuration of divine attributes is reflected. In contrast, a human being reflects God as God. In other creatures, some divine attributes are permanently manifest while others are permanently hidden. In human beings, all divine attributes are present, and any of them can become manifest if circumstances are appropriate.

The Prophet referred to this peculiar characteristic of human beings when he repeated the famous saying found in the Bible—a saying that has also played an important role in Jewish and Christian understandings of what it means to be human—"God created Adam in his own image," though we will employ "form" for "image," in keeping with the Arabic text. Many authorities understand a similar meaning from the Koranic verse, "God taught Adam the names, all of them" (2:31).

It is important to keep in mind that the name *Adam* designates the first human being and, by extension, any and every human being. The Koran and the Islamic tradition in general use the word *Adam* as a synonym for *insan* (human being). The word does not refer to the male as opposed to the female unless Eve is mentioned in the specific context and is understood as designating qualities different from those of Adam. Otherwise, "Adam and Eve" may simply mean, "all human beings, male and female." We will come back to the relationship between Adam and Eve when we discuss the fall from the Garden.

The Koranic story of Adam's creation is of fundamental importance for grasping the Islamic view of human nature. Like most Koranic stories, it is not told in one place in the Koran, so we need to gather bits and pieces from various suras. Here we can summarize some of the important events:

God decided that he was going to place a vicegerent or representative in the earth. The Arabic term for vicegerent here is *khalifa*, from which we have English *caliph*. God told the angels of his plan. In contrast to their usual calm acceptance of everything that God says, the angels in this case seem to have been a bit upset. Their superior knowledge of things allowed them to grasp certain characteristics of this vicegerent that did not please them. They said, "What, will You place in the earth one who will work corruption there, and shed blood?" (2:30). God replied, "I know something that you do not know." The angels may be perspicacious, but their knowledge cannot compare with God's infinite wisdom.

God then molded Adam with his own two hands and blew into him of his own spirit. He taught him all the names. He brought him before the angels to show them his handiwork, but they were not impressed by this lump of clay. Of course, God had known what their reaction would be, and it was all part of his plan. Now God showed all the creatures of the universe to the angels, and these teeming hordes did indeed impress them. At this point, the angels began to understand that God had something up his sleeve. Then God sprung his trap. He said to the angels, "Tell me the names of these if you are truthful" (2:31). The angels were flabbergasted. "We know nothing but what You have taught us" (2:32). In other words, "You know that You have only taught us the names of a few things. How could we know the names of all the creatures of the universe?"

Then God turned to Adam, who had been standing by the sidelines. He said, "Adam, tell them their names" (2:33), and Adam recited one by one the names of everything in creation. (The commentators embellish this a bit and tell us that Adam knew the names of all things in all his children's languages down to the end of time.) Next God rubbed it in a bit. He said, "Did I not say to you that I know the unseen of the heavens and the earth?" (2:33). The angels were duly chastened. God commanded the angels to prostrate themselves before Adam. All of them did so without hesitation, happy to acknowledge his superior knowledge. Only Iblis, as we have heard already, refused to obey God's command.

Like all myths, this myth can be understood in many senses and applied to the human situation in many different contexts.[9] We could not exhaust the meanings of the account even if we wanted to. For present purposes, a number of lessons seem especially important.

Adam was taught the names of the whole of creation, but the angels and other creatures were taught the names of only some of creation. We already know that the term *name* plays an especially important role in the Koran, given that one of the Koran's most basic themes is that "To God belong the most beautiful names" (7:180). Each name of God designates God's reality. By coming to know the names, we come to know God's qualities and characteristics. Hence, the name of a thing designates its nature and reality, especially if that name is taught by God himself.

Clearly, Adam had been taught not only the names, but also their meaning. Through knowing the names of all things, Adam understood what the things were and what they were good for. When God said, "This is an almond tree," Adam knew for certain that it produced almonds and that almonds were good to eat and yielded an oil with fine healing properties. When God said "crocodile," Adam grasped the essence of the crocodile (and would have avoided taking a bath with one).

By teaching Adam the names, God gave him power over the named objects. Even now, after long generations in which meanings and words have tended to become more and more obscure, some of that power remains through knowledge of the names. Having said (whether verbally or mentally), "This is a tree," we know that we can cut it down and use it for firewood. Knowing the name is equivalent to knowing its identity and reality, and without that knowledge, we cannot control and manipulate things. Knowledge is power, and it has always been so.

The myth indicates that Adam's power over creation was at issue from the beginning, since God says that he is placing a vicegerent in the earth. A vicegerent is someone who is given the authority and the means to rule in someone else's stead. When God taught Adam the names, he gave him a share of his own ruling power.

The relationship between God's knowledge and power is an important one, and it is connected directly to what we know about the divine attributes. God controls the cosmos through his knowledge of the cosmos. He knows all things, even the things that he has not yet created. Through his knowledge of things he measures them out. In the typical list of the Seven Leaders (the seven primary divine attributes), knowledge is second. First, there must be life: Dead things do not know. Knowing all things, God desires. In other words, he knows a thing's identity and reality, and he desires to give it existence in such and such a time and place. On the basis of his desire, he exercises his power. One does not exercise power without wishing to do so. There must be a motivation. Then only does God speak. He says to the thing, "Be!" for example, and it comes into existence. Human beings function in a similar way. Since they are alive, they know; once they know something, they may desire to change their relationship to it, for example by bringing it near or sending it far; on the basis of their desire, they exercise their power.

Other living things also have knowledge and act on the basis of their knowledge. But they know only a few names, which is to say that their knowledge of their surroundings is inherently limited. They function in certain fixed ways for certain limited goals. Even the angels, the most luminous beings in the cosmos and the nearest to God, know the names of only certain specific things. Hence, they were happy to acknowledge Adam's superiority when they saw that he knew the names of all things.

The Koran often refers to human power over creation in ways that make it clear that this power is no small affair. After all, only human beings were created to be God's vicegerents. They alone among all creatures were taught all the divine names, since they alone were created in God's form. Hence, everything in the universe exists to be ruled by human beings. Sometimes the Koran refers to human power by pointing to the subjection of creatures to people, a subjection that, of course, was established by God:

> Have you not seen that God has subjected to you all that is in the earth? (22:65)

*Have you not seen that God has subjected to you whatsoever is in
the heavens and the earth? (31:20)*

*It is God who created the heavens and the earth, and sent down
out of heaven water wherewith He brought forth fruits for your
provision. And He subjected to you the ships to run upon the sea at
His command, and He subjected to you the rivers, and He subjected to you the sun and moon constant upon their courses, and
He subjected to you the night and day, and gave you of all you
asked Him. If you count God's blessing you will never number it.
Surely the human being is a great wrongdoer, very ungrateful/
truth-concealing! (14:32-34)*

After Muslims became familiar with Greek philosophical writings, they
borrowed the terms *microcosm* and *macrocosm* as a way of explaining
the relationship between human beings and the rest of the universe. In
effect, all things are present in human beings, because God taught them
the names or realities of all things. A full and complete comprehension of
a thing demands that the reality of the thing be present within the human
subject. Plato had something similar in mind when he said that all
learning takes place through remembering what we already know. We
can only know things because of a certain identity with them. The
colloquialism, "It takes one to know one," conceals a deep wisdom.

When it is said that everything is within human beings, this is not
meant in a literal sense. The principle here is easy to understand if we
return to the discussion of the divine names. God created the universe
as the sum total of his signs. The signs explain the nature of God
inasmuch as he discloses and reveals himself. What does he disclose?
He discloses his attributes, such as life, knowledge, power, and speech.
These attributes work together to produce an infinite diversity of created things; but all things are signs of the same attributes, which in turn
belong to the Real. The cosmos in its full temporal and spatial extension—everything other than God—illustrates all God's manifest attributes. Hence the macrocosm is an image, or form, of God.

The human being was also created in God's form, embracing all God's
attributes. The difference between the whole universe and the human
being is that the signs are infinitely dispersed in the universe, while they
are concentrated into a single, intense focus in each human individual.

The concentration of the attributes within human beings makes
people God's vicegerents, that is, creatures who can perform the same
functions as God, with all due respect to *tanzih*. Human beings manifest
all God's attributes, but in a weakened and dim manner, demanded by
the fact that, although they are similar to God in respect of having been
created in his form, they are different in respect of spatial and temporal
limitations. God remains infinitely beyond any human being.

As vicegerents, human beings possess power over the subjects that they rule in God's stead. These subjects are the creatures of the universe. This power over all things explains, in the Islamic view, why people can destroy the earth as well as protect it. The ecological and social crises of modern times are nothing but signs of misused vicegerency.

Servant and Vicegerent

We mentioned that there are two basic kinds of *islam*: the universal submission that pertains to all created things, and the voluntary submission that pertains to people who have elected to follow the prophets. In the same way, there are two basic kinds of vicegerencies, one pertaining to all human beings, and the second pertaining only to those who have voluntarily chosen to serve God.

Human beings have a natural vicegerency because they have submitted to God's creative power by existing. He created them in his form, and they manifest his attributes in the world. They were taught all the names, and hence they have power over all things. People have access to the second kind of vicegerency only after having submitted voluntarily to God.

Because people are free, they can easily abuse their natural vicegerency. Only by using their freedom to choose God—by surrendering to him through following prophetic guidance—can they act as his true vicegerents in the earth. To be someone's representative, after all, you have to follow that person's commands and instructions.

Following God's instructions, however, is not sufficient to be his vicegerent. On *islam*'s most universal level, everything follows God's instructions. Turtles, demons, scorpions, and mice follow God's instructions just as well as anyone else. But vicegerency is a specifically human quality. God placed Adam in the earth explicitly to be his vicegerent (2:30). Hence, vicegerency pertains to instructions given only to human beings (the jinn may be a special case here, but we will leave them out of the picture). These instructions are the messages brought by the prophets. The proper human response to the prophets is *islam* in the general sense (submission to God by following the message of a prophet) or Islam (following the message brought by Muhammad).

It is clearly not so easy to follow God's instructions. If it were easy, Adam would never have slipped in the first place, and his children would not have run into all the problems that they have. Islam gives high marks to those who succeed in this task. In general, such a person is called a servant (*'abd*) of God, and servanthood is looked upon as the highest and most praiseworthy human condition. In a sense, it is even higher than vicegerency and prophecy, since being God's representative or messenger depends upon being his servant. The most common titles that Muslims accord to Muhammad—titles that are recited during every required *salat*—are "His servant and His messenger." It is no accident that servanthood comes first.

The word *'abd* is one of the most important terms in the Islamic vocabulary, so we need to look carefully at its meaning and connotations. The word is commonly used to mean slave as well as servant, and many would claim that the absolute submission demanded by God means that "slave" is a better translation than "servant." However, freedom is an important quality of a true servant of God. If the word were used only in the sense of the Koranic verse cited earlier, "There is nothing in the heavens and the earth but that comes to the Merciful as an *'abd*" (19:93), then "slave" would be an appropriate translation. In this sense, to be an *'abd* has nothing voluntary about it; it is equivalent to being a *muslim* in the universal sense. Thus, in the broadest sense of the term *'abd*, everything is God's slave, doing his creative work. But in the narrower sense that interests us here, human beings are free to accept or reject to be God's *'abd*. Hence, "servant" is perhaps a better translation.

In short, to be a servant of God is to do his bidding, and his bidding is set down in his scriptures and in the words of his prophets. Hence, to be a servant of God is to submit oneself freely to God, to be a *muslim* or a Muslim.

A servant of God *serves* God. The Arabic verb is *'ibada*, which the dictionaries tell us means "to serve, worship, adore, obey, show humility, be submissive." But in the technical language of Islam, *'ibada* refers to all the obligatory and recommended ritual acts that Muslims perform. Hence the Five Pillars are all *'ibadat*, which can be translated as "acts of worship." To be God's servant is to observe the Five Pillars and the rest of the Shariah, and it is also to imitate the Prophet in his Sunna, which includes many recommended acts of worship.

More than anyone else, the Prophet Muhammad is the servant of God (*'abd allah*), and the Koran itself gives him this title (72:19). Interestingly, the Koran quotes Jesus as saying, "I am the servant of God. He has given me the Book and made me a prophet" (19:30). Hence, Jesus also is looked upon by Muslims as a perfect servant of God.

Notice that the epithet "servant of God" given to Muhammad and Jesus in the Koran becomes one of the most common male names in the Islamic world. Everyone has heard of someone called Abdullah (servant of God). Like Muslim personal names in general, this name marks a grand hope of the parents. Children should live up to their names, and hence the most common names have always been names of prophets, Muhammad in particular. A second popular form of naming follows the pattern of "servant of God," but replaces "God" with some other divine name. Hence, we find Abdul-Hayy (servant of the Alive), Adul-Alim (servant of the Knower), Abdul-Qadir (servant of the Powerful), Abdul-Khaliq (servant of the Creator), and so on. Here the hope is expressed that the person will benefit from the blessing of the divine name.

The concept of *'ibada* plays a central role in the third dimension of Islam, which the Prophet defined as "worshiping God as if you see Him." Hence, we will leave off further discussion of the word's implications to Part III of this book.

In short, Adam was created to be a vicegerent of God. But in order to be God's vicegerent, he first had to be God's servant. In other words, people were created to represent God on the face of the earth. In order to fulfill this function properly, they must submit to God's will as revealed through the prophets. Once people become God's servants, then they can become his representatives. Before they become God's servants, they represent their own personal interests. Without the guidance of divine wisdom, they cannot see the interests of the whole cosmos, and whatever they do will work to the detriment of the subjects over whom they are supposed to exercise vicegerency. Again, this explains why human beings cannot solve social and ecological problems by following their own lights. Their view of things is not broad enough and hence remains disconnected from reality, which is the Real.

Servanthood must precede vicegerency. You cannot represent someone until you follow that person's commands. A king does not appoint a stranger as his ambassador; he appoints someone whom he has tested and whom he knows he can trust.

The Merciful King

In order to grasp some of the implications of the relationship between servant and vicegerent, we can usefully refer back to *tanzih* and *tashbih*. Attributes of *tanzih* demand God's incomparability, distance, and inaccessibility. We suggested earlier that the divine name King brings together in a relatively concrete image the implications of the names that stress *tanzih*. The King—the "oriental despot" if you prefer the old stereotypes—possesses absolute power over his subjects. They are in effect his slaves. The King is mighty, majestic, tremendous, awe-inspiring, inaccessible, powerful. The subjects are pitiful in the extreme.

Suppose this king is a true and worthy king. Then the stereotype is not so bad. And suppose this king is the merciful God, other than whom there is no reality. Then one can grasp that people are in fact God's slaves, since there is no other ruler. Human beings are in fact *muslims*, whether they like it or not. Why shouldn't they accept the actual situation and use their talents to make sure that they do not transgress their proper limits? This is voluntary *islam*, acceptance of the message of the prophets and observance of their instructions. People happily accept to be God's servants.

In short, the attributes connected with servanthood correlate closely with *tanzih*, or the divine attributes of majesty, tremendousness, and inaccessibility. In contrast, discussion of vicegerency stresses the human relationship with God in terms of *tashbih*.

The vicegerent is God's representative. In order to represent God, the person must be chosen by God for the task. The King does not choose the rabble in the street as ambassadors. Rather, he chooses those who have proved their worth by years of dedicated service in the court.

Being a servant is not a one-time affair. People cannot be rebellious truth-concealers today and faithful servants tomorrow. The transition from wandering in error to following the truth is a long and gradual process. Again, it is helpful to think in terms of the imagery of a king's court (though Washington bureaucracy will do). People begin their service to the king as apprentices of a minor official who perhaps never in his life has seen the king. Only gradually do they learn the ropes. Little by little, they are able to put all the proper ways of diplomacy and service into practice. Only in rare instances do individuals work their way up the hierarchy of royal service to become a favorite at court. And only the prime minister has access to the king at all times. This view of things is implicit in the imagery that is employed to express *tanzih*. The transition from being a servant to being a full vicegerent is a long process. At any given stage, one gains certain prerogatives through one's servanthood.

Notice that the most difficult tasks are reserved for the best servants. In other words, the early stages of servanthood are relatively easy, and they carry little of the responsibility of vicegerency along with them. Of course, all *muslims* are vicegerents to some degree. As the Prophet put it:

> Each of you is a shepherd, and each of you will be held responsible for your sheep. The commander who directs the people is a shepherd, and he will be held responsible for his sheep. The man is shepherd over the members of his household, and he will be held responsible for them. The woman is shepherd over the household of her husband and his children, and she will be held responsible for them. The servant is shepherd over the property of his master, and he will be held responsible for it. Verily, each of you is a shepherd, and each of you will be held responsible for your sheep!

As people progress in the path of being God's servant, their responsibility increases. When the Prophet said, "Marriage is half of religion," he was alluding to the responsibilities that accrue to a husband and wife because of their new relationship. Suddenly, a whole range of divine obligations with a social bearing has been added to their servanthood. Before marriage, they had to watch out for their own selves and their parents; now they have responsibilities toward a spouse, the spouse's family, their children, and so on.

The highest degree of vicegerency, which entails ruling the whole cosmos in God's place, is reserved for the most perfect servants. Hence, Muhammad is looked upon as the most perfect human being, the most exalted vicegerent, and the greatest servant.

In sum, God can be viewed from two basic points of view, that of distance and nearness, absence and presence, *tanzih* and *tashbih*. Human beings, in function of their dual relationship with God, have two basic roles: to be God's servant and to be his vicegerent. In order to become a vicegerent, which implies nearness to God, they must first accept their servanthood—their distance from God—and act in accordance with it. God in his mercy desires that human beings not remain distant but rather gain nearness, but they have to choose nearness of their own accord. The route of free choice is to follow the Shariah, the broad road that leads to the water of life.

The Hierarchy of Creation

In respect of *tanzih*, God alone is permanent and real, while everything else is evanescent and unreal. In respect of *tashbih*, all things are real to some degree, but some are more real than others. To be real is to share in God's reality, or to be close to God. This is not meant spatially, since God is not situated in space, nor are angels or human spirits. What is meant is qualitative closeness. In respect of qualitative nearness, we said that heaven is closer to God than earth, because heaven is luminous and earth is dark. So also, angels are closer to God than clay, and spirit closer to him than body. Realities such as fire and soul, because of their ambiguous nature, have to be considered carefully before we can decide where they fit in.

We suggested earlier that human beings are situated at the peak of a hierarchy with inanimate things at the base. In human beings, the divine attributes are more intense than in animals, plants, and minerals; not only are they more intense, but all of them are present, while in other things most are absent.

Angels are luminous and human beings are, at first glance, dark. Hence, one might conclude that angels are superior to human beings. Muslim scholars have often discussed this issue and have frequently disagreed. By and large, the answer depends upon the standards that are employed in comparing the two. Moreover, the problem is made more complex because there are many different kinds of human beings, just as there are many different kinds of angels. Each human being, in fact, represents a unique combination of divine attributes, and hence corresponds to an animal species, each of which also represents a specific combination of attributes.

Like angels, human beings can be divided into categories. Commonly there are said to be five broad sorts of people, given here in ascending order of qualitative nearness to God: truth-concealers, the faithful, the friends of God, the prophets, and the messengers.

The truth-concealers are God's involuntary servants, while the faithful accept his servanthood gladly. But it takes a while before the faithful can be true vicegerents of God, and so we can say that the vicegerents belong to the latter three categories—the friends, prophets, and messengers. When some Muslim authorities maintain that human beings are superior to the angels, they have in mind these three categories of human beings, or perhaps only the last category. They do not have in mind ordinary human beings, who fit into the first two categories.

A good deal of evidence is cited from the Koran and the Hadith to prove human superiority. We have already mentioned the prostration of the angels before Adam. The Prophet is reported to have said, "On the day of resurrection, no one will be greater than the children of Adam." The people wondered at this and someone asked, "O Messenger of God! Not even the angels?" He replied, "Not even the angels. They are compelled like the sun and the moon."

The angels, as indicated earlier, have no freedom of action. They could not disobey God if they wanted to. Hence, they can be only what they are. But human beings can overcome their own limitations and move from distance (*tanzih*) to nearness (*tashbih*), from servanthood to vicegerency. Another hadith makes a similar point:

> God created the angels from intelligence, the beasts from appetite, and human beings from both intelligence and appetite. When a person's intelligence overcomes his appetite, he is higher than the angels, but when his appetite overcomes his intelligence, he is lower than the beasts.

That human beings can be lower than the beasts is a matter of common experience. No one blames a cat for eating a mouse, or a dog for attacking a cat, although the owner of the cat might be upset. Still, it is in the dog's nature, and dogs will be dogs. But everyone knows that human beings should not act like dogs, and when they do, they are worse than dogs. Moral depravity, in fact, is a specifically human characteristic.

That human beings can be higher than the angels, however, is not a matter of common experience, especially in our times. This helps explain why many people nowadays have come to believe that depravity and viciousness belong inherently to human nature. Of course, the depraved and the vicious are happy with this judgment, because they can claim that what they do is simply the natural order of things.

One of the Koranic texts that is cited to prove human superiority over the angels is a reference to the two angels Harut and Marut, who were mentioned earlier. The commentators explain that the angels in heaven continued to be upset after God created human beings. Reading between the lines, one can deduce that they kept on reminding God about their words, "Will you place in the earth someone who will work corruption and shed blood?" (2:30). They were saying, "See, God, we told you so. These human beings are a nasty and vicious lot, always fighting and killing each other."

As befits the divine nature, God was patient with the angels' remarks (after all, he is the Patient, as the Koran tells us). Eventually, God thought that the complaints were going too far and that he had better let the angels find out for themselves that he knew what he was doing. He suggested to them that they would not do as well as the humans if they lived in the earth. This made the angels even more upset, and they protested that they would never rebel against God's commands. God said that they should prove themselves. They chose the two most worshipful and humble angels, Harut and Marut. Before sending them down into the earth, God gave them their commandments: they were to avoid wine, fornication, the unjust spilling of blood, and *shirk*.

To make a long story short, the two angels, newly embodied in order to fit into the earthly world, fell in love with a beautiful and scheming woman. At first, they observed all God's commands, but the woman convinced them that one drink of wine was nothing important, and the rest of the story is obvious. They committed murder for her and ended up worshiping her god.

When God saw how far things had gone, he called the angels to account. They immediately came to their senses and asked forgiveness. God gave them the choice of suffering punishment in this world or in the next. Not being stupid, they chose this world, and to this day they are hanging by their feet at the bottom of a well in Babylon. And of course, the angels in heaven learned their lesson. That ended all the complaints about human excesses. They undertook with renewed vigor one of their basic duties, that of watching out for the well-being of all God's creatures, including the sinful: "The angels glorify their Lord in praise and ask forgiveness for those on earth" (42:5).

Notice that human superiority is connected with the fact that people's bodies are made of earth, and hence the earthly qualities have an effect on their souls. Harut and Marut did not sin—and could not have sinned—until they had bodies. Once the qualities of clay are mixed with light, then darkness, distance, and wrath have to be taken into account. Clay suffers the wrath of God because of its mode of existence, which is to be overcome by the lack of light. To be distant from God is to stand in a relationship of *tanzih*. Hence, it is to be faced with God's majesty, severity, and wrath. In contrast, the angels, who have no clay in their make-up, are pure light, and hence they cannot be so distant from God. It is true that many of the angels manifest God's attributes of majesty and tremendousness, but that is because they are exalted far beyond the creatures with whom they are put in contact. The angels in charge of hell, for example, are angels who manifest wrath. But it is God's wrath that shines through them and, as we shall see in the section on eschatology, wrath and distance from God are inseparable qualities.

At first glance, the body seems negative, because it allows darkness—and therefore disobedience and sin—to find a place in the human constitution. But at second glance, this darkness makes possible the vision of the full splendor of light. Just as white light cannot be refracted into an infinite number of colors without darkness (the removal of certain wavelengths for each color), so also the divine spirit breathed into Adam's clay cannot be refracted into the qualities of his innumerable descendants without the darkness of the body. If not for the body, people would be angels. If they were angels, they could not move further away from God, nor could they move closer to God. They would be fixed in their places, like angels in heaven and toads, figs, and stones in the earth. "None of us there is," say the angels in the Koran, "but has a known station" (37:164). Angels and all creatures other than human beings have known stations and fixed entities. Only human beings are unknown quantities who have been given the freedom to shape their own destinies.

The unique situation of human beings is alluded to in a Koranic verse that was cited earlier. When Iblis refused to follow God's command, God asked him, "What prevented you from prostrating yourself before him whom I created with My own two hands?" (38:75). Many commentators hold that the "two hands" of God mentioned here refer to the two basic kinds of divine attributes, mercy and wrath, or *tashbih* and *tanzih*. Hence, the verse alludes to the fact that Adam was made in God's form. It suggests that other things were created with only one hand, or with God's word instead of his hands. A hadith confirms this interpretation:

> The angels said to God, "Our Lord, Thou hast created the children of Adam and appointed for them the present world, so appoint for us the next world."
> God replied, "I will not make My righteous servant—him whom I created with My own two hands—like him to whom I said, 'Be!' and he was."

Angels, then, were created through God's word "Be!" as were other things. Some commentators maintain that angels of mercy were created with God's right hand and angels of wrath with his left hand. Likewise, God created Iblis and the satans with his left hand. However this may be, the point of such discussions is to bring out the unique status of human beings, a uniqueness that stems from the fact that they were taught all the names. Because of their uniqueness, God sends the prophets to them, but not to the angels or to the animals. (The jinn, ambiguous as always, are able to follow human prophets.) The discussion of prophecy, to which we now turn, is really the discussion of the basic rights and responsibilities of human nature. The underlying question being addressed is, How can people become worthy of the name "human being"? In other words, How do they become God's servants and vicegerents?

Chapter 4

PROPHECY

ع&

THE MESSAGE OF THE PROPHETS

The Second Shahadah

The hadith of Gabriel tells us that Muslims must have faith in "His books and His messengers." The first pillar of Islam includes the verbal witnessing that "Muhammad is the messenger of God." Hence the hadith of Gabriel demands faith in all prophets, while the second Shahadah requires faith in the prophet Muhammad. The seeming contradiction is resolved by Muhammad's message. Having accepted that Muhammad is the messenger of God, Muslims accept the truth of the Koran, and the Koran repeatedly affirms that all God's books and messages are true.

Muslims understand the first Shahadah as expressing a universal truth, one that all human beings know intuitively because they were created in God's form and taught all the names. But the second Shahadah is different. It is connected specifically to Islam, since it expresses the prophecy of Muhammad and the truth of the Koran. If all true religions affirm the first Shahadah, each of them in addition sets down its own specific teachings derived from the message of its own prophet or prophets.

Every prophet speaks a language appropriate for the people to whom he is sent; that is, a language that corresponds with his people's background and world view. As the Koran says, "We have sent no messenger save with the tongue of his people" (14:4). Hence, the details of the message given to every prophet are different. "To every one of you [messengers] We have appointed a right way and an open road. If God had willed, He would have made you one nation" (5:48). But God did not will, because he created the universe for diversity. Hence, he made many nations. "Had your Lord willed, He would have made mankind one nation" (11:118).

Since the first Shahadah is the message of all prophets, religious differences rise up from the domain of the second Shahadah. The specific teachings of Muhammad—his "right way and open road"—are different from those of Moses, Jesus, Confucius, and Buddha. In effect, traditional Muslims have held that each prophet comes with the first Shahadah and with a second Shahadah specific to his own message.

Prophet and Messenger

We noted earlier that one of the meanings of the word *islam* is submission to the will of God as revealed through the prophets. Hence, to be a follower of any religion brought by a prophet is to be a *muslim*. Some Muslims will surely object that the religions brought by prophets other than Muhammad have become corrupted. We would reply that, if this is true, then the people who observe that religion are not in fact following the religion brought by a prophet, but rather a corruption of this religion. It needs to be added that the idea of the corruption of all religions except Islam is not a universal Islamic belief, although many Muslims think it is, and the actual teachings of the Koran on this point are much too subtle to allow for black and white distinctions. We will return to this point later.

The discussion of prophecy hinges on the idea of *nabi* (prophet). The word derives from a root that has two basic meanings: to utter a sound, as a dog's barking, and to become elevated. Most authorities derive it from the first sense of the root. When a dog barks, it lets us know that something unusual is happening. The active verbs from this root mean to inform, to give news. Thus the prophet is he who informs people about God. Other authorities maintain that the meaning of the term *nabi* derives from the second sense of the root; a prophet is someone who has been exalted and elevated by God. In any case, both ideas are present in the Islamic idea of a prophet. A person who becomes a prophet is not an ordinary person. On the contrary, prophets are exceptional human beings who have been chosen by God and given a message. Most often, it is the prophet's duty to pass on the message to other people, but it may happen that the message is a private one.

Although the English word *prophecy* suggests prediction of future events, the Arabic word has no such connotation. It may be that some prophetic messages refer to the future, but there is no necessary connection between the Islamic conception of prophecy and prediction of specific historical events. Very few verses of the Koran have been understood as referring to such events—although many of them do refer to the cataclysmic happenings that will bring about the end of time as we know it and prepare the way for the resurrection.

Hadiths tell us that from Adam down to Muhammad, God sent 124,000 prophets (some accounts say 224,000). Not all of these prophets established communities, but there are obviously enough prophets to allow for all the religions known to modern historians, with plenty to spare.

The Koran employs four main words to refer to prophets: *prophet, messenger (rasul); envoy (mursal);* and *possessors of steadfastness (ulu'l-'azm)*. Many authorities consider *messenger* and *envoy*, two words from the same root, as synonymous. Koranic usage suggests that the term *prophet* is wider in scope than the term *messenger*, and hadiths confirm this when they tell us that God sent 313 or 315 messengers.

Although opinions differ, the following distinctions are often drawn: Everyone chosen by God to receive a message is a prophet. Among the prophets, a relatively small number were chosen to establish religions, and these are called messengers. It is also said that the messengers are those prophets whose messages were detailed enough to be preserved as oral or written scriptures. The prophets modify or reform the religions established by the messengers, or they explain the meaning of their scriptures. For example, Abraham was a messenger, while Isaac, Ishmael, Jacob, and Joseph were prophets but not messengers. The first prophet and messenger was Adam, and the last was Muhammad. The identity of the first and the last prophets is highly significant for the Islamic view of things, as we will see.

A number of opinions are offered about the possessors of steadfastness. The most common opinion is that they are the five messengers who established the major religions of history (a history, of course, that is viewed from within the Judaeo-Christian-Islamic universe): Noah, Abraham, Moses, Jesus, and Muhammad.

The Trust

It is impossible to understand Islam's conception of prophecy without understanding its view of human beings; and likewise, we cannot grasp what a human being is until we grasp the role of prophets in human history.

The story begins with Adam, as it does in Judaism and Christianity, but the Koran's depiction of Adam diverges in important details from that of the Hebrew Bible. The result is an explanation of human nature that can be surprising—and even shocking—to people familiar only with certain Christian interpretations of Adam's fall.

We have already recounted some of the Koranic details of Adam's creation. Here we can provide a few more details that bring into focus Islam's understanding of what it means to be human. Remember that Adam is the first human being and the prototype for the whole race. What is said about Adam has something to do with the situation of everyone.

We learned earlier that human beings have specific characteristics that set them apart from other creatures. In one famous verse, the Koran refers to the sum total of these specific characteristics as "the Trust" (*amana*):

> We offered the Trust to the heavens and the earth and the mountains, but they refused to carry it and were afraid of it. And the human being carried it. Surely he is very ignorant, a great wrongdoer. (33:72)

In order to begin the task of understanding the sense of this verse, we have to remember that a trust is something precious that one person asks another person to hold for safekeeping. In this case, God has entrusted something to human beings, and they are to hold it for him. On the appropriate occasion, they will have to return it, as the word itself implies. The Koran says, "God commands you to deliver trusts back to their owners" (4:58).

What have human beings received on trust from God? Like all other created things, human beings have received everything they have from God. Nothing good belongs to them, since "The good, all of it, is in Thy hands." They will have to give back everything that they have, sooner or later, simply through the natural course of events. However, all creatures are *compelled* to give this kind of trust back to God, and human beings are no different here from anything else. Creatures are all *muslim* and *'abd* in the most general sense of the terms, so they have no choice but to give back to God what belongs to him. Hence, this compulsory trust is not at issue here, since choice does not enter into it. The verse of the Trust is apparently referring to some sort of free choice, and it clearly is talking about something that pertains exclusively to human beings.

The heavens, the earth, and the mountains refused to carry the Trust. The term *heavens* refers to the high and luminous things of the universe and *earth* to the low and dark things. *Mountains* seems to mean everything that is neither high nor low. These three terms can be understood as referring to everything other than human beings. Human beings are neither high like the angels, nor low like the minerals, nor in between like the plants and animals. Or rather, they possess all three qualities: They are high through their spirits, low through their bodies, and in between through their souls. As microcosms, they embrace the heavens, the earth, and the mountains.

In brief, most authorities maintain that the Trust is God's vicegerency. Only human beings are able to carry it because the vicegerency depends upon having been taught all the names. But it is not enough simply to be human to carry the Trust. People have to accept freely to be God's servants before they can become his vicegerents. Hence, carrying the Trust involves human freedom. Compulsory *muslims*—like the heavens, the earth, and the mountains—cannot carry it. One must be a voluntary *muslim* through accepting the guidance offered by God and putting it into practice.

The verse of the Trust concludes by saying that the human being "is very ignorant, a great wrongdoer." The most obvious interpretation of these qualities is that they refer to those children of Adam who do not live up to the Trust. All children of Adam have been given the Trust, but most of them pretend to be ignorant of the truth of their own situation, of the fact that they are, in essence, vicegerents of God. And they are wrongdoers; that is, they put things in the wrong places and overstep the bounds of what is true and right. They arrogate the power and prerogatives of the vicegerency to themselves. They do not treat the divine attributes that they have received from God as a trust. On the contrary, they act as if the attributes belong to themselves and can be used in any way they see fit.

Muslim thinkers have justified this Koranic picture of things in many ways, but we will limit ourselves to commenting on a single Koranic verse that they frequently cite in the context. Having created Adam, God wanted to make clear to him and to his children why they had been created. Hence, he gathered all the children of Adam together and spoke to them. The Koran reports what happened as follows:

> When your Lord took their offspring from the loins of the children
> of Adam and made them bear witness concerning themselves—
> "Am I not your Lord?"—they said, "Yes, we bear witness!" (7:172)

This verse indicates in mythic fashion that human beings, somewhere in the depths of their souls, have all borne witness to God's Lordship. The Arabic word employed for "we bear witness" is the verb from which the word *Shahadah* is derived. The event referred to here is commonly called the Covenant of Alast, the word *alast* being the Arabic for "Am I not?" At this time, all human beings entered into a covenant with God by acknowledging *tawhid* and agreeing to worship none but him.

It needs to be stressed that this intuitive knowledge of all human beings is the knowledge of *tawhid*, not the knowledge of the "right way and open road" that is specific to prophetic teachings. In other words, it pertains to the domain of the first Shahadah, not to that of the second Shahadah, which embraces specific instructions brought by the prophets. The first Shahadah is known by everyone, although they usually have to be reminded about it. In contrast, the truths embraced by the domain of the second Shahadah have to be learned through a divine message.

The verse of Alast continues by explaining God's purpose in calling everyone to witness:

> *Lest you say on the Day of Resurrection, "As for us, we were heed-less of this," or lest you say, "Our fathers associated others with God before us, and we were their offspring after them. What, wilt Thou destroy us for what the vain-doers did?" (7:172-73)*

Interpretations of this verse differ, but many authorities maintain that it means that on the day of judgment, people will be held responsible for recognizing the truth of *tawhid*, whether or not they have heard the message of a prophet. However, they will not be held responsible for the specific teachings of a prophet if such teachings have not reached them.

Innate Human Nature

The idea that human beings recognize *tawhid* innately is often expressed by using the term *fitra*, which is commonly translated as "primordial nature" or "innate disposition." The root meaning of the term is to split or to cleave, and hence it implies opening up and coming out. The verb also means to bring forth and to originate, and, in everyday language, to knead and shape dough. The Koran calls God the *fatir* of the heavens and the earth, which translators usually render as "creator" or "originator." But the meaning of the Arabic word is more concrete than these relatively abstract terms would suggest. One could argue that the expression means the "splitter of the heavens and the earth." This is not unconnected to a verse that employs the metaphor of tearing to explain how the universe was created: "Have not the truth-concealers beheld that the heavens and the earth were all bound up, and then We tore them apart, and out of water fashioned every living thing?" (21:30). This verse of tearing, like the expression *"fatir* of the heavens and the earth," presents us with a picture found in myths from all over the globe. God created the cosmos by separating heaven and earth. Before their separation, everything was uniform and indistinct. To use the Greek expression, there was nothing but chaos; that is, there was no order and no beauty, the two basic senses of the Greek word *cosmos* (from which we also have *cosmetics*). By separating heaven and earth, God brought distinct things into existence.

Heaven, as we have remarked more than once, refers to everything high, luminous, subtle, and active, while earth refers to everything low, dark, dense, and receptive. Once the two are separate, God can let down the water of life from the high realm and bring living things into existence in the low realm. Before the separation, there can be no distinct and discreet things.

The Koran employs the word *fitra* itself only once, along with the verb form of the word. Here we translate the verb as "bring forth." The Koran is addressing Muhammad and, by extension, every Muslim:

> *Set thy face to the religion as one with primordial faith—the* fitra *of God according to which He brought people forth. There is no changing the creation of God. That is the right religion, but most people do not know. [Set thy face to the religion] by turning to Him. And be wary of Him, and perform the* salat, *and be not one of those who associate others with Him. (30:30-31)*

Here the Koran connects religion with the nature that human beings were given when they were created. By being human, they have accepted the Trust and entered into the Covenant of Alast. They were taught the names, created in God's form, and singled out for God's vicegerency. But human freedom is also at issue here. Although human beings have accepted to carry the Trust, most of them turn away from it and become "very ignorant, great wrongdoers." Most of them do not know that carrying the Trust is the right religion, the correct and authentically human path.

To be voluntary *muslim*s, people must turn their "faces" toward God. The Arabic word for *face* is employed for the reality and essence of a thing. The Koran is saying that people should turn their full attention and total being toward God. In other words, they should establish the relationship of *tawhid* and not associate anyone with God. This involves observing the Five Pillars, represented here by the *salat*, and it also involves actualizing Islam's third dimension, to which the expression "to be wary of God" refers.

The Prophet employed the term *fitra* in a famous hadith that encapsulates the Islamic understanding of the term:

> *Every child is born according to* fitra. *Then its parents make it into a Christian, a Jew, or a Zoroastrian.*

This saying suggests that the innate human nature coincides with Islam. Because of the Trust and the Covenant of Alast, people come into the world recognizing the truth of *tawhid*. Then their upbringing and environment distort their original disposition and, instead of serving God alone, they associate other realities with him. If they were to return to their true nature, they would come back to *tawhid*.

One should not conclude from this hadith that Islam considers all non-Muslims as truth-concealers. Certainly the Prophet is implying that the three religions mentioned here have deviated from the straight path of *tawhid*. But other sayings and Koranic verses have to be taken into account before we can draw any final conclusions concerning Islamic beliefs about non-Muslims. We will see in a later section that there is no clear dogma on these points, and that there cannot be, because non-Muslims—like Muslims—may be good or bad, truth-concealing or faithful, right or wrong. But as a general rule, Muslims take the position that followers of any religion take: Our perspective is the right perspective, and other perspectives do not measure up to it. This is as normal for a religion as the fact that you say "I," and you consider your "I" more real and relevant to life than the "I" uttered by your neighbor or by people further afield. It takes a great person indeed to live up to the Christian commandment to love your neighbor as yourself, not to speak of loving people whom you have never met.

Adam and Iblis

The Trust, the Covenant of Alast, and *fitra* all suggest that human beings possess a grand responsibility before both God and his creation, and the Islamic version of the myth of Adam confirms this picture. God taught Adam all the names and commanded the angels to prostrate themselves before him, indicating that this knowledge of the names made Adam greater even than the angels, the most exalted and elevated of God's creatures.

The Koran does not mention the creation of Eve, though the hadith literature follows the Biblical account, according to which she was created from Adam's rib. The Koran does tell us that God placed Adam and Eve in the Garden and gave them instructions as to how they were to live there:

> We said, "Adam, dwell, you and your wife, in the Garden, and eat thereof easefully wherever you desire. But do not come near this tree, lest you be wrongdoers."
> Then Satan caused them to slip therefrom and brought them out of what they were in. (2:35-36)

In the Garden, Adam and Eve's *islam* was to obey the instructions issued by God. They could follow their own desires, so long as they did not approach the tree. Thus we see that human beings, from the moment of their creation, were given freedom and guidance by God. Because of their freedom, they were able to ignore God's guidance. Iblis was present, and he led the two of them astray.

Remember that Iblis had refused to prostrate himself before Adam. When God asked Iblis why he refused, he said, "I am better than he. You created me of fire, and You created him of clay" (7:12, 38:76).

Because of Iblis's disobedience, God sent him down into the earth. But the conversation that takes place between God and Iblis at this point is highly significant for the Islamic understanding of Satan's role in the cosmos. Without thinking about this conversation, we will not be able to grasp the full importance of Adam's fall from the Garden. The dialogue between God and Iblis continues as follows:

> Said He, "Go down out of it. It is not for you to claim greatness here. So go forth, surely you are among the humbled."
> Said he, "Respite me until the day when they are resurrected."
> Said He, "You are among the respited."
> Said he, "Now, because You have led me astray, I shall surely sit in ambush for them on Your straight path. Then I shall come on them from before them and from behind them, from their right hands and their left hands. You will not find most of them grateful."
> Said He, "Go forth from it, despised and banished. Those of them that follow you—I shall assuredly fill Gehenna [i.e., hell] with all of you." (7:13-18)

The Koran adds details to this dialogue in several places. The following seems especially pertinent to the present discussion:

> Said he, "My Lord, because You have led me astray, I shall make the earth seem fair to them and I shall lead all of them astray, except the sincere among Your servants."
> Said He, "This is for Me a straight path: As for My servants, you shall have no authority over them, except those who follow you, going astray. Gehenna is the promised place for all of them." (15:39-43)

This account explains how Satan came to be an enemy of human beings. His motivation is pride, anger, and envy. He is proud because of his fiery nature and high degree among created things. He is angry at God for asking him to prostrate himself before a mere handful of clay. He is envious of Adam because God has shown him special favor. Moreover, it never occurred to Iblis that perhaps God knew something that he did not. He failed to recognize that he himself could be at fault, so he blamed God for his predicament.

One of the most interesting elements in this Koranic account is the bargain that Iblis strikes with God. He asks not to be taken to account until the Day of Resurrection, and God gives him what he wants. Then Iblis says that he will lead all God's servants astray (using the same word that he used when he told God, "You have led me astray"), but the Koran alludes here to Iblis's incapacity and weakness, because Iblis adds, "except those who are sincere." God replies to Iblis that he can do what he wants, but he also stresses that Iblis has no power over good *muslims*. In short, God is involved with Iblis's scheming from the outset.

In reading Christian accounts of Satan, one often gets the impression that Satan is out of control. He has rebelled and set up an empire of his own, where God's laws are not followed. In extreme cases, it seems as if Iblis is a god of evil—doomed to be defeated in the end, to be sure—but free to do as he likes in the meantime.

Islam is too infused with the idea of *tawhid* to allow Iblis to play any sort of independent role. Even Iblis is a *muslim*, though only in the broadest sense of the term. He is a compulsory servant of God, not a voluntary servant. His pride and arrogance, his conviction that "I am better than he," do not allow him to see that he is doing God's work just like everyone else.

When the account of Iblis is read carefully in the full Koranic context, it is easy to understand that one of the central issues is human free will. To begin with, without the error and misguidance that Iblis represents, there can be no wrong choices; or more exactly, there can be no choices whatsoever. For human beings the existence of Iblis sets up a contrast between right and wrong, true and false, guidance and misguidance, salvation and damnation. If there were no wrong path, how could there be a right path?

We saw earlier that in order to create a universe, God separated heaven and earth, the high and the low, the bright and the dark, the subtle and the dense, the light and the heavy. Without these distinctions, there is nothing that can be differentiated from anything else, nor can any created things exist.

The contrast between light and darkness has a physical meaning, but it also has an immaterial meaning, as we pointed out. Light refers to all the divine qualities, while darkness refers to the lack of these same divine qualities. And light has a moral and spiritual meaning, which is to say that it pertains to illumination, knowledge, guidance, and salvation. In contrast, darkness pertains to ignorance, misguidance, and loss. It is sometimes said in Islamic texts that at the end of time, fire will be divided into two parts. Its luminosity will ascend to paradise, but its heat will flow down into hell. Hell is a place of painful, burning darkness, while paradise is a domain of liberating, refreshing light.

In short, Iblis incarnates the darkness of error, ignorance, arrogance, and wrongdoing. Without the powers that Iblis represents, there could be no moral universe. We could not choose the right, because there would be no wrong whereby the right could be distinguished. We could not be saved, because there would be no error and loss to define the nature of damnation and salvation. We could not enter the light, because there would be no darkness to leave. We could not even exist, because our existence depends upon the ambiguity of our situation. Our human status is defined by the fact that we hang midway between light and darkness, heaven and earth, spirit and body.

Iblis represents wrongdoing and evil, but Muslims—at least thoughtful Muslims—also recognize that he was created by God precisely for the work that he does. He is merely doing his job. It is his role in creation to be arrogant, angry, and envious. Hence, God has measured out to him a great deal of such wrathful divine attributes as mightiness and magnificence, but little wisdom or sense of proportion. The Koran itself alludes to this in various verses. When it quotes Iblis as uttering the oath, "Now, by Your mightiness, I will lead all of them astray" (38:82), it connects him to God's name Mighty. When the Koran says that Iblis "claimed greatness," it associates him with the divine name, *al-mutakabbir*—the Great, the Magnificent. Iblis performs a function that is intimately connected to the names of wrath.

Before continuing the discussion of Iblis's nature, let us come back to Adam and Eve. We left the story when Iblis "caused them to slip" in the Garden. People often ask what Iblis was doing in the Garden. By now it should be clear that to be human is to be faced with the choice between right and wrong, obedience and disobedience. God would not have commanded Adam to avoid the tree if he did not want wrongdoing to be a possibility. By commanding Adam, God acknowledged the compact between himself and Iblis. He knew that Iblis would attempt to lead people astray (and he knew, of course, that Iblis would succeed, on one level at least).

When Adam and Eve ate the fruit of the tree, they became aware of their nakedness and took to covering their private parts with leaves from the trees. Here there is a clear parallel with the Biblical idea that the tree was that of the knowledge of good and evil.

By eating the forbidden fruit, "Adam disobeyed his Lord" (20:121). God then said to Adam and Eve, "Did I not prohibit you two from this tree and say to you, 'Verily, Satan is for you two an open enemy'?" (7:22). Their reaction, significantly, resembles that of someone woken from a dream. They were immediately shocked at what they had done, and with one voice "The two of them said, 'We have wronged ourselves, and unless You forgive us and have mercy on us, we shall surely be among the lost'" (7:23). The Koranic account does not allow for ascription of blame to Adam rather than Eve, or vice versa. Both of them slipped, and both of them acknowledged their error and asked to be forgiven.

At this point God sends Adam and Eve down into the earth, telling them that they would find enmity there:

> "Go down, each of you an enemy to each. In the earth a sojourn shall be yours, and enjoyment for a time. . . . Therein you shall live, and therein you shall die, and from there you shall be brought forth." (7:24-25)

The Fall

The word *fall* in the Christian context has a rather negative connotation, while the corresponding term in Arabic, *hubut*, is derived from the verses where God addresses Adam and Eve and tells them to "go down." Muslim thinkers recognize the negative sides of this event. After all, it resulted from disobedience. It was a slip caused by Satan. But rarely do they refer to the fall in terms that would conjure up anything similar to the Christian idea of original sin. Adam and Eve slipped, and as a result, God told them to leave the Garden and go down into the earth.

In the Islamic perspective, it would be wrong to conclude that Adam and Eve would have been better off if they had not slipped. First, everything is measured out. God's wisdom and mercy make sure that everything comes out for the best. Second, God said at the very beginning of Adam's creation, "I am placing in the earth a vicegerent" (2:30). He created Adam for the earth, not for the Garden. The "going down" is a going down *into the earth*. The Garden was situated somewhere else, apparently above the earth. What is above the earth has heavenly qualities, not earthly qualities. It is high, luminous, subtle, and so on.

The general Islamic understanding of Adam's coming down into the earth is captured beautifully by a hadith:

> Moses said, *"My Lord, show me Adam, who brought us and himself out of the Garden."*
>
> *So God showed him Adam. Moses said, "Are you our father Adam?" He said that he was. Moses said, "Are you the one into whom God blew of His own spirit, whom He taught all the names, and before whom He commanded the angels to prostrate themselves, and they did so?" Adam replied that he was. Then Moses said, "What made you bring us and yourself out of the Garden?"*
>
> *Adam replied, "Who are you?" Moses told him. Adam said, "Are you the prophet of the Children of Israel to whom God spoke from behind the veil and whom he appointed to be a messenger from among His creatures?" Moses replied that he was. Adam said, "Did you not find that [my slip] was written in the Book of God before I was created?" Moses replied that it was. Then Adam said, "Then why do you reproach me for something that God had decreed for me before my existence?"*

The Prophet concluded this account by repeating three times, for emphasis, "So Adam won the argument with Moses!" We can conclude that, in general, Muslims believe that the fall may have had certain negative consequences, but these were all part of the divine plan. Without the fall, Adam could not have been God's vicegerent in the earth. In Christian terms, eating the fruit was a *felix culpa*, a "fortunate sin."

Remember that vicegerency depends upon servanthood. Servanthood in turn depends upon standing in a proper relationship with the names of *tanzih* and majesty. In order to be proper servants, people must acknowledge their distance from God and recognize his wrath, severity, magnificence, inaccessibility, and incomprehensibility. However, these attributes cannot be recognized if people see only the merciful and loving face of God. That is why some Muslim thinkers have said that God put Adam and Eve into the Garden so that they could gain strength for the hardships that would follow once they were placed at a great distance from God, in the earth. As long as they remained in the Garden, they were close to God, and he sometimes spoke to them. They experienced his nearness, his beauty, and his gentleness. But once they entered into the earth, they would be far from God, and hence they would have to face up to the consequences of his majestic and wrathful qualities. In order to attain to the full possibilities of human perfection, they had to taste his distance as well as his nearness. To establish *tawhid*, human beings must experience both the attributes of *tashbih* and those of *tanzih*.

In the general Christian perspective, the negative consequences of Adam's fall are epitomized by the idea of original sin. So fundamental was the corruption in Adam's nature brought about by his eating the fruit and disobeying God, that God had to incarnate himself as Christ in order to rectify the divine image. In contrast, there is no concept of original sin in Islam, because God immediately forgave Adam and Eve for eating the fruit. Not only that, but "His Lord chose him" (20:122); that is, God appointed Adam as a prophet. That is why the Koran says, "God elected Adam, Noah, the House of Abraham, and the House of Imran above all the world's inhabitants" (3:33). This then marks a fundamental divergence between the Islamic and Christian views of human nature. The first human being slipped and fell, like all of us do, but in contrast to us, he fell only once. Moreover, he immediately repented and was forgiven. God then appointed him a prophet and kept him free from error and sin. Far from being someone who caused us to suffer, he is the model of human perfection. If people could live up to their father Adam and their mother Eve, they would have nothing to fear. Adam's entrance into the earth as vicegerent and prophet is a sign that God's mercy takes precedence over his wrath, and that his guidance overcomes the misguidance of Satan.

Heedlessness

If Islam does not have a concept of original sin, this does not mean that Muslims believe that everything is fine and people can simply continue on as they were. If that were the case, why would God bother to send 124,000 prophets? Clearly, something was amiss and needed to be rectified.

It is true that the innate human disposition demands the recognition of *tawhid*, but many people associate others with God. What then is the problem? One answer is "Iblis." But that needs some clarification, and we will return to it shortly. Another answer can be found by looking at the function of prophecy. What are the prophets trying to do? If we can understand that, we will have identified the problem that needs solving.

We have already suggested that the message of the prophets has two levels, represented in Islamic terms by the two Shahadahs. The primary message of the prophets is *tawhid*, while the secondary message is that people must follow God's instructions in order to establish the full implications of *tawhid* in their lives.

If the human *fitra* already recognizes *tawhid*, why do the prophets need to speak about it? In one word, the answer is "heedlessness" (*ghafla*). The Koran uses this word as a near synonym for "forgetfulness" (*nisyan*). Iblis rebelled because of pride and arrogance, but Adam slipped because he forgot. "And We made covenant with Adam before, but he forgot, and We found in him no constancy" (20:115). The fundamental difference between Adam and Iblis comes out in their responses to God when he questioned them about their disobedience. Iblis refused to admit that he had done anything wrong and blamed God for leading him astray. Adam and Eve recognized at once that they were at fault, and therefore they asked God to forgive them. Hence, human forgetfulness is one thing, but Satanic refusal to recognize one's own shortcomings is something quite different.

This does not mean that forgetfulness and heedlessness are without blame. On the contrary, they are the fundamental fault of human beings. Hence, they play a role that has certain analogies with original sin in Christianity. To forget God is to forget *tawhid*, and without *tawhid* there can be no salvation.

As noted earlier, the Koran tells us that God can forgive anything except *shirk*, the association of others with him. By forgetting God, people put others in his place. They attribute his qualities to themselves and to the forces of nature and society. They do not know that the whole universe sings his praises and displays his signs. Hence, forgetfulness and heedlessness are in certain ways equivalent to *shirk*. In the following passage, God describes the types of people and jinn who go to hell, and he identifies their sin as heedlessness:

> *We have created for Gehenna many jinn and men. They have hearts, but understand not with them. They have eyes, but see not with them. They have ears, but hear not with them. They are like cattle—no, they are further astray. Those—they are the heedless.* (7:179)

Notice that such people have all the means to see and understand, but they make no use of them. What is it that they should be seeing and hearing? The signs of God. Such people see the natural world, but they do not understand that everything is a sign of God. They hear the sacred texts being recited, but they do not recognize God speaking to them:

Surely many people are heedless of Our signs. (10:92)

*Those who are heedless of Our signs, those—their refuge is the
Fire. (10:7-8)*

When people recognize the signs of God, they consider human existence
in its full scope. They remember where people have come from and
where they are going. Those who ignore the signs are engrossed in the
outward appearances of the present world: "They know an outward
part of the life of this world, but of the next world they are heedless"
(30:7).

Death, as we will see, is a great awakening to reality. From then on,
people can no longer ignore the true meaning of what they see and hear.
No matter how much they would like to return to their blissful ignorance, they will be forced to look at the realities of things. Two angels
will take them before God:

*And every soul will come, with it a driver and a witness. "You were
heedless of this. Therefore We have now removed from you your
covering, so your sight today is piercing."...*
    *"Cast into Gehenna, you two, every stubborn truth-concealer, ev-
ery hinderer of the good, transgressor, doubter, who set up another
god with God!" (50:21-26)*

The Koran and the tradition confirm the close connection between the
fire of hell and forgetfulness in many ways. A number of verses make
this connection especially explicit:

*Today We forget you, just as you forgot the encounter of this day,
and your refuge is the Fire. (45:34)*

*So now taste, because you forgot the encounter of this your day!
We indeed have forgotten you. Taste the chastisement of eternity
for what you were doing! (32:14)*

We said that forgetfulness and heedlessness are fundamental faults
because they negate *tawhid*. One could equally say that to forget God
is to forget oneself, since the human being is the form of God. To lose
touch with God is to lose touch with one's own reality and hence to fall
into unreality, which can only be experienced as painful separation
from everything that is real and good. The Koran alludes to this
perspective in the verse, "Be not as those who forgot God, and so He
caused them to forget themselves. Those—they are the transgressors"
(59:19).

Dhikr

If forgetfulness and heedlessness mark the basic fault of human beings, *dhikr* (remembrance) designates their saving virtue. Just as forgetting God leads to the painful chastisement of being forgotten by him, so also remembering God leads to the joy of being remembered by him: "Remember Me, and I will remember you" (2:152). But *dhikr* means much more than simply the proper human response to God, since it also designates the function of the prophets.

The word *dhikr* has three basic senses: mentioning, remembering, and reminding. To mention something with the tongue is to recall it to the mind, to remember it. And if others are present when you mention something and they already know something about it, then they are reminded of it. The English word *remembrance* also means "an act of recalling to mind" as well as "reminder."

The three senses of *dhikr* are inseparably bound together. God sends the prophets in order to remind people of the Covenant of Alast. They do so by reciting God's signs and mentioning their debt to him. People should respond to the prophets by remembering God, an act which demands that they mention him in prayers of glorification and praise (thus affirming both his *tanzih* and his *tashbih*). Those who respond in this manner are the people of faith, since to have faith is to recognize or remember the truth of *tawhid* in the heart, to mention it with the tongue, and to put it into practice by following the instructions brought by the prophets.

Those people who fail to make the correct response are the truth-concealers. Although they recognize the truth in their hearts, they deny it with their tongues and refuse to follow the prophets' instructions. This, in short, is the drama of prophecy and the human response. All of it is connected explicitly by the Koran to the word *dhikr*, or to closely related words derived from the same root (such as *dhikra*, *tadhkira*, and *tadhakkur*). Here are a few of the many Koranic examples. The first two verses bring out the idea that God's messages to people are reminders:

> *We gave Moses the guidance, and We made the Children of Israel heirs to the Book as a guidance and a reminder to people possessed of minds. (40:53-54)*

> *This is only a Reminder and a Clear Koran. (36:69)*

The correct human response to God's reminders is remembrance. The Koran commands remembering God or remembering his name (which is equivalent to mentioning his name through prayer) in many verses. The result of remembering God is not only to be remembered by God in the next world, but also to achieve peace of heart in this world:

*O you who have faith! Remember God often, and glorify Him at
dawn and in the evening. (33:41)*

*Remember the name of thy Lord at dawn and in the evening and
part of the night; prostrate thyself before Him and glorify Him
through the long night. (76:25-26)*

When the salat *is finished, scatter in the land and seek God's
bounty, and remember God often. (62:10)*

*God guides unto Himself all those who turn toward Him, those
who have faith, their hearts being at rest in God's remembrance—
verily in God's remembrance do hearts find rest. Those who have
faith and do wholesome deeds—theirs is blessedness and a beautiful homecoming. (13:28-29)*

The wrong human response to the prophetic reminders is to deny the
truth of the messages and to carry on business as usual. Looking at the
situation from a slightly different perspective, we can say that becoming preoccupied with all one's worldly affairs and responsibilities is a
sure way to fall into heedlessness:

*Who is a greater wrongdoer than he who is reminded of the signs
of his Lord and then turns away from them? (18:57, 32:22)*

*Woe to those whose hearts are hardened against the remembrance
of God! (39:22)*

*O you who have faith, among your wives and children is an enemy
to you. . . . Your wealth and your children are only a trial. (64:14-15)*

To forget God is to follow the deceptions of Satan, since human forgetfulness is precisely what Satan is striving to achieve. After that, people
are playthings in his hand. But again, Satan is not acting independently
of God, because God himself turns forgetful people over to him and his
minions:

*Whoso blinds himself to the remembrance of the Merciful, to him
We assign a satan who is then his comrade. (43:36)*

*O you who have faith! Let not your possessions, neither your chil-
dren, divert you from God's remembrance. Whoso does that—they
are the losers. (63:9)*

At this point we perhaps need to stress what is at issue in these verses
by recalling the Islamic understanding of human nature: To be human

is to be born with the *fitra*, which is an innate recognition of *tawhid* that is represented mythically by the Covenant of Alast and the Trust. There is nothing extraneous or superadded about this *fitra*—it is precisely what makes people human. But the *fitra* tends to become obscured by upbringing and circumstances, and then people become less than human. They are "deaf, dumb, blind—like the cattle; no, even further astray." *Dhikr* is the all-important remedy that makes possible the actualization of the *fitra*. *Dhikr* is both God's merciful response to heedlessness, and the human response to God's mercy.

In summarizing the importance of *dhikr*, we quote one final Koranic passage that has special significance because it is God's words directed to Adam when he sent him down into the earth. This passage represents God's initial instructions to his servants and vicegerents in the earth. It epitomizes the Islamic view of the contents of the prophetic messages, and the contents of the Koran:

> [After Adam forgot and disobeyed God], his Lord chose him and turned again toward him, and He guided him.
> Said He, "Go down out of it, you two, all together, each of you an enemy to each. Whenever guidance comes to you from Me, then whosoever follows My guidance shall not be misguided, neither shall he be wretched. But whosoever turns away from My remembrance, his shall be a life of narrowness, and on the Day of Resurrection, We shall raise him blind. He shall say, 'O my Lord, why have You raised me blind, when I used to be seeing?'
> "God shall say, 'Even so it is. Our signs came to you, and you forgot them. And so today you are forgotten.'" (20:122-26)

Responding to the Signs of God

The prophets and messengers bring God's signs, just as the heavens and the earth and everything within them display his signs. The proper human response is to remember. The Koran employs a large number of other words that suggest what remembrance involves, such as hearing, seeing, pondering, taking heed, and using the intelligence. The point is always that to be human is not to be misled by appearances. One must understand this world in the context of *tawhid*. The message of the prophets is the message of the whole of existence: People were created to be God's servants and vicegerents.

Each of the words that the Koran employs to indicate the proper human response to the signs has specific implications. Here, of course, we cannot analyze all these words. But we can quote a few representative passages to suggest the flavor of the Koranic text:

This is the path of your Lord, straight. We have differentiated the signs for a people who remember. (6:126)

Even so We list the signs for a people who are grateful. (7:58)

Even so does God make clear the signs for you, so that perhaps you may reflect. (2:266)

Now We have made clear to you the signs, if you have intelligence. (3:118)

Behold how We list the signs so that perhaps they will understand. (6:65)

We have differentiated the signs for a people who know. (6:97)

In that are signs for a people who have faith. (6:99)

In the alternation of night and day, and what God has created in the heavens and the earth—surely there are signs for a people who are god-wary. (10:6)

It is He who made for you the night to rest in, and the day, to see; surely in that are signs for a people who hear. (10:67)

He differentiated the signs. Perhaps you will gain certainty of the encounter with your Lord. (13:2)

Surely in that are signs for everyone patient and grateful. (14:5)

You will not guide the blind out of their error, neither will you make any to hear, except those who have faith in Our signs, and so are muslims. (27:81)

Just as remembering and heeding the signs is a mark of those who have faith, ignoring them and turning away from them is a mark of the truth-concealers. All the positive qualities of human nature appear through remembrance, and all the negative qualities arise as a result of forgetfulness and denial:

Many people are heedless of Our signs. (10:92)

We have sent down on you signs, clear explications, and none conceals their truth but the transgressors. (2:99)

Look how We make clear the signs to them, then look how they are turned away! (5:75)

Who does greater wrong than he who cries lies to God's signs and turns away from them? (6:157)

Who does greater wrong than he who, reminded of the signs of his Lord, turns away from them and forgets what his hands have sent forward? (18:57)

Woe to every guilty impostor who hears the signs of God being recited to him, then perseveres in claiming greatness, as if he has not heard them! (45:7-8)

Those who cry lies to Our signs are deaf and dumb, dwelling in the darknesses. (6:39)

None denies Our signs but the wrongdoers. (29:49)

Those who cry lies to Our signs and claim greatness in face of them—the gates of heaven shall not be opened to them. (7:40)

Guidance and Misguidance

If *dhikr* represents both the function of the prophets and the proper human response to the prophets, guidance (*huda*) represents the divine attribute that is embodied in the prophets. It sums up in a single word both God's motivation for sending the prophets and their activity in the world. If the opposite of *dhikr* is forgetfulness and heedlessness, the opposite of guidance is misguidance (*idlal*) and leading astray (*ighwa'*). Just as the prophets incarnate God's guidance, so also the satans incarnate the quality of misguidance and error.

To guide people is to lead them on a path to a goal. The path in question here is the specific instructions given to each of the messengers or, more specifically, the Shariah given to Muhammad. The goal to which the path leads is salvation or paradise.

We will discuss the nature of salvation in detail when we talk about the Return. For now, we can say that salvation is human happiness on the basis of actualized *fitra*. To be happy is to be fully oneself. Human selfhood is defined by the divine form in which people were created. Hence, happiness and fulfillment depend upon knowing the names that were taught to Adam and living in accordance with their implications.

One of the Koranic names of God is Guide. Hence the formula of *tawhid* demands that "There is no guide but God." All guidance belongs to God, and the prophets simply function as God's representatives. The

Koran and other scriptures are the oral and written forms of God's guidance:

> *God is ever the Guide of those who have faith unto a straight path. (22:54)*

> *Your Lord suffices as a guide and a helper. (25:31)*

> *Say: "Verily God's guidance—that is guidance!" (2:120, 3:73, 6:71)*

> *Whomsoever God guides—he is the guided. (7:178)*

> *He sent down the Torah and the Gospel before, as guidance to the people. (3:4)*

> *These are the signs of the Koran and a Clear Book, a guidance and good tidings to those who have faith. (27:2)*

> *Upon those rest blessings and mercy from their Lord, and those— they are the guided. (2:157)*

God's guidance is tied to his mercy, as this last verse makes explicit. When God guides people, he brings them under the sway of the names of mercy, gentleness, and beauty. The result of guidance is nearness to God, and the Koran refers to those who inhabit the highest degrees of paradise as "those brought near." Nearness to God depends upon *tawhid*, through which human beings establish the right relationship with the Real.

In contrast to guidance, misguidance is closely associated with wrath and severity. Those who go astray turn away from God, not towards him. Hence, they fall into ever greater distance from him. They become more and more overcome by dispersion, multiplicity, separation, disconnectedness, disharmony, and dissolution. To be distant from God is to be under the sway of the divine names that designate his incomparability, inaccessibility, difference, and otherness.

What is the source of misguidance? At first glance, we have to say that it is Satan, the archenemy of human beings. The Koran quotes the prophet Moses as saying, "This is of Satan's doing. He is surely an enemy, a clear misguider" (28:15).

On the Day of Resurrection, the Koran tells us, God will command the sinners to stay in the distance from him that they have chosen:

> *Now, on this day, keep yourselves apart, you sinners! Did I not make a covenant with you, Children of Adam, that you should not worship Satan—surely he is a clear enemy to you—and that you should worship Me? This is a straight path. But he misguided a*

great throng of you. Did you not understand? This is Gehenna,
then, the same that you were promised! (36:59-63)

Besides Satan, others are also said to be the source of misguidance. Among these is caprice, which we have already met as the worst of all false gods: "Follow not caprice, lest it misguide you from the path of God" (38:26). The overall Koranic picture of caprice allows us to say that it represents Satan within ourselves. All of us experience the wind of caprice, which blows us this way and that, though it always blows away from God's guidance. The opposite of caprice is intelligence (*'aql*), and intelligence is understood as the luminous, angelic faculty within us that recognizes God's guidance when it sees it. Intelligence, it is sometimes said, is a prophet within the human soul.

Among human beings, the Koran singles out Pharaoh as a misguider. This is not surprising, given that the Koranic Pharaoh possesses all the qualities of Satan, especially an enormous pride. Just as Moses is mentioned by name 136 times in the Koran, far more than any other prophet, so also Pharaoh, Moses' archenemy, is mentioned seventy-four times, far more than any other wrongdoer. In effect, the Koranic descriptions of his activities summarize all the bad qualities that human beings can possess. Sufficient argument against him is the fact that he claimed divinity for himself by saying, "I am your Lord the Most High" (79:24). But all human beings who follow caprice as their god make the same claim, since caprice is simply their own selfhood.

By attributing misguidance to caprice and Pharaoh, the Koran is, in effect, attributing it to Satan, since caprice and Pharaoh incarnate all the qualities of Satan. But caprice represents Satan within the human soul, while Pharaoh represents him in human society.

The Koran makes clear that Satan is the grand enemy of human beings, referring to him as their enemy in a dozen verses. However, it is quite significant that the Koran never refers to Satan as the enemy of God, although it does imply that he is God's enemy, since it calls the truth-concealers God's enemies. But the Koran easily could have called Satan the enemy of God, since it often calls him the enemy of human beings. This suggests that the Koran is alluding to a point that we have already discussed. Although Iblis disobeyed God, he is still doing God's work by making possible the choice between good and evil. People can have no worse enemy than Satan, because he leads them to hell. But hell also is a creature of God, created for a purpose. The Koran makes clear that even hell has its rights:

Upon the day We shall say to Gehenna, "Art thou filled?" And it
shall say, "Are there any more?" (50:30)

Without Satan, hell would have no inhabitants. So also, without the choices made possible by Satan, there would be no moral domain, since there could be no distinction between good and evil.

The Koran, in fact, explicitly attributes misguidance to God himself. In only five verses does it ascribe misguidance directly to Satan; but in more than thirty verses, it makes God the subject of the verb *to misguide*.

God misguides whom He will and He guides whom He will. (14:4, 74:31)

Whomsoever God guides—he is the guided; and whomsoever He misguides—they are the losers. (7:178)

Whomsoever God misguides, no guide has he. (7:186, 13:33, 39:23)

Some Muslim theologians have always taken pains to interpret this attribution of misguidance to God in ways that protect their idea of what is proper and improper for God. Apparently they have felt that God needs to be defended against people's suspicions, or perhaps they simply feel that God does not mean what he says, since his words go against their ideas of morality. But many Muslim thinkers of classical times had no qualms about letting the Koran say what it is saying. They even drew the conclusion that Misguider (*al-mudill*) is a name of God along with Guide. Of course this point raises sensitive theological issues, and since we have mentioned it, we have no choice but to make some attempt to address them. But first, let us look at the manner in which the Koran attributes misguidance to God.

Guidance is strictly God's attribute, since there is no guide but God. Although the prophets make this divine attribute manifest through the messages that they bring, they have no power to guide people on their own. Lesser mortals are clearly in no position to guide others, given that the prophets themselves cannot do so. The prophets have been given messages to deliver, but guidance itself is God's business:

Obey God, and obey the Messenger, and be cautious. But if you turn your backs, then know that it is only for Our Messenger to deliver the clear message. (5:92)

If they turn their backs, thine is only to deliver the message. (3:20)

This is not to say that Muhammad and the other prophets are not guides. Of course they are. "And thou, surely thou guidest unto a straight path" (42:52). However, Muhammad guides as God's messenger, not as a human being who has personal wishes:

Who shall guide those whom God has misguided? (30:29)

Thou guidest not whom thou likest, but God guides whom He wills, and He knows very well those that are guided. (28:56)

What, shalt thou make the deaf to hear, or shalt thou guide the blind and him who is clearly misguided? (43:40)

What, do you desire to guide him whom God has misguided? Whom God misguides—thou wilt not find for him a way. (4:88)

If on the one hand the Koran attributes misguidance to God, on the other it lays the blame for misguidance on those who are misguided, since God only misguides the wrongdoers:

God would never misguide a people after He guided them until He makes clear to them how they should be god-wary. (9:115)

Even so, God misguides the truth-concealers. (40:74)

Even so, God misguides him who is a doubting dissipater. (40:34)

Thus, God's misguidance is directed against those who have no faith, those who actively and consciously conceal the truth of the prophetic messages and display ingratitude for the blessings God has given them. The wrongdoers cannot blame God for misguiding them, nor can they blame Satan. The Koran reports that on the day of resurrection, Satan will address his followers with these words:

God surely promised you a true promise, and I promised you. Then I failed you, for I had no authority over you. I simply called you, and you answered me. So do not blame me, but blame your-selves. (14:22)

Wrongdoing

That human beings are themselves to blame for their own misfortune in the next world is a constant theme of the Koran. Take, for example, the idea of wrongdoing (*zulm*), which is one of the most common and general terms employed by the Koran to refer to all the negative acts performed by human beings. We said earlier that wrongdoing is the opposite of justice, and that justice is to put everything in its proper place. Hence, wrongdoing is to put things where they do not belong. It is, for example, to associate others with God. The others do not belong in the place of divinity. It is to put false words in the place of true words, or to put someone else's property in the place of your own. It is to put a forbidden or permissible act in the place of an incumbent act as, for example, by doing something else instead of performing the required *salat*.

Against whom does one do wrong? First, it is impossible to wrong God, since all things are his creatures and all things perform his work. Hence, wrongdoing is an activity directed against people, for example. However, you might ask, How can I wrong others by not performing a *salat* that is between me and God? If there is any wrong involved, am I not wronging God? In the Koranic perspective, this is not the case at all. The only person who is wronged in such a situation is oneself.

God has no need for his creatures. What does God want with a bunch of people standing and bowing and mumbling words that they do not understand? God has not prescribed the Shariah for his good, but for the good of human beings. It is they who are being helped, since he is gradually leading them into harmony with what is good and real. When they refuse to follow his instructions, they are simply being ungrateful (*kafir*). Hence, they are doing wrong.

In the 250 verses where the Koran mentions wrongdoing or wrong-doers, it mentions the object of the wrongdoing in only twenty-five verses. In one verse, the object is people: "The way is open only against those who wrong the people, and are insolent in the earth unjustly" (42:42). In a second verse, the object of wrong is the signs of God. God reveals his signs, whether in the natural world or in scripture, in order that people may be guided. When people ignore the signs, they are wronging them, and by wronging the signs, they harm themselves, as they will find out when their deeds are weighed in the scales on the day of resurrection:

> *The weighing that day is true. He whose scales are heavy—they are the prosperers. But he whose scales are light—they have lost them-selves for wronging Our signs. (7:8-9)*

In the remaining twenty-odd verses in which the object of wrongdoing is mentioned, the wrongdoers are said to be wronging themselves. At the same time, the Koran repeatedly affirms that God wrongs no one. He cannot be blamed if people suffer the consequences of their own wrong actions. They themselves are bringing evil upon themselves. And the Koran also tells us in specific instances that wrongdoing has no effect upon God:

> *And they worked no wrong upon Us, but they wronged them-selves. (2:57, 7:160)*

> *God wrongs not people anything, but people wrong themselves. (10:44)*

> *And We wronged them not, but they wronged themselves. (11:101)*

Whoever does an ugly deed or wrongs himself, and then asks for-
giveness from God, he shall find that God is Forgiving,
Compassionate. (4:110)

In the Koranic view, people must recognize that everything they do
counts either for them or against them. They can do nothing that harms
God, just as they can do nothing that benefits God. He is "independent of
the worlds," and nothing done by any created thing has any effect upon
him. People play the game of salvation and damnation to their own
benefit and loss. God is there on the sideline, rooting for them in
compassion and mercy, but he lets them make their own choices. He
cannot force them to make the right choice without taking the Trust
away from them, and if he took the Trust away, they would no longer be
human. Rather, they would stand with the heaven, the earth, and the
mountains, all of whom refused to carry the Trust:

Whoso earns a sin, earns it only against himself. (4:111)

Whosoever is guided is guided only to his own gain, and whoso-
ever falls into misguidance, it is only to his own loss. (10:108, 17:15)

Whosoever shows gratitude shows gratitude only to his own gain,
and whosoever is ungrateful—my Lord is the Independent, the
Generous. (27:40)

Whosoever struggles, struggles only to his own gain. God is surely
Independent of the worlds. (29:6)

The following Koranic verses sum up beautifully the ideas just discussed. We explain each section of the passage to make the meaning
completely clear:

O people, you are the ones who have need of God, and God, He is
the Independent, the Praiseworthy. If He will, He can put you away
and bring a new creation; that is surely no great matter for God.
(35:15-17)

God has no need of creation, but creatures have every need of God. God
could, if he so decided, destroy the whole universe and bring another.
He has no need for these specks of dust who think they are so important.

No one carrying a burden will carry another's burden. If someone
weighed down by a burden calls on someone else to carry it, none
of it will be carried, even if that person be a near relative. (35:18)

All human beings are responsible for themselves. Neither God, nor the prophets, nor anyone else will assume responsibility for their actions.

> *Thou warnest only those who fear their Lord in the Unseen and perform the salat. And whosoever purifies himself purifies himself only for his own good. (35:18)*

Muhammad has come with God's message, but only those who have faith and observe the Five Pillars will heed the warning. Whatever good works they do will have the effect of purifying them of evil and darkness, and this will benefit only themselves.

> *To God is the homecoming. Not equal are the blind and the seeing, the darknesses and the light, the shade and the torrid heat, and not equal are the living and the dead. (35:18-22)*

The whole drama of human existence is being played out before God, the source of all reality, good, wisdom, and justice. People may not be aware of their real situation, but they will face it soon enough. Then they will find that Reality differentiates between those who see and those who do not, since seeing is a divine quality, but blindness is a quality of unreality. If people have not gained the ability to see what is Real, they will remain blind in the next stage of existence. So also, if they do not partake of light, they will remain in darkness. If they have not gained the cooling and soothing peace that derives from harmony and balance, they will fall into the burning dissolution that derives from imbalance and disequilibrium. If they have not gained the life that comes through awareness of the truth, they will remain in the death of ignorance.

Finally, the passage takes the whole drama back to God's guidance and misguidance. Although human free choice is very real and has ultimate importance for human beings, in the last analysis, it is Reality itself that determines what is measured out to each individual.

> *God makes to hear whomsoever He will; thou canst not make those who are in the tombs to hear—thou art naught but a warner. (35:22-23)*

If people are dead to the truth, Muhammad cannot bring them to life. Only the Real gives life and takes it away.

God's Two Hands

To attribute misguidance to God raises profound questions. In traditional Islamic learning, these questions are normally left only for the most advanced seekers of knowledge. Most people find it too difficult to understand how a God, whom they have been told is good and merciful, can misguide people. However, we will not file this question away for someone else to answer, but instead will attempt to provide an idea of how Muslim thinkers justify attributing both guidance and misguidance to God. It is not difficult to show that the basic Koranic position fits in nicely with the underlying insights of *tawhid — tanzih* and *tashbih*.

In order to understand without prejudice the issues connected with the problem of guidance and misguidance, it is helpful to put aside the usual tendency to judge God by our own standards of right and wrong, standards that are normally defined by the spirit of the times. The basic Islamic view on human ideas about God can be stated simply: We cannot judge God by our own lights, since God in his incomparability lies infinitely beyond our abilities to understand. However, we must allow ourselves to be judged by God's standards, since he is the Creator and Lord of the whole cosmos. For Muslims, God's standards for human beings are found primarily in the Koran and secondarily in the Hadith.

Having stated that God's incomparability prevents full understanding, we will not, however, take refuge in mystery and simply say that Muslims have to accept without question. Seeking to understand is fine, provided you know your own limitations, and provided you go to the right sources for the answers. "Enter houses by their doors" (2:189).

We have already learned that when Iblis disobeyed God at Adam's creation, God asked him about his refusal to prostrate himself before "him whom I created with My own two hands." This is one of only two Koranic mentions of God's "two hands," and many commentators feel that it provides an allusion to an idea that has far-ranging implications for the universe as a whole and for the problem of good and evil on all levels.

What are these two hands of God? The Koran offers some help when it speaks of "the Companions of the Right Hand" and "the Companions of the Left Hand" in Sura 56. These are the inhabitants of paradise and hell. There is also a third group of people, called the Foremost, who have advanced beyond right and left and have entered among the ranks of "Those brought near to God."

Many Muslim authorities have maintained that the two hands of God, through which God created Adam, refer to the two basic types of divine attributes that enter into the make-up of human beings, who are created in the form of all the divine attributes. These two types of attributes are of course the names of beauty and majesty, or mercy and wrath, or *tashbih* and *tanzih*. The Companions of the Left live in hell because they are dominated by the names of majesty, which demand God's distance from them. The Companions of the Right live in paradise because the attributes that predominate in their make-up are the names of mercy and beauty, which bring about nearness to God.[1]

You can ask, Why does God allow certain creatures to be far from him and to suffer as a result? This is the same as asking why God has two hands, a left hand and a right hand. Notice that the question has two parts, and that the second part is really a repetition of the first part. To ask why God allows people to suffer is the same as asking why he allows them to be far from himself. To be far from God is to lack the fundamental divine attributes, such as unity, realness, wholeness, goodness, and luminosity. Anyone who lacks such qualities is overcome by multiplicity, dispersion, imbalance, unreality, evil, and darkness. Looked at as descriptions of a human psyche, these qualities all demand disharmony, confusion, suffering, and even madness.

Hence, the underlying question is, Why is anything far from God? The first answer is that of *tanzih*: Everything is far from God, since "There is no god but God." God alone is luminous and real. Everything other than God is dark and unreal.

As soon as we take *tashbih* into account, we see that the things of the universe stand in different relationships to God. Some are nearer to God, and some are farther away from God. Nothing is absolutely near to God, since that could only be God himself. And nothing is absolutely far from God, since such a thing could not exist—it would have no reality, given that reality belongs to God alone.

How are we to judge nearness and farness? That which reflects and manifests the attributes of God is near to God. Angels are near to God because they are made out of light, while bodily things are far from God because they are made out of clay.

You might ask, Why didn't God make everything out of light? We would reply that he did; it is just that some light is brighter than other light. When light becomes very dim, it is called fire. When it becomes so dim that you hardly notice that it is light, it is called clay. But in fact there is nothing but light, since darkness is simply the lack of light. Darkness cannot exist, because all reality belongs to light. Hence, whatever exists represents at least a glimmer of light. There is no darkness.

If you are not satisfied with the example of light, we can substitute any of the names of the attributes and make the same argument. For example: Angels are near to God and bodies are far, because angels are direct manifestations of the divine attribute of knowledge, while bodily things have no knowledge to speak of. However, in the last analysis, we have to say that all things, even stones, have knowledge. It is just that the degree of the manifestation of knowledge differs, so there is always something (or someone) that has more knowledge, and something that has less. The Koran says, "Above everyone who has knowledge is one who knows [more]" (12:76). Hence, below everyone who has knowledge is one who knows less. You might object and ask, How can stones have knowledge? We could reply that they know very well how to stay in one place. And not only that, they are included in the "everything" that the Koran speaks of when it says, "Everything in the heavens and the earth glorifies God" (57:1, 59:1). How can something with no knowledge of God glorify him? Granted, a stone's knowledge is not like our knowledge, but then again, our knowledge is not like God's knowledge, yet we use the same word.

Let us return to the original question, Why does God allow certain creatures to be far from him? By now it should not be surprising if we say that the real meaning of the question is, Why does God not create all things in the same intensity of light or in the same intensity of knowledge, or life, or speech? The first answer is, if he were to do so, he would not have a multiplicity of creatures, he would have one creature. Where would that leave us?

As soon as God creates two creatures, they must be different in some attributes. If they were not different in any respect, they would not be two. Regarding the respects in which they are different, we can contrast them. We would have to say that one is more luminous and the other less luminous, or—and this amounts to the same thing—one is bright and one is dark. It is true that the dark one is bright in relation to a total lack of light, just as a burning match is bright in relation to midnight. But that match is dark in relation to a flashlight, not to mention a 100 watt light bulb, or the moon, or the sun, and so on. Brightness and darkness are relative affairs, as are knowledge and ignorance, life and death, speech and dumbness, power and weakness, happiness and misery.

Let us return to our starting point, the question of guidance and misguidance. Why does God guide some and misguide others? We might as well ask, Why does God have attributes of *tanzih* and attributes of *tashbih*? Why is he both merciful and wrathful? Why can't God be only merciful? The answer should be clear: Because then he would not be God.

God is that reality who comprises everything real, good, positive, and useful, and who displays these qualities through creating an infinite cosmos. Everything in the cosmos is "other than God," and in that respect is governed by God's left hand: it is far from God, while God, in relation to it, is transcendent, inaccessible, majestic, severe, wrathful. At the same time, everything in the universe is governed by God's right hand: it is near to God, while God, in relation to it, is immanent, accessible, beautiful, gentle, merciful.

In order for any given thing to be different from any other given thing, God's two hands cannot have the exact same relationship to the two things. If the two hands dealt with two things in exactly the same way, the two things would be one thing. Since everything is different, the way in which God's hands interrelate is different for each thing. In some creatures (such as bodily things and satans), the attributes of God's left hand display their effects more clearly, while in other things (such as luminous things and angels), the attributes of his right hand predominate.

Human beings are molded with both hands such that neither left nor right takes precedence. But this pertains to those who are fully and completely human, who realize God's form in its full manifestation, and few people attain to this situation. In most people, either the right hand or the left hand predominates. This determines whether the person will end up as a companion of the left hand or of the right hand; that is, an inhabitant of hell or of paradise. A hadith sums up this picture:

> *God created Adam when He created him. Then He struck his right shoulder and brought out his seed white like powder, and He struck his left shoulder and brought out his seed black like coals. Then He said to those in His right hand, "To the Garden, and I don't care," and He said to those in his left hand, "To the Fire, and I don't care."*

What is the human response to this situation? For Muslims, it is to avoid the hand of wrath and seek the hand of mercy. It is to try to keep away from Satan wherever he may appear; that is, to try to keep away from the quality of misguidance, whether it appears as Iblis, Pharaoh, or caprice. Hence, it is to follow the guidance of the prophets and intelligence. It is to observe the Koranic injunction to seek refuge in God from Satan: "If a prompting from Satan should prompt you, seek refuge in God" (7:200, 41:36).

For those who have the eyes to see the ramifications of *tawhid* on every level, the correct human response is to imitate the Prophet in his recognition that God has two hands and that a person should not deal with the two in the same way. As we saw, the Prophet used to pray, "O God, I seek refuge in Thy good-pleasure from Thy anger, I seek refuge in Thy pardon from Thy punishment, I seek refuge in Thee from Thee." In other words, he is saying, "I seek refuge in Thy right hand from Thy left hand." In the last analysis, God alone has reality, so there is nothing else from which and in which people can seek refuge.

Naturally, this explanation of why there must be different types of human beings, some destined for hell and some for paradise, will not satisfy everyone. Typically, someone will immediately protest, "Why me?" But that is to jump the gun. You do not know where you are headed, to the right hand or to the left hand. If you were sitting in paradise, you would not complain. Do not assume that God will place you in hell—that is to despair of God's mercy, which is not a wise move to make. Keep in mind that the worst of sinners can always repent, and the most pious of the pious (like Iblis) can always fall. Everyone is in the same situation, because we are all human. Even the Prophet Muhammad is told to say:

> *I do not own benefit for myself, or loss, but only as God wills. Had I knowledge of the Unseen, I would have acquired much good, and evil would not have touched me. I am only a warner, and a bearer of good news, to a people with faith. (7:188)*

Second, since you do not know where you are going, you are as free as the next person to make your choices. People who object here to God's measuring out frequently have ulterior motives. They want to convince us that the logical response is to say, "Well, it is over and done with, so I am free to go about my business, since it makes no difference what I do. If I am going to hell, there is nothing I can do to prevent it, and if I am going to paradise, there is nothing I can do to help myself along." But this type of argument, as Rumi brings out with great clarity and humor, is simply an excuse to do nothing about one's ultimate destiny. He sums up his view in the verse:

> *The prophets are predestinarians in the work of this world,*
> *the truth-concealers are predestinarians in the work of the*
> *next world.*[11]

In other words, those who learn the lesson being taught by the Koran understand that there is nothing they can do about their worldly lot, so they put their effort into improving their lot in the next world. In contrast, those who quibble about predestination and free will strive to improve their worldly lot, while neglecting the prophetic commands and prohibitions that are designed to improve their future situation.

There is an innate contradiction in claiming that, since all things are predestined, it makes no difference what we do. The contradiction does not lie on the philosophical level, where the argument makes sense: it lies on the psychological and practical level. To see the nature of the contradiction, it is helpful to bring the discussion down to the concrete.

Suppose that you are taking a difficult college course in physics. And suppose that you accept that everything is measured out by God. You can then conclude that the grade you will receive in the course is already determined. But will you then conclude that it makes no difference whether or not you come to class, or whether or not you read the books? Even if you are predestined to pass or to fail the course, if you abandon going to class and you go out and party, you will have eliminated the possibility of passing. If you want to pass, you will have to attend the lectures and do the reading, even though you may end up failing. Most likely, however, if you fulfill the course requirements, you will pass. Having passed, you will come to know that you were predestined to pass. If you had gone out and partied, you would have come to know that you were predestined to fail.

In short, on the practical level, there is no contradiction between the measuring out and human freedom, between guidance and misguidance, between mercy and wrath. People do not know to which group they belong, so therefore they are free to make choices. In the actual living of their daily lives, they not only admit that they possess freedom, but also claim it in most of what they do. God in his mercy, Islam maintains, will hold them responsible only for choices that they claimed as their own. He will not call them to account for what was impossible for them. If people give up all claims — which is precisely the sense of Islam, surrender to the Real — they will still have to exert every effort to put the prophetic model into practice. In no sense does Islamic "predestinarianism" encourage laziness or lack of initiative. Quite the contrary, it stirs up effort and struggle. But it orients effort not toward this world, but toward the next world; not toward dispersion and *shirk*, but toward focus and *tawhid*.

ISLAM AND OTHER RELIGIONS

The Universality and Particularity of Prophecy

Prophecy is the means whereby God offers guidance to human beings through human intermediaries. Just as God's mercy takes precedence over his wrath and thereby determines the nature of wrath, so also God's guidance takes precedence over his misguidance. Guidance itself demands the existence of misguidance. Without the misguidance that is embodied by Satan, the prophetic messages would be meaningless. Without distance, there can be no nearness; without wrong, no right; without darkness, no perception of light. All the distinctions that allow for a cosmos to exist depend upon the diversification and differentiation of the divine qualities. On the moral and spiritual level, this diversification becomes manifest through the paths of guidance and misguidance, represented by the prophets and the satans.

Wherever there have been prophets, there have been satans. The Koran uses the word *satans* to refer both to some of the jinn and to some human beings. To be a satan is to be an enemy of the prophets and an embodiment of misguidance:

> We have appointed to every prophet an enemy—satans from
> among mankind and jinn, revealing fancy words to each other as
> delusion. Yet, had thy Lord willed, they would never have done it.
> So leave them with what they are fabricating. (6:112)

Just as Adam, our father and the first prophet, was faced with Iblis, so also we are faced with Iblis, his offspring, and their followers. Misguidance is a universal phenomenon, found in the outside world and within ourselves. In the same way, guidance is a universal phenomenon. In other words, the human race is inconceivable without both prophets and satans, because human beings are defined by the freedom they received when they were made in the divine form. They are able to choose among the divine attributes, because all the divine attributes are found within themselves. Just as they can choose God's right hand by following guidance, so also they can choose his left hand by following misguidance. Without that choice, they would not have been free to accept the Trust.

As we have seen, the fundamental message of the prophets is *tawhid*. In the Islamic perspective, all prophets have brought the first Shahadah: "We never sent a messenger before thee save that We revealed to him, saying, 'There is no god but I, so worship Me' " (21:25). In contrast to the first Shahadah, which designates a divine guidance that is embodied by all prophets, the second Shahadah refers to the domain of the specific message brought by Muhammad. Other prophets had their own messages that correspond to the second Shahadah:

> *Every nation has its messenger. (10:47)*

> *We have sent no messenger save with the tongue of his people. (14:4)*

> *To every one of you [messengers] We have appointed a right way and an open road. (5:48)*

The Koran insists that Muslims should not differentiate among the prophets of God. Each prophet, after all, was sent by God with guidance, and the primary message of each is the same:

> *Say: We have faith in God, and in that which has been sent down on Abraham, Ishmael, Isaac, and Jacob, and the Tribes, and that which was given to Moses and Jesus and the prophets by their Lord. We make no distinction among any of them, and to Him we have submitted. (2:136; cf. 2:285, 3:84)*

The Koran tells us in several verses that the later prophets came to confirm the messages of the earlier prophets:

> *And when Jesus son of Mary said, "Children of Israel, I am indeed God's messenger to you, confirming the Torah that has gone before me. . . ." (61:6)*

> *He has sent down upon thee the Book with the truth, confirming what was before it, and He sent down the Torah and the Gospel aforetime, as guidance to the people. (3:3)*

At the same time, the Koran makes clear that the details of the messages differ. Any distinction that can be made among the messengers has to be made on the basis of the difference in their messages:

> *And those messengers—some We have preferred above others. Among them was he to whom God spoke, and He raised some in*

degrees. And We gave Jesus son of Mary the clear explications, and We confirmed him with the Holy Spirit. (2:253)

And We have preferred some prophets over others, and We gave David the Psalms. (17:55)

The idea that every messenger comes with a message that is specific to the people to whom he was sent and that differs in details from other messages is deeply rooted in the Islamic consciousness and is reflected in the titles that are customarily given to the great messengers in Islamic texts. Each title designates the special quality of the messenger that distinguishes him from other messengers. Thus, one of the verses just quoted refers to him "to whom God spoke." Most commentators think that this is a reference to Moses, to whom Islamic sources give the title *kalim* (speaking companion), because God spoke to him from the burning bush without the intermediary of Gabriel, and because the Koran says, "And unto Moses We spoke directly" (4:164). But the commentators add that it may also refer to Adam, to whom God spoke in the Garden, and to Muhammad, to whom God spoke during Muhammad's ascent to God (the *mir'aj*). In a similar way, Jesus is usually called God's "spirit," and Abraham his "close friend" (*khalil*).

In Islamic countries, especially among people untouched by modern education, there is a common belief that all religions accept the first Shahadah, but that each religion has a specific second Shahadah that differs from that of the Muslims. Thus it is thought that the Christians say, "There is no god but God and Jesus is the spirit of God," while the Jews say, "There is no god but God and Moses is God's speaking companion."

The Koran recognizes explicitly that, although the first Shahadah never changes, the domain covered by the second Shahadah differs from message to message. Hence, all the laws that are proper to Jews, for example, are not necessarily proper for Christians, nor do the rulings of the Muslim Shariah have any universality (despite the claims of some Muslims). For example, in the following verse, God explains that the Jews have prohibitions that do not apply to Muslims:

And to the Jewry We have forbidden every beast with claws; and of oxen and sheep We have forbidden them the fat of them, save what their backs carry, or their entrails, or what is mingled with the bone. (6:145)

Similarly, the Koran places the following words, which are directed at the Children of Israel, in Jesus' mouth, thus indicating that his Shariah differs from that of Moses.

[I have been sent] to confirm the truth of the Torah that is before me, and to make lawful to you certain things that before were forbidden unto you. (3:50)

An often recited prayer at the end of Sura 2 of the Koran says, "Our Lord . . ., charge us not with a burden such as Thou didst lay upon those before us" (2:286). The commentators say that this refers to the Torah, which is a heavy burden, in contrast to the Muslim Shariah, which, in the words of a hadith, is "easy, congenial" (*sahl samh*).

One of the most delightful expressions of the differing messages entrusted to the prophets is found in the standard accounts of the Prophet's ascent to God, the *mi'raj*. As we saw earlier, Muhammad met a number of prophets on his way up through the heavens. When he met God, God gave him instructions for his community. On the way back down, Muhammad stopped in each heaven to bid farewell to the prophets. In the sixth heaven, right below the seventh, he met Moses. Moses asked him what sort of acts of worship God had given him for his community. He replied that God had given him fifty *salat*s per day. Moses told him that he had better go back and ask God to lighten the burden. He knew from sorry experience that the people would not be able to carry out such difficult instructions. The Prophet continues:

I went back, and when He had reduced them by ten, I returned to Moses. Moses said the same as before, so I went back, and when He had reduced them by ten more, I returned to Moses. . . .

Finally, after Muhammad had moved back and forth between God and Moses several times, God reduced the *salat*s to five. Moses then said to Muhammad:

Your people are not capable of observing five salats. *I have tested people before your time and have labored earnestly to prevail over the Children of Israel. So go back to your Lord and ask Him to make things lighter for your people.*

But by this point, the Prophet was too embarrassed to continue asking for reductions. Hence he said: "I have asked my Lord till I am ashamed, but now I am satisfied and I submit."

Nowadays, discussion of Islamic teachings about prophecy can quickly raise emotions among Muslims. Probably the main reason for this is that in many Islamic countries, religion plays a far greater role in daily life than it does in Europe and America. Hence, generally speaking, political positions are posed in religious terms, and opposition to the policies of other countries can take the form of criticism of other religions.

A second factor that helps keep emotions high in discussions of prophecy is that modernized Muslims commonly take the attitude—as do many people in the West as well—that it is not they who are at fault. Shortcomings must belong to other people, and so whatever the problem may be, the blame must lie in the opponent's court. This attitude is common throughout the world. For those who recognize the truth of myth, it is highly significant that Iblis was the first person to put the blame in the other's court. It is he who said, "Now, because You have led me astray . . ." (7:16). If people followed the example of Adam and Eve, they would look more closely at themselves and find room to recognize that "We have wronged ourselves" (7:23).

Do not think that Iblis's position is found only in politics. It is an everyday reality for all of us. For example, think about the way in which students react when they receive their grades. It is not uncommon to hear someone say, "I got an A in physics, but that lousy English teacher gave me a C −." This is Iblis's reaction—the light is mine, but he led me astray. I did good, but any evil is someone else's fault. The reaction of Adam and Eve would be the following: "How kind of that physics teacher to give me an A, but I really messed up in English and received a C −, so I will have to work much harder to make up for my own shortcomings."

In short, in the contemporary political situation, ideology is often posed in terms of the war of good against evil. In such a situation, those who would stress the universality of the Koranic message rarely meet with much success. It is too easy to think that the other guy is at fault and we are fine. And in order to think that way, it is necessary to forget that God's mercy extends to all creatures. If people did remember that God's mercy takes precedence over his wrath, they might have to start searching for faults in themselves and to leave the others to God. They might have to accept that the C − was a gift and that they should have flunked.

Judaism and Christianity

The Koranic depiction of the role of prophets in human history is highly nuanced. On the basis of the Koranic text, we can neither claim that Islam has exclusive rights to the truth nor that other religions are valid without qualification. Rather, all prophets have come with the truth from God, but their followers do not always observe the teachings that the prophets brought. Hence, the Koran frequently criticizes the followers of the two religions with which the early Muslim community had contact, Judaism and Christianity. It maintains that many Jews and Christians have not lived up to God's message to them, a point that has been made by Jewish and Christian reformers throughout history.

Many Muslims would like to make this a universal judgment against other religions, claiming that Islam is the only valid religion left on the face of the earth and forgetting that there is no reason to suppose that Islam is exempt from the same sorts of distortion. Other Muslims do not agree with the sweeping condemnations that fundamentalists of all religious persuasions issue against their perceived enemies. There is, in short, no consensus among contemporary or past Muslims on the issue of Islam and other religions. But the Koran and the classical commentaries offer plenty of room for a view of things that is full of subtlety and nuance.

Among the general statements the Koran makes about the religions brought by the prophets is the following, found in two places in the text:

> *Those who have faith, and those of the Jews, the Christians, and the Sabaeans—whoso has faith in God and the Last Day and works wholesome deeds—their wage awaits them with their Lord, and no fear shall be upon them, neither shall they sorrow. (2:62, 5:69)*

The key issue here, as should be obvious by now, is faith in God. In the Islamic view, faith in God demands *tawhid*, and *tawhid* is the message of all the prophets. To the extent that *tawhid* is established, salvation is assured. So important is the first Shahadah, through which *tawhid* is expressed, that a hadith found in one of the most reliable sources tells us, "He who dies knowing that there is no god but God will enter the Garden." Notice that this hadith does not even mention faith. Simply to *know* the truth of *tawhid* is sufficient. Another hadith makes a similar point. On the day of resurrection, God will busy himself with weighing good and evil deeds in the scales. The good deeds of each person will be put in one pan and the evil deeds in the other. If good deeds predominate, the person will go to paradise, but if evil deeds predominate, he or she will be thrown into hell. One of the people brought to be judged will be a Muslim who has ninety-nine scrolls listing his evil deeds:

> *God will say, "Do you object to anything in this? Have My scribes who keep note wronged you?"*
> *He will reply, "No, my Lord."*
> *God will ask him if he has any excuse, and when he tells his Lord that he has none, He will say, "On the contrary, you have with Us one good deed, and you will not be wronged today."*
> *A document will be brought out containing "I witness that there is no god but God and that Muhammad is His servant and His messenger." God will say, "Come to be weighed."*
> *The man will ask his Lord what this document is that is being brought along with the scrolls, and He will reply, "You will not be wronged."*
> *The scrolls will then be put on one side of the scale, and the document on the other, and the scrolls will become light and the document heavy, for nothing can compare in weight with God's name.*

When the Koran criticizes the followers of other religions, it is criticizing a perceived distortion of *tawhid*. In doing so, it has recourse to versions of Christian and Jewish teachings to which the followers of those religions do not necessarily subscribe.

To take a simple example, it is commonly said that the Koran rejects the Christian concept of the Trinity. Inasmuch as the Trinity is understood as negating *tawhid*, this is true. But not all Christians think that the Trinity negates *tawhid*. Quite the contrary, most formulations of the Trinitarian doctrine are careful to preserve God's unity. If "three-ness" takes precedence over oneness, then the Koranic criticisms apply. But among Christians, the exact nature of the relationship between the three and the one is a point of recurring debate. One of the actual Koranic verses that are taken as negating the Trinity says, "Those who say, 'God is the third of three' have become truth-concealers" (5:73). Even an elementary knowledge of any Christian catechism tells us that God is not "the third of three." Rather, God is one and three at the same time. Inasmuch as he is three, he presents himself to his creatures as three persons — Father, Son, and Holy Ghost.

Another Koranic verse says something similar, but now we have this first verse to help us understand what is being criticized:

> The Messiah, Jesus son of Mary, was only the Messenger of God,
> and His Word that He committed to Mary, and a Spirit from Him.
> So have faith in God and His messengers, and do not say, "Three."
> Refrain; better it is for you. God is only One God. (4:171)

Notice that this passage gives Jesus an extremely exalted position and recognizes that he has qualities possessed by no other prophet.[12] However, it stresses once again that there is but a single God. If faith in Jesus leads to the affirmation of three gods, then the Koran rejects that. But again, the actual Christian position is highly subtle, and few if any Christians would hold that they have faith in other than a single God.

Some Muslim commentators point out that there is nothing wrong in saying "three" so long as it does not mean that God is the *third of three*. If we say that God is the third of *two*, that is fine. The Koran itself says as much:

> Hast thou not seen that God knows whatsoever is in the heavens,
> and whatsoever is in the earth? Three men conspire not secretly
> together, but He is the fourth of them, neither five men, but He is
> the sixth of them, neither fewer than that, neither more than that,
> but He is with them, wherever they may be. Then He shall tell
> them what they have done, on the Day of Resurrection. Surely
> God has knowledge of everything. (58:7)

Another Christian concept that the Koran criticizes vehemently is that Jesus should be God's son. The verse just cited that negates "three" continues by saying, "Glory be to Him—that He should have a son!" (4:171). Elsewhere the Koran says, "How should He have a son, seeing that He has no female companion, and He created all things, and He has knowledge of everything?" (6:101).

Koranic usage and the general Muslim understanding make clear that by *son*, Muslims understand not a symbol or a metaphor, but a physical son, born of a mother, God's supposed female companion. It may be that some Christians have thought that God has taken a wife, or that he somehow impregnated the Virgin Mary, giving birth to his son. But no Christian theologian has ever imagined such a thing. For Christians, Jesus' sonship is a reality, but it cannot be taken in a physical sense. The fact that Mary is often called the Mother of God does not help clear up the matter for Muslims, who have only the Koranic text and popular misconceptions of an alien religion to go by.

That the idea of sonship is understood by Muslims in a literal sense is obvious, for example, in the short text of Sura 112, often called *Tawhid*. Anyone who thinks about the implications of sonship and fatherhood will quickly understand that these are relative terms. Everyone who is a son is also (potentially at least) a father, and everyone who is a father is also a son, with the sole exception of Adam. Notice that in affirming *tawhid*, the Koran not only negates the idea that Jesus could have been God's son, but also the necessary correlative, that God could have been someone else's son, surely the ultimate absurdity in Muslim eyes:

Say: He is God, One—God, the Everlasting Refuge. He did not give birth, nor was He given birth to, and He has no equal.

Another very commonly repeated Koranic criticism of Jews and Christians is that they have corrupted their scriptures and therefore invalidated the messages brought to them by the prophets. The Koranic text, however, offers a more ambiguous answer to the question of other scriptures than Muslims may admit. The key Arabic term is *tahrif*, which means to turn something from its proper way, to distort, to alter. Do the following Koranic verses refer to the actual *text* of the scriptures, or do they refer to the *interpretation* of the scriptures? Koran commentators take both positions, thus allowing Muslims various alternatives in their attempts to understand the significance of the passage (we translate *tahrif* as "alter"):

Some of the Jews altered words from their meanings, saying, "We have heard and we disobey".... Had they but said, "We hear and we obey,"... it would have been better for them. (4:46)

Notice that in this verse, the Koran does not make a universal judgment, but rather criticizes *some* followers of the Jewish religion. If the point is interpretation, no one could take exception to this statement, since followers of every religion recognize that some of their co-religionists distort the meaning of scripture. Another verse is as follows:

> So, because [the Jews] broke their compact, We cursed them and made their hearts hard; they alter words from their meanings, and they have forgotten a portion of what they were reminded of. (5:13)

Here, the Koran connects the issue of textual distortion with guidance and misguidance. Those Jews who broke their covenant with God suffered hardening of their hearts as a divine punishment. Hardening of the heart is a term that the Koran employs to refer to all the consequences of turning away from God. In general, it signifies a dulling of the intelligence and a weakening of the connection with the divine attributes of gentleness, mercy, and beauty. Those whose hearts became hardened fell into further distance from God and greater misguidance. Hence, they began to pervert the meaning of their own scriptures. The prophets had come to remind them, but they forgot some of what the prophets had told them. Their act of forgetting could possibly mean that some of the scripture was lost, but more likely it simply means that those with hardened hearts were unable to *understand* the meaning of the remembrance; that the divine message embodied in scripture.

In another verse on the same subject, the Koran addresses the Prophet, telling him not to be so eager for the Jews in his environment to listen to his message:

> Art thou then so eager that they should have faith in thee? But there was a group among them who listened to the Speech of God, then altered it knowingly, having understood it. (2:75)

This verse suggests that accepting Islam is not sufficient, if old habits such as reading scripture to one's own advantage are maintained. But again, this verse refers to "a group of them," not to all Jews.

Some of the polemically minded Muslim theologians investigated the Hebrew Bible and the New Testament looking for evidence that Jews and Christians had distorted the text of their scriptures. The first to do this, and the one was the most thorough and systematic in his approach, was the Andalusian scholar Ibn Hazm (d. 456/1064). Given that the Islamic concept of scripture diverges from the Jewish and Christian idea in important respects, and given that the Jewish and Christian canons include a great variety of texts written at many different times and from many different perspectives, it is not surprising that the Muslim scholars found much to criticize. Moreover, these critics were often simply repeating what is found in polemical literature written by Jews and Christian sectarians, or by other, often pre-Islamic, critics of the Bible, who may have been Samaritans, Jewish-Christians, Karaites, Gnostics, Hellenistic philosophers, or Manicheans. Some historians of Islam have even suggested that the modern critical study of the Bible— which, of course, has been far more severe on the Bible than Muslims have—received many of its ideas through the intermediary of the Islamic polemical literature.[13]

The Koran commonly refers to the messages given to messengers as "books"; that is, scriptures. Hence, it refers to the followers of a messenger as "People of the Book" (*ahl al-kitab*). In most of the thirty verses where the Koran employs this expression, it seems to have in view the Christians and the Jews, the followers of the two religions with which the nascent Muslim community had contact. In two verses, it also mentions the "People of the Reminder" in the same meaning.

In many of the verses where the People of the Book are mentioned, the two sides of the Koranic picture of pre-Islamic religion can easily be seen. Those who observe their scriptures are praiseworthy, while those who do not follow the messages that the prophets delivered to them are blameworthy:

> *Many of the People of the Book wish that they might restore you as truth-concealers, after your faith, because of the envy in their souls. (2:109)*

> *Some of the People of the Book are a wholesome nation. They recite God's signs in the watches of the night, prostrating themselves, having faith in God and the Last Day, bidding to honor and forbidding dishonor, and vying with one another in good deeds. They are among the wholesome. Whatever good they do, they will not be denied its reward. (3:113–115)*

The Koran is especially critical of the enmity that Christians and Jews have toward each other. Since they accept the Book—*tawhid* and prophecy—they should not quarrel. The first verse cited is especially interesting, since it makes a general criticism of all those who would say that Judaism and Christianity have no foundation:

> *The Jews say, "The Christians stand on nothing." The Christians say, "The Jews stand on nothing." But they recite the Book. Even so, those who have no knowledge say the like of what they say. (2:113)*

> *Say: "O People of the Book! Come now to a word common between us and you, that we worship none but God, and that we associate*

no others with Him, and that some of us do not take others as
lords, apart from God." And if they turn their backs, say: "Bear wit-
ness that we are muslims."
  People of the Book! Why do you dispute concerning Abraham?
The Torah was not sent down, neither the Gospel, until after him.
What, have you no intelligence? (3:64-65)

There are many more verses of the Koran that refer to Christianity and
Judaism, but a thorough analysis would demand a major book. Enough
has been said to provide the general picture.[14]

One more point, however, needs to be made in order to clarify a major
difference in perspective between the Muslim and Christian view of
things. For Christians, God's word is Christ, the "Word made flesh." The
Gospels are inspired books written about Christ. The whole New Testament can take on the color of God's word, but all this is secondary to
Christ, who is the word incarnate. One can imagine a Christianity
without the New Testament, sustained merely by an oral tradition. But
one cannot imagine a Christianity without Christ.

For Muslims, God's Word is the Koran, and Muhammad is simply the
messenger. True, he is a perfect human being, God's vicegerent, and the
model that God has designated for people to follow. But the message is
the primary issue, not the messenger. One can imagine Islam without
Muhammad, but not without the Koran.

Muslims see other religions in terms of Islam, which in their eyes is
the perfect religion. Of course, followers of other religions also look
from their own perspective; this is not a quality unique to Muslims.
Hence, Muslims expect other religions to have a book like the Koran,
and the Koran provides every reason for them to do so by referring to
the Torah and the Gospel. But note that the Koran mentions Gospel in
the singular, not in the plural. It states repeatedly that Jesus, God's
messenger, was given the Gospel as his message, just as Muhammad
was given the Koran. Hence, Muslims are immediately suspicious when
they hear that there are four Gospels. This difference of perspective on
the role of the human and scriptural elements makes for endless misunderstandings between Christians and Muslims.

In order to sum up the Islamic view of other religions—Judaism and
Christianity in particular—we can say the following: In reading the
Koran, many Muslims prefer to stress the passages that are critical of
other religions and to ignore or explain away the verses that praise
other religions. It cannot be denied that certain Koranic verses provide a strong case for religious exclusivism. However, many Koranic
verses leave plenty of room for openness toward other religions. The
position Muslims take on this issue depends largely on their own
understanding of God's reality. Those who think that God's mercy
really does take precedence over his wrath and embraces all those
who try to follow his guidance find it easy to see God's guidance in all

religions. In contrast, those who prefer to think of God as a stern and somewhat capricious master who issues orders and expects to be obeyed—no questions asked—are much more comfortable thinking that only they (their religious group, their political party) are among the saved.

Sometimes the best way to approach claims regarding exclusive possession of the truth is simply to laugh and to leave things in God's hands. Thus we conclude this section with an anecdote, told to us by one of the ulama many years ago.

Two Iranian scholars were discussing religion. One of them asked the other, "In the last analysis, who goes to paradise?" The other, a poet well known for his sense of humor, answered, "Well, it is really very simple. First, all religions other than Islam are obviously false, so we do not have to consider them. That leaves Islam. But among Muslims, some are Shi'ites and some Sunnis, and we all know that the Sunnis have strayed from the right path and will be thrown into hell. That leaves the Shi'ites. But among Shi'ites, there are the common people and the ulama. Everyone knows that the common people don't care about God and religion, so they will burn in the Fire. That leaves the ulama. But the ulama have become ulama in order to lord it over the common people. That leaves you and me. And I am not so sure about you."

Doesn't this kind of reasoning sound familiar? It is perhaps not wildly inaccurate to say that many of our contemporaries think this way, whether they be Muslims, Christians, Jews, scholars, scientists, politicians, or whatever. And this sort of position sounds suspiciously like that of Iblis, whose motto is, "I am better than he."

The Koran

From the beginning of this book, we have been stressing the utterly indispensable role that the Koran plays in defining the meaning and contents of Islam. The Koran is the message, and the message is Islam. But how may that message be described best in a few words?

The Koran's self-description provides insight into the fundamentals of the Islamic concept of prophecy. On the one hand, most of what the Koran says about itself applies to other revealed books as well; on the other, the Koran makes a case for its own superiority. Hence, in describing itself, it provides the germs of the ideas of both the universality and the particularity of God's messages. Perhaps the best way to grasp the Koranic self-description is to look at the implications of the names and adjectives that it employs in referring to itself, just as the best way to grasp *tawhid* is to look at the implications of God's names.

The word *Koran* itself (Arabic *qur'an*) is employed seventy times in the text. It derives from a root that has two basic meanings that appear unrelated at first: "to recite" and "to gather together." Most commonly, the name is said to mean "recitation." According to one well-known account, the first word of the Koran revealed to the Prophet was *iqra'*, an imperative form from the same root as *qur'an*, meaning "Recite!"

> *Recite! In the name of thy Lord who created, created the human being from a blood-clot. Recite! And thy Lord is the Most Generous, who taught by the Pen, taught the human being what he knew not. (96:1-5)*

In these few verses are found not only the root of the name *Koran*, but also a depiction of the essential relationship between God and human beings. He is their creator and the one who, out of generosity and mercy, teaches them the truth of their ultimate destiny and thereby guides them on the path to fulfillment.

Implicit in the name is an important point whose significance is difficult to grasp in modern times. The Koran is first a *recited* book. It is only a written book as a matter of convenience and as a concession to human weakness. The Koran was recited to the Prophet by the angel Gabriel. The Prophet memorized it and then recited it to his followers, who also memorized it. Those who knew how to write sometimes wrote down what they heard. Those whose memories were still not weakened by dependence on writing learned the text by heart. The Arabs of the time were so confident in their own memories and so accustomed to memorizing everything important that most of them never gave a thought to recording the text on paper. Only several years after the death of the Prophet did people recognize that the environment of Islam was changing so quickly that parts of the text might become lost or corrupted. Hence, the leader of the community ordered written copies prepared and sent to various places to serve as the official text.

We live in a society that has lost the power of memory. We are utterly dependent upon writing and electronic gadgets for learning and information. In preliterate societies throughout the world, people had memories that we would find mind-boggling today. Moreover—we tell ourselves—what an absurdity! What could possibly be worth so much effort at memorization?

We have forgotten many truths that were considered self-evident in former times, in Islam as well as elsewhere. One of these truths is that we are defined by what we know. Muslims have always taken for granted that our humanity is inextricably bound up with our understanding. Life has a purpose, and we are here to achieve that purpose, but we cannot possibly achieve it if we do not understand. The first step in understanding our humanity is assimilating the guidance of the past. There is no simpler way to pass on this guidance than to teach it to children through rote memorization. If we consign it only to written form instead of instilling it into their very bodies, we are abandoning the task of education; we are making sure that most of those who would have had the capacity to understand will now be distracted by other affairs extraneous to the purpose of human life.

We have also forgotten how easy it is to memorize, especially when the techniques of memorization are embodied in the culture itself. Children, as is well known, are like sponges: They can, and do, learn an enormous amount, usually in spite of the formal education that they are forced to endure. When children are fed pap, we are surprised that they then follow comic book characters as role models. In many other civilizations, children were fed the most sophisticated traditional literature from the earliest age, and they grew up knowing that they should model their lives on the greatest human examples of wisdom and compassion. The texts, woven into their flesh and blood, acted as an inexhaustible treasury from which to draw inspiration.

In the traditional Islamic context, education begins with memorization of the Koran, which is the highest possible wisdom. That becomes a source of never-ending inspiration for whatever fields of learning people undertake. The greatest and most sophisticated minds of Islamic civilization freely admit that what they know is merely a few trickles from the Koranic ocean.

One of the keys to memorization and embodiment of the text of the Koran is found in the very meaning of the name: Recitation. People do not *read* the Koran, they recite it. In other words, they read it aloud in a way that brings out its natural music, and they sway back and forth in harmony with its rhythms. How much easier it is to memorize a song than a paragraph from a book, especially on a learned subject. And God himself says, "We have made the Koran easy for remembrance, so is there any that will remember?" (54:17, and elsewhere). One reason it is easy to memorize is that it is a beautifully balanced and rhythmic book, though one would not necessarily assume this from the translations that have been made.

It is an Islamic dogma that the Koran cannot be translated. This is to say that God spoke in Arabic, and the Arabic language itself is the body of his word. As scholars have pointed out, in Islam one cannot talk about the "incarnation" (that is, the "enfleshment") of the word, but rather of the "inlibration" (that is, the "enbookment") of the word. The word did not become flesh in Islam; it became book, and the book was then expanded into uncounted libraries. However, this original book was not written, it was recited. And a recited book is a book that is embodied within human beings. The sounds and rhythms of the recitation have a direct influence on the human body. Through reciting the Koran, people come to embody the book and thereby, indirectly, to "incarnate" the word. The great model of this embodiment of the book is the prophet Muhammad himself, whose Sunna is the ideal to which all Muslims aspire. Once, after the Prophet's death, someone asked his wife A'isha to describe his character. She said, "Have you not read the Koran?" The questioner replied, "Of course I have." She said, "His character is the Koran."

One of the supplications that the Prophet taught to his companions
includes the following words:

> *O God, I ask Thee . . . that Thou givest me the provision of the Ko-*
> *ran and knowledge, that Thou makest it blend with my flesh, my*
> *blood, my hearing, and my sight, and that Thou puttest my body*
> *to work through it.*

We do not mean to deny that the message of the Koran has a rational
and intellectual dimension that can be grasped without recourse to the
recited text itself; otherwise, we would not waste our time writing this
book. However, it is far from true that the whole of the Koranic message can be grasped through study. Faith in Islam, as we have seen,
demands practice. The most fundamental of all Islamic practices, the
salat, consists of cyclic movements and Koranic recitation, all of which
serves to embody the Koran within the person who performs the
prayer. To the extent Muslims live the reality of their religion, the
Koran becomes the reality of their minds, their hearts, *and* their bodies.

We have seen that the body also acts as a vehicle for light; in the last
analysis, it *is* light. We call it darkness only because it is dark in relation
to the light of the spirit. But given the fact that the body itself is a
manifestation of light, its luminosity can be intensified. Recitation (not
reading) of the Koran has the effect of opening up the pores, as it were,
to the luminosity of God's own speech. This, in the traditional Islamic
view, explains the common observation that in Muslim countries — and
elsewhere as well — many people, whether male or female, become
more beautiful as they age. In Islamic languages, it is common to say of
such people that they have a "luminous" presence: Their bodies have
been transmuted by the divine light that infuses them because of their
nearness to God. In Buddhist countries, such people are said to display
the properties of emptiness, or to manifest the hidden Buddha nature
within all of us.

The Koran itself is Light, as it tells us in several verses, and to
embody the Koran through faith and practice is to become transmuted
by this light and to actualize all the qualities of light, which are the
divine qualities.

In the modern context, we find it difficult to imagine how a book could
be so important; dedicating our lives to embodying that book seems as
if it would be a terribly limiting experience. We would have to cut out of
ourselves so many important dimensions of human existence in order
to fit into a narrow mold. But this sort of judgment is based upon our
modern, Western conception of what a book is, and most of us have
nothing more than novels and textbooks as examples. If the Koran bore
any resemblance whatsoever to a novel or a textbook, then we would
have to agree with this criticism.

What sort of thing is this book? This is like asking, What sort of thing is this religion? The scripture is the religion, and the religion is the scripture. And we would *not* say that this is true of other religions as well. Here Islam seems to be a special case, especially if we insist on calling the Koran a book. However, if we universalize our terminology somewhat and say that the Koran is God's Word, and God's Word is his self-expression, then it is much easier to find parallels in other religions. For traditional Jews, the Torah, in its widest sense, plays the same sort of role; and for traditional Christians, it is Jesus, the Word made flesh, who is the all-pervasive reality of the tradition.

From within the Islamic perspective, to live life with the goal of embodying the Koran is far from being a limitation. On the contrary, every other human endeavor involves ignoring human possibilities and closing down our minds and hearts to who we are. This perspective on the meaning of the Koran can only be grasped within the context of Islam's three principles. If we attempt to approach the Koran from the perspective of sociology, history, philosophy, or any other modern discipline, we will end up with an outsider's view of a curious phenomenon or, at best, the recognition that similar ideas are found in other cultures as well. But to discover Islam's own vision of itself, we need to think once again about what it means to be God, what it means to be human, and what the relationship between the two should be in the ideal circumstances.

The Koran is God's Word, his self-expression. Likewise, the human being is God's form—therefore his self-expression. But the Koran takes oral and verbal form, while the human being takes spiritual and bodily form. The Koran's outward form is fully manifest, in the sense that it was received once and for all and never changes. But no human being is fully present in this world at any time from birth to death. The Koran is all there, but none of us is all here. Our infancy has passed, and our old age has not yet arrived. It is difficult to imagine that the infant and the decrepit old man are the same in any real sense, but they are—in some way that is difficult to formulate.

But where, you might wonder, in the midst of this (hopefully) long lifetime is the real you? In fact, an embodiment of the real you is found at every point on the trajectory of life, but the real you itself remains a mystery that correlates with the divine spirit, about which the Koran says:

> *They will ask you about the Spirit. Say: "The spirit is at the command of my Lord, and of knowledge you are given but little."* (17:85)

The point of this comparison between the oral word of God, which is the Koran, and the embodied form of God, which is the human being, is to bring out the Islamic teaching that, in the Koran, we see God's self-expression fully manifest. In the human being, we cannot see the whole because we are situated on a small segment of the historical unfolding of that whole, an unfolding that precedes our life in this world and extends beyond our death. The Koran is thus a full image of God, but we, at any given point, are partial and incomplete images. Made in God's form, we have the potential to bring all God's attributes into externalized and embodied existence through our activities. But in order to grasp what those divine attributes are—attributes which comprise ourselves—we need an external model. That model, for Muslims, is the Koran, which displays the image openly. Muslims must follow the Prophet so that the Koran becomes their character and determines the way they think, feel, and act. This is not a closing down, but an opening up:

> *Whomsoever God desires to guide, He expands his breast to Islam; whomsoever He desires to misguide, He makes his breast narrow, tight. (6:125)*

Islam is to embody the Koran. It is an opening up because, through imitating the Prophet and gaining the Koran as their character, people come to establish real relationships with every attribute of Reality; that is, everything good, beautiful, positive, praiseworthy, and lovable. When people follow any other way—or rather, any nonprophetic way— they constrict themselves; they close down their personalities to many of the diverse dimensions of the divine form that make them what they are. To model themselves upon anything other than God is to fall into *shirk*. It is to be confused about their own reality; to think that they are this or that, or that they should be this or that, and to be unaware that God is not this or that, but the creator of every this and that. Likewise, his image cannot be limited to this and that, but embraces every this and that without being held back by any of them. The vision of human perfection that Islam offers is one of infinite possibility conjoined with total fulfillment, everlasting good fortune, and complete happiness.

All this is implied in the name *Koran* itself, when we take it to mean "recitation." Many authorities have insisted that the other sense of the term was also meant by God when he chose this name for his book. As mentioned above, the other sense is "to bring together." Hence, the Koran is that which brings together. What does it bring together? The wisdom of all the prophets, the guidance that God has given to Adam and all his children. Thus Muslims maintain that all knowledge and wisdom are found in the Koran. The Koran came to confirm the previous messages, and in so doing it did not leave out anything of significance for human beings. A saying of the Prophet's grandson Hasan brings out the Muslim understanding of this sense of the word *Koran*. It also brings out the importance of the Fatihah, the opening chapter of the Koran, which Muslims recite in every cycle of the ritual prayer. By reciting this chapter, they are reciting and embodying the whole of the Koran:

> God sent down one hundred books and four books, and He placed
> the one hundred in the four, that is, the Torah, the Gospel, the
> Psalms, and the Furqan [the Koran]. Then He placed all of them in
> the Koran, and He placed everything in the Koran in its long chap-
> ters, and He placed everything in the long chapters in the Fatihah.

Names of the Koran

Every name and attribute that the Koran applies to itself has divine
and human implications that can be expanded upon indefinitely, just as
is the case with every name of God. In what follows, we cite a few of the
Koran's names and briefly suggest what they imply about the Koran to
Muslim readers.

The saying from Hasan just cited mentions the second most well
known name of the book, *al-Furqan*. The root meaning of the term is "to
separate," or "differentiate," and hence the name has often been translated as "discernment," "discrimination," and "criterion." Many have
held that this name is complementary to the name Koran. Just as *Koran*
means "that which brings together all wisdom," so *Furqan* means "that
which separates truth from error and provides criteria for distinguish-
ing wisdom." The Koran also applies the name Furqan to the Torah:

> And We gave Moses and Aaron the Furqan, and a radiance, and a
> remembrance to the god-wary. (21:48)

> Blessed is He who has sent down the Furqan upon His servant
> [Muhammad], that he may be a warner to the world's inhabitants.
> (25:1)

The Koran often refers to itself simply as "the Book," a term that it
applies, as we have seen, to scripture in general and to the Torah and
the Gospel in particular. In fact, the Koran employs this word as a
generic term for revelation in over two hundred verses, far more often
than it uses other words of similar meaning, such as *revelation* (*wahy*)
and *sending down* (*tanzil*):

> This is the Book, wherein is no doubt, a guidance to the god-wary.
> (2:2)

> O you who have faith! Have faith in God and His messenger and
> the Book He has sent down on His messenger, and the Book which
> He has sent down before. (4:136)

Most of the remaining names and attributes that the Koran applies to
itself can be divided into two groups: Those which emphasize the

knowledge and discernment that the Koran provides, and those which stress God's motivation for revealing the book; that is, his mercy and compassion. The first group of names includes Guidance, Truth, Wisdom, Judgment, Light, Proof, Clear Explication, Elucidation, Admonition, Reminder, and Remembrance. The second includes Mercy, Healing, Generous, and Blessed.

We have already mentioned that the idea of guidance provides a key to understanding the Muslim concept of prophecy. Let us add here that the Fatihah, which is said to carry the whole of the Koranic message in its seven short verses, circles around a prayer that focuses on guidance: "Guide us on the Straight Path" (1:5). If God responds positively to this specific prayer, nothing else is needed; or rather, everything else will be taken care of.

The name Truth (*haqq*) is a term that we have discussed as a name of God, though we translated it earlier as "the Real." The meaning of the Arabic word is broader than that of the English *real* or *truth*, however, since it includes both these meanings along with the sense of right, justice, and appropriateness:

> *We have sent thee with the Truth, as a bringer of good tidings and a warner. (2:119, 35:24)*

> *O mankind, the Messenger has now come to you with the Truth from your Lord. (4:170)*

As both truth and guidance to the Truth, who is God, the Koran is also Wisdom (*hikma*). *Wisdom* is typically defined as "the discernment of truth along with its application to concrete situations." To be wise is to know the truth and to put it into practice in an appropriate manner. The Koran knows the truth—or rather, is the truth—and puts it into practice by revealing it in oral form to human beings; they, in turn, make use of the wisdom presented to them in order to bring themselves into harmony with the Real:

> *God has sent down on thee the Book and the Wisdom, and He has taught thee what thou knewest not. (4:113)*

> *These are the signs of the Wise Book. (10:1, 31:2)*

Since the Koran provides discernment and wisdom, it also judges among things. Judgment (*hukm*), after all, involves drawing a conclusion by applying knowledge to a situation; it is to separate truth out from falsehood and to declare the correct state of affairs. The Islamic concept of judgment is closely connected with that of wisdom, and in fact the two words derive from the same root: "Even so, We have sent it down as an Arabic Judgment" (13:37).

We have already seen how important the idea of light is for grasping the nature of *tawhid*. Light is that which makes the hidden manifest. Hence, the Koran is light, because it displays the divine wisdom hidden in creation and concealed from people because of forgetfulness: "Therefore have faith in God and His messenger and in the Light that We have sent down" (64:8). Light makes everything clear, and judgments are made on the basis of clarity. Hence, the Koran presents itself as a proof (*burhan*), a clear explication (*bayan*), and an elucidation (*tabyin*):

> *O mankind, a Proof has now come to you from your Lord—We have sent down to you a clear Light. (4:174)*

> *We have sent down to thee the Book as an Elucidation of all things, and as a Guidance and a Mercy, and as good news to those who submit. (16:89)*

> *This is a Clear Exposition for mankind, and a Guidance and an Admonition. (3:138)*

Though the quality of guidance has clear connections with discernment and showing the right way, implicit within the concept is the concern of the guide for the guided. Hence, one of the divine names of mercy and gentleness is Guide. This brings us to the second category of Koranic names, those that point to God's motivation in revealing the Koran and other scriptures:

> *Before it was the Book of Moses, as an example and a mercy. (46:12)*

> *These are the signs of the Wise Book, a Guidance and a Mercy for those who do what is beautiful. (31:2-3)*

> *This is clear insights from your Lord, Guidance, and a Mercy for a people who have faith. (7:203)*

The Koran is a mercy because it guides to human wholeness and well-being. Hence, it heals every disease and wound found in the innate human disposition toward *tawhid*:

> *O people, now there has come to you an Admonition from your Lord, and a Healing for what is in the breasts, and a Guidance and a Mercy for the faithful. (10:57)*

> *And We send down in the Koran that which is a healing and a mercy to the faithful. (17:82)*

In short, the Koran manifests everything good in the sense that, without guidance, human beings are lost. The Koran provides them with healing of their own selves, wholeness, and well-being. Hence it is blessed (*mubarak*), a term which implies that it is the source of every blessing, of everything good and desirable: "This is a blessed Book that We have sent down, so follow it and be god-wary so that you may find mercy" (6:155).

In Islamic languages, people do not simply say "the Koran." Normally, they add an adjective out of respect for God's word. Some English-speaking Muslims have taken to calling the book "the Holy Koran" on the model of the Holy Bible, but the linguistic equivalents of "Holy" are not used to describe the Koran in the Koran, or in Islamic languages. Probably the most common adjective applied to it is *generous* (*karim*), a usage derived from the verse, "It is surely a generous Koran" (56:77). Like Truth and Light, Generous is a name of God, and it fits into the category of the merciful and beautiful names. Moreover, temporally speaking, it is probably the first attribute of God revealed in the Koran after creativity. Hence it suggests God's fundamental motivation for offering guidance. As noted already, it is usually maintained that the first verses of the Koran that were revealed are the following:

> Recite! In the name of thy Lord who created, created man from a blood-clot. Recite! And thy Lord is the Most Generous, who taught by the Pen, taught the human being what he knew not. (96:1-5)

Of course, God's generosity is not only manifest in his teaching or guidance. In a more fundamental sense, creation itself is nothing but an act of generosity, since the creatures have no claim on their own existence.

The Prophet Muhammad

If the Koran is Islam, Muhammad is Islam humanly embodied. Devotion to the God who reveals himself through the Koran demands devotion to the perfect embodiment of God's recitation, the one who manifests in his own example God's bringing together and separating out, his guidance, truth, wisdom, judgment, light, proof, elucidation, remembrance, mercy, healing, generosity, and blessedness.

Given the role that Muhammad has played in Islam throughout its history,[15] it is surprising to find Muslims of certain modern persuasions that are often called fundamentalist decrying devotion to the Prophet in the name of *tawhid*. This decrial is accompanied by the almost utter eclipse of the idea of *tashbih*. The result is an excessive *tanzih* that puts God so distant from human affairs that people are free to do whatever they see fit, so long as they do not disobey explicit divine commands.

No doubt, if modernization is to be achieved, such transformations of Islam will have to take place. But now that we in the West, at least, have entered a postmodern era, there is every reason to question the wisdom of throwing out the traditional and the time-honored in order to clear the ground for the paradise promised by technological progress.

In explaining the role of the Prophet in traditional Islam, we will limit ourselves here to bringing out only a few basic elements of the Koranic depiction. What we have to say can only be superficial and cursory. It is sufficient to remember that "Muhammad's character *is* the Koran" to realize that it is not sufficient to glance at explicit references to Muhammad. The whole book, just as it expresses God, also expresses the perfected human substance of God's foremost messenger. Muhammad is the actualized divine form who, for Muslims, stands above the other actualized divine forms, the prophets and friends of God from Adam down to the end of time.

To understand the Islamic view of Muhammad, we have to begin by looking at him in the light of *tanzih*, the fact that God is real and everything other than God is unreal. From this perspective, all good belongs to God. Muhammad is other than God and hence, like all other created things, he is nothing compared to God. In human terms, Muhammad is a mortal like everyone else.

But there is still a major difference between the Prophet and other people. First, the Prophet is God's perfect servant. We saw that everything in the universe is God's servant, but human beings, having carried the Trust, have to choose freely to be God's servant in order to live up to their potential. This free submission of self to God is the outstanding quality of Muhammad's character. Hence the Koran refers to him as "God's servant" and the Muslim consciousness pays this title the highest respect.

But this is not the whole story of Muhammad. As God's perfect servant, he is also God's perfect vicegerent. Having fully actualized *tanzih*, he also embodies *tashbih*. The Koran illustrates these two sides of Muhammad's humanity in the verse, "Say: 'I am but a mortal like you; it has been revealed to me that your God is one God' " (18:110, 41:6). Many commentators in modern times have paid attention only to the first half of this verse and ignored the implications of the second half. Yes, Muhammad is a mortal like everyone else. He is simply a human being. But remember that human beings were taught all the names, and the angels prostrated themselves before Adam. To be human is not exactly ordinary. It is a divine Trust, a special privilege, and very few people live up to it. "Verily," concludes the verse of the Trust, the human being is "very ignorant, a great wrongdoer" (33:72).

What distinguishes Muhammad from others is that he has lived up to the responsibilities of being human, and he has done so—with God's guidance, of course—such that God has chosen him to be a mercy for the whole world: "We have not sent thee save as a mercy to all the world's inhabitants" (21:107). The second half of the previous verse—"it has been revealed to me that your God is one God"—is all important, because it shows that Muhammad is the recipient of revelation. If there was any thought that he is just as imperfect as the rest of us, this thought is removed by the statement that he alone was chosen to receive the Koran.

Yes, Muhammad is a mortal like other people. But no, he is not forgetful and negligent like them, refusing to carry the Trust. He has carried it, and the whole world benefits as a result. The qualities he manifests are not his own qualities. They are the divine names and attributes. We saw earlier that Muhammad, as a human being, cannot guide whomsoever he wishes to guide. Nevertheless, as God's messenger and vicegerent, the one who makes manifest God's light, he is the guide to the Truth and to salvation:

> And thou, surely thou guidest unto a straight path—the path of God. (42:52-53)

> O Prophet, We have sent thee as a witness, and good tidings to bear and warning, calling unto God by His leave, and as a light-giving lamp. (33:45-46)

The light Muhammad manifests is not his own light; "There is no light but God." As mortals, people have no light. But as vicegerents of God, they can be light-giving lamps.

The Koran makes it very clear that Muhammad is a model who is to be emulated; following his example is a means whereby one remembers God—and we already know that remembrance is the desired response to God's reminder. It is not without significance that one of the many titles that have traditionally been given to Muhammad is Dhikrallah, "the Remembrance of God": "You have a beautiful example in God's messenger, for whosoever hopes for God and the Last Day, and remembers God often" (33:21).

We saw that being a Muslim and a servant of God depends upon obeying God. So also, it depends upon obeying Muhammad.

> Whosoever obeys the Messenger thereby obeys God. (4:80)

> Say: "If you love God, follow me, and God will love you and forgive you your sins; God is Forgiving, Compassionate." Say: "Obey God and the Messenger." But if they turn their backs, God loves not the truth-concealers. (3:31-32)

The connection that the Koran makes here between love for God and following the Prophet is especially significant, and we will return to it later. For now, let us simply suggest that love is a quality of soul and heart that bridges the gap between lover and beloved. In this case, the lover is the human being, and the beloved is God. The verse is telling people that if they want to gain nearness to God, they need to follow the example of Muhammad.

Good News and Warning

We have already met the Koranic expression "good news and warning" and passed it by without comment. In order to sum up the Islamic idea of prophecy, however, it may be useful to think about the implications of these words.

The Koran uses the expression "good news" (*bushra* and related terms) in about forty verses to refer to one or more prophetic messages. In half of these verses, it pairs the term with "warning" (*nudhur* and derivatives). In another ninety verses, it refers to prophetic warnings without mentioning good news. The word count suggests that prophecy has more to do with warning than with good news. Since the normal human reaction to a warning is to become fearful and wary, while the reaction to good news is to become happy, the Koran may be telling us that the intention of God in sending the prophets is more to stir up fear than to make people feel happy. This, we think, can be said for the Koran in general, and it follows naturally from the Koranic depiction of the human situation.

In trying to understand the message of the Koran, it is important to keep in view the intention of the author of the book who, in the Islamic view, is God. The author's intention thoroughly colors the text. This author is different from ordinary authors, who certainly write their books with a purpose, but who have no real control over how people will read their books. Given that this author is omniscient and knows his readers far better than they know themselves, he knows exactly how the book will be interpreted. You may object that many people will certainly misunderstand his purpose, but you cannot suggest—at least if you take seriously the idea of *tawhid* and the testimony of the book itself—that God did not anticipate the misunderstanding. In fact, he is making use of the misunderstanding for his own purposes, which do not necessarily coincide with human purposes. This is not unconnected to the concepts of guidance and misguidance:

> God is not ashamed to strike any similitude, a gnat or what is above that. Then those who have faith know that it is the truth from their Lord. But as for those who conceal the truth, they say, "What does God mean by this similitude?" God misguides many by it, and He guides many by it, and He only misguides the transgressors. (2:26)

> And when thou recitest the Koran, We place between thee and those who have no faith in the next world an obstructing veil, and

*We lay coverings upon their hearts lest they understand it, and in
their ears heaviness. (17:45-46)*

*Who is a greater wrongdoer than he who is reminded of the signs
of his Lord and then turns away from them and forgets what his
hands have sent forward? Surely We lay coverings upon their
hearts lest they understand it, and in their ears heaviness, and
though thou callest them to the guidance, yet they will never be
guided. (18:57)*

Why then did God reveal the Koran? There are many ways of answering
this question. One way is simply to say that he revealed it to give people
the good news of the eternal happiness that belongs to them by birthright and to warn them that they cannot count on reaching it. Along
with privilege comes responsibility. If you want to become someone of
real consequence—a servant and vicegerent of God—you have to put
your act together.

Certainly the Koran was not meant to be a history book, if history is
understood as the listing and ordering of historical events. The Koran
often refers to historical events, and there is no reason to doubt God's
veracity in his recitation of what happened. However, he always tells
the story to make a point, and he is a better storyteller than most.
Moreover, the Koranic stress upon signs should make it clear that God
is not interested in what we like to call facts. His message is a promise
and a threat. It is a spur to action, not a disinterested, objective,
historical account. The very idea that objective facts could exist apart
from human intention and interpretation is itself a peculiarly modern
invention that has lost all its appeal, except in popular culture. The
point of the text is not to supply curious bits of information so that our
stock of trivia will increase. Rather, the intention is to remind people of
what it means to be human.

To be human is to be made in the form of God and shaped by his two
hands. It is to embrace all the divine attributes and to manifest God's
beauty and majesty, mercy and wrath, gentleness and severity. It is to
live in accordance with *tawhid*. In respect of the attributes of majesty
and wrath, to be human is to be God's servant. In respect of the attributes of beauty and mercy, it is to be his vicegerent. *Tanzih* demands that
people see God as infinitely beyond themselves and infinitely different;
tashbih demands that they see him closer to themselves than their own
jugular veins.

But the picture of the human being just drawn is the picture of those
who have carried the Trust and actualized their *fitra*. Such people have
heard God's *dhikr* and have taken heed by remembering God. And such
people are extremely rare. Only the prophets and a few of God's friends
live up to *tawhid*. The rest of humanity is either totally overcome by

ghafla, or somewhere on the way to putting their lives together in accordance with prophetic instructions.

Given that most people are heedless of God and of their own innate nature, what they first have to be made aware of is that their situation is far from ideal. They have to wake up to the fact that God is distant from them and will remain distant if they do nothing to change themselves. "God will not change what is in a people until they change what is in themselves" (13:11). Of course, "God is with you wherever you are" (57:4), but that does not mean that we are with God. People have to achieve the awareness of God's presence. And that is not a small task, because in order to achieve it, they must become God's servants on the model of Muhammad.

People are naturally lackadaisical about things that do not seem real to them. Parents, teachers, and physicians can warn about the dangers of alcohol and drugs, but many turn a deaf ear. Scientists can warn as much as they want that pollution is destroying our planet, but most people consider ecology as someone else's problem. Those of us who have become accustomed to turning nature into dangerous waste at a scale unprecedented in human history are not ready to sacrifice anything significant of our precious lifestyle for the sake of our great-grandchildren. We assume that *they*—the people in the Third World—must do something to save their rain forests, because *we*—who have already laid waste to our natural environment—have the right to benefit from the status quo and to continue our extravagant ways.

We could provide many other examples from common experience. The point is simply that, as a general rule, people are too self-centered and ignorant to think beyond today. No matter how much they are told that they will benefit in the long run, they are not ready to sacrifice what they have in hand. In the Islamic view, God knows perfectly well what sort of dunces he has to work with. His task is somehow to wake them up, and he tries to do so by sending the prophets. "Speak to people according to the level of their understanding," the Prophet said. There is a difference between talking to our parents or a little sister, to a friend or a puppy dog, and so messages need to be tailored to the audience.

What is God's technique in addressing human beings? Basically, the carrot and the stick, the technique you would use with anyone with learning difficulties. However, for the theological reasons just mentioned, the stick precedes the carrot. God, who is the Real and the Good, is far away from his creatures, and there is every danger that people will remain distant from all that is real and good. As a result, they will continue to be dominated by the divine names of *tanzih*—majesty, severity, wrath, and vengeance. However, it is possible to move nearer to God, and in that case people will become intimate with the attributes of *tashbih*—beauty, gentleness, mercy, and forgiveness.

If God's intention in sending the prophets is to wake people up, it is beautifully summed up by the terms *good news* and *warning*. God wants to tell people who they are and to warn them that they cannot avoid the Trust that defines their human nature without suffering the consequences:

> *We sent the envoys only to bear good news and warning. (6:48, 18:56)*

> *Say: "God is witness between me and you, and this Koran has been revealed to me that I may warn you thereby and whomsoever it reaches." (6:19)*

God's warning is intimately bound up with *tawhid*. Since there is but a single Reality, everyone who attributes reality to anything other than God stands in *shirk*, the one unforgivable sin: "Give warning that there is no god but I, so be wary of Me" (16:2).

Serving other than God keeps people in distance from God. Hence God warns people of the pain and chastisement that are the human concomitants of divine names such as Wrathful and Vengeful. Besides fire, chastisement, and great violence, the Koran warns specifically of the Day of Judgment, when people will encounter God. They will meet him according to their relationship with him. If they are distant from him, they will meet his wrath and vengeance, but if they have made efforts to travel on the path to him, they will meet his forgiveness and mercy:

> *Now I have warned you of a Fire that flames up, whereat only the most wretched shall be roasted. (92:14-15)*

> *Then the truth-concealers will be driven in companies into Gehenna. . . . "Did not messengers come to you from among yourselves, reciting the signs of your Lord and warning you against the encounter of this day?" (39:71)*

> *. . . that he may warn them of the Day of Encounter, the day they shall come forth, and naught of theirs will be hidden from God. (40:15-16)*

> *And warn them of the Day of the Imminent when, choking with anguish, hearts are in the throats and the wrongdoers have not one loyal friend. (40:18)*

The Koran makes clear that only those with faith will respond to the warning. Others will not take it seriously:

> *Thou warnest only those who fear their Lord in the Unseen and perform the salat. (35:18)*

Alike it is to them whether thou hast warned them or thou has not warned them, they will not have faith. Thou warnest only him who follows the Reminder and who fears the Merciful in the Unseen. Give him the good news of forgiveness and a generous wage. (36:10-11)

Since God knows that they will not listen, one might ask, why does he bother warning them? The answer is God's justice. Wrongdoing is a creaturely attribute, not a divine attribute. No one will be able to blame God for leading people astray. He gives everyone plenty of warning, so if they fail to take heed, they have only themselves to blame. He lets them hang themselves with their own rope:

God is never unjust to His servants. (3:182, 8:51, 22:10)

We have revealed to thee as We revealed to Noah, and the prophets after him . . ., and messengers We have told thee of before, and messengers We have not told thee of . . .—messengers bearing good news and warning, so that people will have no argument against God, after the messengers. (4:163-165)

Even though the Koran stresses the consequences of God's wrath, it often reminds us that God's mercy is his dominant attribute. He may become wrathful toward his creatures, but his wrath is governed by mercy. He expresses his anger only to bring people to their senses. The goal of his severity is to act with his servants in the gentlest manner possible. It is no surprise when love and compassion make people act sternly toward their children. Nor should it be any surprise that God takes his servants to task for their own benefit. The good news brought by the prophets is intimately bound up with the predominant divine attributes of mercy, gentleness, and beauty. The Koran tells people not to give up hope because of the severity of the warning or their own inadequacies in face of the Real:

Say: O My servants who have been immoderate against yourselves, do not despair of God's mercy! Surely God forgives all sins. Surely He is the Forgiving, the Compassionate. (39:53)

Those who heed the message will fear the Merciful. The normal human reaction in the face of danger is to run the other way; but if they fear mercy, they can only fear that they may lose it. People who fear God do not run away from him, they run toward him. In any case, since God alone is real, there is nowhere else to run. Hence they follow the course of the Prophet's supplication: "I seek refuge in Thy good-pleasure from Thy anger, I seek refuge in Thy pardon from Thy punishment, I seek refuge in Thee from Thee." People must run away from God's wrath by clinging to his mercy, which means to flee from *shirk* to *tawhid*, from multiplicity to unity, from the many to the One. Notice how the following verses connect warning both with fleeing *to* God and with establishing *tawhid*, the only means available to bring about nearness to God:

> *So flee unto God! I am a clear warner from Him to you. And set not up another God with God! I am a clear warner from Him to you. (51:50-51)*

Those who can rejoice at the good news brought by the prophets are those who take refuge in God. They are those who submit to God's message. Or rather, they are those who have faith in the message (since mere submission is not sufficient) and who put the message into practice in a way that allows them to develop the character traits and virtues of Adam and the other prophets: humility, patience, god-wariness, and so on:

> *Be wary of God, and know that you shall encounter Him. Give good news to the faithful. (2:223)*

> *Give good news to the humble, whose hearts quake when God is mentioned, and who endure patiently whatever touches them, and who perform the* salat, *and expend of what We have provided for them. (22:34-35)*

> *Those who have faith and are god-wary—for them is good news in the present life and in the next world. (10:63-64)*

> *These are the signs of the Koran and a Clear Book, a guidance and good news to the faithful, who perform the* salat, *and pay the alms-tax, and have certainty about the next world. (27:1-4)*

In short, the intention of God in revealing the Koran only makes sense in the context of *tawhid* on the one hand, and ultimate human destiny on the other. We have discussed *tawhid*, so we now turn to the outcome of human life, which is the return to God.

Chapter 5.

THE RETURN

STAGES OF LIFE AND DEATH

The Return to God lies in the background of all Islamic beliefs and practices. It is impossible to grasp the significance of *tawhid* and prophecy without reference to it, just as it is impossible to grasp the significance of the Return without reference to *tawhid* and prophecy. The three principles of faith amplify the meaning of the basic creed, and that in turn expresses the sense of the word *God* as it has been revealed through the Koran. *Tawhid*, prophecy, and the Return are three faces of a single message. No matter which of the three is investigated, the other two have to be kept in view.

From one point of view, the discussion of prophecy is necessitated by the second Shahadah, "Muhammad is the messenger of God." But the second Shahadah itself is necessitated by *tawhid*, which demands both *tanzih* and *tashbih*. The moment it is understood that God has two hands, and that the right or merciful hand takes precedence over the left or wrathful hand, then it can be seen that God's mercy plays a fundamental role in his relationship with human beings. In order to attract people to his mercy, he sends the prophets with both good news and warning.

The whole of reality—which includes both God and the visible and invisible worlds—is oriented toward human well-being. This orientation can be called guidance. The Real's fundamental intention as Guide is to bring about human happiness and wholeness. Nevertheless, both hands of God are at work. People cannot focus on the right hand and ignore the left. If the right hand gives the good news of everlasting happiness, it also warns people that they dwell in the shadow of the left hand and must rearrange their lives in order to come out from under it.

This, in short, is the meaning of *tawhid* and prophecy. But from the human point of view, the all-important consideration here is that a happy outcome is not guaranteed. Human freedom plays a significant role. People are free enough to delay their passage into the experience of God's all-embracing mercy.

Muslim discussions of the Return are grounded in a specific concept of human nature and happiness. Understanding this concept demands that we also grasp the nature of human misery. We have already discussed the Covenant of Alast, *fitra*, the Trust, servanthood, and vicegerency, and now we turn to the consequences of human responsibility, or of carrying the Trust.

Discussion of the Return is commonly divided into two parts, called the compulsory Return and the voluntary Return. The division parallels the distinction between universal, cosmic *islam* and prophetic *islam*, or between compulsory servanthood and voluntary servanthood.

Human beings are compelled to submit to God in respect of their created nature, but at the same time they are free to accept or reject the prophetic messages. In a similar way, human beings have no choice but to return to their creator. Everyone dies, and everyone meets God. However, some people go happily with the knowledge that they have submitted to the instructions brought by the prophets and that God does not break his promises; others are pulled by the scruff of their necks:

Every soul shall taste death. (3:185, 21:35, 29:57)

O human being! You are laboring laboriously unto your Lord, and you shall encounter Him. (84:6)

God has promised those of them who have faith and do wholesome deeds forgiveness and a tremendous wage. (48:29)

Those that have faith and do wholesome deeds—them We shall admit to gardens through which rivers flow, therein dwelling forever and ever—God's promise in truth. And who is truer in speech than God? (4:122)

Surely God's promise is true, but most of them do not know. (10:55)

Surely death, from which you flee, shall encounter you. Then you shall be taken back to the Knower of the Unseen and the Visible, and He will tell you what you have been doing. (62:8)

If you could only see when the wrongdoers are in the agonies of death and the angels are stretching out their hands: "Give up your souls!" (6:93)

People are compelled to return to God after death, but they can also choose to return to him during their life in this world. Through becoming God's servants, they follow the road that leads to nearness. They may reach God before they leave the world (a goal that is stressed in Islam's third dimension) or, at death, they may simply find that they are situated relatively close to the Real. Hence, they will be more integrated and whole than those people who turned away and went about with what they thought was their own business.

The word *return* should alert us to the fact that authors who focus on the subject do not limit themselves to discussing where human beings are going. They also discuss where they have come from. To say that people are "returning" means that they have already been there. Typically, this discussion of where people come from fits under the heading *Origin (mabda')*. Many books have been written with the title "The Origin and the Return" or have incorporated these two words into their titles.

Both *origin* and *return* are derived from Koranic terminology, although the Koran employs other words as well to make the same point:

As He originated you, so you will return. (7:29)

He created you the first time, and unto Him you shall be taken back. (41:21)

As We originated the first creation, so We shall bring it back again. (21:104)

To Him is your going back, all together—God's promise in truth. He originates creation, then He makes it return, so that He may justly compensate those who have faith and do wholesome deeds. (10:4)

To God belongs everything in the heavens and the earth, and all things are taken back to Him. (3:109)

That "all things" or "all affairs" are taken back to God is a frequent Koranic refrain. Sometimes the Koran provides a few details of the human itinerary, starting from the beginning or near the beginning:

*How can you be ungrateful toward God when you were dead
things and He gave you life? Then He will cause you to die, then He
will give you life. Then you will be taken back to Him. (2:28)*

This verse lists the major stages that are normally discussed in books
on the Origin and the Return: nonexistence, this world, death, life in the
grave, and the resurrection. After the resurrection, people will be
divided into two groups, one of which enters the Fire and the other the
Garden.

Life and Death

In order to discuss the nature of the Return, constant reference has to
be made to the terms *life* and *death*. It is important to have a good idea
of what these two words mean. We just saw that the Koran refers to
people before entering into this world as "dead things." This cannot be
an absolute death, because people had to have existed in some manner
or else they could not have made the Covenant of Alast. Hence, the
world of death before this world is a relative death. In the same way,
life in this world is not an absolute life, because this life does not last
very long, nor can it be depended upon in any way. So also, death at the
end of life is not an absolute death. Rather, it is a transferal from one
mode of existence into another mode of existence, called the grave,
where things continue to happen and where the "dead person" continues to have experiences. Experience is an attribute of living beings,
not dead things. Hence, this is a death in relation to this world, not in
relation to the whole of reality.

The Koran calls God "the Alive, the Self-subsistent" (2:255). In other
words, God alone is alive through himself and subsists through himself. *Tawhid* demands that "None is alive but God, and none is self-
subsistent but God." Everything other than God, considered in isolation
from God, is dead and does not even exist. Only God has life and self-
subsistence. Hence, if things have life, it is because God has given them
life, and if they subsist, it is because God makes them subsist. Compared to God's life, the life of creatures who have been given life is
death. To say that people are alive is to say that they are not completely
dead at this moment, but in a very short time they will be experiencing
death; that is, the cessation of this ephemeral life. We experience this
death in life as the evanescence of life. "Everything is perishing except
the Face of God" (28:88).

If God gives life to things, he also takes it away. Hence, God is not only
called the Alive, he is also called the Life-giver and the Slayer. These are
three of his Koranic names.

Within the cosmos, there is no such thing as absolute life and absolute death. However, outside the cosmos, God is absolute life, while
nonexistence — which in any case does not exist — is absolute death.

God's life is pure and unmixed life with no taste of death. Death is defined as the lack of life or the cessation of life. Human life is an impure and mixed life that, during illness or mental anguish, may seem worse than death. Even during health, life is frail and unfaithful. No one can count on being alive tomorrow. But if human life is mixed with death, so also human death is mixed with life. On the plane of created existence, death and life are necessary to each other, like night and day. To experience one we have to experience the other.

When the Koran speaks of death, it usually means death in relation to the life of this world. In the verse just quoted, the Koran asks, "How can you be ungrateful toward God when you were dead things and He gave you life?" How can people conceal the truth of God and be ungrateful toward him, when the slightest meditation will show them that they have no claim on life? They were once dead, which is to say that they had no share in this world's life. They are now alive through no virtue of their own. Their present life derives from the luminosity of the spirit within them. Like the spirit's light within clay, life within the bodily frame is weak, but it is still life.

This World and the Next World

We have already discussed the structure of the Islamic cosmos. The basic given is that God is Real, and the universe is "other than God." Hence, the universe is unreal. However, there are different degrees of unreality, which is to say that there are different degrees of relative reality. Some things are less real than others, and some things more real. Only pure and simple nothingness is absolutely unreal—everything else has some degree of reality.

The heavens are more real than the earth, because the heavens are a high, luminous world, infused with divine attributes such as light, life, knowledge, desire, power, and speech. The heavens' inhabitants—such as angels and spirits—dwell in nearness to God. In contrast, the earth is a low, dark world, where the divine attributes are reflected only dimly. Those things that are of a pure earthly nature, such as inanimate objects, dwell in relative distance from God.

Between heaven and earth are situated a large number of creatures, such as plants and animals. These creatures have heavenly characteristics through their life, desire, power, and other divine attributes, and they have earthly characteristics through their bodies. They are, in effect, a mixture of the qualities of heaven and earth. Human beings are distinct from other animals in that they have been given a full retinue of the divine attributes, both those that are manifest in the heavens and those that are manifest in the earth. Other creatures lack certain attributes. Only human beings were taught "all the names."

The universe is hierarchically structured. Inanimate things, plants, and animals represent three ascending degrees of nearness to God, who is the Real. In other words, they represent three ascending degrees of reality. Hence, divine attributes, such as life, knowledge, desire, and power, become ever more clearly manifest and more intense as we move up the scale in the direction of the human being. In a similar way, the seven heavens represent ascending degrees of nearness to God. Beyond these heavens lies God's Footstool, then his Throne. On the Throne the Merciful sits, spreading his mercy throughout the universe. The universe itself is nothing but the mercy of God, his generous gift to those who have nothing of their own, not even existence.

This picture of the universe is basically static. It describes the situation of created things in relation to God at the present moment, but the Koran is far more concerned with a dynamic, changing relationship with God that it describes in terms of "that which is close" or "this world" (al-dunya), and "that which is last" or "the next world" (al-akhira). The Koran does not explain the exact relationship between the static and the dynamic pictures of the universe, so a variety of opinions can be found among the commentators.

"This world" is where we are now. "The next world" is where we will be after we leave this world. Some authorities say that the next world begins at the resurrection. From their point of view, the grave, which is the period between death and the resurrection, is an intermediate domain that shares the characteristics of both this world and the next world. It is similar to the soul, which is situated halfway between the body and the spirit. It is so similar to the soul, in fact, that it is often considered to be identical with the soul's existence after death. We will return to this idea later.

In the light of tawhid, we quickly understand that life in this world is ephemeral, since true life belongs to God alone. But the Koran does not make such statements without drawing conclusions. It points to the nature of things in order to bring out the meaning of existence for human beings. All things are signs and hence loaded with significance, but people are heedless and have to be reminded of the meaning. The Koran frequently tells us that the life of this world is ephemeral, either in so many words, or in parables such as the following:

> And strike for them the similitude of the life of this world: It is as
> water that We send down out of heaven, and the plants of the
> earth mingle with it, and in the morning it is straw that the winds
> scatter. (18:45)

The Koran insists that dedicating oneself to straw is to squander one's life and dissipate one's human substance. People should not devote themselves to something that is utterly undependable. They should not act as if life's meaning is found in the affairs of this world, or as if experienced phenomena were anything other than the signs of God.

Reality is not exhausted by what we see with our eyes. In short, the Koran says, do not be deluded by appearances:

> *The life of this world is naught but a sport and a diversion. (6:32)*

> *Surely those who look not to encounter Us, and who are content with the life of this world and at peace with it, and those who are heedless of Our signs, those—their refuge is the Fire. (10:7-8)*

> *They say, "There is only the life of this world—we shall not be raised up." If you could only see them when they are stationed before their Lord! (6:29-30)*

> *"Company of jinn and mankind, did not messengers come to you from among you, relating to you My signs and warning you of the encounter of this day?" They shall say, "We bear witness against ourselves." They were deluded by the life of this world. (6:130)*

> *O people, God's promise is true! So let not the life of this world delude you, and let not the Deluder delude you concerning God. (35:5)*

The life of this world is no life at all. True life is found in God and in nearness to God. The next world, in contrast to this world, will last forever, because it is situated closer to Reality:

> *Surely the abode of the next world is life, did they but know. (29:64)*

> *Are you so content with the life of this world, rather than the next world? Yet the enjoyment of the life of this world, compared with the next world, is a little thing. (9:38)*

> *Whatever you have been given is the enjoyment and adornment of the life of this world, but what is with God is better and more subsistent. Will you not use your intelligence? (28:60)*

Intelligence is a spiritual light that allows for the perception of *tawhid*. Innate to the *fitra*, intelligence immediately perceives that "There is no life but God's life" and that any other life is illusory.

The contrast between the reality of the next world and the illusory nature of life in this world is brought out nicely by a well-known hadith. The Prophet said:

> *On the day of resurrection, the inhabitant of the Fire who had the most blissful life in this world will be brought and dipped once*

*into the Fire. Then it will be said to him, "O child of Adam, have
you ever seen any good? Has bliss ever reached you?" He will reply,
"No, my Lord, I swear by God!"*

*The inhabitant of the Garden who had the most difficult misery
in this world will be brought and dipped once in the Garden. Then
it will be said to him, "O child of Adam, have you ever seen any
misery? Has any hardship every reached you?" He will reply, "No,
my Lord, I swear by God! No misery has ever reached me, and I
have never seen any hardship."*

The Grave

The first step toward the next world, or the first stage of the next
world, is called the grave. People get there through death. Death arrives
because of the activity of God, who measures out death just as he
measures out life. The idea that death is some kind of accident that
could have been prevented if we had been a bit more careful or if
medicine were a bit more advanced is utterly alien to the Islamic way of
looking at things.

The Koran often says that everything is created with a fixed term.
According to the Prophet, the angel who blows the human spirit into the
embryo writes down the person's term of life at the same moment. Not
only is death itself inescapable, but also the very day and hour of death
is forever fixed. Like every other divine quality, life is carefully appor-
tioned: "It is not given to any soul to die save by God's permission, and at
an appointed time" (3:145).

Of course, this does not mean that people should stop being careful.
The appointed time of death is simply one of many instances where free
will meets predestination. Choice plays a role, and no one denies his or
her own ability to make choices. To cease caring whether one is alive or
dead is to make a choice. The Koran commands people, "Do not throw
yourself into destruction with your own hands" (2:195). Muslims are
expected to take reasonable precautions, and since reasonableness is
always difficult to judge, they have to search for guidance, here as
elsewhere, in the Koran and the Prophet's Sunna. Thus, for example,
people's life spans and the way that they will die is fixed, even if they
commit suicide. But the Prophet made clear that suicide is a major sin
when he said, "If someone kills himself, he will remain in the Fire
forever." A person maintains responsibility for and suffers the consequences of the act.

The Koran sometimes refers to the misguided idea that we can
somehow delay death:

*Then, as soon as fighting is prescribed for them, there is a party of
them fearing the people as they would fear God, or with a greater*

*fear, and they say, "Our Lord, why hast Thou prescribed fighting
for us? Why not defer us to a near term?"... Wherever you may
be, death will overtake you, though you should be in raised-up
towers. (4:77–78)*

Death is inevitable, and no one can possibly know how or where it will
take place:

*No soul knows what it shall earn tomorrow, and no soul knows in
what land it will die. Surely God is Knowing, Aware. (31:34)*

The idea expressed in this verse is the theme of an often-told story
about King Solomon the prophet. Once, he was entertaining a friend. As
they were talking, Solomon's vizier entered to announce the arrival of
Azrael, the angel of death, who had come, as he often did, for a chat.
Solomon told him to be ushered in, and they discussed the universal
order and other such matters of prophetic and angelic concern. As soon
as Azrael left, Solomon's friend began asking him to send him on a
mission to India. Solomon asked him why this idea had suddenly
entered his head. He replied that when Azrael had entered the room, he
had given him a strange look. He was afraid that Azrael might be
coming back for him. Solomon was sure that the man was imagining
things, but in order to humor him, he agreed to send him to India on his
magic carpet. A few weeks later, Azrael came on another visit. Solomon
remembered the incident of his friend and asked Azrael if he had given
the man a strange look. Azrael replied, "Well, I may have, since I was
very surprised to see him here with you. Just that morning I had
received instructions to pick up his soul in India the next day."

  Although it is God who gives life and God who takes it away, he
always employs intermediaries in such tasks, and the intermediaries
who are closest to him are called angels. The Koran does not mention
Azrael by name, but it does refer to the "angel of death."

*Nay, but they are truth-concealers concerning the encounter with
their Lord. Say: "The angel of death, who is charged with you, will
cause you to die, then you will be taken back to your Lord."
(32:10–11)*

Having left their bodies behind in this world, souls are taken to a
summary judgment. Then they are made to dwell in the grave, which is
a place not exactly the same as the body's tomb in the earth, and not
completely different from it either. According to the hadith literature,
on the first night in the grave, two angels, called Nakir and Munkar,
examine people, asking them to identify their God, their prophet, and
their scripture. If they provide the right answers, their graves will be
made spacious and comfortable and they will live a delightful existence

until shortly before the day of resurrection, when the angel Seraphiel will blow on the Trumpet and everyone in the heavens and the earth will swoon. However, if people provide the wrong answers, their graves will become very tight and fill up with everything that they hate and fear, such as snakes, scorpions, and spiders, and these things will torment them until the Trumpet is blown.

People remain in their graves until the end of this world, and only God knows when that will be. In any case, existence in the grave is not the same as existence in our world, so things do not follow the same rules. For example, time loses its solidity and externality. In other words, in this world, you can tell how much time has passed by observing the sun and the moon or looking at a clock. But in that world, time is much more closely tied to the subjective perception of what is happening. Even in this world, five minutes under a dentist's drill can seem like an hour, and an hour of intense conversation with a friend can seem like five minutes. In that world, "seemingness" is everything. What things seem like to you will determine how your perception takes place, but the same things may seem different to other people. Everyone perceives in ways that are appropriate to his or her own nature. The period in the grave will seem very short for some people and incredibly long for others, even if they all died on the same day.

The End of the World

Just as the Koran warns of the events that occur after death, so also it warns of the end of time, when the heavens and the earth that human beings experience will be totally altered. The Last Day is not only the day of resurrection in the next world, it is also the end of the world as we know it.

Many events will occur before the Last Day as signs of its approach. The hadith literature is especially rich in describing these signs of the coming end. Certainly, the prophet Muhammad warned that the end was near. According to one hadith, he held up his thumb and forefinger with a tiny space between them and said, "I and the Last Hour are like this."

The idea that Muhammad is the last of the prophets is not unrelated to the idea that little time is left until the end of the world. His message represents the last chance for human beings to put their houses in order. Some in the early Muslim community, like many early Christians, expected the world to end within their own lifetimes. The fact that this world is still hanging on does not call into question the belief in the Last Day's imminence. One is simply reminded that for God, a "day" may last fifty thousand years (70:4). Or, as another Koranic verse tells us, "One day with your Lord is as a thousand of your counting" (22:47). Even if only an hour of a fifty-thousand-year day remained between Muhammad and the end, that could mean that we still have a good deal of time left to wait. What is certain in Koranic terms is that no one knows when the world will end except God himself. Anyone who claims to know is lying.

The end of the world, it should be noted, refers not only to the end of the macrocosm, but also to the end of the microcosm. What happens at the death of this world is similar to what happens at the death of the individual. Some of the following verses can be read as referring both to this world as a whole and to the life of individuals in this world. A hadith tells us, "When a person dies, he undergoes his resurrection." The later tradition calls this individual resurrection the "smaller resurrection" and assures us that it is but a foretaste of the greater resurrection that is still to come. In the following verses, "the Hour" is one of several Koranic designations for the end of time:

And the matter of the Hour is as the twinkling of the eye, or nearer. (16:77)

The Hour is coming, no doubt of it, and God shall raise up whosoever is in the graves. (22:7)

They will question thee concerning the Hour, when it shall arrive. Say: "The knowledge of it is only with my Lord. None but He shall disclose it in its time. Heavy is it in the heavens and the earth, and it will not come upon you except suddenly." (7:187)

The people will question thee concerning the Hour. Say: "The knowledge of it is only with God." What shall make thee know? Perhaps the Hour is near. (33:63)

The Koran is especially eloquent in describing the dissolution of this world that will occur on the Last Day. What the verses make clear is that the order and regularity that we imagine as fixed laws of nature will disappear. The whole universe will be rearranged:

On the day the earth shall be changed to other than the earth, and the heavens, and they come forth to God, the One, the Intensely Severe. (14:48)

On the day the Trumpet is blown, whosoever is in the heavens and earth will be terrified, excepting whom God wills. Everyone shall come to Him, all utterly abject. You shall see the mountains, that you supposed fixed, passing by like clouds. (27:87-88)

When the sun is enfolded, when the stars are darkened, when the mountains are taken away, when the pregnant camels are abandoned, when the wild beasts are mustered, when the seas are set boiling, when the souls are paired [with their deeds], when the buried infant is asked for what sin she was slain, when the scrolls are unrolled, when the heaven is pealed back, when hell is set blazing, when the Garden is brought near, then a soul will know what it has made present. (81:1-14)

The numerous verses that the Koran devotes to describing the Last Day invariably stress the awakening to reality that takes place for human beings. No longer is their any talk of signs, because now the meaning of the signs is being laid bare. People will understand that the world they experienced existed only to allow them to prepare themselves for permanence.

The Resurrection

When Seraphiel blows his trumpet for the second time, all human beings will pour forth from their graves and enter an enormous plain for the presentation to God:

And the Trumpet shall be blown, then behold, they are pouring out of the tombs unto their Lord. They say, "Alas for us! Who aroused us from our sleeping place? This is what the Merciful promised, and the envoys spoke truly!" (36:51-52)

On the day We take away the mountains and you see the earth brought forth, and We muster them so that We leave not one of them behind; and they shall be presented to your Lord in ranks. . . . (18:47-48)

This event is most commonly called *qiyama* (resurrection), the Arabic term meaning literally "the standing up." It is also called by such names as "the mustering" (*hashr*) and "the uprising" (*ba'th*). The events that take place at the resurrection last only for a single day, but some accounts tell us that this day will be equivalent to fifty thousand years of our reckoning. This is not surprising, given that the Koran says, "To Him the angels and the Spirit rise up in a day whereof the measure is fifty thousand years" (70:4). Coming out of the grave is also a rising up to meet God. People ascend from their graves into God's presence, just as the angels ascend up into the heavens. It could be objected that the accounts tell us that God is coming down to meet them. Of course, this is also true, but when God approaches people, they necessarily approach him. God is the Real, the High, the Transcendent, and the Good, and by descending to them, he makes them ascend toward these basic qualities of Reality.

If the earth "shall be changed to other than the earth" on the day of resurrection, this has to do with the fact that God's light will be manifest much more intensely than it was before. When the light descends, the darknesses disappear. There is no more need for signs, because the light has obliterated the obscurities that allowed people to be heedless and made it necessary for them to be reminded. Earth, as we saw earlier, is defined by the qualities that distinguish it from heaven. Heaven is bright and earth is dark. If God's light now fills the earth, it is no longer the earth that people knew:

> *The Trumpet shall be blown, and whosoever is in the heavens and whosoever is in the earth shall swoon, save whom God wills. Then it shall be blown again, and lo, they shall be standing and looking. And the earth shall shine with the light of its Lord, and the Book shall be set in place, and the prophets and the witnesses shall be brought, and judgment shall take place among them through the Truth. They shall not be wronged. Every soul shall be paid in full for what it worked. And He knows best what you are doing. (39:68-70)*

When light shines, people see. When God's light shines, people see themselves with a clarity that was never before possible. They can no longer hide from themselves or from others:

> *And the Trumpet shall be blown, . . . and every soul shall come, with it a driver and a witness. "You were heedless of this. Therefore We have now removed from you your covering, so your sight today is piercing." (50:20-22)*

Light, we always need to remember, is an attribute of God, and "There is no light but God's light." The Koran and other revealed books are light because they are God's self-expressions. All creatures partake of light through their created nature. Human beings increase their share of light inasmuch as they submit to the light that comes through guidance. The Koran, in the Islamic view, is the most intense of revealed lights. Hence, the most direct way of becoming luminous is to model oneself on the Koran. The Koran calls Muhammad a light-giving lamp because "his character was the Koran." The Koran had become his flesh and blood. The hadith collections record the following supplication that Muhammad used to recite during the ritual prayer, especially during the prostration:

> *O God, place a light in my heart, a light in my hearing, a light in my seeing, a light on my right hand, a light on my left hand, a light before me, a light behind me, a light above me, a light below me, and appoint for me a light.*

Not surprisingly, some versions of this hadith replace the last clause with the words "And make me into a light."

Another supplication that has been handed down from the Prophet says, "O God, show us things as they are!" In order to see, people must have light. In order to understand, they must have the spiritual light that is represented by the Koran and other revelations. As al-Ghazali put it, just as the sun allows the eye to see, so the Koran allows the intelligence to see.

All this helps us understand the significance of the shining of the light on the day of resurrection. Obscurities are lifted, and people see things as they really are. If they had become accustomed to seeing things wrongly in this world, their sight will have difficulty adjusting to the intense light of the next world. If they had not strengthened their sight through allowing their inner eyes to adjust to the light of revelation, they will be raised up blind at the resurrection. Their situation is exactly like someone who spent years in a dark cave and is suddenly brought out into the sunlight at noon:

> "My Lord, why have You raised me blind, when I used to be see-ing?" God shall say, "Even so it is. Our signs came to you, and you forgot them. And so today you are forgotten." (20:125-126)

> Are the blind and the seeing man equal, or are the darknesses and the light equal? (13:16)

> Are the blind and the seeing man equal? Will you not reflect? (6:50)

> Not equal are the blind and the seeing man, those who have faith and do wholesome deeds and the ugly-doer. (40:58)

The shining of the light at the resurrection will be a mercy for those who have eyes to bear it; they will be delighted by the encounter with their Lord. But the truth-concealers have dedicated their lives to extin-guishing light. Like bats, they will suffer when they can no longer find a place to hide:

> As for the truth-concealers, their works are as a mirage in a spa-cious plain which the thirsty man supposes to be water, till, when he comes to it, he finds nothing. There indeed he finds God, and He pays him his account in full—and God is swift at accounting. Or their works are as darknesses upon a deep sea covered by a wave, above which is a wave, above which is a cloud—darknesses piled one above the other. When [a truth-concealer] holds out his hand, he can hardly see it. And to whomsoever God assigns no light, no light has he. (24:39-40)

> *Upon the day when you see the faithful, men and women, their*
> *light running before them, and on their right hands. "Good news*
> *for you today! Gardens through which rivers flow, therein to dwell*
> *forever! This is indeed the mighty triumph."*
>   *Upon the day when the hypocrites, men and women, shall say to*
> *those who had faith, "Wait for us, so that we may borrow your*
> *light!" It shall be said, "Return you back behind, and seek for a*
> *light!" And a wall shall be set up between them, having a door in*
> *the inward whereof is mercy, and against the outward whereof is*
> *chastisement. (57:12-13)*

We have seen that the Koran promises in no uncertain terms that
people will encounter their Lord. One of the questions that theologians
often debated was whether or not this encounter implied the vision of
God. Most thought that it did, and they had Koranic verses and hadiths
to support them. The general picture, in fact, is that the vision of God is
the greatest possible bliss, and that all those taken to paradise will
achieve it. However, those who remain in hell will be barred from this
vision, and this will amount to the worst possible chastisement.

The idea of the vision of God should be easy to understand with the
help of *tanzih* and *tashbih*. God's majestic and severe attributes demand
distance from him and the experience of his wrath, while his beautiful
and gentle attributes bring about nearness and joy. To be unable to see
God is to dwell in distance from him and therefore to suffer the burning
fire of severity. To be able to see him is to be near to him and to enjoy the
cool light of his gentleness. The following verses are typically cited to
contrast the situation of those who see God and those who do not:

> *Upon that day faces shall be radiant, gazing upon their Lord, and*
> *upon that day faces shall be scowling, expecting a calamity to fall*
> *on them. (75:22-23)*

> *No indeed, but upon that day they shall be veiled from their Lord,*
> *then they shall roast in hell. (83:15-16)*

To be veiled from God is to be far from the light and overcome by
darkness:

> *As for those who have earned ugly deeds. . . ., abasement will cover*
> *them—and they will have no defender against God—as if their*
> *faces were covered with dark slices of night. Those are the inhabi-*
> *tants of the Fire, therein dwelling forever. (10:27)*

The Koran provides many descriptions of the events that will take place
on the day of resurrection, and the hadith literature adds many more
accounts. Among these events are the weighing in the scales, which has

already been mentioned. The angelic scribes record people's activities during their life in this world. At the resurrection, the angels place their scrolls in the scales. Hopefully, the good deeds will outweigh the evil deeds:

> *And We shall set up the just scales for the resurrection day, so that not one soul shall be wronged anything. Even if it be the weight of one grain of mustard seed, We shall produce it, and sufficient are We for accounters. (21:47)*

> *On that day . . ., whoso has done an atom's weight of good shall see it, and whoso has done an atom's weight of evil shall see it. (99:6-8)*

Another ordeal that people go through is passing over the Path (*sirat*). The Koran refers to Islam as the Straight Path, and Muslims pray to be led upon it when they recite the Fatihah. At the resurrection, the Straight Path is embodied as a bridge stretching over hell, thinner than a hair and sharper than a sword. People will be told to cross it, and some of them will practically fly, while others will gallop over like horses. But many will fall to their destruction at the first step. How one experiences the Path at the resurrection depends upon how one followed the Straight Path in this world.

The overall impression given by the Koran and the Hadith of the day of resurrection is that people experience fully God's awe-inspiring grandeur. Most of the accounts stress God's majesty, power, and overwhelming control of the situation and people's experience of their own nothingness. The situation stands in stark contrast with this world, where people fall into the habit of thinking that they are in control of their own lives. According to the Koran:

> *They measure not God with His true measure. The earth altogether shall be His handful on the day of resurrection, and the heavens shall be rolled up in His right hand. (39:67)*

A hadith explains some of the implications of this imagery:

> *God will roll up the heavens on the day of resurrection. Then He will seize them with his right hand. Then He will say, "I am the King. Where are the tyrants? Where are those who claim greatness?" Then He will roll up the earths in His left hand. . . . He will say, "I am the King. Where are the tyrants? Where are those who claim greatness?"*

People will be mustered "naked"—they will have none of the trappings of authority and power, none of the rich clothing and splendid possessions that gave them so much pride in this world. According to the Prophet, the first person to be given new clothing will be Abraham, the patriarch of Judaism, Christianity, and Islam, whom the Koran describes as the perfect *muslim*. The Prophet said:

> You will be mustered barefoot, naked, and uncircumcised. "As We originated the first creation, so We shall bring it back again—a promise binding upon Us. So We shall do" [21:104]. The first to be clothed on the day of resurrection will be Abraham.

God will judge among the people. Many hadiths say that the majority will be thrown into the Fire. However, as in all the important details of faith, a good deal of ambiguity remains, because other hadiths and Koranic verses stress God's mercy rather than his wrath.

God's mercy comes out most clearly in the question of intercession (*shafa'a*). The Koran tells us that no one can intercede with God without his permission (2:255). The Prophet said that God will give him the "praiseworthy station" (17:79) on the day of resurrection and that the mark of this station is that he will be the first to be given permission to intercede. When he has finished interceding for the members of his community, the other prophets will be allowed to intercede for their communities. Then the friends of God and the faithful will intercede, each in the measure of his or her own station with God. In one hadith the Prophet says:

> The angels will intercede, the prophets will intercede, the faithful will intercede, and none will remain but the Most Merciful of the merciful. Then He will take a handful from the Fire and remove a people who never did any good whatsoever.

According to some accounts, the chastisement of hell plays the role of a purgatory for those who have accepted *tawhid* but have committed major sins. Hadiths tell us that, one by one, the sinners will be plucked from the Fire as if they were burning coals and doused in the Water of Life. There "they will sprout like seeds in the rubbish brought by a flood."

Even those in hell should not give up hope. They might even try shouting a bit louder. The Prophet said:

> Two men who enter the Fire will shout more loudly. The Lord will say, "Bring them out."
> He will say to them, "Why did you begin shouting louder?"
> They will say, "We did that so that You would have mercy on us."
> God will say, "My mercy to you is that you should go from here and throw yourselves wherever you were in the Fire."

> *One of them will throw himself, and God will make the fire*
> *"coolness and safety" [21:69]. The other will stand up, but he will*
> *not throw himself. God will say, "What prevented you from throw-*
> *ing yourself as your companion threw himself?"*
>
> *He will reply, "My Lord, I hoped that You would not send me*
> *back into it after You brought me out of it."*
>
> *The Lord will say to him, "Yours is what you hoped." Then both*
> *of them will enter the Garden through God's mercy.*

God's mercy is frequently associated with his sense of humor. In one hadith, the Prophet said, "God laughs at the despondency of His servant and the nearness of its change"; that is, the fact that his situation is about to change and his despair will turn to joy. Having heard the Prophet say this, one of his companions asked, "O Messenger of God! Does God laugh?" He replied that he does. The companion said, "We will not lack any good from a Lord who laughs."

Several hadiths tell about the last man to be brought out of hell. One version tells us that he will be placed outside of paradise, facing hell:

> *He will say, "O my Lord, turn my face away from the Fire, for its*
> *odor has disgusted me and its blaze is burning me."*
>
> *God will say, "If I do that, what will keep you from asking for*
> *something else?"*
>
> *He will say, "No, by Your might!" Then he will make a pact and*
> *covenant with God as God wishes, and God will turn his face*
> *away from the Fire. When the man has turned his face toward the*
> *Garden and sees its splendor, he will remain silent as long as God*
> *wishes him to remain so. Then he will say, "My Lord, bring me for-*
> *ward to the gate of the Garden."*
>
> *God will say, "Did you not make a pact and covenant that you*
> *would not ask anything beside what you asked?"*
>
> *He will say, "My Lord, let me not be the most wretched of Your*
> *creatures."*

God finally accedes to his request, but again makes him promise not to ask for anything else. Eventually the man asks to be let into paradise. Then God scolds him for being deceitful and treacherous. But the man does not give up:

> *He will continue pleading with God until He laughs because of*
> *him. When He laughs, He will give him permission to enter the*
> *Garden. Then He will say, "State your wish".... Then, when he fin-*
> *ishes stating all his wishes, God will say, "That is yours, and the*
> *like of it as well."*

Hell and Paradise

No scripture devotes as much attention as the Koran to describing the torments of hell and the delights of paradise. Especially eloquent on these themes are the shorter chapters near the end of the book, most of which were revealed toward the beginning of the Prophet's career in Mecca. If you read these passages and try to imagine what they would mean to people with a strong sense that human life has an ultimate significance, then you begin to understand that there is nothing abstract about the Koran's warning and good news. The Koranic descriptions provide extremely powerful evocations of the consequences of human responsibility.

The Koran employs many different words to refer to hell, all of which call to mind the experiences that people undergo when they enter it. These include *fire, blaze, burning, Gehenna* (a word borrowed from Hebrew understood to mean "hellfire"), *crusher*, and *chastisement*. Typically, the Koran juxtaposes descriptions of hell with those of paradise, which it refers to by such words as *garden, peace, refuge, bliss, eternity,* and *everlasting life*:

> God will make those who have faith and work upright deeds enter gardens through which rivers flow. And those who conceal the truth will enjoy themselves and eat as cattle eat, and the Fire shall be their lodging. (47:12)

> The likeness of the Garden that is promised to the god-wary: Through it rivers flow, its produce is perpetual, and also its shade. This is the outcome of those who are god-wary. But the outcome of the truth-concealers is the Fire. (13:35)

> Woe that day unto those that cry lies, those who play at their affairs, the day when they shall be pitched into the fire of Gehenna: "This is the Fire that you cried lies to! What, is this magic? Or do you not see? Roast in it, and bear it patiently, or bear it not patiently, equal it is to you. You are only being recompensed for what you were doing."
> Surely the god-wary shall be in gardens and bliss, rejoicing in what their Lord has given them. . . . "Eat and drink, with hearty appetite, for what you were doing." (52:11-19)

By far, the most common word that the Koran employs to refer to paradise is *garden*, and most Koran translators translate the term as "paradise." After all, the English word *paradise* itself comes from an ancient Persian word meaning "garden." As with any Koranic term, one has to think about the ideas associated with it in order to understand its logic. Even when people are speaking English, it is not uncommon for them to say about an especially beautiful garden, "This is paradise." Paradise, after all, should be a place of happiness and elation. It takes a very jaded human being not to be moved by a garden full of beautiful flowers, singing birds, splashing fountains, bouncing butterflies, and trees weighed down with fruit. Spring, the time when gardens begin to bloom, is the time when sadness is overcome and the earth expands to let heaven enter into its midst.

One could go on and on attempting to describe what it is about gardens that make them attractive to human beings. Of course, one really has to be a poet to express the beauties of spring, and the poets of Islamic languages, especially Persian, have produced some of the most beautiful lyrical descriptions of gardens in world literature.

It might be said that many of these poets are talking about this world's gardens, not the next world's gardens. But by now, it should be obvious that in the Muslim view, beauty is God's attribute. The Prophet said, "God is beautiful, and He loves beauty." This follows naturally upon the Shahadah, "None is beautiful but God." Things made of dust can only borrow beauty, and they must give it back to its owner quickly. After all, why do flowers fade so fast? Even if the poets were describing gardens that they had seen with their physical eyes, this did not prevent their readers from taking their poetry as signs of the beauty of paradise. This was all the more true because some poets left no place for doubt as to where this world's gardens gain their beauty. Listen to Rumi, for example:

O laughing, new spring, you have come from No-place!
    You are like my beloved—What have you seen of her?
Laughing and fresh of face, you are green and musk-scented—
    Are you the same color as my friend? Did you buy some of her dye?
O wonderful season, you are hidden from the eye like the spirit!
    Your effects are manifest, your essence concealed.
Rose, why not laugh? You have been delivered from separation!
    Cloud, why not cry? You have been cut off from your friend!
Rose, adorn the meadow and laugh, for all to see—
    You had to hide among the thorns for many months.
Garden, take good care of all these new arrivals—
    You had heard that they were coming from the thunder.
Wind, make the branches dance in remembrance of the day
    when you blew into the embrace of my beloved.
Look at these trees, all of them joyful like a gathering of the blessed—
    O violet, why are you bent over in pain?
The lily says to the buds, "Though your eyes are closed,
    They will soon open, for you have been given a taste of good fortune."[16]

One of the most common Koranic descriptions given to paradise is "gardens through which rivers flow," a phrase that occurs in about thirty-five verses. Flowing water adds beauty and freshness to any garden. But the Koran lets us know that these are not ordinary rivers:

> *This is the similitude of the Garden which the god-wary have been promised: Therein are rivers of water unstaling, rivers of milk unchanging in flavor, and rivers of wine—a delight to the drinkers—and rivers too of purified honey. . . . Are they as those who dwell forever in the Fire, such as are given to drink boiling water, that tears apart the bowels? (47:15)*

Not surprisingly, the divine names and attributes that the Koran associates with hell are those of majesty, severity, and wrath, while the names it associates with paradise are those of gentleness and mercy:

> *Those who conceal the truth of God's signs, for them awaits a severe chastisement. And God is Mighty, Vengeful. (3:4)*

> *On whomsoever My wrath alights, he has fallen into ruin. (20:81)*

> *Their Lord gives them good news of mercy from Him and good pleasure; for them await gardens wherein is lasting bliss, therein to dwell forever; surely with God is a tremendous wage. (9:21-22)*

THE UNFOLDING OF THE SOUL

Shaping the Divine Form

If you want to learn exactly what the Koran says about the Return, you can find out quickly—if you read the book—that a series of events will occur and that the way in which people will experience these events will depend to a certain extent on human responsibility. However, in order to grasp what the Return has to do with the human role as microcosm and divine form, we need the help of the later tradition. We will see in what follows that just as *tawhid* and prophecy find their human relevance, justification, proof, and verification through the Return to God, so also Islamic teachings on the structure of the macrocosm and microcosm only make complete sense in the context of human destiny.[17]

God created human beings in his own form, which is to say that he taught them all the names. Adam had an actualized knowledge of these names, but he was still susceptible to temporary forgetfulness. The rest of the human race is born into a heedlessness that is more than temporary. The divine qualities are latent within them, but these qualities need to be brought out from latency and be embodied in people's minds and activities.

We said that the names taught to Adam were the names of all things, all creatures. According to many theologians, these names included the names of God. Others hold that the names of the things are themselves names of God, since any name that can correctly be applied to reality also names the Real. In this case, we have to say that besides the ninety-nine most beautiful names, God has an infinite number of other names. Even if we want to insist that the names taught to Adam were only the names of the creatures, we will still have to admit that every creature is a sign of God. Every creature signifies, and hence names, God's reality. Since the creatures are infinite, God's signs are infinite.

However we understand the names taught to Adam, we know that knowledge of these names gave Adam his superiority over other creatures. God told the angels to prostrate themselves to Adam only after Adam had shown them his knowledge of the names. And though Adam was forgetful on one instance, God reinstated him as his favorite and made him a prophet.

God had created Adam to be his vicegerent. Vicegerency is the birthright of his children. However, they will only achieve the vicegerency if they follow the prophets. They must adopt the faith and practice given by God through the scriptures: "God has promised those who have faith and work wholesome deeds to make them vicegerents in the earth, even as He made those who were before them vicegerents" (24:55). To be God's vicegerent means, among other things, to manifest all the divine attributes in the form of which human beings were created. Only by embodying God's own qualities can human beings represent him. But we have also learned that most people do not live up to their potential. Even if they do have faith and work wholesome deeds, they never become dependable servants of God, because caprice and heedlessness often make them ignore or forget their proper duties.

When we take this discussion outside the issue of good works and correct practice, we can look at it from the perspective of cosmology and psychology. This view provides a different way of understanding things that is less anthropomorphic and moralistic.

When a human being is conceived in the womb, we are dealing at first with "clay," but a clay that is being molded by God's two hands. The Koran frequently refers to God's activity in the womb and after:

> It is He who created you of dust, then of a sperm-drop, then of a blood-clot, then He delivers you as infants, then that you may attain your maturity, then that you may be old—though some of you there are who die before it—and that you may reach an appointed term. And perhaps you will use your intelligence. (40:67)

The clay is not sufficiently molded to accept the divine breath until the end of the fourth month. Then the angel blows the spirit into the body.

During the whole period in the womb, the embryo exhibits qualities proper to minerals and plants. The embryo may have other qualities, but none of them would be displayed to our senses. The fact that closer examination, by the use of instruments for example, might yield a different picture, is another issue altogether.

When the infant is born, the first qualities it makes manifest are those proper to the animal kingdom. Animals, in fact, reach maturity much more quickly than human children; hence, they exhibit the full range of the qualities of their species within a few days or, at most, a few months after their birth. But individual human beings practically never exhibit the full range of the qualities of their species, since that range is unlimited.

The divine attributes appear in a very weak form through the vegetal faculties of the embryo. Like plants, the embryo exhibits life. It attracts nourishment to itself, digests, and is able to grow. Gradually, the animal faculties appear within the embryo, and the mother might become aware of these the first time she receives a kick. In former times, her awareness of the embryo's life was known as the "quickening" of the womb. When the child is born, attributes shared with other animals, such as appetite and anger, soon appear. These two manifest the divine attributes of desire and wrath.

It seems safe to say that all cultures have recognized the almost magical power connected with speech. We have already noted that the Koran holds that God creates and reveals through speech. In the same way, through speech, human beings understand God and return voluntarily to him. Learning the Koran and practicing the religion depend upon speech. When the Muslims translated the expression "The human being is a rational animal" into Arabic from Greek, they stressed a part of the meaning of the Greek expression that we have almost lost in English. The literal sense of the Arabic expression is, "The human being is a speaking animal." Rationality is intelligence articulated through speech, and so also, speech is expressed rationality. If speech is not rational, it becomes the barking of a dog or the singing of a bird.

We can take speech as the specific divine attribute that distinguishes human beings from other earthly creatures (but not from angels and jinn, since they also speak). Speech, we have suggested, is self-expression by one who is self-aware. When God speaks, he knows exactly what he is saying and why he is saying it. Animals say many things, no doubt, but their speech and self-awareness are severely limited, so much so that it is fair to say that they do not possess these attributes. Human speech, in contrast, should be self-aware. But in many cases, it may hardly be so. As with other human qualities, the opposition of "what it should be" to "what it is in fact" quickly enters the discussion.

What are human beings able to say and understand by means of speech? There are limits, no doubt, but the limits are not defined by a specific person, a specific language, or a specific historical era. The limits are defined by what it means to be human. To understand human limits, we have to look at the great exemplars of the human race, those who have embodied the divine qualities to the fullest degree. In terms of speech, we will have to think about the greatest speakers of the human race, which includes those who were receptacles for the scriptures and those who produced the finest masterpieces of world literature. Here, one of the meanings of the myth that Adam was taught the names of all things in all the languages of the world becomes obvious. Since human beings know innately all the names, they are able to make manifest all of speech's possibilities.

By meditating upon the way that speech has become manifest within human history, we quickly come to understand that we ourselves represent extremely imperfect embodiments of its possibilities. Where is the greatest contemporary poet compared to a Shakespeare, a Dante, a Hafiz? Where does that leave the rest of us? And on the level of world masterpieces, can a Shakespearean play really compare to the Bible, the Tao Te Ching, or the Bhagavadgita?

Let us consider the infant. Having come into the world, the infant does not begin developing the human quality of speech for several months at least. Once it begins to develop the possibilities of speech, there is no reason to assume that this development will cease before death.

What is the ideal course of development that the human child should follow in bringing speech into actuality? Here, our own culture has no commonly accepted answers. Opinions differ radically according to one's schooling, or lack of it. Everyone has an authority or two to whom he or she appeals. Some will tell us that psychology provides the answers, others sociology, and others philosophy, religion, or their uncle. One child psychologist will tell you something different from the next, and any grandmother will tell you that the child psychologists don't know what they're talking about.

Within the context of traditional Islamic civilization, differences of opinion were much less marked than they are today. People agreed that speech was a divine attribute, that the most perfect language was found in the Koran, and that the Prophet was the most eloquent human speaker. Real speech was God's speech. "There is no speech but the divine speech." If people are serious about developing this divine attribute, they must begin where that divine attribute has taken accessible form, and that is in the Koran. Hence, once again, we see that Islamic culture universally recognized the importance of embodying the Koran and becoming light.

Imagination

The Muslim psychologists gradually developed various theories based on the Koran and the Hadith in order to explain how the human soul grows from a potential divine form to a completely actualized divine form. Their basic approach hinges on the intermediate nature of the soul that we mentioned in our discussion of *tawhid*. To review what we said there, the human being comes into existence compounded of divine breath and clay, or spirit and body. The inherent qualities of spirit are light, life, knowledge (or awareness), desire, power, speech, and so on, all the way down the list of the ninety-nine attributes of God. In contrast, body—inasmuch as it is only clay—possesses none of these qualities to any appreciable degree.

The soul represents the meeting place between spirit and body, or between light and darkness, life and death, awareness and unconsciousness. Any given human being represents a mixture of knowledge and ignorance, power and inability, desire and disinclination. If we meditate upon the different divine qualities, we quickly find that they are found in different people in different degrees. We just discussed how speech can be present in human beings from the level of baby talk to prophetic recitation. In the same way, life is not present to the same degree. We are all alive, of course, but some are ill, aged, or closer to death than others. The discrepancy in the degrees in which the attribute of power become manifest are especially obvious, since our culture has given special importance to power for centuries. By power we mean the ability to control things. On one level, this is physical strength, in which people are extremely diverse. On another level, it is social power, which may be actualized financially, politically, or in other ways.

Each of us is a soul, a breath of God blown into clay, or an embodied spirit. We have no direct awareness either of the spirit or the body. The soul defines what we experience of ourselves. Our experience of our own and other bodies is mediated by the soul, and so also our experience of the spirit. Awareness and perception, through which we know our bodies, are qualities of our souls. The source of awareness is the spirit and, in the last analysis, God, since "None has awareness but God."

The body, as a body, has no perception, since it is simply clay. And the spirit, as spirit, cannot be perceived, since it is the ultimate subject of our awareness. The spirit perceives, and hence it cannot be perceived, any more than we can see our own eyes. Of course, to see the eyes you can use a mirror, and likewise, to see the spirit, you can look into your own soul, which reflects the spirit. But the "you" that underlies all your looking and can never be looked upon itself is the spirit.

We have seen that one of the words that is employed to bring out the nature of the soul is *imagination*. It is characteristic of an image to be identical and different at the same time. Take, for example, a photograph of the White House. The image belongs to the White House, not the Senate or the Supreme Court and hence, in respect to the contents, the image is identical to the object portrayed. But of course, the image is also different, since it is only a chemically established picture on paper. Traditionally, the most commonly cited example of an image is a mirror image.

To come back to the soul, it is an image of both the spirit and the body. Inasmuch as the soul images the spirit, it is light, life, knowledge, desire, power, and so on. But inasmuch as the soul images the body, it is darkness, death, ignorance, and inability.

The intermediateness of the soul is not static. Like a dream image, the soul undergoes constant transformations. It is sufficient to sit down in a quiet place and turn one's gaze within oneself to realize that the objects of our awareness undergo a never-ending flux.

Through the activities of everyday life, people manifest the divine qualities that are latent within themselves. One moment they may put generosity to work, and at another moment they may manifest the divine name Withholder. Their awareness of self and others never stays the same. Ideally, people should actualize more and more of the knowledge taught to Adam through their interaction with God's creatures. The Five Pillars and practices such as the remembrance of God are designed to focus awareness on the actual self-expression of God and allow the divine form within to unfold itself in keeping with the full manifestation of the Real's attributes. But one thing is sure: As an imaginal reality, the soul does not stay the same for two successive instants.

Many other words have been employed to explain the status of the soul as an ambiguous reality situated halfway between spirit and body. For example, the soul is said to be the embodiment of the spirit. Through taking on the contours of the body in the soul, the spirit is able to display its own qualities, such as power and speech. The spirit could not speak without the intermediary of the body. The soul is the meeting place between the spirit and the words that we hear issuing from the mouth of the speaker. The spirit's speech, like God's speech, becomes articulated only when it is externalized through words. The movement from unarticulated awareness to words and sentences occurs through the soul. This is something we all experience.

For example, you are a mathematician and someone asks you a difficult question in your field. You know the answer immediately without thinking, but in order to express the answer, it will take you ten minutes of talking. Here the unarticulated and unembodied spirit— your awareness and understanding—enters into the form of discrete words and sentences by means of the soul.

Words themselves are imagination. They represent the nature of the soul in the domain of speech. The words are neither awareness nor bodily things. Like souls, they are intermediate realities between spirit and body.

One of the qualities of the spirit is its oneness. The divine breath is a single, indivisible reality that is luminous, aware, desiring, and powerful. In contrast to the spirit, the body is infinitely divisible, and neither the body nor any of it parts is a whole unto itself. The oneness of the body has to do with the wholeness that is established by the power of the spirit. Otherwise, the body simply disintegrates into dust. Hence, the spirit is one, while the body is many.

The soul is both one and many. It is one, because each of us is a unique personality who does not deny the fact that "I am I." But the soul is also many, because the one soul has numerous functions through its embodiment. This single I is alive, knowing, desiring, speaking, hearing, seeing, tasting, touching, remembering, and so on. And many of these powers or faculties of the soul are connected to specific bodily organs. In short, the soul is the embodiment of the spirit; without the spirit, there would be no unity, and without the body, there would be no multiplicity.

In the world of our experience, one of the best analogies for the soul as embodied spirit is visible light, which is a single reality. However, as soon as the single reality of light strikes bodily things, it takes on colors. Those colors are present as potentialities within the light from the beginning, but they cannot become actualized without surfaces to strike or some other physical manipulation, such as a prism. In the same way, life, knowledge, and power are present within the spirit, but they cannot become actualized without the body. Hence, in this analogy, light corresponds to the spirit, colors to the soul, and the physical objects that the light strikes to the body.

Just as imagination is often described as being the embodiment of spiritual things, so also it is often called the spiritualization of bodily things. Typically, in this discussion, another dimension of the soul's reality is envisaged. Notice how, through our perception, we take things that exist in the external world and transfer them into our own souls. We see a tree, or a house, or a person, and that seeing is itself an activity of the soul. What was a bodily thing—the tree, the house, the person—becomes a spiritualized thing; that is, a thing that is now present within the luminosity of our awareness. That thing is now part of ourselves. It is alive with our life. What had been dead—inasmuch as it was simply clay—is now alive through us. Hence, it has been spiritualized in relation to what it was.

Notice that the concepts of body and spirit are relative, not absolute. For example, the soul is body in relation to spirit, since—when compared to the spirit—it has all the qualities of body—darkness, death, ignorance, weakness, and so on. But when compared to the body, the soul is spiritual, since it has all the qualities of spirit—light, life, knowledge, power, and so on. Hence, once again, the soul is ambiguous. It is "imagination," an image of spirit and an image of body, but it is neither pure body nor pure spirit.

With this understanding of imagination in the background, we can look again at the development of the soul. All the divine qualities present within the soul are imaginal (not imaginary); that is, they partake of the characteristics of images. Hence, for example, the life of the soul is an image of life. True life is God's life, while unmixed created life belongs to the angels. Human life is an image of true life, which is to say that it is both similar to God's life and different from it. Inasmuch as it is similar (*tashbih*), people are truly alive. Inasmuch as it is different (*tanzih*), people are in fact dead. Are they alive or dead? Both, or neither. Or again, it depends what you mean by the question. Compared to stones, they are alive, but compared to angels, they are dead. To the extent that the image corresponds to the original object, which is God's life, then the life of the soul is true and real.

We could now engage in a similar discussion for other divine qualities, such as knowledge, desire, power, speech, generosity, and justice, but that is an exercise that can be completed by anyone who thinks about what was just said. Hence, we will only make one further point before moving on.

The development of the human soul takes place in an imaginal realm. In other words, all the qualities that pertain to the divine form—all the names that were taught to Adam—remain hanging between spirit and body. However, as each quality develops, it becomes a stronger image of the original, which is God's attribute. At the beginning of human development, *tanzih* dominates over the human makeup. People are extremely distant from God, since the divine qualities are barely discernible within the infant. But as people develop in harmony with the prophetic guidelines, the divine attributes are strengthened. The dim light that was shining at the beginning becomes more and more perceptible. Knowledge and awareness increase. Bodily life may increase only to decrease again, but the true life that pertains to the soul keeps on increasing despite the body's death.

If, as we said above, the spirit can be compared to light, the body to surfaces upon which light shines, and the soul to colors, then we can extend the analogy to explain what happens when the human soul develops in harmony with the divine model.

In infancy, the darkness of the body dominates and the light of the spirit is as yet hidden and undifferentiated. Gradually, colors start to appear. At first, the primary colors appear, corresponding to life, awareness, desire, and power, but they are very dark, since the light is weak. Gradually, the light intensifies and the colors brighten, but along with the primary colors, other colors appear. Eventually, there is no limit to the number of colors that may become manifest, just as there is no limit to the number of divine attributes that can appear. Light has infinite possibilities of display, and so also does the spirit, which is the invisible light of God.

Each unique color that appears from light is latent within light itself. Once manifest, it is an image of light, which is to say that it is both light and not light. It is light because there is nothing else that appears. It is not light because each of the colors represents only a minuscule proportion of light's possibilities. Moreover, when the colors appear, they do so only because the light has become dim. If the light were to shine in its full brilliance, no one would be able to see anything. The veil that prevents us from seeing God is the brilliance of the light itself. As the Prophet said, "God's veil is light." Many of these ideas are implicit in the following hadith, which is often quoted in psychological and cosmological treatises:

> God has seventy veils of light and darkness. Were they to be removed, the glories of His Face would burn away everything perceived by the sight of His creatures.

The Dreamworld

In discussing how the soul develops and what it experiences after death, many Muslim authors appeal to dreams as a kind of foretaste. The world that we experience during dreams is a world of imagination. In dreaming, the soul perceives images. These images are neither the soul itself nor other than the soul, and they are neither the things that are perceived nor other than the things that are perceived. The whole domain is one of ambiguity and wonder.

When you see your sister in a dream, it is truly your sister because it is not your mother or your daughter. On the other hand, it is not your sister, because your sister does not dwell in your soul, nor does she have exactly the same characteristics as the dream image. One could say that the image of your sister is simply yourself. You are seeing your memories of your sister in a form that is appropriate to the psychological state you are in while dreaming. But again, your sister still retains her identity, because she is not your uncle.

Are dream images embodiments of the spiritual, or spiritualizations of the bodily? They may be either, or both, depending on how we look at them. Inasmuch as they are embodiments of your own awareness, the spiritual has become bodily. But inasmuch as your mind has taken perceived images from the outside world, they are spiritualizations of the bodily.

Both the Koran and the Hadith make a close connection between death and sleep. Muslims have traditionally understood sleep and death as two manifestations of a single reality. In both cases, direct awareness of the outside world is cut off, but in both cases, the self-awareness of the soul continues. The basic difference, according to the Koran (39:42), is that after sleep, God puts the soul back in control of the body.

Dreams are phenomena that pertain primarily to sleep. They represent a mode of self-awareness during sleep. Is there anything we experience in death that is similar to the dreams we experience in sleep?

Many Muslim thinkers answer, "Yes, everything." The best way to grasp the nature of the experiences of the soul after death is to understand the nature of dreaming.

How do we understand dreaming? Anyone who has reflected on his or her own dreams knows that they are normally confused and confusing. In Islam, dream interpretation has been considered a gift that is given to the prophets. The most famous example is provided by the story of Joseph and his imprisonment in Egypt, which is retold in Sura 12 of the Koran as "the most beautiful story." Joseph's whole adventure began because he dreamed that the sun, the moon, and eleven stars prostrated themselves before him. When he was finally released from prison in Egypt, it was because he was able to interpret the dream of the king. And only then, once he had saved Egypt from famine and rescued his own family, did God make clear to him the meaning of his own dream: His parents and his eleven brothers prostrated themselves before him in gratitude.

Many hadiths tell of Muhammad's expertise at dream interpretation. His companions would come to him and tell them their dreams, and he in turn would explain the meaning of the dreams to them.

Not surprisingly, dream interpretation has always been a popular branch of learning in Islam. In certain respects, Islamic dream interpretation is similar to the dream interpretation that one finds in popular books today or in tomes on psychology: Always there is attention to the idea that the perceived image is a sign of something beyond itself. The secret in dream interpretation is to recognize what has displayed itself in the specific image, but in order to do that, the interpreter must have a good knowledge of human psychology in general and of the person whose dream is being interpreted in particular.

In Islam, those who were reliable dream interpreters, after the Prophet, were certain holy individuals. It was generally recognized that the understanding of the human psyche is not given to everyone. Ultimately, since the human being is a divine form, one must have direct knowledge from God in order to understand the real significance of dream images. Nevertheless, a certain amount can be understood by anyone.

The most important principle of the science of dream interpretation is appropriateness or correspondence. In order to interpret a dream correctly, one must perceive the qualities manifest in the dream and then understand how these qualities correspond to the qualities of something else that is hidden from the perception of the dreamer.

Al-Ghazali provides an example of appropriateness in an anecdote related from a famous early dream interpreter called Ibn Sirin (d. 110/728–9). A man dreamt that he wore a seal ring on his hand. Seal rings were used to seal letters. Molten wax was placed on the envelope, and then the person sealed the letter with his ring. So long as the seal was not broken, the recipient knew that no one else had read the letter.

In the dream, the person saw that he was sealing not letters, but the mouths and the private parts of men and women. He came to Ibn Sirin and asked him the meaning. Ibn Sirin replied that this was very simple. The man was a muezzin for the local mosque, and it was now the month of Ramadan. Hence, the man had simply dreamed, in an appropriate form, that he was giving the call to prayer in the morning. By giving the call to prayer, he announced to everyone that the fast had begun and they could no longer eat, drink, or engage in sexual relationships.

This is not the place to continue expanding on the Islamic understanding of dreams. It is sufficient to grasp that all Muslims knew that dreams were not to be taken at face value. Dreams had to be understood in terms of some appropriate correspondence between the image and the meaning that had become embodied through the image. And everyone also knew that sleep and death were somehow similar in their characteristics. Hence, to many Muslim thinkers, it was self-evident that we can throw light on the nature of experience after death by investigating the nature of dreams and the correspondences that exist between the perceived images and the meanings that appear in the images.

The *Barzakh*

We said earlier that the grave is one of the stages of human becoming, a stage that extends from the moment of death to the day of resurrection. The grave is often given the name *barzakh*, which means "barrier" or "something that intervenes between two other things." The Koranic source of the term is this passage:

> *Till, when death comes to one of them, he says, "My Lord, return me; perhaps I will work wholesomeness in what I left behind." No, it is but words he speaks. And behind them is a* barzakh *until the day they shall be raised up. (23:99-100)*

In two other verses, the Koran employs the term *barzakh* to refer to an isthmus between two oceans, the sweet ocean and the salty ocean.

> *It is He who let forth the two seas, this one sweet, refreshing, and that one salt, bitter to the tongue. And He set between them a* barzakh, *and a forbidden barrier. (25:53)*

> *He let forth the two seas that meet together, between them a* barzakh *that they do not overpass. (55:20)*

Some Koran commentators say that the two seas are symbols for the
world of spirits and the world of bodies. These two worlds are seas
because, like the ocean, they are full of an enormous variety of living
things, about which we know little. Oceans are water, after all, and "Of
water We made every living thing" (21:30). Sweet water is purity and
clarity, liquid light, angelic freshness. Salty water is mixed with all
sorts of impurities, like the extremely dim light that is reflected in the
world of bodily things. "Not equal are the two seas—this is sweet,
refreshing, delicious to drink, and that is salt, bitter to the tongue"
(35:12).

If we understand the two seas as allusions to spirits and bodies, then
we can understand the *barzakh* as the intermediate world of imagination that keeps the two seas separate. But the *barzakh* itself allows for a
meeting between the sweet and the salty. In Islamic philosophy and
cosmology, the word *barzakh* came to signify any intermediate world or
reality. In the cosmological context, the term has two basic meanings,
depending on which picture of the cosmos we have in mind.

When we look at the cosmos from an atemporal, static perspective,
we see that it is a spectrum extending from light to darkness. At the
summit of the created world stands the world of pure created light,
inhabited by angels, spirits, and intellects. At the bottom is found the
world of almost pure darkness, inhabited by bodies. In between is
found a vast world inhabited by souls, jinn, and satans. The middle
world is the world of imagination or the *barzakh*, because it acts as a
barrier between the sweet sea of the spiritual world and the salty sea of
the corporeal world, or because it partakes of qualities that pertain to
both sides.

When we look at the cosmos in a temporal, dynamic perspective,
then we have two worlds—this world and the next world. This world
extends from the time of Adam to the day of resurrection, when the
next world begins. But where are people who have died? Are they in
this world or in the next world? The answer has frequently been,
neither. They dwell in the *barzakh*, which is an intermediate stage
between the impure and obscure domain of this world (the salty sea)
and the pure domain of light that is the next world (the sweet sea). In
support of this interpretation, commentators cite the first verse on
the *barzakh* quoted above: After death, people cannot return to this
world, because "behind them is a *barzakh* until the day they shall be
raised up."

Those who discuss the characteristics of the *barzakh* after death
agree that it is an imaginal world. In other words, everything that
appears to the soul in the *barzakh* appears to it in an appropriate
form that is neither purely spiritual nor purely corporeal. All *barzakh*
experience corresponds exactly to the works, thoughts, and character
traits that marked the soul's development in this world. Moreover,
given the dynamic and ever-changing nature of imagination, the *bar-*

zakh is not a fixed state, but a continual flux, a river of constantly changing experiences.

What does this mean in concrete terms? It means that after death, the soul experiences itself in forms that are appropriate to its own nature. But its nature after death is determined by its development through life. If the soul had developed in conformity with the *fitra* and had embodied all the divine attributes latent within its divine form, then it will be healthy, harmonious, balanced, unified, and integrated. In other words, it will have developed in keeping with *tawhid*.

In contrast, if the soul had lived the life of a truth-concealer and had refused to conform itself to Reality, then it will be far from unity. Some divine attributes will be partially developed, while others will be atrophied. The result will be a soul that dwells in disharmony, disintegration, and dispersion. In other words, instead of being dominated by the spiritual side of reality (the sweet sea), the soul will be dominated by the bodily side (the salty sea).

The terms we are employing here—harmony, integration, balance—are rather abstract. What do they mean concretely? What is the actual experience of the soul after death? Here the tradition answers by saying that the world after death combines spiritual and corporeal experience into a unity, as in dreaming. In dreams, it is difficult to distinguish between body and soul, since all the dream imagery is both bodily and psychological. We *see* and *experience* our psychological states in concrete form. This is precisely the nature of imagination. In the *barzakh*, harmony is not experienced as some abstract, disembodied, angelic quality, but rather as we would experience it in this world—by walking through a beautiful garden, or meditating upon a beautiful face, or listening to exquisite music.

The world of imagination is the world of the soul, and some would say that it is nothing but the soul. The soul possesses all the senses. It sees, hears, smells, tastes, and touches. It would be a mistake to think that the soul needs physical eyes and ears to see and hear. The soul sees and hears perfectly well in the dreamworld without eyes and ears. So also, in the *barzakh* world, the soul experiences its own reality in sensory form but without the body's sense organs.

As suggested earlier, in the *barzakh*, "seemingness" is everything. If the soul is whole and harmonious, it will perceive the *barzakh* as whole and harmonious. But if the soul is partial and disturbed, it will experience the *barzakh* as partial and disturbed. The more disoriented and distorted the soul's reality, the more horrendous will be its perception of its own *barzakh* dreamworld.

Some authorities maintain that the *barzakh* is simply the soul turned inside out. In other words, in this world, the body is apparent while the soul is hidden. The body is relatively fixed, while awareness is constantly changing. At each moment, thoughts enter and leave the mind, without any volition on our part. These thoughts are nothing but ourselves, of course, just as dream images are nothing but ourselves.

In the *barzakh*, the qualities that pertained to the body in this world are, as it were, turned inward, representing a relative fixity at the inner core of the being. But the soul itself is exteriorized and embodied in images appropriate to its own nature. The soul experiences itself as a world of images, as in dreams. One major difference between dreams and the *barzakh*, however, is that the *barzakh* world is far more real and permanent than this world. Once people enter the *barzakh*, they recognize that the world that they had lived in had been a dreamworld. This is the sense of a famous saying that is often attributed to the Prophet: "People are asleep, and when they die, they wake up." The Koran makes the same point when it says that the sight of people who die is "piercing" (50:22).

The Koran provides many allusions to the imaginal nature of the *barzakh*, but we need the hindsight of the tradition in order to understand them. However, the hadith literature is much more explicit than the Koran. Many of the Prophet's descriptions of experience after death can only be understood as depictions of an imaginal realm where everything that people experience corresponds exactly to their own activities and thoughts. Thus, the Prophet said that negligent prayers will be rolled up like shabby clothes and thrown in the person's face. The deeds of rebels will appear as dogs, and those of skeptics, as pigs. In the grave, good deeds will become embodied as ships in which people sail. Drunkards will be weighed down by pots of wine hanging around their necks. "The molar tooth of a truth-concealer will be like Mt. Uhud, and the thickness of his skin a three nights' journey." "The truth-concealer will drag his tongue a league and two leagues with people treading on it."

This embodiment of people's deeds and thoughts in appropriate forms is not limited to the *barzakh*, since many accounts tell of its taking place on the day of resurrection. So also, the pleasures of paradise and the torments of hell take appropriate form. Many later thinkers place both paradise and hell in the world of imagination, which they picture as infinitely vast. The *barzakh*, then, is only one form of imagination, a temporary form that lasts until the resurrection.

Meeting the Angels

In order to sum up this discussion and illustrate how the Prophet employs a language that is hard to understand without recourse to the imaginal world, we quote the following hadith. Although it is long, it has the advantage of providing the basic beliefs of Muslims concerning the grave in a logical and structured manner. Occasionally, we add comments in order to remind the reader how this ties into previous discussions.

Like many other hadiths concerning the next world, this hadith tells two parallel accounts. The first account pertains to the soul of a person of faith, the second to that of a truth-concealer. The same sorts of things happen, but the person of faith encounters the mercy and gentleness of God's right hand, while the truth-concealer encounters the wrath and vengeance of God's left hand. The first soul is brought into nearness with God, while the second soul is kept in distance. The first experiences happiness and wholeness, while the second experiences misery and dispersion. The two contrasting divine attributes that are mentioned in the hadith itself are "good-pleasure" and "anger." Thus, this hadith provides an explanation for why the Prophet prayed, "I seek refuge in Thy good-pleasure from Thy anger."

At the beginning of the hadith, the companion who is giving the account tells us that he went along with the Prophet and several others to a funeral. The gravediggers had not yet finished their work, so everyone sat down to wait. After a while, the Prophet raised his head and said two or three times, "Seek refuge in God from the chastisement of the grave!" Then he spoke as follows:

> When the faithful servant is being cut off from this world and turned toward the next world, angels descend upon him from heaven. They are white in face, as if their faces were the sun. They bring along one of the shrouds of the Garden and some of the balm of the Garden. They sit with him as far as the eye can see. Then the Angel of Death comes and sits by his head. He says, "O pleasant soul, come out to God's forgiveness and good-pleasure!" The soul flows out as if it were a drop from a water-skin, and he takes it. When he takes it, the angels do not leave it in his hand for an instant before taking it and placing it in that shroud and that balm. It comes out like the most pleasant aroma of musk found on the face of the earth.
>
> They take it up, and they never pass by an assembly of angels without their asking, "What is this pleasant scent?" They answer, "It is so-and-so, son of so-and-so," calling him by the most beautiful names that he was called by in this world.
>
> When they reach the heaven of this world, they ask that the door be opened for him. The door is opened for him. Then in every heaven the angels brought near escort him to the heaven above them until they take him to the seventh heaven.
>
> Then God says, "Write down the book of My servant in Illiyyun, and take him back to the earth, for from it I created them, to it I make them return, and from it I shall bring them forth a second time."
>
> His spirit is then returned to his dead body. Two angels come and say to him, "Who is your Lord?" He will say, "My Lord is God." They will say to him, "What is your religion?" He will say, "Islam."

They will say to him, "What is this man who was raised up among you?" He will say, "He is the messenger of God." They will say, "What is your knowledge?" He will say, "I have recited the Book of God, and I have faith in it and have acknowledged its truth."

Then a caller will call from heaven, "My servant has spoken the truth. So put down a carpet for him from the Garden, clothe him from the Garden, and open for him a gate into the Garden." Then some of its refreshment and scent comes to him, and his grave is made spacious for him as far as he can see.

Then a man of beautiful face, beautiful clothing, and pleasant fragrance will come to him and say, "I give you the good news of what will make you joyful. This is the day of yours that you were promised."

He will say, "Who are you? For your face is a face worthy to bring good."

He will reply, "I am your wholesome deeds."

Then he will say, "My Lord, let the Hour come! My Lord, let the Hour come, so that I may return to my family and my possessions!"

Notice the various qualities that are associated with the wholesome soul in this account. The angels descend with luminosity, appearing like the sun and bringing along a shroud and balm from the Garden. As soon as the Angel of Death speaks to the soul, he announces to it that it is being accepted into God's forgiveness and good-pleasure, two of the attributes of mercy and gentleness. Then the angels wrap the soul in the paradisal shroud, thereby concealing the soul's bodily dimensions, which are dark and dismal in relation to angelic and paradisal luminosity.

The angels also soak the soul in paradisal perfume. To understand the significance of this act we need to recall the importance of perfume and sweet smells in the Islamic consciousness. The Prophet, for example, did not eat garlic and onions—although he did not forbid them—because, he said, the angels were repulsed by the scent. In a well-known saying, he said that God had placed love in his heart for three things of this lower world: women, perfume, and the *salat*. Love in the Islamic context is invariably directed at that which is beautiful, in keeping with the hadith, "God is beautiful, and He loves beauty." The three things that were made lovable to the Prophet represent the most beautiful—and therefore the most divine—elements of this lower world. Female beauty is the most direct visible manifestation of God's beauty, gentleness, mercy, and forgiveness. Perfume is an invisible and subtle beauty which penetrates into the imaginal and spiritual worlds. Moreover, perfume brings with it a sense of the delight of the Garden. It is no accident that most perfumes are made from flowers and that the Prophet's favorite perfume is said to have been essence of rose. Finally, the *salat* that was made lovable to the Prophet represents the embodied Koran, or beauty of character and activity.

In the hadith about the three lovable things, the word used for perfume is *tib*. Likewise, in the long hadith just quoted, the word translated as "pleasant" is *tayyib*, the adjectival form of the same word. From the beginning, the wholesome soul is "pleasant," which means sweet-smelling, attractive, good, and beautiful. That this pleasantness is perceived imaginally both by the olfactory as well as the visual sense is emphasized by what the angels bring: a shroud and balm. These are not the cloth and perfume of this world, but of the Garden, which explains why the soul is perceived by the angels as beautiful.

The angels ask, "What is this pleasant scent?" The word for scent is *rawh*, which is written exactly the same as *ruh*, meaning "spirit." The word itself tells us that this scent is no earthly fragrance, but rather an angelic and spiritual fragrance proper to the heavens; that is, the high worlds.

The angels take the soul on a *mi'raj* that follows the route of the Prophet's *mi'raj*. If the Prophet traveled through the seven heavens already in this life, the faithful are promised that they will ascend through them at death. At the top of the heavens they reach nearness to God. To be near to God is to be near to the Real, the One, the Perfect, the Luminous, the Gentle. By being brought near to these attributes, the soul partakes of them. Thus, the soul comes to actualize more perfectly the divine form in which it was created.

The deeds of the good are written down in Illiyyun, which is usually taken to be a place or a book in the seventh heaven. The word *Illiyyun*, however, means literally something like "high realms." The word itself, derived from the adjective *high* (*'ali*)—which is a name of God—is sufficient indication that what is meant is some form of nearness to God.

At the end of the first section of this hadith, we find one of the more explicit prophetic references to the embodiment of the activity done in this world in an appropriate imaginal form. The dead person sees a man with a beautiful face, beautiful clothing, and "pleasant fragrance." Upon asking, he finds out that this man is his own works. He has been presented with the good deeds that he has performed throughout life in a form appropriate to his situation in the *barzakh*.

In the second half of the hadith, the Prophet describes the death of the truth-concealer. Notice that the text is practically the same, except that all the adjectives are changed, since the truth-concealer represents the direct opposite of the person of faith. To begin with, the soul is described as "loathsome" (*khabith*), an adjective that functions as the opposite of "pleasant." Muslims listening to this hadith will be reminded of several Koranic verses that contrast the loathsome and the pleasant, especially this verse:

The truth-concealers will be mustered into Gehenna, so that God may distinguish the pleasant from the loathsome, and place the loathsome one upon another, and so heap them up all together, and put them in Gehenna. Those are the losers. (8:37)

The hadith about the grave continues as follows:

When the truth-concealing servant is being cut off from this world and turned toward the next world, angels descend upon him from heaven. They are black in face. They bring along with them coarse pieces of cloth. They sit with him as far as the eye can see. Then the Angel of Death comes and sits by his head. He says, "O loathsome soul, come out to God's anger." The soul scatters throughout the body, but the angel pulls it out as a skewer is pulled out from moist wool, and he takes it. When he takes it, the angels do not leave it in his hand for an instant before taking it and placing it in those coarse pieces of cloth. It comes out from them like the foulest stench of a corpse found on the face of the earth.

They take it up, and they never pass by an assembly of angels without their asking, "What is this loathsome scent?" They answer, "It is so-and-so, son of so-and-so," calling him by the most repulsive names that he was called by in this world.

When they reach the heaven of this world, they ask that the door be opened for him, but it is not opened for him. "The gates of heaven shall not be opened to them, nor shall they enter the Garden, until a camel passes through the eye of the needle"[Koran 7:40].

Then God says, "Write down his book in Sijjin in the lowest earth." Then he is thrown down with a throwing. "Whosoever associates anything with God, it is as if he has fallen down from heaven and the birds snatch him away, or the wind sweeps him headlong into a place far away"[Koran 22:31].

His spirit is then returned to his dead body. Two angels come to him, make him sit up, and say to him, "Who is your Lord?" He will say, "Oh, oh, I do not know!" They will say to him, "What is your religion?" He will say, "Oh, oh, I do not know!" They will say to him, "What is this man who was raised up among you?" He will say, "Oh, oh, I do not know!"

Then a caller will call from heaven, "He has lied, so put down a carpet for him from the Fire and open up to him a gate into the Fire." Then some of its heat and burning wind comes to him, and his grave will be made so narrow that his ribs intersect. Then a man of ugly face, ugly clothing, and foul fragrance will come to him and say, "I give you the good news of what will make you miserable. This is the day of yours that you were promised."

He will say, "Who are you? For your face is a face worthy to bring evil."

He will reply, "I am your loathsome works."
Then he will say, "My Lord, let not the Hour come!"

Many of the details of this hadith depend upon the Koranic description of the cosmos. It is especially worthy of note that the truth-concealer is barred entrance into the first heaven. Remember, heaven should not be confused with paradise. Although the Garden and the Fire are discussed in the hadith as existent realities, their location is not specified. Heaven, as we learned under *tawhid*, denotes everything that is high, luminous, spiritual, intelligent, and good. The high things that dwell in heaven have many degrees, represented by the seven heavens. Beyond and outside all the heavens is God, to whom belongs true highness. The souls of the faithful pass into the heavens after death because they have actualized, during their life in this world, the attributes of the heavenly things, which are identical with the attributes of the spirit blown into the body.

In contrast, the souls of the truth-concealers cannot ascend. Rather, they are thrown down into Sijjin. The word *Sijjin*, like its opposite, *Illiyyun*, has been given a number of interpretations. It is said, for example to refer to the place where the books of the truth-concealers are kept, or one of the valleys of hell, or the place of Iblis and the satans below the seventh earth. The word derives from a root meaning "to imprison." The high realms of Illiyyun are a place of freedom and fulfillment, while the low realm of Sijjin is a place of imprisonment and hardship.

Notice also that the truth-concealer says that he does not know the identity of his God, his scripture, and his prophet. The answer comes that he is a liar, that is, he persists in concealing the truth even in the grave.

Final Judgment

Underlying everything that the Koran says about the Return to God is the idea that people will be called to a final accounting for what they do in this life. They will be questioned concerning the acts they performed. They are responsible, that is, they will be expected to give a response when God asks them why they did what they did. As the Prophet's companion Ibn 'Abbas said, people will not be questioned about *what* they did, since that will be written down in the scrolls for them to read. Rather, they will be questioned about *why* they did what they did.

Once God finishes questioning the servants and weighing their deeds in the scales, he will pass judgment. Some will be sent to paradise, and others will be sent to hell. This idea of God judging people and then throwing them into the Fire is especially distasteful to many modern people. One of the common reasons that is given for preferring the Hindu or Buddhist perspectives over that of the Semitic religions is that the former do not ascribe judgment to a capricious and fickle God, but instead make everyone responsible for himself or herself through the idea of karma.

There is no doubt that the Koranic God is a personal God who judges. But most Muslim thinkers have never let themselves get bogged down in anthropomorphic imagery. No one has ever thought that God passes judgment exactly like a judge in a human court. After all, "Nothing is like Him" (42:11), including any judges that any of us have ever seen or heard about.

To say that God judges is another way of saying that reality sorts itself out: Things show themselves for what they are; deception and trickery do not rule the cosmos; everything will end up in its proper place. That which manifests the unity, wholeness, equilibrium, beauty, balance, and gentleness of God will come to rest in proximity to the One, the Beautiful, the Gentle. But that which is overcome by multiplicity, dispersion, partialness, imbalance, ugliness, and severity will remain distant from the One.

From the point of view of universal *islam*, things sort themselves out in complete submission to the Reality of God. Everything is exactly measured out. But there is also the specific *islam*, the free submission of human beings to the messages brought by the prophets. In the final analysis, of course, Muslims have to accept that specific *islam* is simply one aspect of universal *islam*; in other words, voluntary submission is also measured out. However, they accept this on the basis of a vision of *tawhid* and the ultimacy of the Real that does not impinge on their own perceived freedom.

Again, the discussion now turns to free will and predestination. What Muslim thinkers find unacceptable is the idea that God compels people to be truth-concealers and then punishes them for it, or that he compels people to have faith and then rewards them for it. The role of human freedom in this dynamic is sufficient for people to assume responsibility for the choices they make.

People always have reasons for what they do. They do not act because they are forced to act, but because they choose to act. When God comes along on the day of resurrection and tells people to read their books, they will see that "not so much as the weight of a mustard seed" of their works has been left out. And when God asks them why they did one thing and not something else, they will have answers, but they will know perfectly well that many of their answers are lame.

This, again, is an anthropomorphic way of presenting the issue. There are other ways to make the argument, but the anthropomorphic route is normally the easiest to grasp. However, for the purpose of this discussion, it is not necessary to try to plumb what the Muslim thinkers have called "the mystery of the measuring out"—a mystery, they usually add, that people will not be able to understand until they have advanced on the path to spiritual perfection.[18]

The Koran often presents the question of judgment in terms of reward and punishment. More generally, it maintains that every human act brings about an appropriate response from God, and that God never wrongs anyone. People may wrong themselves, but God does not wrong them. The generic term that the Koran employs here is *jaza'*, which means "to repay in kind," whether for good or for evil. In the following, we translate it as "recompense":

> As for him who has faith and does wholesome deeds, he shall have as recompense the most beautiful. (18:88)

> Whosoever comes to Him with faith, having done wholesome deeds, for them await the high degrees—gardens of Eden through which rivers flow, therein dwelling forever. That is the recompense of him who purifies himself. (20:75-76)

> The Fire . . . is the recompense of the wrongdoers. (59:17)

> We shall recompense those who turn away from Our signs with an evil chastisement for their turning away. (6:157)

Along with the term *recompense*, the Koran also refers to "reward" (*thawab*) and "punishment" (*'iqab*). The theme of reward and punishment goes hand in hand with that of good news and warning and, more generally, with that of mercy and wrath. God as named by his gentle and merciful names rewards the soul, and God as named by his severe and wrathful names punishes the soul. In less anthropomorphic terms, this is to say that the soul that has established a firm relationship with the luminous and spiritual dimension of existence thereby enters into nearness to the Real, but the soul that turns away from the luminous and embraces the dark and corporeal dimension of existence is overcome by unreality.

The Koran and the Hadith paint frightful pictures of the plight of the truth-concealers in hell, just as they describe in detail the delights of paradise. Many Muslim authorities have stressed the dangers of hell far more than the promise of paradise. Given that the first priority of Islamic teachings is to establish the Shariah as the framework for life, this stress on God's wrath and severity should not be surprising. In order to be anything at all, people first have to recognize that they are servants of God (whether they want to be or not) and that they have the moral and existential duty to serve God voluntarily. The God who is served, as pointed out already, is the God of *tanzih*, the King who dwells far away and issues commands. This King must be feared, because of his wrath and terrible power.

Despite this general Islamic stress on *tanzih*, servanthood, and God's warning, many authorities of the tradition never forget that God's

mercy precedes and determines his wrath. Mercy pertains to all creatures, whereas wrath pertains only to some creatures in some circumstances. The universal order is oriented toward mercy, and mercy will
win out in the end.

In other words, nearness to God, unity, harmony, equilibrium, and
all the names of gentleness and beauty determine the ultimate nature of
reality. Distance from God, dispersion, disintegration, disequilibrium,
and the creaturely consequences of the names of wrath and severity
pertain to unreality and nonexistence: They cannot subsist. Eventually,
multiplicity will dissipate itself into nothingness, just as shining light
becomes dimmer and dimmer as it moves away from its source. Hence,
that which is real in creatures remains, while that which is unreal
disappears. "Everything is perishing except His face" (28:88). For many
Muslim authorities, this explains why hell cannot be eternal in the
same sense that God is eternal. Paradise will indeed last forever, because paradise pertains to mercy, but the pain of hell will eventually
disappear, though its disappearance may entail unimaginably long
periods of time.

One of the consequences of the predominance of mercy in reality is
that good works are rewarded many times over, while evil works are
paid back only in kind. Wholesome deeds strengthen a person's connection with Reality, and hence they have the effect of canceling out
unreality. In the darkness, a little light goes a long way. The recompense of the real is the real, while the recompense of unreality is
unreality. But the real next to unreality is something next to nothing:
There is no common measure. As for activity that is not rooted in faith,
it simply follows the downward flow of light into dispersion and
darkness.

In more anthropomorphic terms, we can say that God seizes the
opportunity of a wholesome work—that is, a deed that is performed
with the intention of serving God on the basis of prophetic instruction—
in order to pull the person toward himself. "Remember Me, and I will
remember you" (2:152). How can God's remembrance of a person be
equated with the person's remembrance of God, given that God is the
Real and the person is unreal? Hence God's activity in response to the
person of faith is all important. In contrast, God simply ignores the evil
deed and lets it work its ill consequence upon the person who performs
it. The realities of things will manifest themselves in due time, and then
people will realize what they have done:

The recompense of an ugly deed shall be the like of it. (10:27)

*The likeness of those who expend their wealth in the way of God is
the likeness of a grain of corn that sprouts seven ears, in every ear
a hundred grains. So God multiplies unto whom He will. (2:261)*

Surely God shall not wrong so much as the weight of an ant; and if it be a beautiful deed, He will multiply it, and give from Himself a mighty wage. (4:40)

In a well-known saying, the Prophet expressed the disparity between human and divine activity as follows:

God says, "Whoever brings a beautiful deed will have ten the like of it, and I will increase [even more]. But whoever brings an ugly deed, its recompense will be its like, or I will forgive him. Whoever draws near to Me by a handsbreadth, I will draw near to him by an armslength. Whoever draws near to Me by an armslength, I will draw near to him by a fathom. Whoever comes to Me walking, I will come to him running. Whoever encounters Me with sins that cover the earth but associates nothing with Me, I will encounter him with forgiveness the like of them."

Chapter 6.

THE INTELLECTUAL SCHOOLS

୭

W e have just finished discussing some of the implications of the three principles of faith. We are not suggesting that what we have written represents the faith of all Muslims, or even the faith of some specific Muslims. If someone asks, "What exactly do Muslims believe about God or about Muhammad?" it is impossible to provide an answer in any detail that would satisfy all Muslims, whether we mean those who are alive today or those who have left us their writings. The contents of faith are defined by the basic articles with which we began, and which are repeatedly mentioned in the Koran: God, the angels, the scriptures, the prophets, the Last Day, the measuring out. Even this list may be problematic in certain respects. Then we are forced to reduce the universally accepted Muslim creed even further and say that it is, "There is no god but God and Muhammad is His messenger."

However, the moment discussion begins as to what exactly is meant by words such as *God, messenger, Koran, angels, Last Day*, and so on, differences of opinion begin to appear. When we look at the question of how the three principles of faith have been understood over Islamic history, we can see that different people have had different ideas. By and large, Muslims who have thought about these things have agreed on generalities and disagreed on details. The differences of opinion are accentuated by the fact that a number of major schools became established, each of which took a special approach to interpreting the principles of faith.

Just as the Five Pillars and the Shariah became the specialty of a group of scholars known as "jurists," so also the contents of faith became the specialty of three broad groups of scholars who, roughly speaking, fit into the categories of Kalam (dogmatic theology), theoretical Sufism, and philosophy. Each of these categories has several or many subcategories, making the historical development of the interpretation of faith exceedingly complex. In fact, there are few if any scholars today who are equally conversant with all three schools of thought. Most scholars, whether Muslim or non-Muslim, specialize in one of these schools or, what is more likely, in one specific branch or one specific teacher within one of these schools.

The three schools are not always clearly distinct from each other. There are many individual scholars in Islamic history who can be placed in two or three of the schools at once, or who defy classification. Nevertheless, by discussing the three schools separately, as is traditionally done both in the Islamic context and in modern scholarship, we can gain insight into the different directions in which Muslims have developed the ideas of *tawhid*, prophecy, and the Return. At the same time, it is important to recognize that all three approaches investigate the same subject, which is nothing but reality as it presents itself to us; that is, reality as perceived in Islamic terms. Hence, the three principles of faith provide the broad outline of the discussion.

We will look at each school separately and briefly. The first step requires understanding what differentiates their methodologies in studying Islam's three principles. Perhaps the key distinction to be made among these schools lies in their approach to human understanding. The nature of knowledge is one of the fundamental issues for anyone who stops and thinks about anything of lasting importance. "How do I know what I know?" If we are to investigate the nature of reality, the question becomes, "What kind of knowledge allows me to understand reality as it truly is?" Notice that Muslim thinkers all accepted that there is an ultimate reality—as is demanded by the first Shahadah. Without that acceptance, they would not be Muslim thinkers. Hence, in contrast to the modern West, one rarely finds anyone who questions the existence of a supreme Reality or who is skeptical toward the possibility of knowing anything of ultimate significance.

Generally speaking, Islamic experience, like many other forms of religious experience, recognizes three modes of knowing the Real and of understanding the nature of the cosmos and the human soul. One way is simply to use our innate intelligence—this is the path of *reason*. The Koran continually exhorts people to employ their intelligence.

Some Muslims thought that the best way to use the intelligence was the method established by the Greek philosophers, especially Plato and Aristotle. This rational, philosophical approach to reality has many similarities with the Western philosophical tradition before Descartes.

A second way of knowing the Real is through accepting without question the messages that the prophets have brought. This is the path of *revelation*. It is also the path of faith in general, and it is highly praised among Muslims — so long as those who take this position do not generalize and claim that everyone must suffer the same limitations as they do. In other words, it is one thing to say, "I accept, but I really do not understand." It is quite another thing to say, "Since I do not understand, no one can understand." All Muslims accept revelation, since that is precisely the meaning of the second Shahadah. However, some Muslims stress the importance of accepting the literal text of the revelation to a degree that others do not find necessary. By and large the authorities in Kalam follow the path of revelation.

A third way of knowing the Real is to experience reality for oneself without the intermediary of reason or revelation. This path goes by many names, but we will employ the most common term, which is *unveiling* (*kashf*). The image suggested by the word is connected to the idea that God is veiled from his creatures. We have already encountered this idea in a hadith:

> God has seventy veils of light and darkness. Were they to be re-moved, the glories of His Face would burn away everything perceived by the sight of His creatures.

Unveiling takes place when God removes some of the veils between him and a given human being. The sight of the person who experiences unveiling may or may not be burned away. But after the experience, the person has no lingering doubts about the Real behind the veils. In Western languages, the word *mysticism* is often used in a sense that approximates the use of the word *unveiling* in Islamic languages. However, mysticism has unfortunate connotations that tend to confuse the issues rather than clarify them. Hence, we will not employ the word.[19] None of these three approaches should be thought of as exclusive of the others, although some people in Islamic history have made claims for the exclusive validity of one or another of these paths.

As a rule, all three intellectual schools have accepted the validity of revelation on some level. If it is not accepted that the Koran is divine knowledge revealed to human beings, then one has rejected the second Shahadah and ceases to be a Muslim. Those who follow the path of unveiling have been especially careful to take Koranic knowledge as their guide. For them, authentic unveiling can only occur when people follow the Sunna of the Prophet.

Broadly speaking, these three approaches to understanding are found in every human context. However, a given civilization may emphasize one over the others. For example, Christian civilization, while stressing revelation, also witnessed a great flowering of rational approaches to the tradition. At the same time, there have always been Christians who have held that true Christianity lies in personal experience of the truths of faith, or what Muslims would call unveiling. As for modern Western civilization, the dominant form of understanding has for centuries been reason, but the other two forms have never completely disappeared, and they seem to be making a comeback in more recent times.

The Expression of Faith in the Earliest Period

Many modern scholars who have studied Islam have devoted an extraordinary amount of attention to Kalam, so much so that the uninformed reader might suppose that Kalam is the most important form of Islamic thought. However, such scholars have not always been motivated by a concern to bring out Islam's self-understanding. Frequently they have had their own reasons for considering the intellectual approach of Kalam as more important or more interesting than other approaches.

It is true that Kalam plays an important role in Islamic civilization, but the fact that the term is frequently translated as "theology" should not lead us to suppose that Kalam's role in Islam is analogous to theology's role in Christianity. What is of central importance for Islam is the Shariah, not Kalam. The vast majority of practicing Muslims have known nothing about Kalam, although they all have had some degree of familiarity with the Shariah. One can be a good Muslim without Kalam, but it is impossible to be any sort of Muslim without the Shariah. Many of the great Muslim authorities, such as al-Ghazali, warned people against studying Kalam, since it focuses on intellectual issues that are of no practical use for most people.

Why then did Kalam appear in Islam? To answer this question, we need to look at the situation in which Muslims found themselves in the early period of the religion's expansion.

Within the first century of its existence, Islam had spread to much of Iran, North Africa, and what is today the Arab Middle East. The already existing religions in the area included Christianity, Judaism, Zoroastrianism, Mithraism, Manichaeism, and the Sabeanism of Harran; some of these religions were made up of competing sects or schools of thought. In addition, many people were familiar with Greek philosophy, especially Neoplatonism, which itself often played the role of a religion.

Once Muslims began living among peoples who were not Muslim, some of them were naturally drawn into discussions about religion.

The Muslims had the Koran and the Hadith to go by, but the representatives of other traditions, especially the Christians, had centuries of sophisticated theological debates behind them. Remember that Christianity had been nurtured in a region where Greek philosophy was the chief intellectual force. From early on, Christians took a polemical stance against many of the ideas of the Greek philosophers, but in order to discuss philosophy, they had to employ the tools of philosophy. In order to speak with people who had themselves been debating philosophical issues for centuries, the Christians had to learn all the intricacies of logical and philosophical debate.

When the Muslims encountered such representatives of other traditions, some of them reacted by dismissing these people as truth-concealers, but that was not a route that could be taken by anyone with respect for intelligence and for the revelations that preceded Islam. To the extent that individual Muslims had an intellectual orientation, rational issues appeared important to them. They would discuss the nature of religion, prophecy, and God with others who had faith in God, and one of the first things they discovered was that it was not easy to argue successfully against sophisticated thinkers who had thorough philosophical and theological training.

It was only natural that some intellectually inclined Muslims should attempt to learn how to argue out their own positions in terms that would make sense to followers of other religions. They had no choice but to speak the language of the people with whom they were discoursing. They knew full well from the Koran that God adapts his revealed language to the recipients of the message: "We have sent no messenger but in the tongue of his people, that he might make clear to them" (14:4). They knew that the Prophet had advised them to speak to people at the level of the audience's understanding. When they heard their new acquaintances say something about God, or the world, or the divine Word—something that contradicted what they knew to be true on the basis of the Koran—they tried to reply in a language that could be understood.

All the resources for learning Greek philosophy were available within the newly conquered territories. Alexandria, for example, was a major heir to the Greek philosophical tradition, especially Neoplatonism. The early Muslims who discussed these things were not necessarily familiar with Greek philosophy or the local religions. However, these traditions had helped shape the intellectual ambiance.

One of the primary aims of those who undertook to express Islamic teachings in the intellectual language of the times was to defend the tenets of faith against the criticisms of non-Muslims. Gradually, the Muslims adopted certain positions on fundamental issues that were important for theological and philosophical thinking. Muslims who came to be known as *mutakallimun* (specialists in Kalam) took a defensive position vis-a-vis the Koran, the divine Word. Those who came to be known as *falasifa* were more interested in the issues discussed by Greek philosophers such as Plato, Aristotle, and Plotinus. We will return to the philosophical approach later.

There are, in fact, early texts that show a high degree of sophistication in the issues that became central to Kalam. These texts suggest that the intellectual ambiance of the ancient Middle East already had some presence in Mecca and Medina. For example, the sayings of the Prophet's cousin and son-in-law, Ali, were collected together in the fourth/tenth century as the *Nahj al-balagha* (The Path of Eloquence). No doubt the intellectual issues of that century, which included many debates in Kalam, had an effect on which sayings the compiler included and which he left out. It is possible that some spurious sayings crept in, but the relatively uniform style and the high intellectual and spiritual level of the text makes it highly unlikely that it could have been, as some modern scholars have suggested, a fabrication. Moreover, there are earlier sources in which many of the same sayings are found.

In the *Nahj al-balagha*, we see Ali as the most eloquent spokesman for *tawhid* after the Koran and the Prophet himself. But the Koran has its own inimitable style that relies largely on exhortation and direct appeals to the deepest dimensions of the human psyche. It speaks with the authority of God in a manner that Muslims have found convincing from the beginning. The hadith literature also has its own special style, very different from the Koran. Once a person becomes familiar with the styles of the Koran and the Hadith, it is impossible to mistake one for the other. The Prophet speaks with authority, but with humility and deference as well. His sayings are much more expository than Koranic verses. He tends to go into detail, and he delights in repeating the same sentences or the same structures with slight alterations to set up clear contrasts. The Prophet's words are concrete and down to earth. As a rule, he does not employ anything other than everyday words.

Ali's *Nahj al-balagha* represents a third form of expression that is totally distinct from the Koran and the Hadith. If the Prophet delights in the earthly and the everyday, Ali tends to soar into the heavenly and the awesome. His language is much more difficult than that of the Prophet. The Prophet's sayings sometimes employ unusual words, but these are typically nouns that designate concrete things and that, for one reason or another, were not used in later times. Ali employs a wealth of words in intellectual and abstract contexts, making use of the rich resources of the Arabic language in ways that seem unprecedented. He also possessed a genius for pithy and quotable sayings that have a way of summing up volumes of discussion.

The *Nahj al-balagha* presents Ali as a person intimately conversant with all the wisdom of the Koran and the Prophet. More generally, Ali is looked back upon as that companion of the Prophet who was most familiar with the deepest and most hidden dimensions of the divine revelation. The Koran says, "He who has been given wisdom has been given much good" (2:269), and Ali appears as the archetypal man of wisdom. Not that he was wiser than the Prophet, but the Prophet's wisdom is sometimes hidden in his attention to everyday details, while Ali's wisdom is predominantly other-worldly. Its weakness on the worldly level comes out in his career as fourth caliph, a career that was far from successful in the political domain.

What we find in Ali that makes him so relevant to the present discussion is a clear adumbration of the possibilities of intellectual expression contained in the Islamic revelation. The germs of Kalam, theoretical Sufism, and philosophy are all present in his works. To what extent Ali may have been exposed to the intellectual ambiance of the ancient Middle East is an open question. What is certain is that the following generation of Muslims, some of whom were inclined intellectually toward Ali's mode of expression, found every sort of opportunity to discuss theological and philosophical issues.

Kalam

The word *Kalam* itself did not come into use as the designation for a specific approach to the principles of faith until the fourth/tenth century; other words were also used. Abu Hanifa, for example, the founder of the Hanafi school of jurisprudence and an important theological thinker, called this science *al-fiqh al-akbar*, which we can translate as "the greater understanding." Here he uses the word *fiqh*, which we have been translating as "jurisprudence," in its Koranic sense, where it simply means understanding the teachings of the religion. But he distinguishes between the "lesser understanding" (jurisprudence) and the "greater understanding" (the principles of faith). Kalam has also been called *usul al-din*, "the principles" or "roots" of the religion. This name refers to the fact that the fundamental roots of Islam lie in faith, or in understanding the nature of things. Then jurisprudence becomes *furu' al-din*, the "ramifications" or "branches" of the religion, because the practical teachings represent an application of the principles of faith.

The primary concern of the Kalam specialists was to defend the truth of the Koran against anyone who would presume to doubt it, but clearly this "anyone" would have to have something to say. Kalam, we must always keep in mind, was an intellectual exercise undertaken by sophisticated thinkers and addressed to those who considered these issues important.

Of course, for Islamic thought, the issues of Kalam are important, but not as important as is often supposed, especially by those modern scholars who, for one reason or another, have taken the self-evaluation of the Kalam specialists seriously. On the level of faith, what was of monumental importance was the double witnessing—that there is no god but God and Muhammad is His messenger. Without that, there is no Islam, but Muslim intellectuals, including the *mutakallimun*, took that for granted. What the *mutakallimun* felt were matters of life and death were issues such as the following: Is the Koran created, or is it eternal? Are God's attributes the same as God himself, or are they different from God? Are human beings predestined in their activity, or are they free? It would go far beyond the possibilities of this book to enter into any of these discussions from the perspective of Kalam, but we need to say something about why these discussions are important in Islam and why, from another point of view, they are not nearly as important as they might seem.

Discussion of these issues is important because some people are compelled to search for clear cut answers to abstruse questions. Some people are born intellectuals or academics, and a religion cannot ignore such people. They go forward by asking questions, and if they are not provided satisfactory answers, they look elsewhere. We do not mean to say that Kalam provided all the answers; far from it. If it did, Islam would not have witnessed the development of theoretical Sufism and philosophy. However, Kalam provided answers for a good number of people and, because of the rational support provided by Kalam, they were able to commit themselves fully to God and the Koran; in other words, their faith was made firm.

Another side to this whole issue is the fact that theological questions often have direct political consequences, especially when the government claims Islamic legitimacy. Some modern scholars would go so far as to try to explain practically all theological debates in political terms. It is certainly true that the first major group of theological thinkers, known as the Mu'tazilites, were intimately concerned with the exercise of power. They considered the problem of how to differentiate a good Muslim from a bad Muslim a fundamental one and, when they came into political favor for a time under the caliph al-Ma'mun at the beginning of the third/ninth century, they directed an inquisition against scholars who refused to accept their definitions of who good Muslims were.

Later theological schools were also involved with politics, at least indirectly. After all, it is impossible to make statements about the fundamental issues of human existence without these statements having practical implications. This is no less true today than it was a thousand years ago, but people are often unaware that contemporary arguments continue in the same lines as earlier theological debates. Take, for example, the issue of free will and predestination, a central bone of contention among the schools of Kalam. This debate, which has also been important in Christian civilization, lives on in modern secular society, though it is no longer posed in terms of God. For example, many contemporary scholars — biologists, psychologists, sociologists, philosophers, political scientists — are actively involved in the discussion of nature versus nurture. The basic question is simple: Does nature determine human development, or can people change themselves substantially by means of training and education? Among the numerous specific applications of this question are issues of heated debate in contemporary society. For example, do the differences between men and women pertain simply to reproductive biology, or do they extend to intellectual ability as well? Or, in another realm, is sexual orientation innate, or is it socially constructed? Many people are convinced of one position or the other, and the fervor with which they argue makes it clear that theological passions are not alien to modern intellectuals. Of course, the positions that many people take on these issues are complex and subtle, but so also are the positions of many of the Kalam authorities. Free will and predestination, like nature and nurture, is merely a convenient way to refer to one of the most basic puzzles of human existence.

In early Islam, Kalam was made necessary by the intellectual needs of certain types of people and by the social and political realities of the early Islamic community. But it was not considered an appropriate topic of study for everyone, and many scholars thought that it went against the Koran and the Sunna—or at least was dangerous without the proper academic preparation. Al-Ghazali, for example, is highly critical of Kalam in some of his works (even though he himself wrote books in this field). He felt that most people would be much better off if they avoided the nit-picking, overrationalizing approach of the *mutakallimun*. Instead of strengthening their faith, Kalam weakened it. But this is not an argument for doing away with Kalam, and al-Ghazali makes no such suggestion. However, it is an argument against excessive curiosity. The Prophet said, "One of the beautiful traits of a person's Islam is to abandon everything that is not his concern." And he also said, "I seek refuge in God from a knowledge that has no profit." Profitable knowledge is knowledge that prepares a person for the encounter with God, and Kalam does not necessarily do that.

The Kalam specialists themselves maintain that Kalam is important because it preserves the true teachings of Islamic faith from falsifications. If people do not have a right understanding of God, they will not worship him in the correct way, and as a result they will fail to do their duty as God's servants. Faith in Islam is rooted in *tawhid*, and we have seen that the Koran insists that God can forgive everything except *shirk*. But what exactly is the meaning of *tawhid*, and what exactly is *shirk*? If one does not have a firm understanding of Koranic teachings, one will not be able to distinguish between *tawhid* and *shirk*, and the result will be disaster in the next world.

For the *mutakallimun* themselves, Kalam is the most important of sciences because it is the authentic way of establishing true faith, and without faith, works are fruitless. *Islam* without *iman* is simply not sufficient for salvation. Nevertheless, Kalam can be considered to have this great importance only if we accept that there are no other ways to purify and maintain faith. That may seem true to Kalam specialists, but not to philosophers, Sufis, and many jurists. Again, the *mutakallimun* were a tiny minority of Muslims, and although, at times, their opinions had great political implications because of their influence with caliphs or kings, their opinions had little effect on the faith and practice of most people.

Although the issues discussed by the Kalam specialists were important in the first and second century of Islam, there is no clear cut and important body of thinkers who can be classified as *mutakallimun* before the Mu'tazilites, who first appear toward the beginning of the second/eighth century. What characterized the Mu'tazilites more than anything else was their extreme stress upon *'aql* (reason) as the fundamental determinant of how the Koran should be interpreted and defended. If a Koranic verse contradicted logical thinking, then the verse had to be interpreted in a way that showed there was no contradiction.

For a large number of reasons, many of them political, the Mu'tazilites gained prominence with the early Abbasid caliphs in Baghdad. But their influence did not last, and eventually another school of Kalam, called Ash'arism after its founder, Abu'l-Hasan al-Ash'ari (d. 324/935), became dominant. Ash'arism can be seen as a swing of the pendulum back toward the authority of revelation and the recognition that reason has its limits. The Mu'tazilites reveled in the power that reason gave them to understand all things, and in this they were deeply influenced by the Greek philosophical tradition (though they would not necessarily admit it). But Ash'arism appears as a full acknowledgment of reason's limitations.

To help simplify the complex arguments, we can cite as an example the debate over the eternity of the Koran. This discussion goes back to the fundamental theological issue of the exact relationship between the divine attributes and the divine essence. The Mu'tazilites, depending upon rational understanding and the laws of logic, insisted that the answer had to be "either/or": Either the attributes were the same as the essence, or they were different from the essence. Logically, it is impossible for a thing to be the same and different at one and the same time. They opted for making the attributes the same as the essence. Having done so, they concluded that the Koran had to be considered other than God's essence, and hence it was created.

In contrast, the Ash'arites insisted that God could not be made to fit into the constraints of human logic. We cannot claim to understand God in the same way that we understand the things of this world. "Either/or" may work for created things, but it does not necessarily work for the Uncreated, which belongs to an utterly different order of reality. In the end, the Ash'arites adopted a formula that breaks the laws of Aristotelian logic: "They [the attributes] are neither He nor other than He." Inasmuch as God's speech is the same as God and the Koran is God's speech, the Koran had to be eternal. Hence, the Ash'arites argued for its eternity, but they did not deny that the Koran was created inasmuch as it was written in books and recited by tongues.

The Ash'arite formula on the attributes is an early expression of an idea that we have been discussing all along: God is both incomparable and similar at the same time. It is one of many ways of bringing *tanzih* and *tashbih* together into an apparently paradoxical marriage.[20]

Theoretical Sufism

For the purpose of discussing the intellectual character of Sufism, it is sufficient to recall that Sufism focuses upon interiorization (we will not discuss the Sufi perspective in any detail until we reach Part III). The Sufis felt that neither the Shariah, nor faith plus the Shariah, was sufficient for perfect adherence to the Sunna of the Prophet. It is possible to follow the rules of the Shariah for one's own personal purposes and without faith in God; it is also possible to have faith in God without being sincere in this faith and without becoming a person characterized by humility, charity, compassion, and love. The Sufis attempted to bring about perfect practice and faith by developing the inner qualities implied, but not necessarily actualized, by correct activity and correct thinking. In their view, these inner attitudes and character traits marked the Prophet's personality. In brief, they wanted not only to act like the Prophet (*islam*) and to think like him (*iman*), but also to be aware like him of God's presence in all things, including themselves, and to act appropriately (*ihsan, dhikr*).

Early writings possessing Sufi orientation focus on the development of moral qualities. How can one be truly sincere? How can one act as if one sees God present in all things? How can humility be developed when the self is constantly claiming that "I am better than he"? How can one be sure that one is serving God and not serving caprice? How can one have total trust in God when daily bread is also a problem?

The first works with a Sufi orientation did not usually deal directly with the three principles of faith; rather, they brought out the implications of the three principles for establishing a right relationship with God. By the time of al-Ghazali (d. 505/1111), however, some Sufis had begun discussing *tawhid*, prophecy, and the Return in terms that were recognizably different from the approach taken by the *mutakallimun* and the philosophers. Al-Ghazali himself, who is often credited with making the Sufi perspective respectable among those who were suspicious of it, wrote a few minor works that focus on *tawhid* and other issues of faith, but his primary concern was to bring out the inner perfections that needed to be developed if people were able to live up to the Sunna.

Al-Ghazali, whose name was Muhammad, had a younger brother named Ahmad (d. 520/1126), who wrote a classic of Sufism (in Persian rather than Arabic) on divine love. That work began a long tradition of thinking about *tawhid* almost exclusively in terms of the inner experience of love, a love that is identified with God himself.

One of Ahmad Ghazali's disciples, 'Ayn al-Qudat Hamadani (d. 525/1131), employed the language of the Islamic philosophers to bring out the primacy of love in all reality. His detailed explanations of the three principles provide one of the earliest Sufi forays into the domain of explicating the principles of faith, a domain that was occupied mainly by the Kalam specialists and the philosophers.

The greatest of all Sufi theoreticians was Ibn al-'Arabi, who was born in al-Andalus, now known as Spain, in 560/1165 and died in Damascus in 638/1240. His voluminous writings investigate every aspect of the three principles of faith with unparalleled brilliance and penetration. It is probably true to say that no one, after the Koran and the Prophet, has had more influence on the way Muslims have thought about God for the past six hundred years. Only in the past one hundred years have many Muslims chosen to ignore Ibn al-'Arabi's legacy, paying more attention to other intellectual currents. But Ibn al-'Arabi's influence is still very strong and, now that Western rationalism is crumbling in the post-modern age, fewer and fewer Muslims are able to appeal to the rationalistic approach of the Kalam specialists as more modern and more scientific than the approach of Ibn al-'Arabi and his followers.

We do not mean to imply that the various movements known as "Islamic fundamentalism" are now attempting to adopt the Sufi approach as their own—quite the contrary. To the extent that the fundamentalists make any appeal to the Islamic intellectual tradition (as opposed to the juridical tradition), they look to Kalam and, in particular, the more rational approaches in Kalam. Implicit in fundamentalism is a rejection of unveiling and of philosophical reasoning, and a rejection of most of the great thinkers and sages of the Islamic tradition. At the same time, most fundamentalist movements feel quite at home with the scientific rationalism of the modern West. However, they feel that the West has betrayed the rational approach by letting morality slip out of center stage. They cannot imagine that scientific rationalism and amorality are two sides of the same coin.[21]

Philosophy

Islamic philosophy developed parallel with Kalam. Both approaches are indebted to the Greek heritage for much of their terminology and for the important role given to rational inquiry. But the Kalam specialists give pride of place to the Koran and to their own understanding of the Muslim creed, while the philosophers give pride of place to reason and the Greek intellectual heritage.

By and large, the Muslim philosophers maintain that rational inquiry provides a sufficient means to understand the nature of reality. The *mutakallimun* had constant recourse to the Koran to bolster their opinions. Most early philosophers tend to avoid Koranic references and instead appeal to observation and logical reasoning. Moreover, the philosophers were proud of their knowledge of the Greek tradition. They called Aristotle the First Teacher and accepted many of the findings of the Greek philosophers as true. In contrast, the *mutakallimun* were rather embarrassed by their own indebtedness to the Greek tradition, if they admitted it at all. They claimed that the Koran itself established the route of reason as the primary means to understand its message.

While the Kalam specialists focused on God and his attributes, the philosophers focused on reality itself. Nevertheless, in practically every form in which Islamic philosophy developed, *tawhid* was an underlying theme. The philosophers typically discussed *wujud*, which can be translated as "existence" or "being." Practically all of them agree that *wujud* can be divided into different kinds. *Wujud* in its purest form is pure "is-ness": It cannot not be. It is what the prophets refer to as "God." *Wujud* also takes other forms, but these other forms may come and go. In contrast to *wujud* itself, the forms in which *wujud* appear have no inherent reality and hence are contingent upon it. These forms are what we experience in the cosmos, the existent things or the creatures.

Islamic philosophy looks back to al-Farabi (d. 339/950) as the Second Teacher, though there were other important Muslim philosophers before him, especially al-Kindi (d. 252/866). But the greatest philosopher of the early period, if not of the whole of Islamic history, is Ibn Sina (d. 428/1037), known in the West as Avicenna. It was he who brought the Greek tradition to its peak of sophistication within the Islamic context. He was not only a great philosopher, but also one of the greatest physicians of history, both in practical and theoretical medicine. Many of his works were translated into Latin at an early date, and he was well known in the West as a great philosopher and physician until recently.

Avicenna produced a masterly synthesis of Greek and Islamic wisdom. However, in the opinion of many of the *mutakallimun* and Sufis, his theories were too heavily freighted with Greek terminology and Greek ideas. In modern terms, we could say that Avicenna was too much of an academic for the taste of most Muslims. They wanted Islamic wisdom to be expressed in Islamic terms, which meant that the Koran and the Sunna had to be respected above all else. If there appeared to be a contradiction between what the Koran said and what Aristotle said, then one should come right out and say that Aristotle was wrong.

Al-Ghazali mounted an influential attack on Avicenna's philosophy. A second attack was launched a hundred years later by Fakhr al-Din Razi (d. 606/1209), one of the last of the great Muslim authorities who limited themselves almost exclusively to the perspective of Kalam. But other currents of thought were also developing during this period. We already saw that the Ghazali brothers had begun expressing the three principles of faith in Sufi terms, and others followed their lead. The great Ibn al-'Arabi was a contemporary of Razi, and had even corresponded with him, but he was far from agreeing with his approach. In Ibn al-'Arabi's view, Razi had far too much confidence in reason and no grasp of unveiling.

In philosophy itself, a new perspective was opened up by Shihab al-Din Suhrawardi, who died in prison in 587/1191 at the age of thirty-eight. A remarkable sage and thinker, he took over Avicenna's system and rewrote it with a new orientation, emphasizing the importance of unveiling far more than Avicenna had. Suhrawardi presented his "Illuminationist Philosophy" as a synthesis of the rational thinking of the Greeks and the unveiling of the ancient sages of Persia, whose hearts had been opened to the light of God. Suhrawardi maintained that this synthesis alone was able to bring out the full significance of the Islamic revelation, which needed to be read in terms of both reason and unveiling.

In many respects, Suhrawardi's teachings resemble those of Ibn al-'Arabi. However, Suhrawardi holds that the rational training provided by the philosophical tradition was a necessary prerequisite for intellectual and spiritual perfection. In contrast, Ibn al-'Arabi felt that a true sage would acknowledge the truths that reason was able to perceive, but that rational inquiry itself was more a hindrance than a help. Unveiling alone was the way of the prophets and their authentic successors.

One of Suhrawardi's most famous contributions to Islamic philosophy is his metaphysics of light. Instead of taking the usual philosophical position and talking about *wujud* as the underlying reality of all things, Suhrawardi employed the term *light (nur)* to designate ultimate reality. Light could be analyzed rationally, and at the same time the Sufis had long employed the term to express what they perceived through unveiling. Moreover, Light is a Koranic name of God, and it plays a major role in Zoroastrian mythology, to which Suhrawardi made frequent reference.

After Suhrawardi, the Muslim philosophers tended to be broad-based. They studied Avicenna, Suhrawardi, and many of the *mutakallimun*. They frequently made room for unveiling in their philosophical investigations, and they often studied Ibn al-'Arabi as a great fountainhead of theoretical teachings about the principles of faith. This philosophical tradition has continued down to modern times in some Islamic countries, especially Iran.

Probably the greatest of the later philosophers was Mulla Sadra of Shiraz (d. 1050/1641). He is known for a vast synthesis of all the currents of Islamic thought, though his terminology is dominated by Avicenna's philosophy. In taking revelation into account, Mulla Sadra paid close attention not only to the Koran and the Hadith, but also to the sayings of the Imams of the Shi'ite tradition. He also studied the theoretical elaboration of unveiling achieved by Ibn al-'Arabi and his followers. Finally, Mulla Sadra himself devoted much of his life to Sufi practice and utilized his theoretical teachings to explain the significance of his own unveilings.

Mulla Sadra represents the culmination of an appeal to all three modes of knowing as an avenue to understanding the principles of faith. He respected and utilized every intellectual approach in Islam, and he saw them all as valid ways of understanding *tawhid*. This is not to say that he accepted everything said before him uncritically—far from it. He was first and foremost, at least in the manner in which he formulated his ideas, a representative of the philosophical tradition. Hence, he was deeply concerned about weighing every object of knowledge in the scales of reason. He criticized many of the ideas of the *mutakallimun*, the philosophers, and the Sufis, but he also accepted many ideas—after having proved their validity through rational arguments. His approach was thoroughly rational, but at the same time his rational faculty was illumined by unveiling and the Koranic revelation.

The Two Poles of Understanding

We said that Kalam, theoretical Sufism, and philosophy stress— respectively—revelation, unveiling, and reason. However, we have also pointed out that in each case, the other two approaches play, or may play, a significant role.

It is important to grasp what is implied in the different approaches to knowledge. Otherwise, we may be tempted to think that these schools are antithetical, when in fact, we are dealing with complementary modes of human understanding. People with an intellectual bent are naturally attracted to one or more of these approaches. The three schools provide us with the social and institutional embodiment of the human capacity for understanding the objects of faith.

We can find a certain analogy to the role played by the three schools in the various approaches to knowledge found in the modern world. People may be innately attracted, for example, to philosophy, or to science, or to the arts. In the Islamic case, the three approaches are grounded in faith and *tawhid*, whereas in the modern case, there are no underlying common principles (except perhaps the principle of the lack of principles).

Since *tawhid* is the common theme of Islamic intellectuality, we should be able to categorize the various modes of human understanding in terms of *tawhid*. In other words, if we have three different approaches to *tawhid*, we should be able to discern what it is—in terms of *tawhid*—that distinguishes them.

We already know that *tawhid* demands two complementary perspectives on reality, known as *tanzih*, the declaration of incomparability, and *tashbih*, the declaration of similarity. Ideally, these two should be kept in balance. However, we also know that *tanzih* has the right to a certain precedence in the initial stages of human development. Why?

Because *tanzih* establishes the greatness of God and the smallness of the human, or the reality of the Real and the unreality of the unreal. It situates people in their proper relationship with their Lord. It allows them to understand that they are servants of God, and that they must act like servants. Therefore, they come to realize that *islam* is incumbent upon them. They must freely recognize their imperfect nature and set about to rectify it by following the divine guidance brought by the prophets.

At the early stages of human development, *tashbih* has to be kept in the background, if not denied altogether. If *tanzih* alerts us to the difference between the human and the divine, *tashbih* tells us that the human *is* the divine. However, this identity with God will not help at the beginning. Even mud, maggots, and poison ivy can make the same claim.

If identity with the Real is to have any profit, it must be established in the way in which the Real wants it to be established. In other words, people must understand it just as the prophets – the messengers of the Real – have understood it. In order to reach this understanding, people have to submit to God's guidance. God does not lift people up to his presence in one stroke. First, people become his voluntary servants. Only then is it possible to enter into nearness to him and represent him in the cosmos. Vicegerency depends upon servanthood, which is to say that the true perception of *tashbih* follows upon the true understanding of *tanzih*.

If two different but complementary modes of being human – servanthood and vicegerency – can be described in terms of *tanzih* and *tashbih*, so also two different but complementary modes of human understanding can be described in the same terms. To understand *tanzih* is to grasp God's distance, otherness, transcendence, and inaccessibility. To understand *tashbih* is to grasp God's nearness, sameness, immanence, and accessibility. From the first point of view, the primary emphasis is placed upon otherness; from the second point of view, the primary emphasis is placed upon sameness.

Muslim thinkers who have analyzed these two modes of understanding associate *tanzih* with reason, while they see a close connection between *tashbih* and unveiling as well as imagination. This needs some explanation, but once it is understood, we should be able to see how each intellectual approach within Islamic civilization can keep *tawhid* in view while criticizing or contradicting the findings of other approaches. Moreover, this way of understanding may throw some light on parallel bifurcations that we find in our own civilization, like that between art and science, myth and reason, mysticism and logic, or intuition and ratiocination.

Tanzih involves understanding the Real as other. Through it, people affirm that they are one thing and God is something else, far beyond them. Reason is a mode of understanding that works through analysis;

that is, taking apart and separating out. To understand rationally, we establish the principle of either/or. What we try to understand must be one thing or another; it cannot be both. This is simple logic, and logic expresses the innate nature of reason.

When people look at the Real with the help of reason, they establish difference and separation; that is, *tanzih*, because reason can see in no other way. Reason looks at phenomena and recognizes that God is different from the phenomena. To the extent that it can recognize God's attributes in the things, it separates the attributes out from the things. The rational perspective can see that, for example, mercy is a divine attribute. It can also see that a mother manifests mercy in her relationship with her child, but it "abstracts" mercy from the mother. *Abstraction*—which means literally "to draw away, to withdraw"—is a characteristic of rational operations. Reason draws qualities away from the things within which they appear and, in the theological case, places them far away in God. The net result is separation, difference, distance, *tanzih*.

In more practical terms, rational processes lead naturally to greater stress upon analysis and difference. By separating things out from each other and from God, reason focuses on multiplicity and manyness. Mathematics, inasmuch as it allows people to deal with separate and discrete things, is reason's ideal tool. However, the more attention people pay to difference, the more their endeavors and occupations become separate from each other.

If people think only about God's transcendence, difference, and otherness, they will end up considering the universe as distant from oneness and unity, since oneness and unity are God's attributes. If they keep on stressing the idea of God's remoteness, they will be left with a universe that has no relationship with God whatsoever. This can only mean that they will lose even the concept of God, and they will then find it logical to be atheists or agnostics.

Exclusive stress upon God's distance leads to the point where thinking in terms of God becomes unnecessary, but without a concept of God—the absolute center, the One, the Real—there will be no way to see how the universe holds together. The result will be that human knowledge and activity will become more and more dispersed and disharmonious. We see an example of this in the modern West, which has been obsessively preoccupied with reason for the past several hundred years: God has long since been banished from the field of serious knowledge. As a result, there is no unifying principle, despite the efforts of various philosophers and scientists to come up with one. The various fields of science and learning have become more and more specialized, and more and more disconnected.

This increasing dispersion of knowledge is witnessed most clearly in the never-ending proliferation of information. As a result, communication becomes more and more difficult, because each person's understanding can grasp only a small portion of the plethora of available details. No one can possibly see how all the scientific information that has been and is being gathered is interconnected. Fields of knowledge that used to be considered small are themselves splintering and losing coherence. On the scientific and university level, this leads to an ever-increasing number of specializations. Each discipline sets up its own field of expertise, but experts in different fields speak utterly different languages and find it impossible to communicate with each other.

Scientists are no longer just "physicists," but rather particle physicists, or astrophysicists, or some other kind of physicist. In order to keep up with the proliferating information available in any subfield of physics, the specialists have to read scores of journals in their own narrow field. As a result, it becomes increasingly difficult to communicate with physicists in other specialties, even if laymen think that all these people work in the same field. And we are still talking only about physics. What about biology, or geology, or any of the other hard sciences? What about neuroscience, for example, where the experts tell us that the "explosion of research has turned the field into a Tower of Babel."[22] What about the social sciences? And what about the various branches of the humanities? Even in philosophy, where the uninitiated might imagine that rational beings should certainly be able to speak to each other, we find intense and acrimonious differences of opinion. Thus, it is not surprising to find contemporary observers claiming that the defining characteristic of modern intellectual life is fragmentation.

On the level of human activity, this splintering of knowledge demands that people will be working at cross-purposes in society. The social fabric cannot hold together, and more and more groups form subsocieties. Each group is forced to choose ever-narrower ideals in order to preserve its unity.

It is more difficult for modern people to gain an insight into the nature of unveiling because reason has been stressed so exclusively in our own culture. An analysis of the English word can be helpful. A *veil* is something that separates, that prevents seeing and understanding: It can be a piece of cloth hanging down, a wall, a bush, a cloud, a facial expression, night. It can be the human body itself, which prevents a vision of the soul. It can be darkness, which is the lack of light. It can be ignorance, which is mental darkness. It can be arrogance, envy, jealousy, cupidity, and a hundred other vices, which narrow down the soul and make it impossible to see beyond our own limitations.

The veil can also be light. An excess of illumination has the same effect as not enough illumination: It prevents vision. Clarity of explanation may go right over the head of someone whose understanding is not prepared. (This, in the Islamic view, explains why the Koran—the clearest and most manifest of lights—is not grasped by human beings. As the Gospel of John puts it, "The light shines in the darkness, but the darkness does not comprehend it.") A veil, in short, is that which separates us from the other, that which prevents our understanding of the other.

To *unveil* is to remove the separation that prevents vision and understanding. It is to overcome, in some manner and to some degree, the difference between us and the other. As a mode of knowledge, unveiling works not by dividing things, but by bringing them together. Characteristically, unveiling perceives identity, sameness, wholeness, oneness. It perceives that all things are signs of God and manifest his reality. It does not perceive this rationally and abstractly, but directly. It looks at things—whether of the external or internal worlds—and perceives the things subsisting through God.

The word *unveiling* is used for a specific kind of perception and understanding that depends upon devoting oneself to the way of the prophets. As a rule, it is available only to those who have strong faith (including meticulous observation of the Shariah) and who develop their sincerity in a particular way (which will be discussed when we come to Part III).

There is another word that is broader than *unveiling* and designates every sort of understanding that establishes identity, whether or not it is achieved through following the prophets, and whether or not the perception of God's presence is involved. That word is *imagination*, about which we have already said a good deal. In the present context, we should be able to see that what we already know about imagination throws light on the difference between the approaches of reason and unveiling.

We learned earlier that imagination pertains to the realm of intermediateness and ambiguity. An image is neither the thing that it images nor wholly other than the thing. From the point of view of cosmology, *imagination* is a term that can be applied to everything that is neither completely unseen nor completely visible, neither pure light nor pure clay, neither spirit nor body. In the perspective of Islamic psychology, the term imagination can be applied to the soul, which is neither spirit nor body, but something in between.

In the present context, the word *imagination* refers to a kind of understanding that perceives sameness. Sameness involves the combination of two sides. Imagination sees images, and the images it sees represent a meeting between the viewer and the object that casts the image. Thus, a mirror image is the union of the mirror and the reflected object; a dream image combines the soul and the object seen.

In theological terms, imaginal understanding correlates with *tash bih.* Unveiling, which invariably sees things in appropriate images, perceives God as immediately present in the soul or in the cosmos. In contrast, reason patiently explains that God is absent. Imaginal vision knows that the signs *are* God, even if reason tells us that the signs are signs *of* God. When reason hears the Koranic verse, "Wherever you turn, there is the Face of God" (2:115), it provides us with many clever interpretations to show that the Koran does not mean what it says. God does not have a face, and God cannot be seen, and God is in fact distant from us. But unveiling sees the face of God wherever it turns; it understands that God is actually present right there and right here.

On the broad plain of human endeavors, imagination is a mode of understanding that bridges gaps and perceives sameness, whereas reason perceives difference. Understanding through imagination appears most clearly in poetry, music, and art in general. Artists and poets see connections where the rest of us see difference. Poetic imagery typically depends upon understanding a subtle sameness that reason could never work out on its own. To the extent that our imaginative faculty is alive and well, it appreciates the truth of sameness, even if our rational faculty tells us that things are not really the same.

Reason understands *tanzih*, and without *tanzih* there can be no *islam* and no servant, and hence there can be no *tashbih* and no vicegerent. But imagination allows for the realization of *tashbih*. It is through imaginal understanding that the Koran enters into the flesh and blood of Muslims. Reason sees God and the Koran as distant, while imagination finds them near. Reason insists on keeping God at arms length, while imagination embraces him. Reason establishes a subject and an object, while imagination understands that the subject is the object.

It needs to be stressed that if either point of view is forgotten, we fall into distortion and falsification of *tawhid*. To negate *tawhid* is to establish *shirk*, which is to associate other realities with God. One cannot say, "God is distant" and leave it at that. Nor can one say, "God is near" and be done with the discussion. One has to waffle back and forth in order to keep the different points of view distinct. The human reality demands both servanthood and vicegerency, both *tanzih* and *tashbih*. To forget either is to destroy the integrity of faith and knowledge.

If we stress *tanzih* and forget about *tashbih*, the result is the permanent perception of God's distance from creation. If God is forever distant, he is in effect cut off from his creation. This is one version of what in the West has been called Deism and in Islam is known as *ta'til* (divesting God of his function). When God is kept permanently at arms length, this world, and especially the human presence within this world, take on independent reality. We are now in charge; hence, we have associated ourselves with God. In other terms, excessive stress on *tanzih* leads to a proliferation of lesser divinities that are seen to determine the priorities of our world. In keeping with the proclivities of reason, the names of these divinities—such as "progress," "democracy," "socialism," "communism," "science," and "development"—are abstract, but they are real enough for their worshipers. In fact, they are so real that it is dangerous to question their sacredness. It is true that some of them have been discredited by the mass destruction that has followed their worship in the modern world, but others have quickly taken their place.

If *shirk* arises because of forgetting *tashbih*, it arises for even greater reason when *tashbih* is affirmed and *tanzih* is ignored. From the perspective of *tashbih*, everything is divine. *Tanzih* lets people see things as disharmonious, discrete, and distinct, whereas *tashbih* allows them to see them as harmonious, unified, and united. Each perspective works as a check on the possible excesses of the other point of view.

Sufis, for example, like to emphasize *tashbih*. They often play down the differences among things and see all diversity as the self-expression of God. In their view, the various branches of learning and science appear as so many approaches to the same truths. Difference appears as insignificant, while sameness becomes the overriding attribute of things.

However, if people push this sort of Sufi perspective too far, they will forget that the Real is different from the world and consider the world in itself as real, good, valuable, and worthy of ultimate concern. Each thing in the world becomes divine. However, it quickly becomes impossible to sustain a vision of equal divine reality for all things, so certain things are singled out as being the prime divinities. Most commonly, people settle upon themselves as real: "I am divine; I am real, and others cannot have the same rights as I, since they are real only inasmuch as they depend upon my reality." To take this position and follow through on its logical consequences is a path toward madness; it is no accident that insanity has traditionally been understood as the loss of rational discernment and the uncontrolled expansion of imagination.

The constant insistence that God is near may also lead toward a type of gushy sentimentalism that is familiar nowadays. Proponents of this view tell us that all is one, so we should love everyone and everything equally. In other words, we must ignore our God-given ability to judge the difference between good and evil, right and wrong, paradise and hell.

In practice, few people take *tashbih* to its logical extreme, because it is difficult to live and function only in one's own imagination. Nevertheless, overdependence upon imagination is one of the most common of human characteristics, and the Koran refers to it as "following caprice," an expression we have already discussed: "Have you seen him who has taken his own caprice to be his god?" (25:43).

In short, excessive stress upon *tashbih* leads people to serve many gods—many objects of devotion and concern—or to serve their own egos in place of God. In either case, this is *shirk*, the loss of *tawhid*. The net result of focusing too much on *tashbih* is practically the same as paying exclusive attention to *tanzih*.

We have discussed reason and unveiling (and imagination) in some detail, but let us not forget about revelation. We learned that the primary function of the prophets is to remind people of *tawhid*.

Having been reminded by the prophets of *tawhid*, reason makes contact with the Real. It recognizes that nothing is real but God, and that everything other than God is a false divinity, an unreality, a nothingness.

For its part, imagination, having been reminded of *tawhid*, also makes contact with ultimate reality. But it does not see difference, it sees sameness. It recognizes that everything other than God is in fact present with God. All things are real, all things are something, but only in respect of God's presence within them. Thus, on the basis of the Shahadah, reason sees *tanzih* and imagination sees *tashbih*.

Without being reminded of *tawhid*—without revelation—reason and imagination go their own ways, sometimes working together and sometimes functioning at cross-purposes. There is no escape from these two ways of understanding, since they permeate human existence. In the Islamic view, only revelation allows them to play their proper and harmonious roles.

Turning back to the three intellectual schools, we can now suggest that their differences and similarities have to do with their appreciation of the different facets of *tawhid*, or the respective roles that they accord to revelation, reason, and imagination.

Kalam's Rationality

In theory, Kalam gives pride of place to revelation. However, most of those known as *mutakallimun*, or Kalam authorities, interpret the revelation on the basis of reason. Since reason establishes difference, Kalam stresses *tanzih*. God is different from all things, and hence everything we say about God has to be interpreted in a way that makes it different from what we say about anything else. God is discussed in terms of abstractions: He is always "drawn out" from the world of appearances and placed far away. The language and thinking that Kalam employs are typically abstract, and most people find Kalam dry and boring.

To talk about something that is basically incomprehensible often demands the use of language that is itself difficult to comprehend. Most people do not see things in terms of abstractions, but rather in terms of the concrete and the present; that is, in terms of *tashbih*. In the perspective of Kalam, *tashbih* is dangerous, because it suggests that God is not different. In the eyes of the Kalam specialists, *tashbih* is the error of the common people, those without intellectual training, without a proper understanding of God, or without healthy rational faculties. It is irrational—and hence wrong—to think that God is present. When the Koran seems to say that God is present, Kalam insists on reading the verses in a way that establishes his absence.

We said that one of the primary aims of Kalam is to defend Muslim dogma. Kalam takes a protective role vis-a-vis the Muslim community and Islamic teachings, but given the fact that its approach stresses *tanzih*, Kalam envisages the human role fundamentally in terms of servanthood. God is the distant King and Master, and human beings are his servants who must, under threat of severe punishment, obey his commands. The God of Kalam is not the type of God that anyone could love. One can fear and respect him, yes, but not love him. Some *muta-kallimun* maintained that love for the Creator was impossible, and they explained away the Koranic verse, "He loves them, and they love Him" (5:54) with their usual rational dexterity. Ibn al-'Arabi, after explaining that the rational approach to God must end up with *tanzih*—a God who is infinitely distant from his servants—remarks that fortunately, religious teachings were not monopolized by the rational thinkers. If that had been the case, no one would ever have loved God.

One final characteristic of Kalam is its contentiousness. The word *kalam*, which means "speech," is often used to mean "debate" or "dispute." Typically, most of the discussion in Kalam texts is aimed at disproving the opinions of other schools of Kalam, the philosophers, and various sectarian groups. To provide a taste of the Kalam style, we quote a passage from the founder of the Ash'arite school, Abu'l-Hasan al-Ash'ari. In it, he is criticizing the Qadariyya, who maintained that people are in complete possession of free will.

> The Qadariyya suppose that God created good and Satan created evil, and they suppose that God willed that which did not come to be, and that something came to be which He did not will. This opposes the consensus of the Muslims, which is, [as the Prophet said,] "What God wills will be, and what He does not will will not be." They reject the words of God, "You will not will unless God wills" [76:30]. . . .
>
> The Messenger of God called them the Magi of this community, because they follow the religion of the Magi and copy their words. They suppose that good and evil have two creators, as the Magi supposed. They think that among evils are those that God did not will, as the Magi say. They suppose that they have power over loss and benefit for themselves, aside from God, thereby rejecting the words of God, "Say: I do not own benefit for myself, or loss, but only as God wills" [7:188]. . . . They suppose that they have exclusive power over their own works, aside from God. Hence they affirmed that their selves are independent of God. They describe themselves as powerful over something over which they describe God as having no power. In the same way, the Magi affirmed that Satan has a power over evil that God does not have.[23]

Philosophy's Abstraction

The philosophical approach to Islamic teachings has both deep differences with Kalam and certain similarities. One major difference is on the issue of revelation. The philosophers refuse to accept uncritically the necessity for the Koranic revelation. Whether or not the Koran is God's word is one of the issues that needs to be discussed. By and large, the philosophers were Muslims who observed the Shariah. Most of them were able to prove to their own intellectual satisfaction that prophecy was a fact of existence. However, the very act of posing the question of prophecy's validity was enough to raise the ire of most Muslims, the Kalam specialists in particular. Moreover, some philosophers reached the conclusion that prophets attained divine wisdom through personal effort and that it was therefore possible for others to reach the same station. To many critics, they seemed to be saying that philosophers did not need prophets, since they themselves were prophets.

The experts in Kalam based their perspective on their own understanding of the Koranic revelation. In contrast, the philosophers considered themselves the heirs to the Greek tradition of Plato, Aristotle, and Plotinus. They saw no basic contradiction between Islam and Greek wisdom, while the Kalam specialists, in keeping with their protective stance, found this idea practically heretical.

What the *mutakallimun* and the philosophers shared was an appreciation of the role of reason. Theoretically, most theologians put revelation above reason, but in practice, many of them insisted that the Koran had to submit to the laws of rational inquiry. But the philosophers, both in theory and in practice, placed reason at the pinnacle of values.

One of the many differences between the approach of Kalam and philosophy is evident in the auxiliary sciences that each group considered important. By and large, the *mutakallimun* focused their attention on such sciences as Koran commentary, Hadith, Arabic grammar, and jurisprudence. In contrast, although the philosophers would usually study these sciences, they devoted their primary attention to philosophy proper, which included not only metaphysics and logic, but also natural philosophy (the sciences of nature, such as physics, optics, and mechanics), mathematics (including astronomy and music), psychology (the science of the relationship between spirit, soul, and body), and medicine. We have already noted that Avicenna, often considered the greatest of the Muslim philosophers, was arguably the greatest physician of Islamic history as well. Al-Farabi, the Second Teacher, is the author of a monumental work on music theory. Nasir al-Din al-Tusi (d. 672/1274), who was learned in all the intellectual sciences including Kalam and theoretical Sufism, revived Avicenna's philosophy and was one of the greatest mathematicians and astronomers in human history.

The speculative and theoretical side to philosophy was always important. But in stark contrast to many modern philosophers, the Muslim philosophers applied their metaphysics and cosmology to everyday life. All of them were deeply interested, for example, in the science of ethics. For most of them, ethics was the training of the soul in order to bring it into harmony with the Real in preparation for the Return to

God. But they discussed this science in the terminology inherited from Greek philosophy, not primarily in terms of Koranic categories.

To gain an idea of the abstract reasoning typical of the philosophical approach, we can look at the following passage. Avicenna is discussing good and evil in terms of *wujud* (existence, or being). The basic point maintained by the philosophers was "None has true *wujud* but *wujud* itself," which is to say that nothing is real but the Real. In the same way, nothing can be absolutely good but God alone, because, in religious language, "There is no good but God." The philosophers call this *wujud* that is identical with the Real and the Good the "necessary *wujud*," since it cannot not be. In the following, Avicenna shows that evil is simply the lack of good, or the lack of *wujud*:

> *Everything that is a necessary* wujud *through itself is sheer good and sheer perfection. "Good" is, in short, that which everything desires and through which each thing's* wujud *reaches completion. But evil has no essence, because it is either the nonexistence of a substance or the nonexistence of the wholesomeness of a state. Hence* wujud *is goodness, and the perfection of* wujud *is the goodness of* wujud. *That* wujud *which is not accompanied by nonexistence—whether the nonexistence of substance or the nonexistence of something that belongs to the substance—and which, rather, is perpetually actualized, is sheer good.*
>
> *Anything which is a possible* wujud *through its essence is not a sheer good, because its essence, in itself, does not necessitate that it have* wujud. *Hence, its essence, in itself, allows for nonexistence. That which allows for nonexistence in any manner is not free of evil and imperfection in every respect. Hence sheer good is only the necessary* wujud *through itself.*
>
> *"Good" may also be applied to that which is beneficial and useful for the perfections of things. We will explain later that it is necessary that the necessary* wujud, *through its very essence, benefit every* wujud *and every perfection of* wujud. *Hence, in this respect also it is a good into which no imperfection and evil can enter.*[24]

Although philosophers felt that reason was the key to understanding, many of them knew that imagination opened up the mind to certain perspectives that reason could not grasp. As psychologists, the philosophers were always interested in the role of imagination as a faculty of the soul, but as thinkers who applied their theories to life, they also made use of imagination to gain insight into the divine nature. This was not true of all the philosophers, but a significant number—including Avicenna and Suhrawardi—had understood that imagination provided a different mode of knowing reality and expressing the truth. Most works of the philosophers are dry, abstract, and pedantic, like the works of the theologians, but both Avicenna and Suhrawardi wrote what have been called "visionary treatises." In these works, reason is given a secondary role, and imagery is utilized to open up the reader's understanding. These works often seem more like poetry than prose. They attract by their beauty and by a certain sense of wonder, rather than by logical arguments.[25]

Suhrawardi was especially concerned about keeping reason and imagination in balance while attempting to explain the nature of things. The fact that he chose "light" rather than *wujud* as the main object of philosophical investigation reflects his concern for maintaining this balance. Although the word *wujud* is not used in the Koran, by his time it was well-established as a philosophical term. As employed by the philosophers, the word encouraged abstract thinking; it became a means to express *tanzih* rather than *tashbih*. But Suhrawardi knew that the experiential wisdom gained through unveiling had an important role to play: Without the direct experience of the presence of the Real, people were locked into *tanzih*.

The term *light*, as we have already pointed out, is a Koranic name of God. In contrast to *wujud* as employed by the philosophers, *light* designates ultimate reality, both as something known and as something that knows. Light is that which uncovers, unveils, and reveals: It brings about awareness. To be illuminated is to be aware. Light is not only the Real as object, it is also the Real as subject. Our experience of light is our experience of awareness. Sufis typically describe unveiling in terms of light: When the divine light shines, the darkness of ignorance is removed.

Suhrawardi expresses the importance of reason in his many philosophical treatises, which are written in the style of Avicenna. As for his visionary recitals, they express his ability to see through light, or his identity with light. Through reason, the Real is kept at arm's length, but once the seeker tastes and experiences light, the distance between God and the servant is erased. However, this identity of Light and its radiance (that is, the human being) cannot be expressed rationally without setting up the barrier of abstraction and distance. In contrast, imagistic writing speaks directly to the imagination. The imagery allows the soul to experience, through recognition of its own imaginal substance, that it is not different from the Real's imaginal apparition.

As an example of Suhrawardi's visionary recitals, one episode can be cited from "The Language of the Ants." The title refers to a Koranic verse that mentions Solomon overhearing a conversation among the ants (27:19). In this passage, it seems that Suhrawardi takes Solomon as a symbol for God, and he presents the nightingale — in Persian, often called "the bird of a thousand tales" — as the symbol for the human being, who was taught all the names but then fell into forgetfulness:

> *All the birds were gathered together in the presence of Solomon, except the nightingale. Solomon chose a bird to act as messenger. He should tell the nightingale, "It is necessary for the two of us to meet."*

Solomon's message reached the nightingale, who had never been out of his nest. He referred to his friends, saying: "Solomon has commanded such and such, and he does not lie. He has promised a meeting. If he is outside, and we are inside, it is impossible for us to meet. But he cannot fit into our nest, and there is no other way."

There was an old one among them. He called out, "If the promise of 'The day they meet Him' [9:77] is correct, and if the situation of 'Each one will be made present with Us' [36:32] and 'Surely to Us is their return' [88:25] and 'In the sitting place of truthfulness with a powerful King' [54:55] is to be actualized, then the way is as follows: Since King Solomon cannot fit into our nest, we must leave our nest and go to him. Otherwise, no meeting will be possible."[26]

In short, the characteristic philosophical mode of expression circles around *tanzih* and abstract thinking. But many philosophers were perfectly aware of the limitations of reason and hence they employed images—or, if you prefer, symbols—to express *tashbih* and the nearness of the Real.

Sufism's Vision

We said earlier that theoretical Sufism stresses unveiling, or the direct vision of the divine light, or seeing God's actual presence in the world and in the self. But Sufism is equally rooted in revelation. Even more than Kalam, the Sufi theoreticians based their experience on the Koran and the Sunna. The Prophet did not achieve his knowledge through his own rational and imaginative powers. Quite the contrary, God chose him as an appropriate receptacle and taught him the Book and wisdom:

God has sent down on thee the Book and the wisdom, and He has taught thee what thou knewest not. God's bounty to thee is ever great. (4:113)

The Sufis accepted without question that Muhammad was the last of the prophets and that no scripture would appear after him. However, they did not accept that following the Prophet meant simply conforming to his Sunna and memorizing the Koran and the Hadith. On the contrary, it was possible for people to be so utterly sincere and devoted in their imitation of the Prophet that God would teach them directly, without the intermediary of rational learning. The Sufis frequently quote the Koranic verse, "Be wary of God, and God will teach you" (2:286), to prove their point. The prerequisite for unveiling is god-wariness, and god-wariness (as we will see in Part III) is the perfection of faith and practice through sincerity. But it does not necessarily entail the disciplined exercise of the rational faculty in the mode of the Kalam experts or the philosophers. In fact, according to many Sufis, such rational endeavors are more of a barrier to understanding than an aid.

This is not to say that Sufis rejected reason as a valid means of understanding. The Koran repeatedly admonishes people to use their *'aql*; that is, their intelligence or reason. The Sufis understood that reason was a human faculty that had to be developed in order for perfection to be achieved. What they did not accept was that either Kalam or philosophy was the best way to train one's rational thinking. Again, they felt that following the Sunna of the Prophet and exercising god-wariness would result in a perfected rational faculty.

Sufi writings are by no means irrational, even in terms of philosophy and Kalam. Many of the Sufis had training in one or both of these sciences and employed theological and philosophical arguments in their writings. It is often difficult to know what sort of label one should place on a given author: Was he a Sufi or a *mutakallim*, or perhaps a philosopher, or perhaps all three?

Al-Ghazali is a good example of the difficulty of categorization. In many of his writings, he appears as a master of Ash'arite Kalam, but in others he is highly critical of Kalam, and in others he takes a thoroughly Sufi approach. He was also well versed in philosophy, and the Latin West knew him as "Algazel" the philosopher. The seventh/thirteenth century philosopher Afdal al-Din Kashani wrote works on logic and had an extremely acute rational perception of things, but at the same time, he spoke from the vantage point of unveiling. Many other individuals can be cited who do not fit neatly into any of the categories we have set up. This is as it should be, for these are simply three different yet complementary modes of knowledge, and none of them contradicts or excludes the others.

Although Sufism made use of all three types of knowledge, its stress upon unveiling meant that Sufis were more concerned to explicate *tashbih* than *tanzih*. The type of imaginal knowledge provided by unveiling allowed them to see the presence of God in themselves and the world. This was a direct and immediate experience of God's identity with the things. At the same time, they saw no contradiction between God's presence and his absence. Just as they knew imaginally that God is near, they knew rationally that God is far, that he is not any specific thing but stands beyond all things.

Sufism did not disagree with the *mutakallimun* that God is far. However, since Kalam placed almost exclusive stress upon *tanzih* and God's attributes of wrath and severity, the Sufis felt it necessary to bring out the other side of the picture. Their writings stress *tashbih* and God's mercy and gentleness.

If Kalam writings are mainly abstract, as befits a rational approach, Sufi writings tend in the direction of concreteness, as befits the imaginal perception provided by unveiling. This helps explain why Sufism has been far more pervasive a presence in Islamic civilization than either Kalam or philosophy. Many Sufi theoreticians made full use of the possibilities of imagery, symbolism, and storytelling, and hence they were able to speak to everyone. Anyone can understand a story, even if the point of the story is a subtle theological or metaphysical teaching, but very few people can understand the abstract reasoning involved in the typical arguments of the Kalam specialists and the philosophers. Moreover, Sufi authors used poetry to great advantage. Many of the greatest poets of Arabic, Persian, Turkish, and other Islamic languages were Sufis. They employed their poetry to celebrate the presence of God in all things. In contrast, no outstanding jurist, *mutakallim*, or philosopher was ever a first-rate poet. This in itself says a great deal about the success of the Sufis in expressing their vision of reality, all the more so when we remember that poetry has always been by far the most popular form of literature throughout the Islamic world.

This is not to deny that some Sufi theoreticians wrote difficult works that were inaccessible to the vast majority of the populace. These works did make use of the imaginative faculty, but they also employed the techniques of the philosophers and *mutakallimun*, who were often part of the intended audience. In any case, Sufism has always made use of imagination and imagery in expressing its teachings, while Kalam limited itself almost totally to abstract reasoning. We will provide examples of Sufi writing in the next part of the book.

Part III:

IHSAN

Chapter 7.

THE KORANIC ROOTS OF *IHSAN*

❧

Having looked at *islam* and *iman*, the first two dimensions of Islam as delineated in the hadith of Gabriel, it is now time to turn to the third and deepest dimension, *ihsan*, or "doing what is beautiful." We suggested that discussions of *islam* focus on activity, while those on *iman* look closely at understanding. As for discussions of *ihsan*, they focus on human intentionality. Why do people do what they do? *Islam* tells us what they should do and *iman* provides them with an understanding of why it is necessary to do what they do, but neither of these domains concerns itself with how it is possible to bring one's motivations and psychological qualities into harmony with one's activity and understanding. This is the concern of those who focus on *ihsan* and related concepts as the ideal qualities of the human soul. We now turn to a discussion of a few of the Koranic ideals that are connected with correct motivations, and some of the ways in which Islamic institutional forms reflect these concerns.

The Word *Ihsan*

In the hadith of Gabriel, the Prophet said that *ihsan* is "to worship God as if you see Him, for if you do not see Him, He sees you." Before investigating the meaning and implications of this saying, it will be useful to look at how the word *ihsan* is used in the Koran and the Hadith.

Ihsan derives from the word *husn*, which designates the quality of being good and beautiful. Dictionaries tell us that *husn* means, in general, every positive quality (goodness, goodliness, beauty, comeliness, pleasingness, harmony, symmetry, desirability). Its opposites are *qubh* (repulsiveness) and *su'* (ugliness or evil).

The dictionaries do not consider *husn* a synonym of *khayr* (which we discussed earlier in opposition to *sharr*: "good and evil"). *Husn* is a good that is inseparable from beauty and attractiveness, while *khayr* is a good that provides a concrete benefit, but it may not be beautiful and attractive; or it may simply be "better" than its alternative. We saw that *khayr* is often used as a comparative adjective.

Husn needs to be distinguished from *jamal*, which we also translate as "beauty." We have encountered the term *jamal* in the hadith, "God is beautiful, and He loves beauty." Sometimes *jamal* is practically synonymous with *husn*. Some lexicographers say that in the case of human beauty, *husn* refers to the eyes, while *jamal* refers to the nose. In religious terminology, *jamal* has no opposite. Instead, it is employed as the correlative of *jalal*, or "majesty." Thus we have the beautiful and the majestic names of God.

The Koran employs the word *hasana*, from the same root as *husn*, to mean a good or beautiful deed or thing. Its opposite is *sayyi'a*, an ugly deed or thing. A *hasana* may be done by both human beings and God, but a *sayyi'a* cannot be performed by God:

> *Whatever beautiful thing touches you, it is from God, and whatever ugly thing touches you, it is from yourself. (4:79)*

> *He who brings something beautiful shall have better than it, but he who brings something ugly—those who worked ugly things shall be recompensed only with what they were working. (28:84)*

Perhaps the most significant Koranic usage of words derived from *husn* is found in the adjective *husna*, "most beautiful," which is applied to God's names. We have noted that the Koran mentions God's "most beautiful names" in four verses. This means that God's attributes are more beautiful, more attractive, and more praiseworthy than the attributes of anything else. In effect, the adjective *husna* expresses the first Shahadah, because it means that each of the most beautiful names designates a superlative quality. Or rather, each divine name designates an attribute possessed by God alone. God is beautiful, and none is beautiful but God. God is majestic, and none is majestic but God. All the most beautiful names can be placed in the formula of *tawhid*.

The Koran also uses the word *husna* as a noun, meaning "the best, the most beautiful," that which comprises all goodness, beauty, and desirability. *Husna* is the recompense given to those who have faith. By following the prophets and living up to the Trust, human beings actualize God's most beautiful names in themselves and come to participate in everything that is most beautiful. Hence the word *husna* is used to designate both the attributes of God and the ultimate goal of human beings, the felicity that they experience in the next world.

> *As for him who has faith and does wholesome works, his recompense shall be the most beautiful. (18:88)*

> *For those who answer their Lord, the most beautiful, and for those who answer Him not, . . . theirs shall be an ugly reckoning, and their refuge shall be Gehenna. (13:18)*

The word *ihsan* is a verb that means to do or to establish what is good and beautiful. In the Koranic verses that follow, we will translate it as "to do what is beautiful" or "to make beautiful." The Koran employs the word and its active particle *muhsin* (the one who does what is beautiful) in seventy verses. Significantly, it often designates God as the one who does what is beautiful, and *al-muhsin* is one of the divine names. God's doing the beautiful began with creation itself, while the crowning glory of creation is the human being, made in God's most beautiful form:

> *He is the Knower of the unseen and the visible, the Mighty, the Compassionate, who made beautiful everything that He created. And He created the human being from clay, and made his progeny an extraction of mean water. Then He proportioned him and blew into him of His own spirit. (32:6-9)*

> *It is God who made the earth a fixed place for you, and heaven a building, and He formed you, made your forms beautiful, and provided you with the pleasant things. (40:64)*

> *He created the heavens and the earth with the Real, formed you, and made your forms beautiful, and to Him is the homecoming. (64:3)*

If God does what is beautiful through creating human beings, human beings have the obligation to do what is beautiful in their relationships with God and other creatures. In other words, they should act in accordance with their *fitra*, the original disposition that God placed within them: "Do what is beautiful, as God has done what is beautiful to you" (28:77).

When people do what is beautiful, this of course does not benefit God. People themselves gain by conforming to their own deepest nature: "If you do what is beautiful, you do what is beautiful to your own souls, and if you do what is ugly, it is to them likewise" (17:7). But of course, people will not be able to do what is beautiful until God helps them to do so. In the last analysis, human activity depends upon God's initiative. God made all things beautiful, just as he made all things *muslims*. But only his guidance allows people to become Muslims, and so also, only his blessing and mercy can turn a person's ugly character traits into beautiful character traits. This helps explain the sense of the supplication taught by the Prophet: "O God, Thou hast made my creation [*khalq*] beautiful, so make my character [*khuluq*] beautiful too."

The Koran repeatedly commands human beings to do what is beautiful, and at the same time, it promises that those who do what is beautiful will be brought under the sway of God's gentle, merciful, and beautiful names. The following two verses are especially significant in that they connect *ihsan* with *husna*. We are reminded that the ugly is recompensed only with its like, but the good and the beautiful are recompensed not only with their like, but with increase as well. Human qualities gain their reality from the most beautiful divine qualities. When human beings return to God, their beautiful qualities become indistinguishable from God's own qualities.

> To God belongs whatsoever is in the heavens and whatsoever is in the earth, so that He may recompense those who do the ugly for what they have done, and recompense those who do what is beautiful with the most beautiful. (53:31)

> Those who do what is beautiful will receive the most beautiful and increase. (10:26)

A hadith brings out the beautiful's power to efface the ugly with special clarity:

> When the servant submits, and his submission is beautiful, God will acquit him of every ugly thing he approached. After that, the requital for the beautiful will be the like of it ten to seven hundred times over, and for the ugly its like, unless God should disregard it.

In the following Koranic verses, notice that the first beautiful act that human beings must perform after *tawhid* is to do what is beautiful and good to their own parents, those who brought them into existence. It is parents who provide the means that God employs in creating people, in making them beautiful. God takes credit for creation—this is the demand of *tawhid*. But he expects his creatures to act appropriately toward the human intermediaries of creation. Only then can people hope that other creatures—and their own children—will act beautifully toward them.

Worship none but God, and do what is beautiful toward parents.
(2:83)

*Say: "Come, I will recite what your Lord has forbidden to you: You
must not associate others with Him. And do what is beautiful toward parents. Slay not your children because of poverty; We will
provide you and them. Approach not any indecency, outward or
inward. . . ." (6:151)*

*Set not up with God another god, or you will sit condemned and
forsaken. God has decreed that you shall worship none but Him.
And do what is beautiful toward parents, whether one or both of
them reaches old age with you. Say not to them, "Fie," neither
chide them, but speak unto them respectful words, and lower to
them the wing of humbleness, and say, "My Lord, have mercy upon
them, as they raised me up when I was little." (17:22–24)*

*We have charged the human being that he do what is beautiful to-
ward his parents. His mother bore him painfully, and painfully she
gave birth to him. . . . When he is fully grown, and reaches forty
years, he says, "My Lord, dispose me that I may be thankful for
Thy blessing wherewith Thou hast blessed me, my father, and my
mother, and that I may do wholesome works that will please
Thee. And make my offspring wholesome toward me." (46:15)*

The Koran always depicts those who do the beautiful as good and
praiseworthy human beings. They share in God's quality of *ihsan*, and
hence they are near to him and participate in his gentleness and mercy.
Since they do the beautiful, they themselves are beautiful. Hence, it is not
surprising that in five out of sixteen Koranic verses where God is said to
love human beings, they are described as *muhsin*, while in the remaining
eleven verses, they are given other good and beautiful qualities (we will
come back to the significance of this point when we discuss love):

*God is with those who are god-wary, and those who do what is
beautiful. (16:128)*

*Do what is beautiful. God loves those who do what is beautiful.
(2:195)*

*Pardon them and forgive; God loves those who do what is beauti-
ful. (5:13)*

*Have patience. God will not leave to waste the wage of those who
do what is beautiful. (11:115)*

*Those who struggle for Us—We shall guide them on Our paths, and
God is with those who do what is beautiful. (29:69)*

*Who is more beautiful in religion than he who submits [islam] his
face to God while he does what is beautiful? (4:125)*

The mercy of God is near to those who do what is beautiful. (7:56)

*God rewards them ... with gardens through which rivers flow,
therein dwelling forever. That is the recompense of those who do
what is beautiful. (5:85)*

*They shall have whatsoever they want with their Lord—that is the
recompense of those who do what is beautiful. (39:34)*

The word *ihsan* is used in a wide variety of ways. Doing what is beautiful is important on every level. One place where Muslims have always paid close attention to this rule is in giving names to their children. Like people in practically every other civilization, Muslims have chosen names that represent ideals that they hope their children will achieve. A number of hadiths make explicit the importance of choosing names, and the Prophet sometimes changed people's names if he felt they were inappropriate. Typically, people who convert to Islam adopt a Muslim name as a sign of the identity they hope to achieve. The Prophet said that the most beloved names to God are 'Abd Allah (servant of God) and 'Abd al-Rahman (servant of the Merciful). He summed up the importance of names in the saying, "You will be called on the day of resurrection by your names and the names of your fathers, so make your names beautiful."

On one level, this is a command to choose beautiful names for children. On another level, of course, it is a command for people to rectify their own character traits so that they will be called by names such as generous, kind, compassionate, and so on, which are among God's most beautiful names. The long hadith we quoted toward the end of the section on the Return mentions that, after death, people will be called by the most beautiful or the most repulsive names by which they were called in this world, depending on their character traits.

One indication of the importance of *husn* in the Islamic world view is the fact that the Prophet's two grandchildren were called Hasan and Husayn. We have already met the first word, the adjective from *husn*, meaning "beautiful." *Husayn* is the diminutive of the same word. Hence, the two names can be translated as "the beautiful one" and "the little beauty." The fact that we do not think that these would be appropriate names for men says something about different conceptions of beauty in the West and in Islam. What is certain is that the two names were chosen, or at least approved, by the Prophet himself.

One of the most interesting hadiths concerning *ihsan* is the following, which is found in most of the standard hadith collections:

God has prescribed doing what is beautiful for everything. When you kill, do the killing beautifully, and when you slaughter, do the slaughtering beautifully. You should sharpen your blade so that the victim is relieved.

The first sentence is of special importance, because it sets down a universal rule. Just as God has created the cosmos as beautiful, so human activity, which must follow the divine model, has to be performed beautifully. Then, the hadith turns to the specific instance which probably occasioned the saying in the first place. The Prophet is telling his companions that they know the Koran and that it has commanded doing the beautiful. They should not think that acts that are normally considered ugly are in any way exempt. Killing is ordinarily an ugly act, and killing a human being without just cause is sufficient reason to end up in hell: "Whoso slays a soul not to retaliate for a soul slain, nor for corruption done in the earth, is as if he had slain all people" (5:32; cf. 4:93). In the same way, slaughtering animals for food is not an act that most people find pleasant and attractive, and with good reason. Nevertheless, God has allowed it, and hence it should be done in the best way possible.

In the third sentence of the hadith, the Prophet gives a specific example of what doing the beautiful involves on this level, where a certain ugliness is inevitable. The knife should be sharp, so that the animal's throat can be slit quickly, and the animal will not suffer. Likewise, if it is a question of killing a human being, whether in war or as retaliation, it should be done with a sharp sword. This command is not unrelated to a large number of prohibitions found in the Shariah concerning war. For example, women, children, priests and monks, and noncombatants in general must not be harmed. (This means, of course, that the Shariah prohibits all the means of mass destruction employed in modern warfare.)

Worship

The Koran and the Prophet consider *ihsan* as one of the most desirable of human qualities. The Koran connects *ihsan* to everything good and praiseworthy and makes its possessors the inhabitants of paradise. The Prophet's definition of *ihsan* in the hadith of Gabriel is especially interesting in that it gives us an insight into the quality's interior dimension, its psychology. It explains the human attitudes and motivations that go hand in hand with *ihsan*. We begin by considering the word *'ibada* (worship): "To do what is beautiful is that you *worship* God as if you see Him."

As noted earlier, the word *'ibada* comes from the same root as *'abd* (servant). We can also translate it as "to serve," or "to be a servant." To worship God is to be his servant and to do what he asks you to do. Here we are not talking about compulsory servanthood, mentioned in this verse: "None is there in the heavens and earth but comes to the Merciful as a servant" (19:93). Rather, *ihsan* demands servanthood that is voluntary, free, and truly devoted.

When the word *worship* is employed in a narrow sense in Islamic texts, it refers to the Five Pillars of Islam and the other acts — such as supplication and remembrance (*dhikr*) — that have a specifically ritual and devotional nature. In this sense of the term, its plural is often employed, and we can translate it as "acts of worship." Jurisprudence frequently divides human activity into two broad categories: Acts of worship and transactions. The first are ritual activities that relate people directly to God, while the second have to do with human interrelationships — such as marriage, inheritance, and contracts — that must be accomplished in keeping with God's instructions.

The Koran uses the term *worship* in a much broader sense than observing the Five Pillars. The word means to take something as one's god and hence to obey the commands and prohibitions of that god. It is to orient one's life and existence in terms of what one considers to be Real. It is to appeal to one's god for guidance and aid, and to give gratitude to one's god for blessings received.

The object of correct worship, of course, is God, and God alone. This is demanded by *tawhid*. In fact, worship is simply the first practical implication of *tawhid*. Since there is no other reality, people must orient themselves to the Real. That orientation of self to a reality that is personal and makes moral claims upon human beings is called worship. Since the necessity of worship follows directly upon *tawhid*, and *tawhid* is the vision inherent in the *fitra* of human beings (and, apparently, in that of the jinn as well), the Koran connects creation directly with worship: "I created the jinn and mankind only to worship Me" (51:56).

In the same way, worship of the one God is the message given to all the prophets, since worship is demanded by *tawhid*:

> *We sent forth in every nation a messenger: "Worship God, and avoid false gods." (16:36)*

> *We never sent a messenger before thee except that We revealed to him, saying, "There is no god but I, so worship Me." (21:25)*

> *Ask those of Our messengers We sent before thee: Have We appointed gods to be worshiped apart from the Merciful? (43:45)*

According to the Koran, when God spoke to Moses from the Burning Bush, he said:

Verily I am God. There is no god but I, so worship Me, and per-form the salat *in remembrance of Me. (20:14)*

The Koran vehemently criticizes the worship of anything other than God, for there is nothing else that is worthy of worship. A god is precisely that which deserves worship and service, and *tawhid* tells us that this quality is possessed by God alone. Only people devoid of intelligence could fail to grasp *tawhid*:

A Book whose signs are made firm and then differentiated, from One Wise, Aware: Worship none but God. (11:2)

Say: "I have only been commanded to worship God, and not to as-sociate anything with Him. To Him I call, and to Him I turn." (13:36)

Why should I not worship Him who gave me my fitra, *and unto whom I shall be returned? (36:22)*

Fie upon you and what you worship apart from God! Have you no intelligence? (21:67)

Those who worship others have associated others with God and hence have fallen into *shirk*. The god whose worship is criticized is sometimes "caprice," that most dangerous of inner gods that pulls people this way and that according to the whim of the moment.

Say: "I have been forbidden to worship those whom you call upon apart from God." Say: "I do not follow your caprices, or else I would have been misguided." (6:56)

Made I not covenant with you, Children of Adam, that you should not worship Satan—surely he is a clear enemy to you—and that you should worship Me? (36:60)

In short, the Koran considers voluntary servanthood of God a human imperative, and it makes those who serve him properly, who worship him as is his due, the best of human beings. We already know that being a servant is the prerequisite for becoming God's vicegerent. However, this is not ordinary servanthood, but pure, undefiled, and sincere ser-vanthood. Such servants achieve their sincerity through dealing with God as he deserves to be dealt with. But of course, in the last analysis, it is God who purifies the servant. Hence the Koran sometimes refers to those who have been "made sincere": "God's servants made sincere—for them awaits a known provision . . . in the gardens of bliss" (37:40-43).

Seeing God

The Prophet's definition says, "To do what is beautiful is to worship God as if you *see* Him, because if you do not see Him, He sees you." Here the Prophet focuses on the attitude and intention behind the outward activity that is demanded by *islam*. His point is easily understood by thinking about the way we do things in everyday life. For example, the law tells you not to drive over the speed limit. Many people observe the law, but others observe it only because they are afraid there may be a patrol car lurking around the next bend; and if a patrol car happens to be right behind them in traffic, they would not think of exceeding the limit.

The Prophet is saying that people should worship God—that is, observe the Five Pillars and, more generally, do everything that they do—as if God were in a patrol car right behind them. Even if you do not see the patrol car, you can be sure that he is employing devices that no radar detector will ever be able to foil. "God is with you wherever you are" (57:4), and there is no escape.

The attitude demanded by *ihsan* may be dominated by *tanzih* or by *tashbih*, or it may combine the two qualities in equal measure. In the example of the patrol car, we appealed to severity and wrath, the attributes of *tanzih*. "The sultan is the shadow of God"; that is, God viewed as king and commander. The police are the arms of the sultan— the strict enforcers of the law. From this perspective, people worship God because of fear of the consequences if they do not follow the commands that he has issued. They are the Lord's servants and must obey him on penalty of prison—Sijjin, the lowest pit of hell.

But not all activity is motivated by fear. It often happens that people do things out of love and the wish to be close to the object of their love. Then, the motivation is a hope and a trust that is rooted in the attributes of *tashbih*, such as mercy, gentleness, and bounty. When a young man does everything his girlfriend asks him to do, it may be that he is motivated by his desire to marry her. He has a goal in mind that he wants to achieve. What is certain is that he will act differently if she is right there with him, or if she has gone off with her family on vacation. Naturally, when the girlfriend is not around, the boy's efforts relax. But when she returns, his efforts increase.

In these two examples, the motivation for activity is fear of loss and hope for gain. But many Muslims authorities maintain that worshiping God as if you see him means that you forget all thought of either loss or gain. It is sufficient that God is Real and the servant unreal. One must focus upon what is Real and forget the unreal. One must, in other words, have no thought of oneself whatsoever, and think only about God. This is the perfection of remembering God (*dhikr*). It is one thing to remember someone who is far away, and quite another to remember a person who is present. By living in God's presence, one not only remembers God constantly, but one cannot possibly forget him.

The definition of *ihsan* says that you should worship God "as if you see Him, for, if you do not see Him, nonetheless He sees you." He sees you because He is with you wherever you are. But notice that the definition says, "if you do not see Him." What if you do see Him? That is the goal of worship. Then, without question, one's worship will be for God's sake alone.

How does one see God? This is a complex issue, one that has been discussed and debated throughout Islamic history. Briefly, we can say that the authorities have answered the question differently depending upon whether their perspective was dominated by *tanzih* or *tashbih*. The Kalam experts, who stress *tanzih*, rejected the possibility of seeing God in this world, although most of them accepted that he can and will be seen in the next world. In contrast, the Sufis, who stress *tashbih*, said that it was possible to see God in this world, not with the eye of the head, but with the eye of the heart. Most of them, however, said that people can never, whether in this world or the next world, see God as he sees himself: They can only see God to the extent that he chooses to show himself to them. If "He is with you wherever you are," then you can see him inasmuch as he is with *you*, but you cannot necessarily see him as he appears to others or the angels, and certainly not as he appears to himself.

One can say that the goal of *ihsan* is to worship God while actually seeing him. The significance of this goal becomes clear when we remember that the vision of God is the highest bliss of paradise. Nothing in the next world can compare with seeing God. So also, nothing in this world can be compared with the vision of God that is achieved through true *ihsan*.

Sincerity

Ihsan is to act as if one is seeing God. In such a situation, one is aware that nothing can be hidden from God. But the goal is not simply to act as God wants you to act; rather, it is to do things for God's sake alone. This is *tawhid* put into practice. Since there is no reality but the Real, all activity and thought should conform to the Real. One of the motivations for achieving this conformity is the understanding that God is present, which means not only that he sees what you do, but also that he sees what you think. God knows everything, whether manifest or hidden, including your most secret thoughts:

> God knows what is in your hearts; God is Knowing, Clement. (33:51)

> What, does God not know best what is in the breasts of all the world's inhabitants? (29:10)

He knows what you conceal and what you proclaim. (27:25)

Ihsan demands that people be aware of God's presence and act appropriately, but it also demands that they think, feel, and intend appropriately. It is not enough for outward activity to be correct (that would be simple *islam*); rather, inward thoughts and attitudes must conform exactly with outward activity. There should be no contradiction between what people think and what they do, or between what they are and what they think. The human personality needs to be harmonious, balanced, and whole, without tendencies and impulses pulling in different directions.

This harmony of the person is often called *ikhlas*, which is usually translated as "sincerity." Sincerity is to be the same inside and outside. When a sincere person says something, the words are true and correspond exactly to the person's understanding and faith. So also, the activity of a sincere person displays what the person actually feels and is.

The Arabic word *ikhlas* is never used in the loose sense that the word *sincerity* is used in English. In modern usage, sincerity becomes an excuse for doing anything that makes you feel good. It is to be yourself, to do your own thing. As long as you are sincere—that is, as long as you are true to yourself—whatever you do is fine. This way of looking at things is utterly foreign to Islamic thinking, because *ikhlas* must be established in relationship to God. But the type of sincerity just mentioned is established in relation to the false god that the Koran calls "caprice"; hence, it is a form of *shirk*.

The meaning of *ikhlas* can be grasped with the help of its antonyms. First, it is the opposite of *nifaq*, which is usually translated as "hypocrisy," but which comes from a root that means "to sell." Literally, *nifaq* means "trying to sell oneself." A hypocrite, in Islamic terms, is someone who tries to convince people that he is something that he is not. He tries to sell them goods that are not what they seem to be.

A group known as "the hypocrites" played an important role in the Prophet's community at Medina. Outwardly they accepted Islam, but their only real interest was in furthering their personal goals. They did not have faith in God or the Prophet, but they saw that, in that situation, it was expedient to follow the new religion. The Koran employs the word *hypocrite*, often with explicit reference to this group, in thirty verses. But the picture that the Koran draws of hypocrites in general makes them the worst sort of truth-concealers, the lowest of the low. Notice how the verses imply that the hypocrites may be able to deceive the people, but God knows what they really are. He sees into their hearts, and they have forgotten that God is with them wherever they are:

When the hypocrites come to thee they say, "We bear witness that thou art indeed the messenger of God." And God knows that thou

*art indeed His messenger, and God bears witness that the hypo-
crites are truly liars. They have taken their oaths as a covering,
then they have blocked the way of God. (63:1-2)*

*The hypocrites, men and women, are as one another: they bid to
dishonor and forbid honor. They keep their hands shut. They have
forgotten God, and He has forgotten them. The hypocrites—they
are the transgressors. God has promised the hypocrites, men and
women, and the truth-concealers, the fire of Gehenna, therein to
dwell forever. That is enough for them. God has cursed them, and
there awaits for them a lasting chastisement. (9:67-68)*

The second word that is employed as the opposite of *ikhlas* is *riya'*,
which comes from a root meaning "to see" and which means "to make a
false show of something," or "to display oneself in a way that one is not."
Again, the sense is that people do good deeds outwardly that are belied
by the intention behind the activity. They are not acting for God's sake,
but to impress people or to curry favor with someone. The Koran uses
the term to describe the activity of the hypocrites:

*The hypocrites seek to trick God, but God is tricking them. When
they stand up for the ritual prayer, they stand up reluctantly, to
make a show for the people, and they remember God only a little.
(4:142)*

Sincere activity must be done for God's sake alone. Thus, for example,
the Koran recommends giving charity to people in addition to the
obligatory alms tax. But for this to be true charity, it must be given for
God's sake, not for the sake of showing people how generous and pious
you are. Moreover, you must never make those to whom you give
charity feel indebted to you. After all, it is God who gives them the gift.
They should feel indebted to God for everything good. But if you try to
make them feel indebted to you, your act is sullied by an ulterior
motive. Both you and they lose sight of *tawhid*.

In this context, the Koran sometimes employs the verb *manna*, which
means "to try to make people feel that they owe you a favor." For
example, you give your friend a nice compact disc player as a birthday
gift. Then, you keep on reminding your friend how generous you were,
hoping, of course, to gain some benefit for yourself, or simply to have
the feeling of satisfaction that you are such a wonderful person. Your
activity toward your friend shows that the gift was not actually a gift,
but a payment for favors expected. The Koran explicitly prohibits this
kind of wrongdoing, saying that to make people feel obliged and to hurt
them by reminding them of your kindness is to negate the gift:

*O you who have faith, do not void your acts of charity by imposing
favors and hurting, as does he who spends his wealth to make a
show for the people and has no faith in God and the Last Day.
(2:264)*

Part of sincerity, then, is not to make a show for people, but to do
things for God's sake alone, and without telling anyone about it. A
hadith tells us that "Acts of charity in secret extinguish God's wrath."
People must neither show people how good they are, nor try to show
God and his Prophet how good they are. If trying to make people
acknowledge the favor they owe you is bad, it is far worse—and far
stupider—to try to make the Prophet or God feel obliged because you
have followed the revealed message. In fact, you are the one who is
being benefited by submission and faith, not they; you should be showing gratitude, not they:

*They count it as a favor to you that they have become Muslims.
Say: "Do not count your submission as a favor to me. No, God con-
fers a favor on you in that He has guided you to faith, if you are
truthful." (49:17)*

Let us come back to the word *ikhlas* itself. *Ikhlas* derives from a root
that means "to be clear, pure, and free from admixture." Literally,
ikhlas means "to purify, to clarify, to refine, to remove all impurities."
The Koran uses the word itself in only one passage, in the phrase
"purify their religion for God." It tells us that the hypocrites can reform
themselves by freeing their religion—that is their practice and their
faith—from all extraneous elements. One might say, "Well, this applies
only to the hypocrites, not to me." But this is to forget that everyone is a
hypocrite, so long as caprice and other false gods have the slightest
influence on their thinking and activity:

*Surely the hypocrites will be in the lowest level of the Fire—you
will not find for them there any helper—save such as repent, do
what is wholesome, hold fast to God, and purify their religion for
God. They are with the faithful, and God will give the faithful a
mighty wage. (4:145-46)*

Notice that the Koran places the hypocrites in the deepest pit of hell.
This certainly indicates the ugliness of hypocrisy in Muslim eyes, and,
by contrast, the beauty of sincerity. A hadith makes the same point in
more colorful language.

One day the Prophet was sitting with a few of his companions when
suddenly there was a loud crash. Everyone was startled except the
Prophet. They looked around, and one or two of them exclaimed, "What
was that?" The Prophet said in a matter-of-fact way, "Oh, that was a

stone that was thrown into hell seventy autumns ago and has just hit bottom." His companions looked at each other in bewilderment. A few moments later, someone ran up and said that so-and-so, one of the well known hypocrites, had just died: He was seventy years old.

In several verses the Koran employs the terms *mukhlis* and *mukhlas*, which are adjectives derived from *ikhlas*. The first means "purifying," or "having sincerity," and the second means "purified," or "having been given sincerity [by God]." In ten of the eleven instances where the former adjective is employed, it is associated with the word *religion*, as in the above verse, and it is also associated with worship:

> We have sent down upon thee the Book with the Truth. So worship God, purifying thy religion for Him. (39:2)

> Say: "I have been commanded to worship God, purifying my religion for Him." (39:11)

> Set your faces in every place of prostration and call upon Him, purifying your religion for Him. (7:29)

> He is the Alive, there is no god but He. So call upon Him, purifying your religion for Him. (40:65)

Even sincerity is not necessarily pure. In some verses the Koran describes how people can be faced with danger and then turn toward God, "purifying their religion for Him." Then, when the danger is past, they go back to their old ways. This is not true sincerity, since it has no constancy:

> When they embark in the ships, they call on God, purifying their religion for Him. But when He has delivered them to the land, they associate others with Him, that they may be ungrateful truth-concealers in what We have given them and take their enjoyment. They will soon know! (29:65-66)

In the last analysis, real sincerity cannot be achieved by human beings: It has to be given by God. Just as none guides but God and none misguides but God, so also none establishes the purity of religion but God. This is suggested especially in one of the eight verses in which the Koran employs the term *mukhlas* (purified). It says about Moses, "He was purified, and he was a messenger and a prophet" (19:51). To be God's prophet, a human being must first have been purified by God himself.

In the remaining seven verses where the Koran employs the term *mukhlas*, it uses the expression "purified servants." These are human beings who enter paradise or are protected from Satan's deceptions. The fact that they are God's "servants" gives us further insight into what servanthood involves. It is a total devotion to God alone, in which all one's faith and practice are focused upon the One. There is no place left for caprice or the worship of others.

Ikhlas, in short, is the human embodiment of *tawhid*. This helps explain why sura 112 of the Koran is called both the sura of *ikhlas* and the sura of *tawhid*. When human beings live *tawhid* to its fullest, they are *mukhlis* and *mukhlas*; they both purify their religion for God alone, and God in turn aids them by purifying them of attention to everything other than himself.

God-wariness

Among the near synonyms of *ihsan*, perhaps the most important is *taqwa*, which we have been translating as "god-wariness." Koran translators have rendered the term with such expressions as *dutifulness, piety, righteousness, good conduct, guarding against evil, godfearing*, and *god-consciousness*. The Koran refers to the god-wary in far more verses than it mentions either the sincere or those with *ihsan*. The word itself means "to protect, to be wary, to be careful, to take good care of." It is clearly an attitude that epitomizes every human good and, in the Koranic context, this good must be focused upon God. The Koran says, "The noblest of you in God's sight is the one with the most *taqwa*" (49:13).

The Koran frequently commands people to have *taqwa*, and commonly the verb takes God as object. Then we translate it as "Be wary of God." Others might render it as "Be dutiful toward God, be conscious of God, be pious toward God, be godfearing." The implication of the term is that one protects oneself by always keeping God in view. In other words, whenever you say something or do something, you do it "as if you see God." You are very careful about this, because you know that God sees not only your actions, but also your thoughts:

> *If you do what is beautiful and are god-wary—surely God is aware of what you do. (4:128)*

> *Be wary of God, and know that God sees what you do. (2:233)*

> *Be wary of God. Surely God knows the thoughts in the breasts. (5:7)*

One of the implications of the word *taqwa* is that people have to protect themselves from something dangerous. Hence, the Koran often makes the object of the word not God himself, but his threats, punishment, chastisement, and warning. And the Koran reminds people that they will have to face God and answer to him for their actions:

> *Be wary of the Fire, whose fuel is people and stones. (2:24)*

Be wary of God, and know that God is severe in punishment. (2:196)

Be wary of God, and know that you will be mustered to Him. (2:203)

Be wary of God, and know that you will encounter Him. And give good news to the faithful. (2:223)

Be wary of a day when no soul shall give satisfaction for any other soul. (2:48, 2:123)

O people, be wary of your Lord, and fear a day when no father shall give satisfaction for his child, and no child shall give any satisfaction for his father. Surely God's promise is true. So let not the life of this world delude you, and let not the Deluder delude you concerning God. (31:33)

Say: "God I worship, purifying my religion for Him. Worship then what you like apart from Him." Say: "Surely the losers are they who lose themselves and their families on the day of resurrection. . . . Above them they shall have shadows of the Fire, and below them shadows. With this God frightens His servants: 'O My servants, be wary of Me!' " (39:14-16)

The path of god-wariness is clearly the path brought by the messengers, the path delineated by God's signs:

In the alternation of night and day, and what God has created in the earth—surely there are signs for a god-wary people. (10:6)

God makes clear His signs to the people. Perhaps they will be god-wary. (2:187)

Even so, We have sent it down as an Arabic Koran, and We have turned about in it something of threats. Perhaps they will be god-wary. (20:113)

This is My path, straight. So follow it, and follow not [any other] paths, lest they scatter you from His path. This then He has charged you with. Perhaps you will become god-wary. (6:153)

When people protect themselves from God's wrath and severity by following the prophets, they are brought under the wing of God's mercy and gentleness. In other words, the fruit of god-wariness is paradise:

*Be wary of what is before you and what is behind you. Perhaps you
will find mercy. (36:45)*

*The faithful are brothers, so make things wholesome among your
brothers. Perhaps you will find mercy. (49:10)*

*If you do what is wholesome and are god-wary, surely God is For-
giving, Compassionate. (4:129)*

*Whoever is god-wary and does what is wholesome—no fear shall
be upon them, neither shall they grieve. (7:35)*

*Have faith in God and His messengers. If you have faith and are
god-wary, there shall be for you a mighty wage. (3:179)*

*O faithful, be wary of God, and have faith in His messenger. He
will give you a twofold portion of His mercy, and He will appoint
for you a light whereby you shall walk, and forgive you. God is Forgiving, Compassionate. (57:28)*

*For those that are god-wary, with their Lord are gardens through
which rivers flow. (3:15)*

*The Garden . . . is the ultimate abode of the god-wary, and the ulti-
mate abode of the truth-concealers is the Fire. (13:35)*

The way to achieve god-wariness is to "worship God"; that is, to establish *tawhid* by being God's perfect servants:

*Worship God! You have no god but He. Will you not be god-wary?
(7:65, 23:32)*

*O you who have faith, worship your Lord who created you and
those before you. Perhaps you will be god-wary. (2:21)*

The picture of *taqwa* drawn by the Koran provides a clear illustration
of the relationship between the attributes of *tanzih* and *tashbih*. God-
wariness focuses on God's threats and punishment. Hence, it exem-
plifies the correct relationship between the servant and his Lord, the
subject and his King. The God of which people should be wary is the
God of severity and wrath. He is the God who is far away from them and
worthy of the utmost awe and fear.

Once people establish the relationship of *tanzih*, the result is not that
they stay distant from God, but rather that God brings them close to
himself. His mercy and gentleness respond to the lowliness of the

servants by raising them up into his presence. Only in terms of their nearness to him can they be worthy of being his vicegerents.

Those who are wary of God will be taken into the proximity of the Merciful, but those who fail in their duties will remain under the sway of the Severe in punishment: "On the day that We shall muster the god-wary to the Merciful as guests, and drive the wrongdoers into Gehenna as herds . . ." (19:85-86).

In one verse, the Koran draws a clear distinction between two kinds of divine mercy. In the broader sense, mercy refers to God's kindness and gentleness to all of creation, for he brings it into existence through no merit of its own. In a narrower sense, mercy refers to the nearness that is given to the god-wary. Then it is contrasted with God's chastisement, which he inflicts upon those who have chosen to stay distant from him. Or rather, as we have already seen, their distance from God is itself chastisement, because to be far from the wholeness and harmony of the Real is to be overcome by the partiality and chaos of the unreal. Mercy is achieved by the god-wary, and god-wariness in turn demands both submission and faith:

> *I strike with My chastisement whomsoever I will. And My mercy embraces all things, but I will prescribe it for those who are god-wary and pay the alms tax, and those who have faith in Our signs, those who follow the Messenger, the prophet of the unlettered, about whom they find written in the Torah and the Gospel. He bids them to honor and forbids them dishonor, making lawful for them the pleasant things and making unlawful for them the loathsome things, and relieving them of their burdens and the fetters that were upon them. Those who have faith in him, venerate him, and help him, and follow the light that has been sent down with him—those are the prosperous. (7:156-57)*

Love

One of the words that is most closely connected to everything implied by *ihsan* is *hubb* (love). Especially in later times, when *ihsan* comes to be discussed as one of Islam's three dimensions, love is placed at center stage. In one word, what is the right attitude of the human being toward God? Love.

To understand the Islamic conception of love, we first must see how the Koran employs the term. Most importantly, what does love have to do with God? Once we have an understanding of God's love, it becomes easier to grasp what human love implies.

The Koran ascribes love to God in about fifteen verses, and in several more verses, it tells us what God does *not* love. If human love is to have any meaning in relation to God, it certainly has to follow God's example.

A hadith that we have already quoted helps situate the concept of love in the context in which it was understood by the tradition. The Prophet said, "God is beautiful, and He loves beauty." In later times, the object of love is invariably said to be something beautiful and, conversely, if something is beautiful, it is worthy of love. There is no reason to suppose that this understanding of love is not already implicit in the Koran. *Jamal*, the dictionaries tells us, is practically synonymous with *husn*. To have *ihsan* is to do what is beautiful. Five of the fourteen Koranic verses in which God is said to love something mention those who have *ihsan*. If God loves them, it is surely because, by doing what is beautiful, they themselves have beautiful character traits and are worthy of God's love.

In every Koranic instance where God is said to love something, the objects of his love are human beings. But these are specific human beings, not the human race in general. God loves those human beings whose character traits and activities are beautiful:

> *Do what is beautiful! Surely God loves those who do what is beautiful. (2:195)*

> *Vie with one another, hastening to forgiveness from your Lord, and to a Garden whose breadth is the heavens and the earth, prepared for the god-wary, who give alms in both ease and adversity and who restrain their anger and pardon people. God loves those who do what is beautiful. (3:133-34)*

> *Whoso fulfills his covenant and is wary of God—surely God loves the god-wary. (3:76)*

> *There is no fault in those who have faith and do wholesome deeds in what they eat, if they are god-wary, have faith, and do wholesome deeds, and then are god-wary and have faith, and then are god-wary and do what is beautiful. God loves those who do what is beautiful. (5:93)*

> *Truly God loves those who repent, and He loves those who cleanse themselves. (2:222)*

> *Trust in God. God loves those who have trust. (3:159)*

> *Make things wholesome among them equitably, and be just. Surely God loves the just. (49:9)*

Such verses provide a good idea of which character traits are desirable and praiseworthy. In contrast, the twenty-three Koranic verses that mention what God does *not* love speak of blameworthy human qualities. Thus, for example, we are not surprised to learn that God does not love the truth-concealers, the wrongdoers, the workers of corruption, the transgressors, the immoderate, the proud, and the boastful.

One of the most significant points about the Koranic use of the word *love* is that the quality is ascribed to God and to human beings, and to nothing else; and God's love is always directed at human beings. Many authorities maintain that, more than any other quality, love designates the special relationship between God and human beings, or the real meaning of the Trust given only to human beings. Human beings alone can be the object of God's love, and only human beings can love him.

However, God does not love human beings whose love is not directed at him. Human beings can love God, but usually their love is directed at others:

No indeed, but you honor not the orphan ... and you love possessions with an ardent love. (89:17-20)

Surely they love this hasty world. (76:27)

Made attractive to people is the love of things they crave—women, children, heaped-up heaps of gold and silver, horses of mark, cattle, and tillage. That is the enjoyment of the life of this world. But God—with Him is the beautiful homecoming. (3:14)

In other words, people should not love the fleeting beauty that attracts their cravings, but they should love the permanent beauty of God. The cure for everything that ails human beings can be found in redirecting their love toward its true object.

Here, once again, we encounter the fundamental significance of prophecy. How can people love a God about whom they know nothing? And once they come to know that God is lovable, what do they do next? In the Koranic view, once the first spark of love for God lights up, the way is clear. The person must follow the Sunna of the Prophet. Only then can people move toward God through right practice, right faith, and doing what is beautiful. Having imitated the Prophet not only in activity, but also in character, they will be worthy of God's love. Through God's love, they will reach salvation. Thus God commands the Prophet to utter these words:

Say: "If you love God, follow me, and God will love you and forgive you your sins. God is Forgiving, Compassionate." Say: "Obey God and the Messenger." But if they turn their backs, God loves not the truth-concealers. (3:31-32)

Though the Koran rarely mentions love for God, the few verses in which
it does mention it take on a great deal of importance for the later
tradition. One verse in particular is constantly quoted. In it, two points
are made that are especially significant: First, that God wants people to
love him. And second, that their love for him follows upon his love for
them. Although in the just quoted verse, human love is mentioned as
preceding divine love, the vision of *tawhid* does not allow anyone to
imagine that human love is possible, unless it has been instigated by
God. How could anyone love God without the intervention of his mercy,
compassion, and guidance? How could anyone even exist without God's
mercy and love?

> *O you who have faith, should any of you turn back on your reli-
> gion, God will bring a people whom He loves and who love Him,
> who are humble toward the faithful and disdainful toward the
> truth-concealers, who struggle in the path of God and fear not the
> blame of any blamer. That is God's bounty—He gives it to whom-
> soever He will. He is All-embracing, All-knowing. (5:54)*

The gift of love, this verse tells us, is God's bounty, and hence it is tied
back to the attributes of gentleness, mercy, and beauty.

Wholesomeness

Islam or the Shariah is concerned with differentiating right activity
from wrong activity and explaining how to do things correctly. It
discusses sin inasmuch as sin means breaking the commandments of
God. It deals with the issue of good works inasmuch as good works
mean following God's instructions and imitating the Prophet.

Iman adds a dimension of understanding. It allows people to see that
the meaning of activity transcends the domain of everyday life and
reaches back into the divine reality. It lets them understand that everything in the universe is governed by *tawhid*, yet human freedom of
choice can upset the balance. It tells them why they should be God's
servants and explains which path they should follow to become his
vicegerents. It makes clear that human activity is deeply rooted in the
Real, and that this has everlasting repercussions after death.

Ihsan adds to *islam* and *iman* a focus on intentionality. It directs
human beings to reorient their desiring and their choosing on the basis
of an awareness of God's presence in all things.

The Koran and the Islamic tradition sometimes differentiate among
these three dimensions—*ihsan, islam, iman*—and sometimes they do
not. The Koran in particular frequently employs terminology that can
be understood as emphasizing two or three dimensions of Islam at
once, and it would be helpful to look at one of these terms in order to
show how the very idea of "good works" as discussed in the Koran is

inseparable from Islam's third dimension, even if the discussion seems to be focusing on the first dimension. The term we have in mind is *salih*, from a root that means "to be sound, wholesome, right, proper, good." We have been rendering the root as "wholesome" in the attempt to find an English equivalent that can be used both to refer to people and to acts, since the Koran uses both the form *salihat* (wholesome deeds) and *salihun* (wholesome people).

According to the Koran, doing wholesome deeds, along with faith, will yield paradise. In the first verse cited below, the formula employed—"There is no fear upon them, nor shall they grieve"—is the same the Koran employs for God's friends (10:62). Notice that in some of the verses, wholesome is associated with beautiful:

> *Whoever has faith in God and the Last Day and does wholesome deeds—they have their reward with their Lord, and there is no fear upon them, nor shall they grieve. (2:62; cf. 5:69)*

> *Give good news to those who have faith and do wholesome deeds that they will have Gardens through which rivers flow. (2:25)*

> *Whoso does wholesome deeds, be it male or female, and has faith, We shall assuredly give him a pleasant life, and We shall recompense them with their wage according to the most beautiful of what they did. (16:97)*

> *Whoso does wholesome deeds, be it male or female, and has faith—those shall enter the Garden, therein provided for without reckoning. (40:40)*

> *Those who have faith and do wholesome deeds, them We shall admit to gardens through which rivers flow. (4:57, 4:122)*

> *Whoso has faith in God and works wholesome deeds, He shall acquit him of his ugly deeds and cause him to enter the Garden. (64:9)*

> *Who is more beautiful in speech than he who calls to God and does wholesome deeds, and says, "Surely I am among the muslims"? Not equal are the beautiful deed and the ugly deed. Repel [the ugly] with that which is more beautiful. (41:33-34)*

Another fifty verses could be quoted that say basically the same thing. However, let us look at what the Koran says about wholesome people, that is, those who have faith and do wholesome deeds. First, it is not without significance that this word is the name of an ancient, non-Biblical Arab prophet, whom the Koran mentions in eight verses. The

Koran also enumerates several of the prophets as being among the wholesome, including Abraham, Jacob, Isaac, Ishmael, Idris, John, Zachariah, Elias, and Jesus. In one verse the Koran places the wholesome, the prophets, the sincere devotees, and the witnesses among those whom God has blessed (4:69). But any sincere *muslim* can be one of the wholesome, whether or not the person is a Muslim.

> *Some of the People of the Book are an upright nation, who recite God's signs in the watches of the night while prostrating themselves. They have faith in God and the Last Day, they bid to honor and forbid dishonor, and they vie with one another in good deeds. They are among the wholesome. (3:113-14)*

> *Those who have faith and do wholesome deeds, them We shall surely admit among the wholesome. (29:9)*

Wholesomeness clearly derives from God's mercy, since it results in nearness to God (cf. 21:75, 21:86, 27:19). Interestingly, in three verses where the Koran mentions Abraham as being among the wholesome, it adds "in the next world." Abraham is the model of human perfection, embodied *fitra*, the father of monotheism, and the prophet who is understood as the closest in character traits to Muhammad. The implication is that all *muslim*s who attain to fullness of *fitra* will be among the wholesome in the next world, and that wholesomeness is predominantly a next-worldly quality. After all, to do wholesome deeds is to integrate one's activity into the One; it is to establish *tawhid*. Its full ramifications cannot be seen until vision becomes clear after death.

In short, when the Koran employs the term *wholesome deed*, it is saying that not only is the deed correct, but the intention is also correct. Hypocrites can act correctly, but their reward is to be thrown into the deepest pit of hell.

The Koran employs other words from the same root that are significant if we want to understand the full import of wholesomeness for the Islamic consciousness. For example, the word *islah* is used in thirty verses to mean "establishing wholesomeness." In modern times, the word has often been used to mean "reform." Likewise, the word *sulh* is used in one verse in the sense of the "peace" and "harmony" that should ideally be established between husband and wife. In later times, the word comes to mean "peace" in a political sense.

More implications of the Koranic use of the word *wholesome* can be understood if we look at how the Koran employs its opposite, *fasid*, which means "corrupt, ruined, evil, wrong." The wholesome are those who live in harmony with the Real and establish wholesomeness through their activity. In contrast, the *mufsidun* (workers of corruption) are those who destroy the right relationships among things.

The Koran makes the connection between corruption and the upsetting of *tawhid* rather explicit. First, it insists that the order and wholesomeness of the universe depend upon its having a single principle. If there were more than a single source of reality, the universe would disintegrate into chaos: "Why, were there gods in earth and heaven other than God, these two would surely be corrupted" (21:22).

We know that among the worst false gods that people worship is caprice. If God followed people's caprices—their desires and personal judgments about what is right and wrong—this would take the universe to ruin: "Had the Real followed their caprices, the heavens and the earth and everyone within them would have been corrupted" (23:71).

On one level, the order and wholesomeness of the universe are preserved by God, the One. All things are *muslim*s and God's servants. On another level, that of voluntary *islam* and voluntary servanthood, people are able to upset the wholesomeness of the earth and work corruption. The Koran never suggests that human corruption can extend into the heavens, since that is the domain of the angels, who can only submit to God. This helps explain why the angels protested at Adam's creation and said, "What, wilt Thou place therein one who will work corruption and shed blood?" (2:30). As angels, they were incapable of working corruption. Corruption is only a possibility among those made of clay. If the angels had bodies of clay, they too could work corruption—as Harut and Marut found out, to their regret.

In the universal order, corruption is a human prerogative. Vicegerency alone gives creatures the freedom to work against the Creator. Only the misapplied Trust can explain how moral evil can appear in the universe. Even Iblis worked no corruption before the creation of Adam. The freedom of the jinn to disobey God is somehow bound up with human vicegerency. The following verse seems particularly appropriate in the modern world. Its full significance could hardly have been grasped before modern technology and industrial pollution made the self-destruction of the human race a distinct possibility:

> *Corruption has appeared on the land and in the sea because of what people's hands have earned, so that He may let them taste some part of what they have done, and so that perhaps they may return. (30:41)*

Why should corruption have appeared as the result of modern science and technology? From the Islamic point of view, this should be easy to understand, even if most modernized Muslims have embraced science and technology as their own, accepting its value without question. What, after all, is the self-professed goal of the fathers of modern science and the proponents of technological progress? We have all heard it said a thousand times that the modern West has finally learned how to conquer nature, and this gives us our superiority over all other civilizations. Underlying this type of statement is the assumption that we as human beings have a right to do with nature what we want. Yet, in the Islamic view, nature is the theater in which God displays his signs. Every attempt people make to change the way things naturally happen is an act of insubordination to God's will in creation. For people to attempt to control nature is for them to reject submission to God's will; it is to be ungrateful toward God for the situation in which he has placed them and to claim that his wisdom is not present within events. By nature here we do not mean simply that which is outside the cities — the whole visible cosmos is "nature," and that includes society and human individuals.

Here people will naturally protest that our own human gifts are part of nature. God himself has given us the power to control nature and to improve society, so how could we not make use of it? Why should we simply submit to whatever catastrophe befalls us? The Islamic answer is that God sets down the limits for the use of this power, because this power is nothing but the outward manifestation of human vicegerency. People in fact are not free to act any way they think best; or rather, they are free to try to do so, but they have to accept the consequences of their activity. When action is a rejection of both the universal *islam* that rules all of creation as well as the more specific, prophetic *islam* that is embodied in religious forms, the result can only be disaster in this world and the next.

What then is the remedy for the problems of human society? How can hunger, disease, oppression, pollution, and a thousand other human-produced ills be cured? In the Koranic view, there can be no other route than to return to God through religion (*islam, iman,* and *ihsan*): "So set your face to the upright religion before there comes a day from God that cannot be turned back" (30:43). God measures out both the good and the evil, the wholesome and the corrupt. But, as we have already seen, people have enough freedom to make their own choices and to be called to account for what they have done. To the extent that they choose the wrong and the corrupt, they displease God. God loves those who do what is beautiful, not those who do what is ugly:

> When he turns his back, he hurries about the earth to work corruption there and destroy the tillage and the stock. God loves not corruption. (2:205)

The Koran frequently stigmatizes the workers of corruption. Among the worst of them are the hypocrites, who claim to be doing good deeds but whose outward demeanor is belied by their inner intentions. The following verses show clearly that wholesomeness, like sincerity, demands that the good deed be motivated by faith and god-wariness:

Among the people are some who say, "We have faith in God and the Last Day," but they do not have faith. They seek to deceive God, but they are deceiving only themselves, and they are unaware. In their hearts is a disease, so God increased their disease, and theirs is a painful chastisement because they are liars. When it is said to them, "Work not corruption in the earth," they say, "We are only doing wholesome deeds." Surely they are workers of corruption, but they are unaware. (2:8-12)

Corruption comes about in the earth when human beings, God's vice-gerents in the earth, turn away from his commands and forget the messages of the prophets:

And those who break God's covenant after His compact, and who snap what God has commanded to be joined, and who work corruption in the earth—theirs shall be the curse, and theirs is the ugly abode. (13:25)

Corruption in the earth is effaced when people orient themselves toward God through *tawhid*; when they set up priorities in this world in terms of the next world. Only by taking the next world into account can people have a grasp of the whole of reality and understand the ultimate significance of their activity:

Seek, amidst what God has given you, the abode of the next world, and forget not your portion of this world. And do what is beautiful, as God has done what is beautiful to you. And seek not to work corruption in the earth. Surely God loves not the workers of corruption. (28:77)

What God does love is doing what is beautiful. Because of his love for those who do the beautiful, he brings them near to himself, and this nearness is typically called "the Garden" or "God's mercy":

Work not corruption in the earth after it has been made wholesome, and call upon God in fear and hope. Surely the mercy of God is near to those who do what is beautiful. (7:56)

In sum, the Koran presents us, through the concepts of "wholesomeness" and "corruption," with a picture of the human role in creation that distinguishes right activity, right thought, and right intention from their opposites. It provides one more example of how the two hands of God—his mercy and his wrath—are reflected in the human domain, the domain of the earth, this lower realm where people have been appointed God's vicegerents. It associates wholesomeness with mercy, paradise, and the beautiful, while it connects corruption to wrath, hell, and the ugly.

Establishing wholeness, wholesomeness, and beauty depends upon the full engagement of the human being with the Real. The truly wholesome are those who act both as God's perfect servants and his perfect vicegerents.

Chapter 8.

THE HISTORICAL MANIFESTATIONS OF *IHSAN*

୧୬

Supplication

I t is difficult to find doorways into peoples' souls, especially in a civilization that does not encourage the writing down of inner experiences. Autobiography is a relatively rare genre in Islamic literature, and what little there is seldom analyzes the authors' motives and intentions, especially not in terms of religious categories. However, there is one genre of writing where people do open themselves up; not to others, but to God. This is "supplication" (*du'a*), the personal calling upon God. Of course, as soon as a supplication is written down, one can assume that it has lost some of its spontaneity. Nevertheless, supplications voice the concerns that Muslims have in trying to establish a right relationship with God.

Supplication is an important subgenre already in the Hadith. Many of the Prophet's personal prayers were remembered and written down. In many cases, he taught others how to call upon God, and in other cases, people heard him repeating the same prayer on several occasions and memorized it. Many of the Prophet's descendants also left supplications, especially his great-grandson, Ali ibn al-Husayn, whose *al-Sahifat al-sajjadiyya* is considered the classic text of the genre and provides unparalleled insight into the world of early Muslim personal relationships with God.

The recitation of the supplications that have been transmitted from the Prophet and other great Muslims is one way for people to imitate their predecessors in talking with God and in trying to establish the right attitudes toward God. In addition, they may feel that they are establishing a personal nearness to the author of the prayers.

One of the first things that one notices in reading supplications is that the abstract language and perspective of *tanzih* that is are typical of early Muslim theological writing are totally lacking. God is not a distant monarch who simply issues commands to his slaves and expects them to be obeyed. Quite the contrary, he is present with the worshiper, listening to the supplications, and responding to them. Does he not say in the Koran, "Supplicate Me, and I will respond to you" (40:60)? The God of supplication is, in short, a God who is conceived predominantly in terms of *tashbih*. It is a God to whom people can relate through love and intimacy. This is a God who is concerned with every detail of human life. People cannot have two domains, one for unimportant things that God does not care about, and another for God's affairs: *Tawhid* demands that God cares about all human affairs. As the Prophet said:

> Each of you should ask your Lord for all your needs. He should even ask Him for the thong of his sandal when it breaks.

In many forms of modern Islam, the depth of the personal relationship with God that is encouraged by the Koran and the Islamic tradition is pushed into the background. This is natural as soon as we remember that modernist Islam typically stresses the rational side of Islamic teachings, partly as an apologetic device to fend off Western criticisms of Islam, and partly as a theological principle to allow the integration of modern forms of knowledge—technology in particular—into Islamic countries. We must always remember that theological rationality, by its very nature, stresses *tanzih*, and hence the impersonal and distant sides of God's reality. Nevertheless, supplication still plays a major role in the religious life of Muslims, especially those who have not had the traditional world view altered by modern education. In keeping with the earliest examples, supplication is eminently personal and allows people to see their intimate relationship with God in every dimension of life. Take, for example, this supplication, chosen at random from Ali ibn al-Husayn's *al-Sahifat al-sajjadiyya* and entitled, "His Supplication in Asking for Water during a Drought":

O God,
   water us with rain,
   unfold upon us Thy mercy
     through Thy copious rain
       from the driven clouds,
     so that Thy goodly earth may grow
       on all horizons!
   Show kindness to Thy servants
     through the ripening of the fruit,
   revive Thy land
     through the blossoming of the flowers,
   and let Thy angels—the noble scribes—be witness
     to a beneficial watering from Thee
       lasting in its abundance,
       plenty in its flow,
       heavy, quick, soon,
     through which Thou revivest what has vanished,
       bringest forth what is coming,
       and providest plentiful foods,
     through heaped up, wholesome, productive clouds,
       in reverberating layers,
     the rain's downpour
       not without cease,
     the lightning's flashes
       not without fruit!
O God,
   give us water
   through rain,
     helping, productive, fertilizing,
       widespread, plentiful, abundant,
     bringing back the risen,
     restoring the broken!
O God,
   give us water with a watering through which Thou wilt
     make the stone hills pour,
     fill the cisterns,
     flood the rivers,
     make the trees grow,
     bring down prices in the lands,
     invigorate the beasts and the creatures,
     perfect for us the agreeable things of provision,
     make grow for us the fields,
     let flow for us the teats,
     and add for us strength to our strength!
O God,
   make not the cloud's shadow over us a burning wind,

allow not its coldness to be cutting,
let not its pouring down upon us be a stoning,
and make not its waters for us bitter!
O God,
  bless Muhammad and his Household,
  and provide us with the blessings of the heavens and the earth!
  "Thou art powerful over everything"[3:26].[1]

Art and Poetry

Islamic art is a vast field, and every beginning student of Islam should make a point of examining one or more of the numerous illustrated books that present some of the treasures of Islamic civilization. For the purpose of our discussion, we will only cover a few of the reasons for the specific developments that took place in various art forms in Islamic civilization and the significance of these developments from the perspective of Islam's three dimensions.[2]

The major contours of Islamic art are implicit in the form of the Koran, the Word of God. God expressed himself to the Islamic community through speech. In order to preserve and maintain God's speech, the Muslims had three fundamental duties: To recite the Koran, to copy the Koran, and to embody the Koran through the *salat* and other rituals.

As we already know, "God is beautiful, and He loves beauty," and "God loves those who do what is beautiful." Muslims with any sensitivity toward beauty have attempted to do things beautifully. Recitation of the Koran gave rise to the arts of the voice, copying the Koran gave rise to the arts of the pen, and embodying the Koran gave rise to the arts of the ritual environment. To be more explicit, the three major arts in Islam are rhythmical recitation and poetry, calligraphy, and architecture.

The Koran, we said earlier, is not just read; it is recited. Beautiful voices are highly prized, since everyone recognizes that the more beautifully the Koran is recited, the more awe-inspiring and joy-inducing it is for everyone concerned and, of course, the more the message will be appreciated. Most people were taught at least some of the Koran from a very early age. Children went to Koran school, where they would learn recitation (not reading) and calligraphy (not writing).

In dealing with the Koran, there is a proper mode of conduct (*adab*) that people observe. A book that is God's own speech deserves the highest possible respect. The Koran is never placed directly on the ground. In a library, it is put on the highest shelf, in a place of honor. People should not touch the Koran if they are ritually impure. They often kiss it or place it upon their eyes after picking it up and before putting it down. Before reciting, they say (in accordance with the command of Koran 16:98), "I seek refuge in God from Satan the accursed." When they recite it, they try to do so with proper courtesy. Since the Koran is the most eloquent of books, it should be recited in a mode in which its eloquence comes out; every letter and every vowel must be pronounced impeccably; the beautiful ways of reciting it, handed down orally by Koran reciters from earliest times, are much studied and imitated.[3]

If the Koran deserves the utmost respect in recitation, so also is the case with writing it. Arabic calligraphy developed into the primary visual art of Islamic civilization because Islam is built on the Koran, and the form in which the Koran is presented must accord with the beauty of its Speaker.[4]

Finally, the Koran needs a worthy building in which to be recited and embodied. The mosque (place of prostration) became an institution in Islam from the beginning. Any place that is ritually pure can be a mosque, of course, and the Prophet said that one of the ways in which his prophecy was distinguished from that of earlier prophets was that the whole face of the earth was designated as the mosque of his community. Nevertheless, the faithful need a place to gather for the incumbent Friday communal prayer, and it is highly recommended at all times to pray the five prescribed *salat*s in community; so the mosque soon developed into a place worthy for the recitation of God's Word. The Koran resonated within its walls, and much of the decoration of the mosque is typically provided by Koranic calligraphy.

Beautiful recitation is naturally rhythmic. Rhythm, in turn, depends upon harmony and balance. Behind every attractive rhythm lurks at least an intuitive understanding of the nature of number, or more precisely, of the nature of the relationship of the many to the one. So also, Islamic calligraphy expresses the spoken word through visual harmony and balance. It demonstrates in sensory form the beauty of the divine Word.

What strikes Westerners the first time they encounter Islamic art is the relative lack of naturalism and representationalism in general, and the total lack of sculpture. Partly, this has to do with the prohibitions of figurative art issued by the Prophet, but the Prophet's prohibitions themselves simply manifest the implications of *tawhid* in its Islamic form. The divine art that people can and should imitate is the Koran, which is God's self-expression, the aural and oral embodiment of the divine form in which human beings were created. All attention needs to be focused on the revelation, since that is the sole route of guidance. To the extent that people's attention is distracted from the divine Word, they will fail to actualize their divine form and fall into *shirk*.

Most observers remark on the abstract nature of Islamic art; that is, Islamic art tends not to represent things, but rather ideas. The reason for this becomes clear as soon as we remember that abstraction is a function of reason, and reason, illumined by *tawhid*, sees *tanzih*; reason disengages the divine reality from every created reality. However, art is by nature imaginal, since it presents us with images. Hence, art is closely connected to *tashbih*, the vision of God's presence in the world. In order to express *tawhid*, artistic forms—which by nature are imaginal and therefore connected to *tashbih*—must be offset by representations of abstract, distant qualities. In other words, the forms must somehow represent beauty as belonging not to themselves, but to God. Islamic art reminds people of the divine beauty by detaching that beauty from this world; that is, from the things that figurative art attempts to represent.

In other words, since there is nothing beautiful but God, Islamic art attempts to represent God's beauty without making the world beautiful in itself; it tries to display the signs of God's beauty while reminding people that these are only signs. *Tanzih*'s abstraction balances *tashbih*'s imagery by detaching beauty from the objects within which it becomes manifest. When an artist represents a figure, the observer will tend to associate the artistic beauty with the figure itself—the face is beautiful, the flower is beautiful, and so forth. When relatively abstract designs are represented in place of created things, this introduces an element of *tanzih*, of separation of the beauty from the representation. One sees that the harmony of forms produces the beauty and can never think that a person or object is beautiful, since none is represented.

Even when representational art begins to play a rather important role in certain parts of the Islamic world, especially Persia and India, it is rarely of a naturalistic sort. Rather, the scenes depicted are usually representations of things not found in the physical world. Often, they recall instead the Koranic accounts of paradise, or sometimes hell. Both paradise and hell are located in the imaginal world. When people look at a Persian miniature, for example, they seldom think that the artist is representing a scene that he has observed with his eyes. It is clearly a landscape, or perhaps a portrait, with otherworldly qualities. For Muslims sensitive to the spirituality that informs their religion— that is, sensitive to the fact that all beauty and all reality belong to God—artistic forms become a way of perceiving the signs even more directly than they are found in the natural world.

In short, Islamic art combines the concreteness of imagination with the abstraction that is implicit in *tanzih*. It represents God's beauty in imaginal forms, yet it manages to disengage these forms from the physical world. It offers a picture of the soul within which the divine image is becoming manifest: The artistic forms are neither spiritual nor bodily, but something in between; something that can only be imagination, which combines the qualities of the two sides.

The Islamic avoidance of figurative representation in the visual arts contrasts sharply with the artistic traditions of the Christian, Hindu, and Buddhist civilizations. These three major civilizations developed depiction of the human form in painting and sculpture as great art forms. In all three cases, the original impulse was to depict the Real in its human embodiment. Christian art began with icons of Christ, who is considered an incarnation of God. In a similar way, Hindu art depicts the avataras, or the gods themselves (who always have certain human features), while Buddhist art focuses on the enlightened human being: the Buddha, or the boddhisattva. From the Islamic perspective—and remember that Muslims look at these civilizations from the outside— all three of these religious civilizations place too much emphasis upon *tashbih*, both in their myth and in their art. In practical terms, this is reflected in the general revulsion among Muslims toward idol-worship and the general refusal to try to understand that the statues in Hindu and Buddhist temples may not be idols in the Islamic sense. Few are sympathetic with the line by the great Sufi poet Mahmud Shabistari (d. ca. 720/1320): "If the Muslim were to understand what an idol is/he would know that religion is found in idol-worship."

We do not mean to imply that Islamic art is limited to representations of the Koran and its message. We simply want to bring out that the central role of the Koran in Islamic life turned the attention of Muslims toward rhythmic sound, calligraphy, and architectural forms, such that other art forms became secondary.

Music, for example, is a form of rhythmic sound, and it was highly developed in Islamic civilization. In some parts of the Islamic world, it has remained slightly peripheral because of the understanding of some of the ulama that music was prohibited by the Prophet. However, there is no agreement on this prohibition. What the ulama all agree upon is that music has an extremely powerful effect upon the soul, and that it can represent both the beautiful (that which reflects the divine beauty) and the dispersive and fiery (the satanic), not to mention every other human possibility. Hence, music has always remained suspect in the eyes of many Muslims, but the same Muslims may recite the Koran with heavenly voices. If we tell them that this is music, they will reply that music is instrumental, but this is recitation. The Koran is practically never recited with instrumental accompaniment. There is no worthy vehicle for the divine Word but the voice of God's own vicegerent.

The most widespread manifestation of the arts of rhythmic sound in the Islamic world—more widespread even than recitation of the Koran itself—is recitation of poetry. Without doubt, poetry is the prime means of literary expression in Islamic civilization. But many people forget, because of modern habits, that poetry, like the Koran, was never read: It was recited. Even today, a native speaker of a language like Persian or Urdu finds it very difficult to *read* a line of poetry out loud, unless it is bad poetry. The rhythmic power of good poetry practically forces the reader to recite or chant it. Only people who have lost a sense for the beauty of their own language are not moved by their own classical poetry.

Relatively little Islamic poetry has anything to do with the explicit message of the Koran. The stereotypes are quite accurate: The Persian, Turkish, and Urdu poets never cease talking about nightingales and roses, winedrinking and drunkenness, and love for their beautiful beloved. When people read this kind of poetry in translation, they quickly get bored, unless the translator happens to have a remarkable poetic gift, or unless the poetry has an epic or didactic content that carries some interest.

In the original languages, however, the situation is quite different. Anyone who has heard a good reciter reciting poetry in one of the Islamic languages knows that the content of the poetry is not the only important element. In the hands of an accomplished artist, poetry captures the imagination through its sound and music, and poetry, in contrast to the Koran, is often recited to the accompaniment of instrumental music, which enhances its power.

Historians of Islamic literature often speak of the secular nature of much of the poetry produced by Muslims. This judgment, however, is usually a bit premature. First, Muslims do not make the same distinction between the religious and the secular, or the sacred and the profane, that has been made in the West. Everything, after all, is a sign of God, but it takes eyes to see the signs. The Koran frequently employs expressions like, "O you who have eyes!" or "O you who have minds!" and it makes clear that it is only the faithful or the god-wary who have these eyes and minds. Scholars of literature may not always fit into this category, and as a result they are likely to see literary forms in secular terms.

The Koranic message, as we have seen, is not limited to commands, prohibitions, and theological pronouncements. On the contrary, one of its primary messages is that people should recognize the beautiful and do what is beautiful. This is not simply a moral beauty, but a visual and auditory beauty as well. Conduct should be beautiful, writing should be beautiful, speaking should be beautiful. For many Muslims, especially the theoreticians of the third dimension — that is, the Sufi authorities — beauty is divine, wherever it is found: It can only serve to remind people of God. By its nature, it stirs up love, and love can never be satisfied by the temporal or the temporary. Love leads to God, the only true beauty. "God is beautiful, and He loves beauty." So also, to the extent that people realize their own divine form, they will love God's beauty and recognize that "There is no beauty but God." Every other beauty can be nothing but a ray of his beauty. Every love for anything at all can only be a love for a ray of beauty and hence, in the last analysis, for God.[5]

But this is a relatively abstract, academic way of explaining why love plays an important role in Muslim experience. Poets speak a language that is much more direct. Rumi, one of the greatest of the Persian Sufi poets, can do a better job of telling us about the true nature of love and beauty. Unfortunately, the entrancing music of his language is impossible to reproduce in English — you simply have to imagine that someone is singing one of the most beautiful melodies you have ever heard — but pay attention to what the singer is saying:

Anyone madly in love with the dead
  has hope for something that lives . . .
Strive in the hope of a Living One
  who does not die in a day or two.
Choose not a mean companion out of meanness,
  for intimacy of that sort is a borrowed thing.
If your intimates other than God are faithful,
  what happened to your father and mother? . . .
Your intimacy with milk and breasts has gone,
  your dread of grammar school has gone.
That was a ray upon their being's wall—
  the ray has gone back to the Sun.
When that ray falls upon something,
  you become its lover, O champion!
Whatever you love in existence
  has received a gold plating from God's attributes . . .
The beauty of the counterfeit coin is a borrowed thing—
  beneath its beauty lies the substance of ugliness . . .
From now on take water from heaven—
  you have seen no faithfulness from the drainpipe![6]

To summarize this extremely brief discussion of Islamic art, let us say that the Koranic stress upon goodness and beauty as divine attributes and as desirable human qualities encouraged the development of a great variety of art forms among Muslims. Although the jurists sometimes questioned the legitimacy of some of these forms, by and large Muslims were sufficiently sensitive to Islam's third dimension to recognize that formal beauty is as important and as essential to life as beauty of activity, character, and soul. Human beings were placed in this world to develop their own selves in harmony with the divine form, and thereby to gain nearness to God. This desired nearness has standards on every level. Activity has to measure up to the rulings of the Shariah, understanding has to harmonize with the sciences of faith, and character needs to be shaped by *ihsan*, sincerity, and god-wariness. Such an all-embracing vision of things could not leave the physical environment outside its view. There, the standard by which everything needs to be judged is beauty, but a beauty defined and shaped by the implications of *tawhid*.

The outward beauty manifest in the artistic domain simply reflects the inward beauty of God. The human soul should measure up to its divine form not only by doing what is morally beautiful, but also by doing what is formally beautiful. Conversely, external beauty is a support for beauty of the soul. A beautiful environment gives people a sense of harmony, balance, equilibrium, and joy that can act as the model for the soul's own qualities.

Practical Sufism

We have already dealt in some detail with the theoretical dimensions of Sufi teachings, and we explained how the Sufi perspective differs from that of Kalam and philosophy. Here, we want to look at Sufism as one manifestation of *ihsan*, of doing what is beautiful or, more accurately, of *being* what is beautiful.

Practical Sufism — like jurisprudence, Kalam, philosophy, and theoretical Sufism — is an extremely widespread and complex phenomenon. Uncounted books have been written by the Sufis themselves, and recently by Western scholars, investigating the various manifestations of Islamic society and civilization that fit under the umbrella of Sufism. We cannot begin to deal with the complex issues that appear as soon as we look at Sufism in its historical forms. Instead, we simply want to suggest that Sufism is a convenient name for many of the manifestations of Islam's third dimension. It is convenient mainly because it is an indigenous term that is typically used in the way we are using it — though of course, other understandings have also been proposed. As an indigenous term, it avoids the connotations of the English words that have been proposed as its equivalent; chief among these, as mentioned earlier, is *mysticism*, which we consider particularly inappropriate.

What then is practical Sufism? First, it is to put theoretical Sufism into practice through one's everyday activities. Theoretical Sufism offers a vision of *tawhid* based on unveiling, firmly grounded in the Koranic revelation, and, in many of its manifestations, respectful toward, though not enthusiastic about, rational investigation. This vision sees human beings as imperfect because of *tanzih*, and it understands human perfection to lie in the actualization of all the divine qualities associated with *tashbih*. To be fully human is to actualize the divine form. In order to achieve this, Sufis follow the Sunna of the Prophet and seek to embody the Koran. They want the Koran to be their character, just as it was the Prophet's character.

Practical Sufism is fundamentally concerned with human character traits. One of the standard definitions holds that Sufism is the rectification of character; another tells us that all of Sufism is *adab* (a word we will discuss in detail). In the spirit of these definitions, Ibn al-'Arabi tells us that Sufism is to assume God's character traits as one's own (*al-takhalluq bi akhlaq allah*). Consideration of the implications of these few statements can provide us with a basic insight into the goal of Sufi practice.

Before explaining the implications of the term *rectification of character*, we should point out that this same term designates one of the major practical goals of the philosophers. The whole field of ethics as a subdiscipline of philosophy investigates the nature of character traits and how they can be rectified, and without doubt Muslim philosophers did not consider this simply a theoretical issue. They felt that philosophy was a tool to be used for the eminently practical aim of becoming a better person. What differentiates the philosophers from the Sufis is the stress that the latter place upon the Prophet as the embodiment of perfect character and on his Sunna as the framework within which beautiful character traits can be actualized. The early philosophers, in keeping with the philosophical perspective in general, did not emphasize the necessity of following prophetic guidance. Often they referred only to the Greek philosophers, Aristotle in particular, in discussing ethics. Whether or not, in their personal lives, they considered Islam a necessary component for achieving a good character is not always clear; for the Sufis, Islam was the sine qua non.

The word that the philosophers use for "ethics" is *akhlaq*, which is the plural of *khuluq*, or "character," as in "rectification of character." The word *khuluq* means not only character in general, but also character trait; so the study of ethics is the study of character traits. It is extremely significant that in Arabic the word *khalq* (creation) is written the same way as *khuluq* (character). A person's character has to do with the way a person is created. A hadith that is often cited in support of the measuring out tells us that "God has finished with creation [*khalq*] and character [*khuluq*]." Nevertheless, people are not finished with character until they die. In effect, people participate through their own free choices in the creation of their character through the way they live their lives. That is why, as we saw, the Prophet used to pray, "O God, Thou hast made my creation beautiful, so make my character beautiful too." Without the possibility of the rectification of character, the whole idea of a voluntary return to God loses its meaning.

The expression "rectification of character" indicates that in the case of any given human being, character and its various traits are not yet finalized: People can change themselves, they can become better people. This discussion, however, focuses not on their activity, but rather on the qualities that make up their character; what we would today more likely call "personality." We ask, "What kind of person is he?" and we expect to be told about the person's character traits. But nowadays, we are more likely to use extremely general expressions such as "nice" or "nasty," "normal" or "strange," "regular" or "obnoxious." In the Islamic context, there are a large number of attributes that the Koran applies to the faithful and god-wary, and these are all desirable. Many more are applied to the truth-concealers, and these should be avoided. For their part, the philosophers are likely to use terms derived from Greek texts, though many of them overlap with Koranic terms.

The basic meaning of the word we have translated as *rectification* is "to prune, trim, cleanse, polish." We begin with a personality that needs work. All the nasty and obnoxious characteristics have to be trimmed away, and the good characteristics have to be cleaned and polished. Strictly speaking, there are no good character traits to be acquired, since every good quality is already found in the human *fitra*, made in the form of God.

We cited the famous maxim from an early Sufi authority that Sufism is all *adab*. *Adab* is an extremely rich concept that can be employed to bring out the whole ethos of Islam. The primary meaning of the root is "to invite, to gather together for a banquet." The secondary meanings of the term suggest how important entertaining guests was in pre-Islamic times and within Islamic civilization itself. "Children of the road"—that is, travelers—are specified by the Koran as one of the categories of people to whom *zakat* should be given. Throughout Islamic history, it was considered a religious and social duty to invite travelers into the home and to take care of them.

Caring for travelers and strangers is only one small facet of *adab*, as the concept eventually developed. Early in Islamic history, the word had come to signify proper discipline of the soul and correct modes of activity. Primarily, this meant proper training and education in all the domains of Islamic learning and practice that were necessary for a person to achieve the ideals of the religion. Hence, *adab* was identified with the Prophet's Sunna in the broad sense, as including both his character and his activity.

However, *adab* was certainly not limited, for example, to the ideas discussed by the jurists or the specialists in Kalam; that is, to those of the ulama who delineated the rules for following the Shariah and defended the Koran and the Hadith. Rather, it was adopted as an ideal by all the learned and, to a large extent, by everyone who underwent an Islamic education.

In Islamic languages, to say that a person has *adab* means that he or she is cultured, well-mannered, sophisticated, and, in general, has good breeding. The word *adab* is also applied to belles lettres, especially poetry. Not uncommonly, a person with *adab* knows thousands of verses of the best poetry by heart and is able to recite them on the most appropriate occasions. It is almost impossible to imagine that a person should be described as having *adab* in classical times and not have beautiful handwriting. In several Islamic languages, one of the worst things that you can say about a person is that the person is without *adab*. One might as well say that the person is a monkey or a pig.

The term *adab* was applied to the proper mode of conduct for every group of people in society and to all the appropriate activities considered individually. Many books detail the *adab* of judges, Sufi novices, princes, courtiers, physicians, musicians, and even housewives. Barbara Metcalf writes the following about South Asian Islam, but what she says is true about Islam wherever it has become established:

> *Expressed in ṣūfī writings, implied in the practices of scholars*
> *and saints, embedded in the widely varied literatures of the* adab
> *of kings and courtiers, the* adab *of judges and* muftis, *the litera-*

ture of everyday pleasurable instruction, and manuals of reli-
gious and moral advice for ordinary people, the concept of adab
proves to be a key to central religious concepts of South Asian
Islam.[7]

Metcalf suggests that one can define three conceptually distinct domains of Islamic teaching—the Shariah, the Sufi path (Tariqah), and
adab, each of which has its own specialists. She sees each of these three
domains as expressing the same realities of Islam: "Yet since all
emerge, at core, as attempts to codify and embody the practice of the
Prophet, they are ultimately the same in mainstream Islam." But she
also recognizes that "*Adab* itself is based on the teachings of the other
two domains,"[8] and it is this point that we would stress. Rather than
picture *adab* as a separate domain, we prefer to see it as one of the areas
where the ideals of Islam's third dimension are integrated with those of
the other two.

Adab is a codification of right activity that, depending on the context
and the focus, may be concerned strictly with the Shariah, or with
philosophic ethics, or with the moral implications of the Sufi stress
upon the inward domain of doing what is beautiful. Unlike works on
jurisprudence, which are limited to Islam's first dimension, works on
adab combine attention to activity with attention to right attitudes and
morality. Hence, they combine Islam's first and third dimensions.
Moreover, they are usually grounded, explicitly or implicitly, in one or
more of the intellectual perspectives of the second dimension.

Adab always brings along with it a sense of beauty, refinement, and
subtlety. One could even say that *adab* represents in the domain of
human character what rhythmic sound represents aurally and what
calligraphy and architecture represent visually. The underlying motivation in all these domains is to embody the beautiful, to bring out the
inner harmony, oneness, and balance demanded by *tawhid*. As Metcalf
points out, the word *adab* is often employed to refer to outer behavior,
but "it is understood as both cause of and then, reciprocally, fruit
of one's inner self. Knowing, doing, and being are inescapably one."[9]
Adab represents, in other words, one of the forms in which Islam's
three dimensions coalesce harmoniously to express the concrete human ideals of the religion.

If Sufis have said that Sufism is all *adab*, the point is that every
activity needs to be correct—that is, based on the prophetic model—
and that this can only come about when the soul is harmonized and
integrated through sincerity, god-wariness, and doing what is beautiful. Moreover, doing what is beautiful cannot be forced or affected—
that would destroy its spontaneity, which is one element of its beauty.
Doing what is beautiful must well up in the soul—our poets might say—
as fragrance wells up from the rose. Beautiful activity must be rooted

in beautiful being. To repeat Metcalf's words, "Knowing, doing, and being are inescapably one."

To embody the beautiful is to embody the qualities of God. This is Ibn al-'Arabi's point when he defines Sufism as "assuming the character traits of God as one's own." Ibn al-'Arabi explains that this is only a manner of speaking. In fact, those character traits are all latent within human beings because of the divine form, but they belong to God, and as long as people remain heedless of their own nature, the divine qualities within them will not become manifest in proper harmony and balance.

It is important to keep in mind that Muslims never understood sincerity and *ihsan* simply as attitudes, feelings, or psychological states. Rather, they looked upon them as modes of being that bring the unreal creature into harmony with the Real itself, thus transforming the actual mode of existence of the creature. Only this ontological transformation can explain how human beings can attain nearness to God, who is the Real.

To go to paradise is not like moving from this room to the next room, as the imagery might suggest. Rather, it is a transmutation of human nature that allows for a new mode of existence. Muslim authors often use alchemical imagery to explain the change that takes place. In alchemy, you do not take a piece of lead from this room to the twentieth story, where it lives happily ever after. On the contrary, you transmute lead, molecule by molecule, so that nothing is left but pure gold. Then only can the lead, which is no longer lead but gold, become a worthy ornament for the King. The King has no concern for a piece of lead that insists on keeping its own dark nature. He throws it back into the molten depths of the earth where it belongs.

Through *ihsan*, God's servants worship him as if they see him. They gradually turn their gaze away from the unreality of themselves and focus it upon the Real. They remember God constantly, and as a result, they forget their own selves, their own caprices, their own ignorance and folly. Created in the form of God, they contain within themselves all God's attributes, but only latently or mutedly. By focusing upon the Real and forgetting the unreal, people in effect awaken the real dimension of themselves.

Rumi provides us with an image for what happens when the Real is awoken within the soul. The human being is a compound of spirit and body. You can say that God has stuck an angel's wing on a donkey's tail. When people focus on their own angelic and divine qualities, God gives them the power to fly into his own presence, but if they forget about their angelic nature and dwell on their asininity, they remain in the stable. In the same sort of context, Rumi often compares the human being to Jesus mounted on his donkey. Thus he says:

> *Have mercy on Jesus, not on the ass!*
> *Let not your animal nature rule your intelligence!*[10]

The Ethos of Love

We said earlier that the various manifestations of *ihsan* focus on the quality of love. This is especially true of poetry, where love is the dominant theme with an infinite variety of images.[11] It is also true of Sufism, where love is typically presented as the key to Islamic life and practice. In other words, for a large body of Muslims, love has always been Islam's life-blood. In their view, without the animating spirit of love—Islam's third dimension—the religion dries up and desiccates, and we are left with sterile debates over the fine details of activity, or polemical attacks on anyone who does not toe the dogmatic line concerning issues of faith.

Muslims who focus on Islam's third dimension recognize that the Shariah is necessary for faith to develop, and that faith along with practice then provides the ground in which the flower of *ihsan* can blossom and flourish. Neither faith nor practice can ever be abandoned, because they are *ihsan*'s framework and support, but faith and practice are not their own raison d'etre. They exist in order to give fruit, and that fruit, in one word, is love. In order to understand the perspective of Muslims who think this way, we need to discuss their understanding of love in some detail.

As Rumi, the greatest poet of love, tells us, love is both indefinable and infinitely explainable. One can neither say what it is, nor can one be done with speaking about it. Nevertheless, we can follow Rumi, and many of the other Sufi authors, and suggest some of what love implies.

We have already explained that love is a divine attribute or, in other words, that God is love. Love needs to be distinguished from mercy. God's general mercy is directed toward all things, while his specific mercy becomes manifest in paradise, which is given to the god-wary. The opposite of God's specific mercy is wrath, which finds its clearest reflection in hell.

The Koran associates God's love with his specific mercy, not with his general mercy. God loves those who do what is beautiful, but he does not love those who conceal the truth and do what is ugly. If he did love them, he would not place them in hell. None of this is to deny that God's mercy takes precedence over his wrath, and that hell itself is a mercy for those who enter it, but this is another issue that would lead us too far from the question of love.

The Sufi stress on love for God grows out of their emphasis on the priority of *tashbih* over *tanzih*, of mercy over wrath. When the theologians and jurists discuss God, with their rational categories and their commands and prohibitions, the result can only be a human feeling of distance and fear. But Sufis place their emphasis on God's nearness and his love for human beings. Instead of stressing rational arguments and abstract discourse, they employ every sort of analogy and image to make the experience of God concrete. Their underlying message is that God loves us and desires the best for us. To bring this home, they stress God's beautiful and lovable qualities in the language of everyday speech. It is only human to love someone who loves you. Anyone who has that much sense has to be lovable. The Sufis were supremely aware of this psychological tendency. Moreover, they were fully informed of the metaphysical fact that God's goal in creating human beings was to actualize love, given that no other creature can truly love God.

Innumerable Sufi texts could be quoted to support these points. Given the limitations of space, we will only suggest that the most accessible English language texts on the role of love in Islam are the various translations of Rumi's works.

Instead of quoting what is already available in English, we present below a short text that has not previously been translated. It is from one of the greatest classics of Sufi literature—a work, however, that has largely been ignored by modern scholars—known as *Kashf al-asrar* (The Unveiling of the Mysteries) by Rashid al-Din Maybudi. This is a Koran commentary which, the author tells us, he began writing in the year 520/1126. Since it fills eight thousand pages in its modern edition, one can suppose that it took a few years to complete. Only about one-quarter of *Kashf al-asrar* is devoted to Sufi interpretations of Koranic verses, since the main body of the text is concerned with translating the Koran into Persian, explaining its apparent meaning, and then explicating its literal and historical context and significance. Then the author turns to the more hidden meaning of the text. He often quotes in these sections from his teacher, the famous Sufi and jurist, Khwaja 'Abdallah Ansari (d. 481/1088). Ansari is noted for important works in both Arabic and Persian. His Persian prose is among the most beautiful and poetic of the language, and hence it is especially difficult to translate. In the sections from Ansari quoted below, we try to bring out the rhythm of the text by translating it as if it were poetry.

The author is explaining the meaning of the most commonly cited Koranic verse about love, already quoted above: "O you who have faith, should any of you turn back on your religion, God will bring a people whom He loves and who love Him . . ." (5:54). Here then is Maybudi's text:

> *"O you who have faith, should any of you turn back on your religion." This verse contains an allusion for the knowers and good news for the faithful.*
>
> *The allusion is that God is the protector of the community of Islam, the primordial religion, the Muhammadan Shariah, and that it will always remain. Nothing will be lost if some people turn their back on this religion and become apostates. The Lord of Mightiness will bring others who embrace this religion with soul and heart and nurture it lovingly. God will preserve the signposts*

of His commandments and the pillars of His prohibitions through them. He will decorate the carpet of the Shariah by their dignity. He has inscribed them with the letters of love, for He says, "whom He loves and who love Him." He has written upon the page of their hearts with a divine script: "He has written faith in their hearts" [58:23]. He has illuminated their inmost eye with the lamp of true knowledge, "So he is upon a light from his Lord" [39:22]. The Divinity is their upbringer, the lap of prophecy is their cradle, eternity without beginning and eternity without end are their warder, the playing field of gentleness is the lodging place of their gaze, and the carpet of awe is the resting place of their aspiration.

God makes the same point when He says in another place, "So if those cover its truth, we have already entrusted it to a people who do not cover its truth" [6:89]. The Prophet said, "A group among my people will never cease to support the Truth. None who oppose them will harm them until God's command comes."

The good news is that whoever does not turn his back is counted among the objects of love. They are the people of love and faith. Those who do not fall into the abyss of apostasy have the good news that the name of love will fall on them. God says, "Should any of you turn back on your religion, God will bring a people whom He loves and who love Him." First He affirms His love, then the love of the servants. Thus you come to understand that as long as God does not love the servant, the servant will not love . . .

Khwaja 'Abdallah said,
The sign of finding love's well is contentment,
    that which increases love's water is faithfulness.
The substance of love's treasure is light,
    the fruit of love's tree is joy.
If you fail to separate yourself from the two worlds
    you are excused from love,
If you seek recompense from the Friend,
    you are ungrateful.
Love is love for God,
    the rest is all idle fancy.
"Whom He loves and who love Him" is a great work,
    a marvelous bazaar—it lifted up water and clay.
Thereby God became love's kiblah
    and the target of union's arrows.
How could the traveler not be delighted
    that love is the nearest house to the Lord?
Love is a tree that produces only joy's fruit,
    an earth that grows nothing but intimacy's flowers,
a cloud that rains nothing but light,
    a wine whose potion is nothing but honey,

a road whose earth is nothing but musk and ambergris.
Love was written in eternity without beginning,
   love's brand lasts till eternity without end.
         From the time when love
            for the Friend
         became my habit
            and character
         all of me comes
            from the Friend,
         and the Friend comes
            from my all.
Behold how long love's fortune lasts!
   Hear how beautiful is the tale of lovers!
Love's playing field is as wide as the heart,
   paradise is one branch of the tree of love.
Those who drink love's wine are promised the vision,
   whoever is sincere will reach the goal.[12]

The Embodiment of the Spirit

We have come a long way since discussing the Five Pillars, but enough references have been made to the Shariah for the reader to understand that practice is the foundation and the most necessary element of Islam. Human beings are embodied spirits. Body and spirit meet in soul, which is both body and spirit. Who we are, in other words, is inextricably connected with our embodiment, and our embodiment is inextricably connected with what we do.

A certain type of religious orientation, commonly found incorporated even within post-Christian sensibilities, would place the body and spirit at loggerheads. It has not been uncommon for Christians to set up a duality, according to which the spiritual is good, the bodily is evil, and the latter has to be overcome or avoided. In today's post-Christian environment, it is also common to meet the opposite extreme, where everything has to be judged by the body, and the idea that there could be a spiritual reality somehow unaffected by the body is utterly rejected.

The traditional Islamic view, as discussed earlier, accepts both spirit and body as significant components of the human being. The spirit is more real, because it pertains to the divine side of things; it is God's own breath. However, human beings cannot possibly exist as human beings without bodies, and hence, in a very important sense, the spirit depends upon the body. The myth is clear on this point: God first shaped Adam's clay with his own two hands; only then did he blow the spirit into the clay and create the human being.

The drama of human existence is played out on the level of the soul, which combines the inherent luminosity of the spirit with the darkness of the body. Our own individualities are inseparable from both spirit and body, and this is precisely the meaning of *soul* as we have been employing the term. The soul, as the Muslim psychologists often express it, is the child of a spiritual father and a corporeal mother. The perfection of the soul lies in allowing the paternal heritage to dominate over the maternal heritage; or, in other terms, to let the heavenly rule over the earthly, the luminous over the dark.

The earth yields its fruits only when it receives light and water from heaven. The woman gives birth only when she is impregnated by the man. Colors appear only when light shines in darkness. If the earth rejects light and water, it withers and dies. If the woman rejects the man, she remains barren. If darkness refuses the light, it has nothing to show.[13]

Such imagery is employed by the Muslim authors to explain that the soul has to submit itself to the influence of the spirit, just as human beings have to submit themselves to God. To turn away from the spirit and focus exclusive attention on the body is to reject the light and pursue the darkness. The soul's luminosity pertains to the divine attributes, while its darkness derives from the bodily receptacle that is absolutely necessary so that the light may have a place in which to shine. The soul is embodied light, or spiritualized darkness.

The soul is not static: It changes instant by instant with the flux of God's creativity. At every moment, the soul is faced with new situations, and the spirit's freedom from all constraint gives the soul a relative freedom of choice. Every act, and in particular every voluntary act, has an effect on how the divine form unfolds within the human being.

One of the most common ways in which the development of the soul is discussed is in terms of three ascending levels, called "the soul that commands to evil," "the blaming soul," and "the soul at peace."

At the first level, souls find little of the spirit's light within themselves: They tend toward forgetfulness and heedlessness; caprice rules; people do what they feel like doing, simply because they feel like it. For infants, this is the natural, normal, and good situation. Nevertheless, everyone knows that the child must gradually be trained to accept that there are authorities higher than its own wishes, but as long as the child has not yet developed a healthy rational faculty, there is little use employing the arguments of reason.

The Koran, however, is not addressed to children. It is addressed to adults in full possession of their rational faculties. It tells them that following caprice is irrational, because rational beings know that there are authorities higher than their own feelings. Of course, the Koran does not propose a program of logical reasoning and philosophical discourse so that people can come to this understanding; that is fine for a modern philosophy department, but hardly a reasonable position for God to take when he is speaking to every adult human being, not just those who enjoy philosophizing. The purpose of the revelation is to guide people to a mode of happiness that would be unimaginable without divine aid. "No soul knows what comfort is laid up for them secretly, as a recompense for what they were doing" (32:17).

The Koran, in short, addresses human beings and tells them that it is utterly absurd for them to follow the dictates of caprice as if they were children. Not only is it absurd, it is dangerous, since it may eventually lead to the dissolution of the divine form in which they were created. However, the Koran recognizes that many, if not most, people dwell at this level. Their souls are overcome by the darkness and heedlessness that pertain to the bodily dimension of reality. The Muslim psychologists employ the Koranic term "the soul that commands to evil" (12:53) to refer to this lowest stage of human becoming, the stage where truth-concealing and heedlessness come naturally. At this stage, the person rejects everything that goes against caprice with no thought of the consequences. To mix Rumi's metaphor of the angel's wing and the donkey's tail, this is the stage where the tail wags the wing.

There is no reason to suppose that human beings will necessarily pass beyond this stage. The Koran frequently addresses the Prophet, telling him not to waste his breath trying to reason with the truth-concealers. If someone is blind, no one can make him see but God:

> Those who cry lies to Our signs are deaf and dumb, dwelling in the darknesses. Whomsoever God will, He misguides, and whomsoever He will, He puts on a straight path. (6:39)

Significantly, the Koran frequently compares those who are deaf and blind with animals. The stage of the soul that commands to evil is precisely the animal level of the soul, unilluminated by the light of intelligence. As the tradition tells us, those who remain at the animal level will experience themselves as animals in the *barzakh* and at the resurrection. The vast distance separating their human potential from their animal actuality sets up a profound disequilibrium in the soul that can only be experienced as blazing torment:

> The truth-concealers take their enjoyment and eat as the cattle eat, and the Fire shall be their lodging. (47:12)

> Be not as those who say, "We hear," and they hear not. The worst of beasts in God's sight are those who are deaf and dumb and have no intelligence. (8:21-22)

> Hast thou seen him who takes his caprice to be his god? Wilt thou be a guardian over him? Or deemest thou that most of them hear or understand? They are but as the cattle. No, they are more misguided from the path. (25:43-44)

We have created for Gehenna many of the jinn and mankind.
They have hearts, but they think not intelligently with them; they
have eyes, but see not with them; they have ears, but hear not with
them. They are like the cattle—no, they are more misguided.
Those—they are the heedless. (7:179)

As children grow up, standards of judgment and activity are gradually instilled into them by their family and surroundings. Typically, these standards have a moral dimension—things are presented as good or bad, right or wrong. Western civilization has tried—without much success—to give those standards a rational and scientific basis. Islam holds that true standards are innate, because they stem from the divine form within us. This is one of the senses of the already quoted hadith, "Every child is born according to *fitra*. Then its parents make it into a Jew, a Christian, a Zoroastrian"—or, as we would add today, an agnostic, a scientific humanist, a New Ager, and so on.

Whatever may be the source of our values, we have them. The Koran addresses only those with a sense of values (having given up on the animals among them). It reminds them of their *fitra*, their innate recognition of *tawhid*. Those who respond to the reminder remember God. They have faith in him and his messenger, and they submit to his commandments by following the Shariah. But this does not mean that the soul is at once irradiated with the light of the spirit or catapulted into the divine presence. Quite the contrary, it simply means that people have now become aware that, within this embodied spirit that is the soul, the luminous and intelligent dimension is more fundamental and more real. The outward reflection of the spirit known as revelation has been acknowledged, but its inner reality has yet to be fully realized.

This is the second stage of the soul. Muslim psychologists call it "the blaming soul" (a term derived from Koran 75:2). The conscience is awake, but this is a conscience informed by the prophetic message. People at this stage of development observe the Shariite rulings as best they can. More than that, they are attempting to be sincere in their activity and to do what is beautiful in every situation. Naturally, they often fail to live up to the Koranic ideal or the Prophet's Sunna, but they do not shrug their shoulders as if nothing was wrong. Instead, they blame themselves for not struggling harder in God's path. They have a sense of shame before God, because they are worshiping him "as if they see Him." This explains one of the senses of the Prophet's saying, "Every religion has its character trait, and the character trait of Islam is shame [*haya*]."

Most of the faithful never pass beyond the stage of the blaming soul. This is not to say that they are all equal, simply that they never reach the perfection that is embodied in the Prophet and the great exemplars of the tradition. Each of the faithful will reach a different stage of development. No two souls are the same, and any given soul never ceases undergoing transformations. To dwell at the stage of blaming oneself is to dwell in hope and trust. It is to turn oneself over to God, since only the awareness of God in the first place allows one to blame oneself. Rumi makes this point in answer to one of his disciples who was upset at the way in which people had to kowtow to the Mongol rulers of the time, who were not even Muslims:

> "In former times [said the disciple], the truth-concealers worshiped idols and prostrated themselves before them. Today we do the same thing. We go before the Mongols and prostrate ourselves and show all kinds of respect to them. Then we consider ourselves Muslims! And we have many other idols within ourselves, such as greed, caprice, spite, and envy. We obey all of them. Hence, outwardly and inwardly we act the same as the idol-worshipers, but we consider ourselves Muslims!"
>
> The master answered: "But there is one more thing. It enters your mind that 'This is bad and cannot be approved of.' Hence the eye of your heart has certainly seen some ineffable, indefinable, and tremendous thing that shows these to you as ugly and shameful. Salt water appears salty to someone who has drunk fresh water. 'Things become clear through their opposites.' Hence God has placed the light of faith in your soul, and it sees these things as ugly. After all, they appear ugly in comparison to that light's beauty. If not, why don't others have this pain? They are happy in what they are doing and say, 'This is the thing.' God will give you what you seek for. Wherever your aspiration lies, that you will become. 'The bird flies with its wings, and the person of faith flies with his aspiration.' "[14]

Those who have faith should have a constant awareness of their own faults and blame themselves for not overcoming them. The flip side of this coin is that they have to hold before themselves an ideal to which they aspire. They will never reach it until they try; and when they do try, they will not reach it through their own effort, but, as Rumi and many others who stress God's gentleness and mercy tell us, God will give it to them, in his own good time.

The final stage of the soul is called "the soul at peace," on the basis of this Koranic verse: "O soul at peace, return to thy Lord, well-pleased, well-pleasing! Enter among My servants! Enter My paradise!" (89:27) This is the soul that has returned to God in this world. Such a soul belongs to those who have established *ihsan* to such a degree that they worship God not "as if" they see him, but while actually seeing him present in all things, including themselves. This, in the Sufi view, is the station of Muhammad, who is the first among God's servants, and the other prophets, as well as anyone else whom God chooses. It is the ideal toward which Muslims should be striving.

The Koran addresses itself neither to the soul that commands to evil, which is deaf and blind, nor to the soul at peace, which has reached the goal and has rejoined the spirit's light. Rather, it is addressed to the blaming soul, which wavers between spirit and body, light and darkness, good and evil, right and wrong. The Koran tells people where they stand—in an ambiguous domain halfway between God and nothingness—and shows them the way to choose the Real over the unreal. To the extent that their freedom is real, they will be able to choose where they will go. They choose whether the angel's wing will lift them to the highest heaven, or the donkey's tail will drag them to the lowest earth.

All of Islamic thinking about God and the human being draws this picture of an ambiguous reality hanging between pure light and utter darkness, but this ambiguous reality can never escape embodiment. The "bodily resurrection" is not only a dogma in Islam, it is also the only possible way to explain how people can be divine and human at the same time. God alone has no embodiment as this or that; human beings are embodied forever.

In no sense does bodily resurrection mean that this physical body will last forever. The body, which everyone knows is ephemeral, is merely the vehicle for the embodied spirit, the soul. The soul—the spirit manifest in forms—lasts forever, not the material body. The soul itself *is* a body, just as it is a spirit. Sometimes it does not recognize itself as a body, imagining that it is only spirit, but the dreamworld dissolves this illusion, as does the *barzakh*, the resurrection, paradise, and hell. In all these worlds, the soul experiences its embodiment without a bodily garment of the type that it wears in this world.

To return to what we said earlier, Islamic theoretical teachings support and deepen the practical teachings, but given the fact of the soul's embodied reality, the practical teachings take on a fundamental importance. It is not accidental that Islam presents itself most clearly and obviously in the Shariah. The Five Pillars are called pillars because the religion has nothing to stand upon without them: Only through the practices set down in the pillars and in the Shariah in general is it possible to embody the Koran in the actual experience of life.

Part IV:

ISLAM IN HISTORY

Chapter 9.

HISTORY AS INTERPRETATION

❧

S urely one of the deepest gulfs separating the modern Western perspective from the traditional Islamic world view lies in the understanding of history. In order to grasp the difference in perspectives, let us look at the word *history* in English. The word has two sides to its meaning: In one respect, it is simply a narrative of events; in a second respect, the narrative is inseparable from an explanatory account.

We say, "That is history," meaning that something happened in the past, and that we know about it. Through this use of the term, we imply that events that occurred in the past had an objective reality about which we are informed; we discuss history as a dimension of reality; we think of past events as we think of places: They are there and they are fixed.

From the second point of view, we use the word *history* while recognizing that there is a subjective element involved in its study. When we say, "History teaches us that . . .," we have recognized, as least implicitly, that a certain perspective on the past allows us to perceive its meaning. If we ask why we should learn lesson *x* instead of lesson *y*, we will soon realize that historians—those who make it their profession to write about the past—have points of views, presuppositions, and ideologies. Of course, this is no less true for the study of contemporary society, or psychology, or bacteria. When we find meaning, we do so on the basis of preconceived ideas about what can be meaningful; otherwise, we are left with a disconnected jumble of information.

In the modern world, we have witnessed the birth of the critical study of history. A host of new methods for studying the past have given many scholars confidence that human beings, for the first time, are able to look at the past "objectively" and "scientifically." The self-congratulation involved in this view of things should be obvious, and it should also be enough to put us on our guard.

This is not the place to investigate the belief systems of contemporary scholarship. One point, however, needs to be stressed: Historians and many philosophers consider history to have an enormous importance, and looking at history in this manner has no precedent in any previous civilization. As has often been observed, this attention paid to history is not unrelated to the nature of the Judeo-Christian tradition. Judaism was differentiated from other ancient religions partly by the significance that it gave to historical events. Following in Judaism's wake, Christianity situated its founding myth *within* history, not outside of it, thus giving a special character to the historical process. In modern times, many Western intellectuals, having lost religious faith, nevertheless have held on to certain Christian attitudes, including the divinity of history. Hegel is the grand example of a thinker who found the divine only in the historical process.

We do not mean to suggest that all modern historians are Hegelians, but we do think that the belief that has commonly been found among historians (though much less today than a few years ago)—that they are able to find out what *really* happened in the past and to draw conclusions from it—means that they have, in effect, assumed a prophetic role. In this view, the historians tell us of the significance of the past. They alone are able to understand the "signs" that have been recorded as occurring before the present. In an anthology of religious texts from Judaism, Christianity, and Islam, one of our finest historians of the early Islamic environment, F. E. Peters, called attention to this prophetic role—only partly tongue in cheek—while disclaiming any similar role for himself:

I have made here almost no judgments about authenticity: these are the received texts, scriptural and otherwise. . . . Thus there are no traces here of the revelations of Julius Wellhausen or Ignaz Goldziher, no echoes of the prophetic voices of Rudolf Bultmann or Joseph Schacht, of Jacob Neusner or Patricia Crone.[1]

It is not only historians who make claims that have prophetic implications. If religion involves establishing guidelines for right activity, right thought, and right intentions, any human enterprise that deals with one or more of these domains has religious significance. Many of our modern academic disciplines—the hard sciences in particular—dictate thinking and activity to the public: Their revelations are eagerly devoured in popular magazines, and people look forward to the establishment of paradise on earth.

We have already suggested the implications of the almost exclusive stress upon rationality in the modern world: To focus on reason is to focus on the quantitative dimension of reality; it is to divide, dissect, and take apart. Herein lies the genius and the power of modern civilization, but also its nemesis. The underlying thrust of all critical scholarship (not simply the school that has adopted the term as its own) is to *deconstruct*. The net result is the exponential increase of information, and the ever receding possibility of holding things together. In the midst of this world without a *center* and without an *origin* (as Eliade uses these terms), all sorts of claims are made for every subdiscipline of learning. Among historians, the claim is simply "We know better," whatever the specific methodology that is pursued.

One cannot object to the idea that modern methodologies have uncovered information that has heretofore been unknown or ignored. One can object, however, when a historian speaks of significance in terms that have religious or cosmic repercussions.

To discuss the meaning of history is to discuss what it means to be human. Some historians may declare that they are simply recording events, but in this day and age, most are willing to admit that objective history is an illusion: It is impossible to record an event without making judgments about its significance. When information has been handed down from the remote past, such judgments are made at every stage. The historians set for themselves the laudable goal of uncovering the actual event under the accumulated layers of interpretation, but this simply means that they present us with their own interpretations: To conceptualize is to interpret.

The self-congratulation that too often accompanies the academic mindset has led to the rejection of the plausibility of all nonmodern ways of looking at history, in particular those that are found in religious civilizations. Lawrence E. Sullivan alludes to this fact while speaking about the eschatological meanings that religions typically find in historical events:

> Our own historical visions of time have often served to eliminate
> the relevance of our contemporaries' proposed solutions to the
> enigma of our common historical condition. We shrink from
> these visions of the end because they relativize history, the mode

*of time that has licensed the accumulation of symbolic currencies
in the forms of wealth, land, labor, written word, and science.*[2]

Islamic Interpretation of the Past

Muslims have always exhibited interest in the past. Understanding
the Koran and the Sunna—the twin foundations of the religion—
demands that the present traces of past events have a critical importance for human life. Some Muslim scholars made it their profession to
record past events, whether or not they had any direct relevance to the
Koran and the Prophet. They often wrote "universal histories," from
Adam down to their own time, not to mention other kinds of historical
accounts.

Modern historians have often employed the writings of the Muslim
historians. Typically, they have noted the interpretative stance of the
author, tried to discount the resulting distortion, and taken whatever
passes through their own methodological sieves as grist for their mills.

We are not interested here in the history of historiography in Islam.
We note that historical writing has played a role, but we do so simply to
emphasize that, for the vast majority of Muslims, academic history—or
what passes for such in a given epoch—was of no concern. Their
sensibilities toward the past were largely shaped by the Koranic world
view. Everything that happened in the past was a sign of God. Hence,
the *significance* of the past was already established before people
learned anything about the details.

Not that the situation has really changed in the modern world. Most
historians have already limited the possibilities of meaning before they
begin their research. However, in the Islamic case, it is very clear that
significance depends upon signs, and signs depend upon God. In other
words, significance is determined by *tawhid*.

The Koran repeatedly admonishes people to learn the lessons of the
past. We saw how much attention it pays to the prophets: In practically
every case, the Koran recites the trials and tribulations undergone by
the prophets to illustrate that people have not changed. The Meccans
were treating Muhammad the way that the Israelites had treated their
prophets. Moreover, the point is clearly universal. In other words, it is
not simply a question of Muhammad's time; it is a question of all times
and all places, because heedlessness of God and his messages is rooted
in the human condition. In the Islamic view, people are always missing
the significance of history, and they always have to be reminded.

The Koran does not simply take the tales of the prophets as signs of
God's work in history; it takes all the lore that has reached its listeners
as signs of the past, and it takes the omnipresent ruins of previous
cultures and civilizations as signs. "Everything is perishing but His
face" (28:88). Human civilizations are fleeting and illusory; God alone is

real; refuge from time's disasters must be sought in God, not in the ephemeral fabrications of human minds and hands. The Koran speaks about the outcome or ultimate end (*'aqiba*) of past peoples in some twenty verses. It asks its readers to think about how many past peoples and civilizations God has destroyed because of their wrongdoing. In this context, it recommends "traveling in the earth" as a means of widening one's horizons and coming to understand the vanity and ephemerality of local ties and local issues. Only by opening themselves up to a broad view of things can people begin to see the simultaneous nothingness and grandeur of the human race:

Many ways of life have passed away before you. So travel in the earth and consider what was the end of those who cried lies. (3:137)

Those cities We relate to thee tidings of, their Messengers came to them with clear explications, but they were not the ones to have faith in what they had cried lies to before. . . . So consider what was the end of those who worked corruption! (7:101–103)

What, have they not traveled in the earth and considered what was the end of those before them? Those were more intense than they in strength, . . . and their messengers came to them with clear explications. And God would never wrong them, but they wronged themselves. (30:9)

The Koran makes clear that God has frequently brought down destruction on cities and towns, and that this stems from people's rejection of the prophetic messages:

Like Pharaoh's folk, and the people before him, who cried lies to the signs of their Lord, so We destroyed them because of their sins. (8:54)

Have they not seen that We have destroyed before them many a generation that We had established in the earth, as We have never established you? (6:6)

We destroyed many generations before you when they did wrong, and their Messengers came to them with the clear explications, but they would not have faith. (10:13)

How many a city We have destroyed in its wrongdoing, so it has fallen down on its roofs! How many a deserted well, a tall palace! (22:45)

We never chastise, until We send forth a messenger. And when We desire to destroy a city, We issue commandments to those who live there in ease, and they perform acts of transgression there. Then the Word is realized against it, and We destroy it utterly. How many generations We have destroyed after Noah! (17:15-17)

This destruction of towns and cities for wrongdoing is not simply a matter of past history, it is also a promise for the future:

No city is there, but We shall destroy it before the day of resurrection, or We shall chastise it with a terrible chastisement. That is inscribed in the Book. (17:58)

In threatening the Prophet's enemies with destruction, the Koran says plainly that God holds back because of the presence of Muhammad among them, or the presence of those who seek nearness to God: "But God would never chastise them, with thee among them; God would never chastise them while they asked forgiveness" (8:33). For later thinkers, this sets down the principle that God will not destroy the world so long as even one faithful Muslim remains, doing therein what is beautiful. They cite in support the hadith, "The Hour will not come as long as there is someone on the earth saying, 'God, God'."

The Marks of the End

With this brief introduction to Koranic teachings about human history, let us turn to the last part of the hadith of Gabriel. The text reads:

The man said, "Tell me about the Hour."
The Prophet replied, "About that he who is questioned knows no more than the questioner."
The man said, "Then tell me about its marks."
He said, "The servant girl will give birth to her mistress, and you will see the barefoot, the naked, the destitute, and the shepherds vying with each other in building."

We have seen that the Koran declares that God alone knows when the Last Day will occur, and that anyone else who claims to know is a liar. Apparently, the Prophet took Gabriel's question about the Last Day as asking for specifics about the time of the Hour's occurrence, and he answered that he knew no more than the questioner did, since none knows about it except God. But the question does not necessarily refer to the time of the Hour. In any case, the Prophet's answer can have another significance, once we recognize that he knew all along who the questioner was. He can be saying, "You, Gabriel, know as much about that as I do, but it is neither my place nor yours to reveal this knowledge, since it is not part of the message that God has commanded us to reveal."

As for the marks (*amarat*) of the Hour, this was a topic of major interest for the Prophet and his companions. The books on Hadith devote a good deal of space to the many sayings of the Prophet relevant to the signs that will presage the end of time. The Koran frequently talks about the terror of the Hour, and in a few instances it mentions events that are taken as its precursors. For example, a beast will appear shortly before the final destruction: "When the Word falls on them, We shall bring forth for them out of the earth a beast that shall say to them that people had no faith in Our signs" (27:82). Another verse warns that the barbarian tribes Gog and Magog will be unleashed to do their work:

> When Gog and Magog are unloosed, and they slide down out of every slope, and the true promise draws near—then the eyes of the truth-concealers will stare: "Woe to us, we were heedless of this! No, we were wrongdoers." (21:96-97)

In the hadith of Gabriel, the Prophet mentions two marks that would tell people that the end of time is near. The first is that "the servant girl will give birth to her mistress." Like many sayings referring to the last times, this sounds like a riddle, but it is not too difficult to understand: The basic meaning is that the social order will be disrupted.

In normal times, there are acknowledged social relationships that preserve order. The Koran provides indications of these relationships through the great attention it pays to the necessity of honoring and obeying one's parents. Another normal relationship is that between rulers and the ruled: Certain people give instructions, and others obey. "Obey God, and obey the Messenger and those in authority among you" (4:59). We have already cited the hadith, "Each of you is a shepherd, and each of you will be held responsible for your sheep. . . ."

The proper relationship of mistress to servant girl is for the mistress to issue commands and the servant girl to obey (there may of course be other relationships as well, but this specific relationship is at issue here). One of the places where this relationship holds is mother and daughter. The mother raises and nurtures the daughter, and the daughter in turn obeys the mother. However, if the "servant girl gives birth to her mistress," then mother has become servant and daughter has become mistress: This is a reversal of the right social order; it is a profound disequilibrium, and its seriousness in the Islamic consciousness can perhaps best be judged by the fact that in several verses the Koran makes reverence to one's parents the first practical application of *tawhid*, as we have already noted. If the mother-daughter relationship is upset, and if that is one of the most fundamental relationships of society, then surely the relationship of *tawhid*, not to mention other relationships, will also be upset: Religion and society would fall apart.

The second mark mentioned by the Prophet is simply another example of social disintegration. In Islam, poverty is paid great respect. The
Prophet said, "God loves His servant who is faithful, poor, chaste, and
father of a family." The hadith of Gabriel is clearly not talking about
people who lack material possessions. Rather, the reference is to those
who have the moral qualities and character traits of the meanest and
most despicable members of society: They may be Muslims in appearance, but inwardly they are truth-concealers and workers of corruption. In a normal society, such people live at the peripheries and are
powerless. Toward the end of time, they will be the designers and
builders of grandiose structures, and they will be very proud of their
accomplishments.

There is no reason to suppose that "building" in the hadith refers only
to physical structures. Koranic usage of the term suggests that it may
just as well refer to anything that humans can build, including houses,
machines, societies, nations, philosophies, and ideologies.

> *Why, is he better who founded his building upon wariness of God
> and His good-pleasure better, or he who founded his building
> upon the brink of a crumbling bank that has tumbled with him
> into the fire of Gehenna? (9:109)*

> *Those who were before them contrived, then God came upon their
> building from the foundations, and the roof fell down on them
> from over them, and the chastisement came upon them from
> whence they were not aware. (16:26)*

In short, this last part of the hadith of Gabriel suggests that when the
last times draw close, every social order instituted by the prophets will
be disrupted and overthrown. Human life and society will be ruled by
fabrications of human cleverness that grow up out of the basest instincts of the soul.

We pointed out earlier that from the beginning of Islam many Muslims thought that the end of the world was imminent. The Prophet
himself held up his thumb and forefinger with a tiny space between
them and said, "I and the Hour are like this." But we also pointed out
that one of God's days may last one thousand or fifty thousand years, or
even more. The only thing that Muslims can say for sure about the time
of the Last Day is that it is 1400 years nearer than it was when the
Prophet warned of its imminence and that many of its marks are
apparent for all to see. They can also be sure that the religious order of
things will not improve before the return of Christ. In other words,
islam, iman, and *ihsan* will be increasingly difficult to actualize within
the individual and society.

Chapter 10.

THE CONTEMPORARY SITUATION

ஒ

P ractically every introductory book on Islam provides details of
the historical unfolding of the Islamic community and its situation
in the modern period. There are far more studies of contemporary
political events in Muslim countries than there are of classical Islamic
civilization or Islam's religious teachings. Our purpose here is not
to repeat what others have said or to describe the modern scene
from within a framework that makes sense to contemporary sensibilities. Rather, we will try to throw light on how history can be read as
signs from the perspective of a world view still dominated by *tawhid*.
What, in short, does Islam's vision of itself tell us about contemporary
history?

Until recently, most Westerners simply took it for granted that progress was a fact of human existence, and that the non-Western world
would have to follow on the heels of the West to survive in the modern
world. Given the events of the twentieth century, more and more reflective people have come to doubt whether progress is indeed an intrinsic
good. Many people now ask if the course of technological development
pursued by Western society was a wise choice. Scientists in all sorts of

fields ask whether the present course of progress is not the quickest way for the human race to commit suicide.

The word *progress* itself begs many questions. It implies a direction, a goal, and standards whereby it can be judged. But when we look at human affairs, the only domain within which undeniable progress has been made is in the accumulation of power through technology: Our computers and our bombs are definitely better. In practically every other field of human endeavor, even those in which popular opinion takes progress for granted—such as medicine and scientific learning in general—serious doubts about the reality of progress are being raised.

As soon as the human side of the historical process is taken into account, skepticism toward self-congratulatory claims of progress is only natural. Do people become better through the technological concentration of power? Are those who live in the First World better people than those who live elsewhere, or who lived in former times? Here we need standards by which to judge our humanity, standards that modern academic approaches—whether the hard scientific, the sociological, the psychological, or the philosophical—have practically abandoned.

As soon as the contemporary situation is considered from within the value system of a traditional religion such as Islam, it becomes easy to conclude that "the barefoot, the naked, the destitute, and the shepherds are vying with each other in building."

We pose these issues to remind the reader of the presuppositions that go into judgments about the nature of history, society, and human welfare. When we decide that a particular political process or a specific event is good or bad, we are judging on the basis of preconceived ideas whose truth is not self-evident. If we want to judge the contemporary Islamic world, we should make clear from the outset which standards we are employing. Most books, especially those that deal with contemporary affairs, take popular prejudices about the purpose of human life as the unquestioned ground from which judgments can be made. That progress is a good thing is simply one example of these unquestioned presuppositions.

The Declining Fortunes of Islam

Western scholarship has typically read Islamic history as the story of rise and decline. In what is commonly called Islam's "Golden Age"—the high period of the Baghdad caliphate—a *pax islamica* had been established throughout most of the civilized world; scientific, philosophical, literary, and artistic endeavors reached peaks that had few precedents in human history. Gradually, however, because of a decline in creativity and a steady stream of barbarian invaders, Islam lost its creative power. By the eighteenth century, it was ripe for conquest by the

European nations, whose scientific and technological revolution was just getting off the ground.

This, by and large, has been the received wisdom in modern times. More recent historians, of course, are questioning every finding of earlier generations. For example, since the idea of decline is intimately tied up with the ideology of progress, once progress is called into question, what appears to have been a decline may simply be a peaceful equilibrium that is highly efficacious for achieving a civilization's goals. The goals of Islamic civilization have never been scientific and technological progress, but rather perfection of the human soul. How has Islamic civilization fared in terms of its own standards? That is a question that few historians have ever asked.

A Western-educated intellectual class began appearing in Islamic countries in the second half of the nineteenth century, and it has continued to gain in influence. These Muslims, who have been familiar with modern ideologies and presuppositions, have taken a variety of positions on the situation of the Islamic world. The initial reaction of most of those who gained a Western-style education was an enormous sense of inferiority in the face of political domination by Western powers; this domination was, of course, powered by technology. Muslims wanted to be free of domination by the colonial powers, and the only course of action that appeared possible to the modern educated classes was to learn modern science and technology in order to gain political power. Many Muslims felt that traditional Islam was nothing but a hindrance to this goal, and so they adopted two basic courses: abandoning the religion, and reforming it.

Those who abandoned Islam are not our concern. As for those who set out to reform Islam, they were of course reforming it in accordance with their own ideas of how political independence could be achieved in an era of concentration of power in the hands of the technologically endowed.

Reformist Islam typically appeals to those dimensions of Islamic teachings that can be harmonized with modern science and technology. This means that the reformers stress rationality and devalue imagination and unveiling. The apologetic works of this group, English versions of which began appearing in India in the nineteenth century and continue to be written, never tire of telling us how rational, scientific, and humane Islam is. In brief, the thrust of their message is as follows: The whole program of modern science is simply the logical development of the Koranic teachings. On the level of human values, the United Nations charter was simply plagiarized from the Koran and the Hadith. Muslims, because of outside influences and internal decadence, lost sight of the true goal of the Koranic teachings—that is, technological progress and a democratic society (again, defined UN style)—and as a result, the West picked up the Muslim birthright and ran with it. It is now time for Islam to reclaim its own heritage. (We may be guilty of a bit of caricature here, but not much.)

The net result of this kind of thinking has been that the power elites in the Islamic countries—and these have typically been educated in the Western mold, for a variety of reasons—have set out to emulate the West. Even today, the "Islamic" revolutionaries have not lost faith in science and technology: They know perfectly well that keeping political power demands technological control over the masses, and they justify their own claims to technological power with any means at their disposal, including appeal to the Koran and the Hadith.

Reading the Signs of History

We have just made certain implicit judgments about those who have sought out political power in the Islamic world in modern times. We suggested that many of them have lost sight of authentic Islamic teachings: Those among them who are called "fundamentalists" are no exception. Let us now suggest why we feel that the vision of Islam demands skepticism about modern Islamic political movements.

We have proposed from the beginning of this book that Islam's self-vision requires that human affairs be considered on three different but interdependent levels: *islam, iman,* and *ihsan* (submission, faith, and doing what is beautiful; or activity, knowledge, and intentionality). What does Islamic history look like when we judge it from this point of view?

Answering this question in any detail would require writing another book; we can only suggest very briefly how the contemporary situation might be judged. Before doing so, however, we need to point out a fact that is self-evident for Islam's vision: The only time in history when an optimum balance was established among these three dimensions of human existence was when the Prophet was ruling the community at Medina; from then on, it was downhill (with occasional upswings of course). As the Prophet said, "No time will come to you which will not be followed by one that is more evil until you encounter your Lord."

Muslims in general recognize that the institution of the caliphate—the political rulership of the community—was in decline as soon as it became hereditary with the Umayyads in the first/seventh century. The first four caliphs have traditionally been called *al-khulafa' al-rashidun,* the "rightly guided caliphs," or perhaps better, the "caliphs of moral integrity." The political fortunes of Islam rose with the Umayyads and Abbasids, but the moral integrity of both the community leaders and the community as a whole declined. Innumerable pious people over the centuries have pointed to this decline of Islam and urged the community to reform. Until recently, the reform of Islam was envisaged within a world view such as that we have been describing.

In the traditional view, reform of society depended upon reform of the individual, and reform of the individual depended upon observance of Islam in all three of its dimensions. Individual perfection was always connected with nearness to God, or actualizing the divine form within each and every person. Only in modern times has reform been taken to mean the remaking of human beings, not in the form of the God of the Koran, but rather the form of the gods of progress and democracy (as revealed to the modern West).

Islam is still very much alive, but it is not difficult even for outside observers to see that, in most of those who vocally acclaim their Islamic affiliation, the three dimensions of Islam are not kept in balance. Almost without exception, those groups that are labeled fundamentalist by outside observers are typified by stress upon the Shariah without a corresponding emphasis upon intentions, moral attitudes, and spirituality. *Islam* is typically discussed as if it were the whole of Islam, while *ihsan* is at best given lip service. At the same time, a utopianism that flies in the face of the traditional understanding of history animates fundamentalist political activities.

Islam, in the broad sense we have in mind, has been and still remains both an individual and a social ideal. Individuals who want to be good Muslims must strive to observe the Shariah carefully, deepen their *iman*, and develop the divine and human virtues that make up a balanced human personality, such as wisdom, generosity, patience, gratitude, justice, and love. Any one of these three tasks is difficult, especially in today's world. It is all the more difficult to devote attention to all three tasks at once.

The individual ideal of a balanced Islam producing a balanced personality runs parallel to the social ideal of a community functioning organically in mutual harmony. Muslim authorities have been perfectly aware from the beginning of Islam that not everyone will be able to actualize all three dimensions of the religion. Human beings represent a bewildering variety of capacities for growth, perfection, and deviation. The Koran stresses the idea that "God charges no soul save to its capacity" (2:286). Not everyone can be expected to devote his or her life to learning or to spiritual practices, though people must do so "to their capacity." In a healthy Islamic society, people will follow the Shariah with a maximum degree of sincerity, devote themselves to the Islamic sciences and arts, and undertake the rigors of the spiritual life to the extent of their individual gifts. If such a society has ever fully existed, it was at the time of the Prophet; since then, most societies in the Islamic world have participated in this ideal to some degree, at least until very recent times.

Though it is difficult to judge from the outside the health and wholeness of Islam in this broad sense, there are many criteria which would point to it, such as observance of the Shariah without coercion by government or religious officials, cultivation of both the transmitted and the intellectual sciences, and a flowering of beauty through calligraphy, architecture, poetry, and music.

One of the saddest signs of the dissolution of Islamic norms over the past fifty years is the loss of a sense of beauty. No one who has visited the cities of the Islamic world can help but be struck by the extraordinary contrast between the remaining traditional structures and the monstrosities of contemporary architecture. That the sense of beauty has disappeared in architecture (with a few exceptions of course) is simply one symptom of the fact that a sense of beauty has disappeared from everyday life. People think nothing of tossing exquisitely hand-wrought copper and wooden utensils into the garbage to replace them by gaudy plastic goods.[3] This outward "plasticizing" of society is a symptom of a much deeper parallel process on the mental and spiritual planes.

There are many other signs of the distortion of integral Islam in modern times. One is the tremendous stress placed upon *tanzih* and the almost total eclipse of *tashbih*, at least among those who speak up vocally for Islamic values, especially those with political agendas. In some cases, the celebration of God's wrath and anger is used to justify methods of warfare—such as mass killing and terrorism—that are explicitly forbidden by the Shariah.

Modernist Islam typically rejects the intellectual understanding of the tradition, unless it is posed in political terms. Islam does have its own political teachings, but these have always remained peripheral: To place them at the center is to break with the tradition. Of course, the political ideologies of contemporary Muslim movements are seldom rooted in Islamic teachings; rather, they are reinterpretations of the Koran and the Hadith based on modern presuppositions concerning democracy or other "good" forms of government, though of course, as elsewhere, Marxist interpretations are now on the wane.

To the extent that modernist Islam appeals to the schools of faith, it limits itself to the most rationalistic of the theologians and the philosophers. Rationalism is easy to harmonize with love for science and technology, but a stressing of imagination, beauty, and unveiling immediately brings forward issues of human nature that few people feel comfortable with in the modern world.

Kalam, especially in its Mu'tazilite version, is easy to pose in terms that do not question the legitimacy of modern science. Stress on *tanzih* allows the theologian to disengage God from anything but specific commands; reason establishes God's difference from the cosmos and the human world, and then it gives the theologian relatively free rein to set up a "rational" program of human improvement. So long as God is not present within the cosmos itself—as *tashbih* teaches us that he is—human beings are free to deal with it as they like: There are no reasons not to follow the West in raping nature. Massive economic development and industrial pollution become God's approved way to establish the "Islamic" goal of a rational society.

Islam is a great religion. We do not mean to imply that nothing is left but deviation from the harmonious balance of *islam*, *iman*, and *ihsan*. There are Muslims throughout the Islamic world who know that Islam needs to be lived on all levels. If they are not apparent before the public gaze, this should not surprise anyone. We all know what is important in the eyes of the modern world, and we all know that the very nature of the modern media demands noise and tumult. Peace, harmony, and equilibrium do not make news.

Select Glossary

All foreign words are Arabic unless otherwise indicated. The correct transliteration, if different from the form used in the text of the book, is indicated in parentheses according to the standard, modified *Encyclopedia of Islam* system.

A

'abd: Servant, worshiper, slave. All things in the universe are God's compulsory servants because they are created by him. Human beings also need to be God's voluntary servants in order to achieve the purpose for which they were created. The term *'abd* is often paired with *khalifa*.

Adam (*ādam*): The first human being, or simply, "the human being." God molded his body out of clay, blew his own spirit into him, taught him all the names, and appointed him vicegerent in the earth.

Allah (*Allāh*): The Arabic word for God.

amana (*amāna*): Trust. The special responsibility that God offered to the heavens, the earth, and the mountains, but they all refused. Then human beings agreed to carry it. The Trust is often identified with the vicegerency or with love.

aya (*āya*): Sign. The Koran employs the term to refer to anything in the universe that gives news of God, including all natural, human, and social phenomena; scriptures; the extraordinary acts and miracles of the prophets, and its own verses. *Aya* is thus the standard term that is employed to refer to the subunits of the *suras*, or the chapters of the Koran.

ayatollah (*āyatallāh*): Sign of God. Anything in the universe is a sign of God. More specifically, the term was adopted as a designation for high ranking ulama in Iran in the early twentieth century, but nowadays any prominent mullah in Iran is likely to be called an ayatollah.

C

companions (*ṣaḥāba*): Those who met the Prophet and accepted his message. Often contrasted with "followers," those who met any of the companions.

D

dhikr: To mention, to remind, to remember. Reminding people of God is the primary function of the prophets and the scriptures. The human response is also called *dhikr*, that is, remembering God and one's responsibilities toward him. More specifically, a special form of prayer is also called *dhikr*. This usually entails the repetition of certain names of God or certain formulae containing God's name, such as the first Shahadah.

du'a (*du'ā*): Supplication. A form of prayer in which people make personal requests from God.

F

fitra (*fiṭra*): The original human nature as created by God. Its fundamental attribute is the understanding of *tawhid*.

G

ghafla: Heedlessness. The basic human shortcoming; contrasted with *dhikr*.

ghayb: Absent, unseen, invisible. This is an attribute of God, the angels, and the jinn. *Ghayb* and *shahada* (the witnessed, the visible) make up the two main worlds of the cosmos.

H

Hadith (*ḥadīth*): The sayings of the Prophet himself or of his companions concerning his activities. Hadith is contrasted with Koran, which is the word of God. A hadith is one of the sayings found in the Hadith. The Hadith are gathered together in a number of collections. In Sunni Islam, the six collections considered the most reliable are called the "sound" collections; they are typically cited by the names of their authors, such as Bukhari, Muslim, Tirmidhi, Abu Dawud, etc.

hadith qudsi (*qudsī*): Holy saying. A hadith of the Prophet in which God's word are quoted directly. For example, "The Prophet said that God has inscribed on His Throne, 'My mercy takes precedence over My wrath.'" Like other hadiths, these are clearly distinguished from the Koran.

hajj (*ḥajj*): The pilgrimage to Mecca that is incumbent on all Muslims at least once in their lifetime if they have the means to go; one of Islam's Five Pillars.

halal (*ḥalāl*): Permissible according to a ruling of the Shariah; contrasted with *haram*.

haram (*ḥarām*): Forbidden by the Shariah; contrasted with both *halal* and *wajib*.

hijra: The emigration from Mecca to Medina by the Prophet in the year 622 C.E. Because of the importance of this event in Islamic history, it marks the first year of the Islamic calendar.

I

'ibada (*'ibāda*): To worship, to serve, to be a servant. This is the basic duty of human beings, failing which they cannot achieve vicegerency.

Iblis (*iblīs*, **akin to Latin** *diabolus*): The proper name of Satan. Like the other jinn, he was created of fire. Through pious devotions he was brought into nearness with God along with the angels, but he refused to prostrate himself before Adam when God commanded him to do so, and as a result he was sent down out of God's presence in disgrace.

ihsan (*iḥsān*): Doing what is beautiful, the third dimension of Islam.

imam (*imām*): Leader; the person who leads the *salat* when Muslims pray together; the prayer-leader in a mosque. In Shi'ite Islam, the Imams are certain descendents of the Prophet who are looked upon as the legitimate leaders of the Islamic community.

iman (*īmān*): Faith, the second dimension of Islam. Its objects are God, the angels, the scriptures, the prophets, the Last Day, and the measuring out. Typically, these are discussed in terms of the three principles: *tawhid*, *nubuwwa*, and *ma'ad*. The opposite of *iman* is *kufr*.

islam (*islām*): Submission to God. The word has four basic meanings. In the broadest sense, it refers to the fact that every created thing submits to God by being God's handiwork. In this sense, no choice is involved, but in the next three senses, people can choose whether or not to accept *islam*. Second, *islam* means submission to God's guidance as brought by the prophets. In the third meaning, for which we use the word Islam as a proper noun, it means submission to the guidance of God as brought in the Koran. In the fourth and narrowest sense, *islam* means observing the Five Pillars in general and the Shariah in particular.

J

jihad (*jihād*): Struggle in the path of God. In the most general sense of the term, jihad is the personal struggle against one's own shortcomings that is required of all Muslims so that they can perfect their submission. In a more specific sense, it is battle against the enemies of Islam as regulated by the Shariah, as in defensive warfare. In its most common usage, it simply means a war that is perceived by those who participate in it as just; this perception is totally separate from the question of whether or not the Shariah would in fact sanction such a war.

jinn: Creatures of an ambiguous and somewhat mysterious nature who were created out of fire, which combines the qualities of light and clay. Their luminosity makes the jinn somewhat similar to angels, but their darkness makes them similar to bodily things. The most famous of the jinn is Iblis, also known as Satan. Like human beings, the jinn are divided into two main groups—the followers of Iblis (the truth-concealers) and the followers of the prophets (the faithful).

jism: Body. Anything that can be perceived by the five senses. In a general sense, the body is that which God pairs with the spirit in order to bring a creature into existence. Thus, angels have bodies of light, jinn have bodies of fire, and human beings and other animals have bodies of clay. In the case of human beings, the body's attributes are understood as opposite to those of the spirit. Hence, the spirit is high, the body low; the spirit is luminous, the body dark, and so on. The soul (*nafs*) is situated half-way between the body and the spirit.

jurisprudence (*fiqh*): The science that takes the Shariah as its object of study.

jurist (*faqīh*): An expert in jurisprudence.

K

Kaaba (*ka'ba*): Literally, "cube." The main Islamic sanctuary in Mecca, also called the "House of God." It marks the kiblah, or the direction in which people face when they perform the *salat*, and it is the focus of the rites performed during the hajj.

kafir (*kāfir*): Truth-concealer. A person who has the attribute of *kufr*.

Kalam: Dogmatic theology. One of the three intellectual schools that investigate the meaning of the objects of faith. Kalam takes a defensive stance toward the Koran and is generally polemical. Its major tool is reason or rational investigation.

khalifa (*khalīfa*): Vicegerent or representative of God. Adam was created to be God's vicegerent, and hence vicegerency is a privilege and responsibility given exclusively to human beings. Becoming a vicegerent depends upon being a proper servant (*see `abd*). In Islamic political thought, the *khalifa*s are the vicegerents or successors of the Prophet. Thus the Umayyad and Abbasid rulers were known as *khalifa*s or, in English, "caliphs."

kiblah (*qibla*): The direction of Mecca. Muslims face toward the kiblah when they perform the *salat*.

Koran (*qur'ān*): The scripture of Islam, the word of God revealed to the Prophet Muhammad by means of the angel Gabriel.

kufr: Ungrateful truth-concealing; literally, to cover over and conceal. In Koranic usage, it is the opposite of both *iman* (faith) and *shukr* (gratitude). Most Koran translators have rendered the word as "unbelief" or "infidelity" in the first meaning and as "ingratitude" in the second. In general, *kufr* is considered one of the worst of sins, because it involves being ungrateful to God through rejecting His guidance.

M

ma'ad (ma'ād): The return to God, the third principle of *iman*. The word is often translated as "eschatology."

madhhab: A school of jurisprudence. In Sunni Islam, there are four: Hanafi, Hanbali, Maliki, and Shafi'i. The vast majority of Shi'ites follow a fifth school, called Ja'fari.

madrasah (madrasa): School, place of study.

malak (pl. malā'ika): Angel; literally, "messenger." A kind of creature typically contrasted with human beings and animals, and often with jinn as well. Angels were created with bodies made out of light. They never disobey God, in contrast to both human beings and jinn. Animals are similar to angels in that they never disobey God.

mi'raj (mi'rāj): Literally, "ladder." The ascent of the Prophet to God, an event that plays an important role in Muslim conceptualizations of the nature of the cosmos and of human perfection.

mullah (Persian *mullā*, from Arabic *mawlā*): One of the professional ulama.

mushrik: One who has the attribute of *shirk*.

muslim: One who has the attribute of *islam*. The word has four basic meanings in keeping with the four levels of *islam* (*see islam*). In the third sense of the term, we render it as "Muslim," meaning a follower of the religion of Islam.

mutakallimun (mutakallimūn): The ulama who specialize in Kalam.

N

nabi (nabī): Prophet. A human being who brings guidance from God to other human beings. God is usually said to have sent 124,000 prophets from Adam down to Muhammad. *Nabi* is often used synonymously with *rasul* (messenger), but when the two are contrasted, the *rasul* is understood to have a higher rank with God.

nafs: Soul, self. This word is used in various ways by different Muslim thinkers. In general, it refers to the human self as a whole. Frequently, its qualities are described as standing half-way between those of spirit and body (*see jism* and *ruh*).

nubuwwa: Prophecy, the second principle of *iman*. It is derived from the word *nabi*.

P

Pillars (arkān), Five: The five basic activities that are made incumbent upon Muslims by the Koran and the Hadith: Shahadah, *salat*, the fast of Ramadan, *zakat*, and hajj.

principles (aṣl), three: The fundamental ideas that undergird Islamic thinking and form the basis of Islamic faith: *tawhid, nubuwwa*, and *ma'ad*.

Q

qadar: Measuring out. One of the objects of *iman*.

R

Ramadan: The ninth month of the Islamic calendar. Fasting every day during this month from dawn until sunset is one of the Five Pillars.

rasul (rasūl): Messenger, a specific kind of prophet (see *nabi*). Typically, the messengers are said to number 313. They establish religions, whereas prophets who are not messengers modify or reform already established religions.

ruh (rūh): Spirit. The divine breath that God blew into Adam's clay. Angels are said to be spirits, or spirits blown into bodies of light. All visible things have invisible spirits. When spirit is differentiated from soul, it is typically understood as lying on a higher level and partaking of all the attributes of God in a direct manner.

S

salat (*ṣalāt*): A form of Islamic prayer. The five daily *salat*s are one of the Five Pillars.

Shahadah (*shahāda*): The "witnessing." The testimony of faith, which consists of the pronunciation in Arabic of two formulas, "There is no god but God," and "Muhammad is the messenger of God." Pronouncing the Shahadah is the first pillar of Islam, while the first formula of the Shahadah is the basic definition of *tawhid* and hence the foundation of faith, Islam's second dimension. *Shahada* also means the visible world, as contrasted with the invisible world (*ghayb*).

Shariah (*sharī'a*): Literally, the "road leading to water"; the revealed Law, which establishes the commands and prohibitions of the religion. It provides detailed explanations of Islam's first dimension. It is based on the Koran and the Sunna of the Prophet, to which other sources such as consensus and argument by analogy are added.

Shi'ism: One of the two major branches of Islam, making up about fifteen percent of Muslims. Generally speaking, Shi'ites are distinguished from Sunnis both by the *madhhab* they follow and by certain objects of faith, in particular the Imamate, or the belief that certain descendents of the Prophet called Imams play an intermediary role between human beings and God.

shirk: Associating others with God, the only unforgivable sin. It consists of thinking or acting as if anything other than God shares in the attributes of God. Its opposite is *tawhid*.

sign: *See aya.*

Sunna: The way of living and acting set down by the Prophet; hence, the model that Muslims follow in order to lead a life that is pleasing to God. The basic source for the Sunna is the Hadith.

Sunnism: The larger of the two major branches of Islam, making up about eighty-five percent of Muslims. Contrasted with Shi'ism.

sura (*sūra*): Chapter of the Koran, of which there are 114. Literally, the word means fence or enclosure.

T

tanzih (*tanzīh*): God's incomparability with his creatures; his transcendence. The complement of *tashbih*.

taqwa (*taqwā*): God-wariness, one of the most highly praised human qualities in the Koran. Closely connected to *ihsan*.

tariqah (*ṭarīqa*): Literally, "the path." The path that leads to the encounter with God here and now. The *tariqah* is looked upon as a narrow path that is followed by a relatively small number of people. It is contrasted with the Shariah, which is a broad path followed by all Muslims, including those who follow the *tariqah*. The Sufi orders refer to themselves as *tariqah*s, because they attempt to put into practice all three dimensions of Islam, not simply the Shariah.

tashbih (*tashbīh*): The similarity of God with his creatures; his immanence within creation. The complement of *tanzih*.

tawhid (*tawḥīd*): Literally, "asserting unity." The affirmation of God's oneness, which is the first principle of faith and the ruling idea in Islam. It is given its most succinct verbal expression in the first formula of the Shahadah. Perfect *tawhid* involves simultaneous affirmation of both *tanzih* and *tashbih*.

U

ulama (*'ulamā'*, **plural of** *'ālim*): The learned, those who have knowledge. This is the most general term used for all those Muslims who devote their lives to learning about their religion. Most typically, the word refers to the jurists, those who are experts in the Shariah. Typically, the ulama undertake public religious duties such as leading prayers in mosques, performing marriage ceremonies, or interpreting the Shariah. Often, they have formed a class of professional religious functionaries. Strictly speaking, all those who become learned in any of the Islamic sciences — such as Koran commentary, Hadith, Kalam, philosophy, and Sufism — are ulama. In some languages, the ulama are often called mullahs.

V

vicegerency (*khilāfa*): The attribute of the *khalifa*.

W

wajib (*wājib*): Incumbent according to the Shariah, as, for example, the daily *salat*. One of the five categories into which acts are placed.

Z

zakat (*zakāt*): Alms-tax, one of the Five Pillars.

Appendix:

Sources of the Hadiths

The appendix lists all hadiths cited in the book in the order of their first appearance. In each case, one or two Arabic sources are mentioned, though many more usually could have been provided. As is customary, the books on Hadith are indicated by author name; they follow the reference format given by the standard source (A. J. Wensinck et al., *Concordance et indices de la tradition musulmane*, Leiden: E. J. Brill, 1936–69). If a hadith is not indexed in Wensinck, we have provided a reference to al-Ghazali or some other author who cites it (for bibliographical details of these works, see the end of the appendix). Those interested in English versions of hadiths should consult James Robson, *Mishkat al-masabih* (4 vols., Lahore: Sh. Muhammad Ashraf, 1963–65), which provides relatively accurate translations and covers a broad range of hadiths selected from the standard sources (in the following, MM refers to this work). The available translations of Bukhari and Muslim — each in several volumes — are not reliable.

xxv–xvi. (The hadith of Gabriel). Muslim, Iman 1; Bukhari, Iman 37; MM 5-6.
xxxv. The search for knowledge is incumbent. . . . Ibn Maja, Muqaddima 17; MM 54.
11. (The *salat* as centerpole). Tirmidhi, Iman 8; Ahmad 5:231.

11. (God loves the *salat*.) Bukhari, Mawaqit 5; Muslim, Iman 138; MM 114–15.

15. If one of you had a river. . . . Bukhari, Mawaqit 6; Muslim, Masajid 283; MM 114.

16. A person who marries achieves one-half of his religion. al-Ghazali, *Ihya* 2:44; MM 660.

17. Five things break the fast of the faster. . . . al-Ghazali, *Ihya* 1:350.

21. We have returned from the lesser jihad to the greater jihad. . . . al-Ghazali, *Ihya* 3:14.

28. I came to know everything in the heavens and the earth. Tirmidhi, Tafsir sura 38, 2.

30. My companions are like stars. . . . Maybudi, *Kashf* 1:561.

37. Faith is a knowledge in the heart. . . . Ibn Maja, Muqaddima 9.

40. Did you open the heart and look? Muslim, Iman 158; Abu Dawud, Jihad 95.

41. The good, all of it, is in Thy hands. . . . Muslim, Musafirin 201.

51. Abandoning the *salat* throws a man into *shirk*. . . . Muslim, Iman 134; MM 115.

51. Shall I tell you about something that is more frightening to me. . . . Ibn Maja, Zuhd 21.

51. The most frightening thing that I fear for my Community. . . . Ibn Maja, Zuhd 21.

56. You should have the religion of old women. al-Ghazali, *Ihya* 3:118.

57. God created human beings in his own image. Bukhari, Isti'dhan 1; Muslim, Birr 115.

60. God created a hundred mercies. . . . Muslim, Tawba 21.

60. There is no power and no strength but in God. . . . Bukhari, Adhan 7; Muslim, Salat 12.

70. God will only chastise the one who is defiant. . . . Ibn Maja, Zuhd 35; MM 505.

70. I seek refuge in Thy good-pleasure. . . . Muslim, Salat 222; Abu Dawud, Salat 148

74. Praise belongs to God in every situation. Abu Dawud, Adab 91.

76. My mercy takes precedence. . . . Bukhari, Tawhid 55; Muslim, Tawba 14; MM 502.

82. (Hadiths of the *mi'raj*). Bukhari, Anbiya 5; Muslim, Iman 264; MM 1264–70.

90. This world is accursed. . . . Tirmidhi, Zuhd 14; Ibn Maja, Zuhd 3.

96. He is a Light. How could I see Him? Muslim, Iman 291.

102. Satan cannot imaginalize himself in my form. Bukhari, Ilm 38; Muslim, Ru'ya 10.

102. The Garden and the Fire were imaginalized for me in this wall. Ahmad 3:259.

114. (A person's place in the next world). Bukhari, Tawhid 28; Muslim, Qadar 1; MM 23–24.

117. I am with My servant's opinion of Me. Bukhari, Tawhid 15; Muslim, Tawba 1.

127. Each of you is a shepherd. . . . Bukhari, Jum'a 11; Muslim, Imara 20.

129. On the day of resurrection, no one will be greater. . . . Maybudi, *Kashf* 2:783–4.

129. God created the angels from intelligence. . . . Rumi, *Mathnawi*, book 4, page 366 (text).

131. The angels said to God, "Our Lord. . . ." Maybudi, *Kashf* 2:783–4

138. Every child is born according to *fitra*. . . . Bukhari, Jana'iz 80; Muslim, Qadar 22.

143. Moses said, "My Lord, show me Adam. . . ." Bukhari, Qadar 11; Muslim, Qadar 13; MM 23.

162. God created Adam when He created him. . . . Ahmad 6:441.

167. Easy, congenial. al-Ghazalis, *Ihya* 4:222; cf. Ahmad 6:116.

167. I went back, and when He had reduced them by ten, . . . Bukhari, Salat 1; Muslim, Iman 259; MM 1266–67.

169. He who dies knowing that there is no god but God. . . . Muslim, Iman 43.

169. God will say, "Do you object to anything in this?". . . . Tirmidhi, Iman 17; MM 1176.

177. His character is the Koran. Muslim, Musafirin 139.

178. O God, I ask Thee. . . . that Thou givest me the provision. . . . al-Ghazali, *Ihya* 1:471–2.

189. Speak to people according to the level of their understanding. al-Ghazali, *Ihya* 1:147.

199–200. On the day of resurrection, the inhabitant of the Fire who had. . . .
Muslim, Munafiqin 55; Ibn Maja, Zuhd 38; MM 1210–11.

200. If someone kills himself. . . . Bukhari, Tibb 56; Muslim, Iman 175.

202. I and the Last Hour are like this. Bukhari, Riqaq 39; Muslim, Jum'a 37.

203. When a person dies, he undergoes his resurrection. al-Ghazali, *Ihya* 4:94

206. O God, place a light in my heart. . . . Muslim, Musafirin 187.

207. O God, show us things as they are! Hujwiri, *Kashf*, 231.

208. God will roll up the heavens. . . . Muslim, Munafiqin 24; MM 1165.

209. You will be mustered barefoot. . . . Bukhari, Anbiya 8; Muslim, Janna 58; MM 1169.

209. (The Prophet will be given) the praiseworthy station. Ahmad 1:398, 3:456.

209. The angels will intercede, the prophets will intercede. . . . Muslim, Iman 302; Ahmad 3:94; MM 1184–86.

209. They will sprout like seeds. . . . Ibid.

209–210. Two men who enter the Fire will shout more loudly. . . . Tirmidhi, Jahannam 10; MM 1193.

210. God laughs at the despondency of His servants.... Ibn Maja, Muqaddima 13.
210. Turn my face away from the Fire.... Bukhari, Riqaq 52; Muslim, Iman 299; MM 1187.
212. God is beautiful, and He loves beauty. Muslim, Iman 147; Ibn Maja, Du'a' 10.
221. God's veil is light. Muslim, Iman 293.
221. God has seventy veils.... al-Ghazali, *Ihya* 1:144; cf. MM 1227.
226. People are asleep, and when they die, they wake up. al-Ghazali, *Ihya* 4:35.
226. The molar tooth of a truth-concealer.... Muslim, Janna 44; Ahmad 2:328; MM 1211.
226. The truth-concealer will drag his tongue.... Tirmidhi, Jahannam 3; Ahmad 3:182; MM 1212.
227–231. (The faithful servant and the truth-concealer in the grave). Ahmad 4:287; MM 340–42.
228. (God placed love for three things in his heart....). al-Ghazali, *Ihya* 2:48.
235. Whoever brings a beautiful deed will have ten the like of it.... Muslim, Dhikr 22.
244. One of the beautiful traits of a person's Islam.... Tirmidhi, Zuhd 11.
244. I seek refuge in God.... Muslim, Dhikr 73; Abu Dawud, Witr 32; MM 524.
270. O God, Thou hast made my creation beautiful.... Ahmad 1:403.
270. When the servant submits, and his submission is beautiful.... Bukhari, Iman 31.
272. You will be called on the day of resurrection.... Abu Dawud, Adab 61.
273. God has prescribed doing what is beautiful.... Muslim, Sayd 57; Abu Dawud, Adaji 11.
280. Acts of charity in secret.... al-Ghazali, *Ihya* 1:321.
280–281. That was a stone that was thrown into hell.... Muslim, Janna 31.
296. Each of you should ask your Lord for all your needs.... Tirmidhi, Da'awat 117; MM 474.
299. (The whole face of the earth was designated as a mosque). Muslim, Masajid 4; MM 1231.
305. God has finished with creation and character. al-Ghazali, *Ihya* 5:239.
315. Every religion has its character trait.... Ibn Maja, Zuhd 17.
326. The Hour will not come as long as.... Muslim, Iman 234.
328. God loves His servant who is faithful, poor.... Ibn Maja, Zuhd 5.
332. No time will come to you.... Bukhari, Fitan 6.

al-Ghazali, *Ihya' 'ulum al-din*, 6 vols., Beirut: Dar al-Hadi, 1992.

Hujwiri, *Kashf al-mahjub*, ed. V. Zhukovsky, Tehran: Amir Kabir, 1336/1957.

Maybudi, *Kashf al-asrar*, 10 vols., ed. A. A. Hikmat, Tehran: Danishgah, 1952–60.

Rumi, *The Mathnawî*, 8 vols., ed. R. A. Nicholson, London: Luzac, 1925–40.

Notes

Preface

1. Among the books that we recommend to our students are the following: Victor Danner, *The Islamic Tradition: An Introduction* (Warwick, N.Y.: Amity House, 1988); F. M. Denny, *An Introduction to Islam* (New York: Macmillan, 1985); G. Eaton, *Islam and the Destiny of Man* (Albany, N.Y.: SUNY Press, 1985); J. Esposito, *Islam: The Straight Path* (New York: Oxford, 1988); H. A. R. Gibb, *Mohammedanism* (London: Oxford, 1949); S. H. Nasr, *Ideals and Realities of Islam* (London: George Allen & Unwin, 1966); J. Renard, *In the Footsteps of Muhammad* (New York: Paulist, 1992); Annemarie Schimmel, *Islam: An Introduction* (Albany, N.Y.: SUNY Press, 1992).

Introduction

1. Those interested in learning more about some of the criticisms we have in mind might begin by looking at the books cited by Lawrence E. Sullivan in his masterly study, *Icanchu's Drum: An Orientation to Meaning in South American Religions* (New York: Macmillan, 1988), pp. 884–85. What he says in the passage leading up to the suggested reading applies also to Western perceptions of Islam: "One of the great disservices to our understanding of South American religions [read: Islam] has been the perception of tribal peoples [read: Muslims] as slavishly dedicated to an unchanging order revealed in the images of myth and handed down unquestioned and unmodified from one generation to the next.

This attitude accompanies the evaluation of 'myth' as a banal and inane narrative. Tribal peoples (representing 'archaic' modes of thought) childishly cling to
their myths, infantile fantasies, whereas mature contemporaries jettison myths
with the passage of 'historical time' and the 'entrance' into 'modernity.' It would
be fascinating to study these and other justifications proffered for avoiding a
serious encounter with the reality of myth [read: Islamic thought] and symbolic
acts. . . . This is not the place to carry out a history of the 'modern' ideas of myth
and religion. It is enough to suggest that the Western cultural imagination
turned away when it encountered the stunning variety of cultural worlds that
appeared for the first time in the Age of Discovery. Doubtless this inward turn
sparked the appearance of all sorts of imaginary realities. The Enlightenment,
the withdrawal of Western thinkers from the whirling world of cultural values
into an utterly imaginary world of 'objective' forms of knowlege, and its intellectual follow-up coined new symbolic currency. These terms brought new meanings
and new self-definition to Western culture: 'consciousness/unconsciousness,'
'primitive/civilized,' 'ethics/mores,' 'law/custom,' 'critical or reflective thought/
action.' "

2. For the English retelling that is closest to the story as told by the classical
texts, see Martin Lings, *Muhammad: His Life Based on the Earliest Sources*
(London: Allen & Unwin, 1983).

3. F. E. Peters, *Judaism, Christianity, and Islam: The Classical Texts and Their
Interpretation* (Princeton: Princeton University Press, 1990), p. 5.

4. In citing from the Koran, we usually follow the translation of A. J. Arberry
(*The Koran Interpreted*, London: Allen & Unwin, 1955), which is the most careful,
accurate, and eloquent translation available. On occasion, however, we modify
Arberry's translation in order to maintain consistent usage for important terms.
In addition, the chapter and verse that we cite follow the standard Egyptian
order, used in most translations, but not in Arberry's. Hence there are sometimes small discrepancies between our numbering of verses and that of Arberry's translation.

5. On the significance of this genre of hadith, see W. Graham, *Divine Word and
Prophetic Word in Early Islam* (The Hague: Mouton, 1977).

6. See for example Ahmad ibn Naqib al-Misri (d. 769/1368), *The Reliance of the
Traveller: A Classic Manual of Islamic Sacred Law*, translated by N. H. H. Keller
(Dubai: Modern Printing House, 1991), pp. 807–15. For an interesting example of
a twentieth-century African Muslim who used this model to teach the basics of
Islam to illiterate tribespeople, see L. Brenner, *West African Sufi: The Religious
Heritage and Spiritual Search of Cerno Bokar Saalif Taal* (Berkeley and Los
Angeles: University of California Press, 1984), pp. 187–92.

7. Sources for hadiths are provided in the appendix.

8. When God speaks in the first person in the Koran, he sometimes refers to
himself as "I" and sometimes as "We." One could say that "We" simply reflects the
imperial usage of time immemorial: A king refers to himself as "we" because he
speaks for everyone in his kingdom. Some Muslim theologians, however, maintain that when God says "I," he is referring to his own self, which is one. In
contrast, when he says "We," he is referring to his many names and attributes,
which bring about diversity in creation.

9. Here we have followed the text as given by Muslim in his *Sahih*. If we had
instead followed the text as given by Bukhari, we would have dealt with faith
before submission, and the details would have differed somewhat.

10. Jonathan Berkey, *The Transmission of Knowledge in Medieval Cairo: A Social History of Islamic Education* (Princeton: Princeton University Press, 1992), p. 217.

11. For a good presentation of the range of Muslim commentaries on the Koran, see Mahmoud Ayoub's ongoing work, *The Qur'an and its Interpretors*, 2 vol. (Albany, N.Y.: SUNY Press, vol. 1, 1984; vol. 2, 1992).

Part I: *Islam*

1. A sympathetic observer of Islam, John Esposito, writes, "Islam is not a new religion with a new Scripture. Instead of being the youngest of the major monotheistic world religions, from a Muslim viewpoint it is the oldest religion" (*Islam: The Straight Path* [Oxford: Oxford University Press, 1988], p. 22). Many Muslims do indeed believe this, but they do so by conflating the meanings of the term *islam* as found in the Koran.

2. The traditional method of determining the time of dawn mentioned in the Koran involves trying to see the difference (on a moonless night) between a black string and a white string. This works out to roughly one or one and one-half hours before sunrise, varying according to latitude. In Islamic countries, most people live within earshot of a mosque and therefore hear the morning call to prayer at this time.

Part II: *Iman*

1. See Wilfred Cantwell Smith, *Faith and Belief* (Princeton: Princeton University Press, 1979).

2. Ibid., p. 109.

3. To gain a visual idea of the symbolic nature of the *mi'raj* narrative, one should look at some of the many miniature paintings in which it is represented. There it becomes clear that the worlds that are depicted lie on other planes of existence. See, for example, M.-R. Séguy, *The Miraculous Journey of Mahomet* (New York: George Braziller, 1977), which provides fifty-eight color reproductions from a fifteenth-century Turkish manuscript.

4. For more details on these angels, see Murata, "Angels," in S. H. Nasr, ed., *Islamic Spirituality: Foundations* (New York: Crossroad, 1987), pp. 324–44.

5. For some of the basics of the Islamic understanding of earth, water, and clay, see Murata, *Tao of Islam: A Sourcebook on Gender Relationships in Islamic Thought* (Albany, N.Y.: SUNY Press, 1992), chapter 4 and passim.

6. For an early version of this story, see Franz Rosenthal, *The History of al-Tabari*, vol. 1 (Albany, N.Y.: SUNY Press, 1984), pp. 258–59.

7. On the basis of this teaching a tiny minority of Muslim jurists have considered abortion permissible, though reprehensible, if it takes place before the end of the fourth month of pregnancy. The majority of jurists, however, consider abortion forbidden in any case, though most of them allow contraception. See B. Musallam, *Sex and Society in Islam: Birth Control Before the Nineteenth Century* (Cambridge: Cambridge University Press, 1983).

8. This is why most Muslim theologians maintain that anyone who has not heard a prophetic message is not responsible to follow a Shariah; of course the

issue is more complicated, since God reveals his signs not only in scripture, but also in nature. Hence, many theologians hold that there is a certain degree of responsibility with or without the intervention of prophecy because people are free beings with the ability to read the signs.

9. We of course use the term *myth* in the sense that it is used by Eliade and other specialists in religious studies. In no sense do we use it according to everyday usage, where a myth is a false story. On the contrary, a myth is more true than any facts, since it is always and forever true, while facts come and go, depending on changing scientific and historical paradigms. To say that the Koranic account of Adam is a myth means that it is the criterion by which Muslims must judge the truth about human beings. If people do not grasp the foundational nature of the myth, they have not made the effort to understand its lessons. The timeless truth of the myth does not contradict the possibility of its historical factuality, though one wonders why God would bother telling what actually happened to the satisfaction of a materialistic historian. Even supposedly objective historians do not tell it exactly as it happened. They tell the story as they understand it. The Koran in particular and prophecy in general have a clear intention, which is to bring about human salvation. Hence the truth of the message depends upon its ability to effectuate this intention, not upon satisfying human curiosity about origins or settling disputes among scientists and historians. In any case, such disputes have meaning only within the worlds of meaning established by science and historiography. These worlds have no privileged claim to universality, objectivity, or truth, and they certainly have almost nothing to do with human salvation.

10. As for the Foremost, they are the prophets and the friends of God, who are ruled by neither set of attributes because they have perfected the divine form within themselves and manifest God's beauty and majesty as God manifests them. They are just as much at home with the majestic attributes as they are with the beautiful attributes. It goes without saying that this does not mean that they suffer distance from God as a result. Quite the contrary, it means they are like God himself in this respect. In the same way, although the Companions of the Right Hand are dominated by the attributes of mercy, they are not nearer to God than the Foremost, because they have not fully actualized the attributes of wrath, so they lack certain perfections.

11. R. A. Nicholson, ed., *The Mathnawî of Jalâlu'în Rûmî* (London: Luzac, 1925–40), book 1, verse 638 (our translation).

12. Christians are often struck by this and other Koranic passages about Jesus, and some of the evangelically minded among them would like to find here an opening to convert Muslims to the right religion (i.e., their version of Christianity). The typical Muslim response, however, is a yawn. They cannot get excited about any human qualities when "There is nothing real but the Real." After all, they say, so what if Jesus was born of a virgin? That does not make him divine. Adam was created without father or mother, so that should place him a notch above Jesus. The Koran itself compares Jesus to Adam: "Surely the likeness of Jesus, in God's sight, is as Adam's likeness. He created him of dust, then said unto him 'Be!', and he was" (3:59).

13. See the readable and informative study by H. Lazarus-Yafeh, *Intertwined Worlds: Medieval Islam and Bible Criticism* (Princeton: Princeton University Press, 1992).

14. Excellent recent studies on the Islamic understanding of Christianity include Jane Dammen McAuliffe, *Qur'ânic Christians: An Analysis of Classical and*

Modern Exegesis (Cambridge: Cambridge University Press, 1992) and Neal Robinson, *Christ in Islam and Christianity* (Albany, N.Y.: SUNY Press, 1991).

15. The reader who wishes to gain understanding of the importance that Muhammad has always played in the Islamic tradition is referred to Annemarie Schimmel's fine study, *And Muhammad Is His Messenger* (Chapel Hill: University of North Carolina Press, 1985).

16. Adapted from W. C. Chittick, *The Sufi Path of Love* (Albany, N.Y.: SUNY Press, 1983), pp. 283–84.

17. Relatively little has been written by modern scholars on the way in which Islamic eschatological teachings developed. The best example in English of a sophisticated presentation of Islamic eschatology is found in James Morris, *The Wisdom of the Throne: An Introduction to the Philosophy of Mulla Sadra* (Princeton: Princeton University Press, 1981). A more general study of the tradition is found in W. C. Chittick, "Eschatology," *Islamic Spirituality: Foundations*, pp. 378–409.

18. We are not seeking refuge in mysteries, but simply saying that an introductory text is not the place to get into the most subtle domains of Islamic thought. For some explication of principles behind the mystery of the measuring out, see W. C. Chittick, *The Sufi Path of Knowledge* (Albany, N.Y.: SUNY Press, 1989), Chapter 17; and idem, *Faith and Practice of Islam*, pp. 213–14.

19. For a detailed discussion of the reasons we avoid the word, see Chittick, *Faith and Practice of Islam*, p. 168ff.

20. We do not mean to imply that the terms *tanzih* and *tashbih* as we have been employing them were used by al-Ash'ari and his immediate followers. Our usage did not come into vogue before the seventh/thirteenth century. For al-Ash'ari, *tanzih* represents the correct position, while *tashbih* is a heresy, but his understanding of the terms does not coincide with the way they were used in much of the later literature.

21. For a powerful argument showing the intimate links between reason and the dissolution of human values in the modern world, see John Ralston Saul, *Voltaire's Bastards: The Dictatorship of Reason in the West* (New York: The Free Press, 1992).

22. *The Chronicle of Higher Education*, November 11, 1992, p. A8.

23. al-Ash'ari, *al-Ibana*, in *al-Risalat al-sab'a fi'l-'aqa'id*, 3d ed. Hyderabad-Daccan: Da'irat al-ma'arif al-'Uthmaniyya, 1980), pp. 5–6.

24. Ibn Sina, *al-Najat* (Cairo: Maktabat al-sa'ada, 1938), p. 229.

25. For a good study of the complementary roles played by *logos* and *muthos*— that is, rational and imaginal thought—in Avicenna, see Peter Heath, *Allegory and Philosophy in Avicenna (Ibn Sina)* (Philadelphia: University of Pennsylvania Press, 1992).

26. Suhrawardi, *Majmu'a-yi athar-i farsi*, ed. S. H. Nasr (Tehran: Imperial Iranian Academy of Philosophy, 1977), pp. 297–98. See also W. M. Thackston, *The Mystical and Visionary Treatises of Suhrawardi* (London: Octagon Press, 1982), p. 78.

Part III: *Ihsan*

1. Ali ibn al-Husayn, *The Psalms of Islam: Al-Sahîfat al-Kâmilat al-Sajjâdiyya*, trans. W. C. Chittick (Oxford: Oxford University Press, 1988), pp. 65–67.

2. Especially useful for understanding the relationship between Koranic teach-ings and Islamic art are the writings of T. Burckhardt, such as *Art of Islam: Language and Meaning* (London: World of Islam Festival Trust, 1976) and *Fez: City of Islam* (Cambridge, U.K.: The Islamic Texts Society, 1992); see also S. H. Nasr, *Islamic Art and Spirituality* (Albany, N.Y.: SUNY Press, 1987). For an outstanding study that amply illustrates how Islamic ideals are integrated into the everyday activities of contemporary artists, see H. Glassie, *Turkish Tradi-tional Art Today* (Bloomington & Indianapolis: Indiana University Press, 1993).

3. Recitation of the Koran is still, in the age of cinema and video, one of the major art forms of the Islamic world. There are Koran reciters who command salaries greater than movie stars. For an understanding of what recitation involves, see K. Nelson, *The Art of Reciting the Qur'an* (Austin: University of Texas Press, 1985).

4. On the importance of calligraphy, see Annemarie Schimmel, *Calligraphy and Islamic Culture* (New York: New York University Press, 1984). For specimens of Koran calligraphy, see M. Lings, *The Quranic Art of Calligraphy and Illumination* (London: Art of Islam Festival Trust, 1976).

5. Earle H. Waugh has explained many of the reasons for the efficacy of poetry in stirring up love for God in his fine study of the way in which music and poetry are utilized by contemporary Egyptian Sufis: *The Munshidîn of Egypt: Their World and Their Song* (Columbus: University of South Carolina Press, 1989).

6. Nicholson, op. cit., vol. 3, verses 545–60

7. Barbara Metcalf, *Moral Conduct and Authority: The Place of Adab in South Asian Islam* (Berkeley: University of California Press, 1984), p. 4.

8. Ibid., p. 9.

9. Ibid., p. 10.

10. Nicholson, op.cit., vol. 2, verse 1853.

11. For an explication of some of the typical imagery, see Annemarie Schimmel, *A Two-Colored Brocade: The Imagery of Persian Poetry* (Chapel Hill: The Univer-sity of North Carolina Press, 1992).

12. Rashid al-Din Maybudi, *Kashf al-asrar*, edited by A. A. Hikmat (Tehran: Danishgah, 1952–60), vol. 3, pp. 154–55.

13. On the implications of employing gender symbolism in such discussions, see S. Murata, *The Tao of Islam: A Sourcebook on Gender Relationships in Islamic Thought.*

14. Adapted from Chittick, *Sufi Path of Love*, pp. 152–53, 212.

Part IV: Islam in History

1. F. E. Peters, op. cit., p. xix.

2. Sullivan, op. cit., pp. 678–79.

3. If, more recently, people have refrained from simply throwing them out, it is not because of an awareness of their beauty, but because of the discovery that Western tourists are willing to buy these things. Frequently those Muslims with sensitivity toward the beauty of their own heritage have acquired it through modern Western education. It is the Westernized elite who run the museums, not those few Muslims who never lost their sense of beauty.

Index

Arabic words and proper names listed in the index, in contrast to those mentioned in the text, are transliterated phonetically (in keeping with the standard modified *Encyclopaedia of Islam* system).